The ethics of researching the far right

Manchester University Press

RACISM, RESISTANCE AND SOCIAL CHANGE

Previously Published in this Series

The ethics of researching the far right

Critical approaches and reflections

Edited by
Antonia Vaughan, Joan Braune,
Meghan Tinsley, and Aurelien Mondon

MANCHESTER UNIVERSITY PRESS

Published by Manchester University Press
Oxford Road, Manchester, M13 9PL

www.manchesteruniversitypress.co.uk

British Library Cataloguing-in-Publication Data
A catalogue record for this book is available from the British Library

ISBN 978 1 5261 7387 4 hardback

First published 2024

Typeset
by Deanta Global Publishing Services, Chennai, India

The ethics of researching the far right

Critical approaches and reflections

Edited by
Antonia Vaughan, Joan Braune,
Meghan Tinsley, and Aurelien Mondon

MANCHESTER UNIVERSITY PRESS

Published by Manchester University Press
Oxford Road, Manchester, M13 9PL

www.manchesteruniversitypress.co.uk

British Library Cataloguing-in-Publication Data
A catalogue record for this book is available from the British Library

ISBN 978 1 5261 7387 4 hardback

First published 2024

The publisher has no responsibility for the persistence or accuracy of URLs for any external or third-party internet websites referred to in this book, and does not guarantee that any content on such websites is, or will remain, accurate or appropriate.

Typeset
by Deanta Global Publishing Services, Chennai, India

Contents

Contributors

Jean Beaman (she/her) is an Associate Professor of Sociology, with affiliations with Black Studies, Political Science, Feminist Studies, Global Studies, and the Center for Black Studies Research, at the University of California, Santa Barbara. Her research is ethnographic in nature and focuses on race/ethnicity, racism, international migration, and state violence in both France and the United States. She is the author of *Citizen Outsider: Children of North African Immigrants in France* (University of California Press, 2017), as well as numerous articles and book chapters. She is also an Associate Editor of the journal, *Identities: Global Studies in Culture and Power* and a Corresponding Editor for the journal *Metropolitics/Metropolitiques*. She was a 2022–2023 fellow at the Center for Advanced Study in the Behavioral Sciences at Stanford University, and a Co-PI for the Mellon Foundation Sawyer Seminar grant, 'Race, Precarity, and Privilege: Migration in a Global Context', for 2020–2022.

Elsa Bengtsson Meuller (she/they) is a PhD Candidate at the Department of Politics and International Relations at Goldsmiths, University of London. Elsa holds an MSc in Comparative Political Thought and a BA in Politics from SOAS, University of London. Elsa's research focuses on misogyny, online gender-based violence, and anti-feminist and male supremacist extremism, and explores feminist theory and approaches to the politics of cyberspace. In their doctoral research, Elsa develops a feminist methodology for researching anti-feminist online cultures through the use and theorisation of emotions and affect.

Joan Braune (she/her) is a Lecturer in Philosophy at Gonzaga University. She is the author of *Erich Fromm's Revolutionary Hope: Prophetic Messianism as a Critical Theory of the Future* (Sense Publishers, 2014) and co-editor with Kieran Durkin of *Erich Fromm's Critical Theory: Hope, Humanism and the Future* (Bloomsbury, 2020). Her current research applies the Frankfurt School's critique of fascism to contemporary resurgent far-right movements. She is active in the Gonzaga Institute for Hate Studies and serves on the editorial board of the *Journal of Hate Studies*.

Katy Brown (she/her) has recently completed her doctorate at the University of Bath, where her research focused on the mainstreaming of the far right in Europe. Her thesis aims to theorise mainstreaming and analyse the role of elite discourse in this process, using the Brexit referendum as a case study. She has published articles on far-right opposition to Turkish accession to the EU, the *Guardian*'s use of populism with Aurelien Mondon, and the mainstreaming of the far right with Aurelien Mondon and Aaron Winter.

Laura Connelly (she/her) is a Lecturer in Criminology at the University of Sheffield, UK. She works on or at the intersections of race, gender, migration, and criminalisation, and often explores these issues within the context of the sex industry. She is co-author (with Remi Joseph-Salisbury) of *Anti-Racist Scholar-Activism*, published by Manchester University Press in December 2021. Laura sits on the steering committee of the Northern Police Monitoring Project and organises as part of the No Police in Schools campaign.

Luc S. Cousineau (he/him – they/them) is the Co-Director of Research at the Canadian Institute for Far-Right Studies and an instructor in the Department of Recreation and Leisure Studies at the University of Waterloo. His work focuses on the intersections of masculinities, technologies, and power, and the influences of far-right masculinism on social structures and youth.

John Drury (he/him) is a Professor of Social Psychology at the University of Sussex. His research focuses on collective behaviour – in protests, riots, and social movements; mass emergencies and disasters; and less dramatic crowd phenomena such as at festivals, music, and sports events. He has published over 100 peer-reviewed journal articles on these and other topics, including events such as the 2011 English riots, the London bombings of 7 July 2005, the Hillsborough disaster, and the 2010 Chile earthquake. He teaches crowd psychology to the UK Fire and Rescue Service and to crowd safety managers around the world. His findings on collective resilience in mass emergencies have informed the training of over 2,000 stewards across Europe and informed the Civil Contingencies Secretariat's National Risk Assessments. He is the Director of Research in the School of Psychology and is a former editor of the *British Journal of Social Psychology*. As part of the response to the COVID-19 pandemic, he participated in the UK government SAGE behavioural science subgroup SPI-B and is a member of Independent SAGE.

David Farrell-Banks (he/him) is an interdisciplinary researcher and museum practitioner currently based at the Fitzwilliam Museum, University of Cambridge. His research is primarily interested in the role of the past in our present-day lives, drawing on critical heritage, critical discourse, cultural memory, and the digital humanities in his work. His first monograph, *Affect* *and Belonging in Political Uses of the Past*, engages with the relationship between the representation of particular historical moments in heritage and right-wing political discourse. This work focuses on the capacity of the past to move people emotionally and provide confidence in engaging in political action. Since completing his doctoral studies at Newcastle University, he has worked on the AHRC COVID-19 response project *Museums, Crisis and Covid-19* at Ulster University. He currently is currently supporting the development of participatory practice at the Fitzwilliam Museum, Cambridge.

Andrew Fergus Wilson (he/him) is a Senior Lecturer in Sociology with research interests in extreme forms of nationalism, marginalised beliefs, and conspiracy theory. His work largely focuses on the use of symbolic forms and tropes by extreme political groups in a digital setting. He is interested in how these groups use and reuse stigmatised knowledge and mythopoetic visual codes in the production of a collective identity with a particular emphasis on conspiracy theory, apocalyptic beliefs, and notional understandings of religious and quasi-religious imagery.

Isis Giraldo (she/her), a committed non-white feminist and a cultural studies scholar, is interested in the connections between culture and power and this constitutes the main focus of her research and intellectual endeavours. She teaches at the English Department of the University of Lausanne.

Sadia Habib (she/her) is a Lecturer in Education at the Manchester Institute of Education (MIE) in the School of Environment, Education, and Development (SEED). Since May 2019, Sadia has been the young people's programme coordinator at the Manchester Museum leading a three-year British Council/Heritage Lottery Fund international multi-partnership project entitled *Our Shared Cultural Heritage*. She has set up a Young People's Collective with over fifty young people regularly leading activities, campaigns, and events that matter to themselves and their communities, and changing the heritage sector for the better. She also works as a Researcher in Social Sciences at the Centre on the Dynamics of Ethnicity. Sadia's research interests lie at the intersection of identities, arts, culture, education, social justice, critical pedagogy, and anti-racism. In 2020, Sadia was in the top three finalists for the Museums Association's Radical Changemaker Award; in 2021, Sadia won the Manchester Culture Award for Promotion of Equality and Social Justice. In 2018, she co-founded The Riz Test which has fast become a popular tool used by the arts and culture industries, academics, and students to measure the representation of Muslims in film and on television. The Riz Test sit on the BFI's Muslims on Screen Advisory

Panel, and Sadia is also on the BAFTA Equality, Diversity, and Inclusion steering group. Sadia has written extensively about identities, young people, and belonging in her own books, as well as in edited collections.

Carina Hoerst (she/her) has a PhD in social psychology from the University of Sussex. Under the supervision of Prof John Drury, she examined the connection between electoral events and subjective power in the enactment of a far-right identity. She focused on providing a social-psychological explanation for the sharp rise in racially and religiously aggravated hate crimes in 2016 in the UK and the US after Brexit and the US Presidential election, as well as the increase of US-based far-right street mobilisations in the same context. She has published findings from her own work and collaborations in multiple outlets including academic journals, blog posts, and podcasts. She has further contributed to an Independent SAGE report on racialised stigmata and inequalities during the COVID-19 pandemic as well as to a draft for the advisory report for the US House Committee investigating the Capitol insurrection.

Miranda Jeanne Marie Iossifidis (she/her) is a Lecturer in Sociology at Newcastle University, UK. Her research interests are around the collective and creative negotiation of environmental present(s) and future(s) through speculative fiction, everyday urban culture and collective action. She is currently working on a project that uses creative methods in workshops exploring speculative ecofascist presents and futures.

Rae Jereza (they/them) is a non-binary, Filipino-American anthropologist working in North America. They are currently a Senior Researcher at the Polarization and Extremism Research Innovation Lab (PERIL) and a Research Assistant Professor at the School of Public Affairs at American University. They are a core committee member of the Society for Linguistic Anthropology's Language and Social Justice Committee.

Daniel Jones (he/him) completed his PhD (2021) at the University of Northampton, examining how far-right and antifascist print media developed, communicated, and used identity. He has run the Searchlight Archive at the University of Northampton since its creation in 2012 and is also an Associate Lecturer in History, having taught since 2014. He currently sits within the Humanities Department within Culture in the Faculty of Arts, Science, and Technology at the University of Northampton. Having been responsible for building up the Searchlight Archive, Daniel has taken a keen interest in the emerging field exploring the questions of ethics and engagement around these collections. He has given talks on ethics surrounding extremism to

PhD training consortia, advised on collection ethics around extremism within academia and commercially, spoken at international conferences about the experiences of the Searchlight Archive, and undertaken several public engagement talks as well. Daniel's wider research interests focus on antifascist and far-right cultures. His works include 'The National Socialist Group: A Study in the Groupuscular Right' (2017), co-authored with Prof Paul Jackson, and an upcoming chapter with Manchester University Press, 'The National Socialist Movement of the United States and the Turn to Environmentalism: Greenfingers or Brownshirts?', and he is currently working on ecofascism and its links to accelerationist cultures. Daniel is an associate fellow of the Royal Historical Society and the section editor for Modern Ideologies and Faiths in the *Blackwell Religion Compass* journal.

Remi Joseph-Salisbury (he/him) is a Senior Lecturer in Sociology at the University of Manchester, with interests in the study of racisms and anti-racisms, particularly in the contexts of education and policing. He is a member of the Centre on Dynamics of Ethnicity at the University of Manchester. Remi is the co-author of *Anti-Racist Scholar-Activism* (2021, Manchester University Press) and co-editor of *The Fire Now: Anti-Racism in Times of Explicit Racial Violence* (2018, Zed Books) and *Black Mixed Race Men* (2018, Emerald Publishing), winner of the Philip Leverhulme Prize for best first book in sociology. He has recently written on issues including the presence of police in schools, the policing of the pandemic, police abolition, and the enduring nature of racism in British education. Remi is also a steering group member of the Northern Police Monitoring Project, a police abolitionist group based in Greater Manchester, and the No Police in Schools campaign.

Imo Kaufman (she/they) is a PhD student at the University of Nottingham. Their project is in collaboration with the National Videogame Museum and explores a lived experience of gaming in the UK, looking at gamer subjectivities, performativity, and ideologies through an oral history lens. Imo's research interests also include the intersection of the alt-right and gaming spaces.

Balša Lubarda (he/him) is a Fulbright Fellow at the Institute for the Study of Societal Issues, UC Berkeley (United States), and the Head of DAMAR Research Institute (Montenegro). He was previously the head and founder of the Ideology Research Unit at the Far-Right Analysis Network (previously the Centre for Analysis of the Radical Right). He is also the author of *Far-Right Ecologism: Environmental Politics and the Far Right in Hungary and Poland* (Routledge, 2023), a monograph based on his doctoral research, conducted at Central European University (Hungary/Austria). His work predominantly focuses on the odd bedfellows and political idiosyncrasies as well as environmental politics and green theory.

Richard McNeil-Willson (he/him) is a Research Fellow in terrorism and political violence at the Institute of Security and Global Affairs (ISGA) at Leiden University, Netherlands. His work critically examines concepts of extremism and counter-extremism legislation, with a focus on Europe. He is also a former Max Weber Research Fellow at the Robert Schuman Centre for Advanced Studies, at the European University Institute, Florence, Italy, and holds a UK Research Council PhD from the Institute of Arab and Islamic Studies, Exeter University. Dr McNeil-Willson has worked as the main researcher for several European Commission Horizon-funded projects and has advised the European Commission directly in developing policy responses to far-right violence. He has published academic journal articles, as well as the *Handbook of Violent Extremism and Resilience* (Routledge, 2023).

Anna A. Meier (she/her) is Assistant Professor of Politics and International Relations at the University of Nottingham. Her work focuses on institutional responses to white supremacist violence in the United States and Europe, employing critical ethnographic and relational approaches.

Aurelien Mondon (he/him) is a Senior Lecturer in politics at the University of Bath. His research focuses predominantly on the impact of racism and populism on liberal democracies and the mainstreaming of far-right politics through elite discourse. His latest book *Reactionary Democracy: How Racism and the Populist Far Right Became Mainstream*, co-written with Aaron Winter, is out with Verso.

George Newth (he/him) is a Lecturer in Politics at the Department of Politics, Languages, and International Studies, University of Bath. His research focuses on populist articulations of regionalist, nationalist, and far-right ideologies, with a particular focus on the history of the Italian Lega (Nord). Recent publications have examined left-wing, centrist, and right-wing articulations of populism (*Politics*, 2021), how the concept of 'nativism' represents blurred lines between the mainstream and the extreme (*Identities*, 2021), the latent nature of populist discourse (*Social Movement Studies*, 2022), and Matteo Salvini's Eurosceptic discourse (*Journal of Language and Politics*, 2022). His forthcoming book with Routledge Studies in the Modern History of Italy, *Fathers of the Lega: Populist Regionalism and Populist Nationalism in Historical Perspective* (September 2023), rethinks the roots of populist and far-right politics in North Italy.

Chloe Peacock (she/her) is a Lecturer in Criminology at the University of Sheffield, where she teaches in the School of Law and the Department of Sociological Studies. As a Research Associate at the University of Manchester, Chloe was part of the Centre on the Dynamics of Ethnicity's research on anti-racist organising around statues and monuments. Chloe's research concerns how criminality and criminal justice are constructed in media, political policy, and professional discourses. She is especially interested in the role of ignorance, amnesia, and denial in legitimising criminal justice policy and practice, and its racialised and classed harms. She is a member of the Secrecy, Power, and Ignorance Research Network. Chloe has also been a Postdoctoral Fellow at the University of Bristol and holds a PhD in Sociology from Goldsmiths, University of London.

Kayla Preston (she/her) is a PhD student in sociology at the University of Toronto. Her areas of interest are the far right, gender, political sociology, and race. She has published research in the journals *Postcolonial Studies* and *Men and Masculinities* and in the edited collection *Gendering Globalization, Globalizing Gender: Postcolonial Perspectives*.

Ruth Ramsden-Karelse (she/her) is a Research Fellow at the ICI Berlin Institute for Cultural Inquiry and an Associate of the University of Manchester's Centre on Dynamics of Ethnicity (CoDE) and the Stuart Hall Foundation. In 2022, Ruth received her DPhil in English from the University of Oxford. Centring on South African communities that were legally classified 'Coloured' under apartheid, the key focus of her interdisciplinary research is the worldmaking work of self-described gays and girls from 1950 to the present, with a focus on depictions of Cape Town's District Six and, in particular, the GALA Queer Archive's Kewpie Collection. Ruth's writing has appeared in publications including *GLQ: A Journal of Lesbian and Gay Studies* and *Gender, Place & Culture: A Journal of Feminist Geography*.

Lorna-Jane Richardson (she/her) is a Lecturer in Digital Humanities and Heritage in the School of Art, Media, and American Studies at the University of East Anglia. Her research and teaching are focused on digital media, cultural heritage, and digital research ethics. She is interested in how the use of digital technologies might support creativity, discussion, and the repurposing of expert knowledge in communities. She researches how the use of social media can support, damage, exclude, and contain public discourse, expertise, and alternative ideas. She works predominantly with data drawn from public digital discussions and online communities, most recently working with data about film heritage, archaeological sites, ancient DNA and material culture, as well as the lived experience of online patient communities.

Kurt Sengul (he/him) is a media and communications scholar in the Department and Media and Communications at the University of Sydney. He has published widely on the topic of far-right populist communication in journals such as Critical Discourse Studies, Media International Australia, and Communication Research and Practice.

Alice Sibley (she/her) is a final-year PhD candidate at Nottingham Trent University in the United Kingdom. She focuses on the demographics and grievances of the British far right. She has published in edited collections, such as *The Handbook for Non-Violent Extremism* in 2023, and journals, such as *The British Journal of Political and International Relations* in 2022. Her research interests include the populist radical right, far-right extremism, and far-right terrorism.

Omran Shroufi (he/him) is a Postdoctoral Researcher at the Vrije Universiteit Brussel where he is investigating how far-right youth engage with audiovisual fiction. Omran recently completed a PhD in Politics at the University of York where he examined the emergence of pro-Israeli far-right parties in Western Europe. His research interests include far-right studies, far-right ideology, German politics, and (discourses about) populism and anti-populism.

Ryan Switzer (he/him) is a PhD candidate in Stockholm University's Department of Sociology. He researches space, emotion, and stigma in the Nordic far-right social movement through ethnographic methods.

Vanessa Tautter (they/them) is a PhD researcher at the Centre for Memory, Narrative, and Histories at the University of Brighton with a focus on oral history, memory studies, and cultural studies. Currently, they are also a junior fellow at the International Research Centre for Cultural Studies (IFK) in Vienna. Their PhD project critically explores experiences of transnational change in public memory politics in Europe since the 1980s among those who grew up in previously dominant, now largely residual memory cultures, using Austria and Northern Ireland as case studies. During their PhD, Tautter has been a visiting researcher at the Austrian Academy of Sciences, Queen's University Belfast, and the University of Vienna. They previously studied History and English at the University of Graz, Maynooth University, and West Virginia University.

Catherine Tebaldi (she/they) is a failed tradwife. She is a postdoctoral researcher in digital and linguistic anthropology at the University of Luxembourg, a member of the Far Right Analysis network and the Institute for Research on Male Supremacism, and the digital media manager of the Society for Linguistic Anthropology.

Meghan Tinsley (she/her) is a Lecturer in Sociology at the University of Manchester. Her research brings together themes of nationalism, racialisation, state violence, and memory. Her work has been published in a number of international sociological and interdisciplinary journals, including *Memory Studies*, *Current Sociology*, *Critical Sociology*, *Postcolonial Studies*, and *Ethnic and Racial Studies*. Her first book, entitled *Commemorating Muslims in the First World War Centenary: Making Melancholia* (Routledge, 2021), examines how a century-old conflict widely perceived as a European civil war remains a catalyst for constructing collective identity in two post-imperial, multicultural nations. She argues that the dominant narrative of Muslim colonial subjects at war writes the nation's own idea of its contemporary self onto the past. In this narrative, empire is rewritten as multiculturalism, and colonial soldiers establish the conditions under which contemporary Muslims might belong to the nation. Meghan's current research engages with contesting statues, imperial nostalgia, and decolonising the museum. She convenes the Decolonial Reading Group, which draws staff and students from across the Faculty of Humanities. She is also co-founder and co-convenor of the British Sociological Association's Postcolonial and Decolonial Transformations Study Group. Meghan is a Member of the Editorial Boards of *Sociology* and *The Sociological Review*.

Antonia Vaughan (she/her) is a PhD student in Politics at the University of Bath. Her research focuses on the ethics of researching the far right and the mainstreaming of the far right online.

Michael Vaughan (he/him) completed his PhD at the University of Sydney on the contentious politics of international tax, before working as a Postdoctoral Researcher at the Weizenbaum Institute for the Networked Society in Berlin with a focus on far-right digital communication. He is currently a Research Officer at the International Inequalities Institute at the London School of Economics and Political Science. His research interests include digital political communication and participation, far-right politics, and the communicative dimension of mobilisation around economic inequality.

Katherine Williams (she/her) is a final year PhD candidate in the School of Law and Politics at Cardiff University, UK. Her research investigates women's engagement with the populist radical right, with a specific focus on the role and motivations of women in Alternative for Germany (AfD).

Aaron Winter (he/him) is a Senior Lecturer in Sociology (Race and Anti-Racism) at Lancaster University. He is co-editor of *Discourses and Practices of Terrorism: Interrogating Terror* (2010), *Reflexivity in Criminological Research: Experiences with the Powerful and the Powerless* (Palgrave, 2014), *Historical Perspectives on Organised Crime and Terrorism* (2018), and *Researching the Far Right: Theory, Method and Practice* (2020), and co-author, with Aurelien Mondon, of *Reactionary Democracy: How Racism and the Populist Far Right Became Mainstream* (Verso, 2020). He is also co-editor of *Identities: Global Studies in Culture and Power* and the Manchester University Press series Racism, Resistance and Social Change.

Jackson Wood (he/him) is a PhD candidate in Criminology at the University of Melbourne. His research concerns far-right 'extremism' in virtual space, with a focus on the social media platform called Discord. More broadly, Jackson's research interests also include qualitative methods, ethics, and the intersection between technology, harm, and justice.

Yutaka Yoshida (he/him) is a Lecturer in Social Sciences at Cardiff University. He has expertise in researching far-right movements in Japan and psychosocial studies. He previously taught the undergraduate Hate Crime module at London South Bank University and is currently coordinating the Crime in the Digital World module for postgraduate students at Cardiff University. While continuing to explore nationalist civil movements, Yutaka has also developed an interest in studying fraud victimisation in Japan.

Gary Younge (he/him) is Professor of Sociology at the University of Manchester. He was previously a columnist and editor-at-large of the *Guardian*. Throughout his career, both his journalism and books have covered social movements in general (and the civil rights movement in particular), inequality, race, immigration, identity, and politics. He is currently concentrating his research on the Black presence in post-war Europe.

Michael C. Zeller (he/him) is an Assistant Professor of comparative politics at the Geschwister-Scholl-Institute for Political Science at Ludwig-Maximilians-Universität München. He completed his PhD in Political Science at Central European University. His research interests include social movements, far-right socio-politics, political violence, and qualitative methodologies. Dr Zeller worked as an Associate Researcher on the EU Horizon-2020 BRaVE (Building Resilience against Violent Extremism and Polarisation) project and as a principal investigator for the Proscribed Right-Wing Extremist Organisations (PREO) project. His research has been published in the journals *Mobilization*, *Intersections: East European Journal of Society and Politics*, and *Social Movement Studies*.

Series editors' foreword

Series Editors: John Solomos, Satnam Virdee, and Aaron Winter

The study of race, racism, and ethnicity has expanded greatly since the end of the twentieth century. This expansion has coincided with a growing awareness of the continuing role that these issues play in contemporary societies all over the globe. *Racism, Resistance and Social Change* is a new series of books that seeks to make a substantial contribution to this flourishing field of scholarship and research. We are committed to providing a forum for the publication of the highest quality scholarship on race, racism, anti-racism, and ethnic relations. As editors of this series, we would like to publish both theoretically driven books and texts with an empirical frame that seek to further develop our understanding of the origins, development, and contemporary forms of racisms, racial inequalities, and racial and ethnic relations. We welcome work from a range of theoretical and political perspectives, and as the series develops we ideally want to encourage a conversation that goes beyond specific national or geopolitical environments. While we are aware that there are important differences between national and regional research traditions, we hope that scholars from a variety of disciplines and multidisciplinary frames will take the opportunity to include their research work in the series.

As the title of the series highlights, we also welcome texts that can address issues about resistance and anti-racism as well as the role of political and policy interventions in this rapidly evolving discipline. The changing forms of racist mobilisation and expression that have come to the fore in recent years have highlighted the need for more reflection and research on the role of political and civil society mobilisations in this field.

We are committed to building on theoretical advances by providing an arena for new and challenging theoretical and empirical studies on the changing morphology of race and racism in contemporary societies.

Introduction

*Antonia Vaughan, Joan Braune, Meghan Tinsley,
and Aurelien Mondon*

At a time when far-right and even fascist politics are becoming increasingly mainstream globally – often with deadly direct and indirect consequences – research is essential to understand the most effective ways to combat such ideologies. To do so, it is crucial to undertake this research first and foremost in defence of and in solidarity with those targeted and harmed by these ideologies, while also acknowledging the threat posed to broader democratic principles and commitments to equality, human rights, and dignity. We must also contend with the reality that such research engages with texts and movements that do physical and verbal violence, raising a number of urgent ethical issues for researchers.

As such, this book fills a significant gap in an otherwise incredibly diverse and extensive literature (see Ashe et al. 2020 for a good overview). Indeed, while academic research on the far right has been booming, little to no attention has been paid to the ethics of researching what is clearly a particularly sensitive and politically urgent topic (Conway 2021). These ethical dilemmas are extensive, whether regarding the politics itself and the threat it poses, the safety and well-being of research participants and researchers, or the dissemination of findings and risks posed to communities at the sharp end of such politics. Beyond explicitly ethical questions, this book also offers a critical intervention into the field of research on the far right to address issues such as racism, sexism, white supremacy, colonialism, and positionality, which must be core to any ethical approach to social research.

As we explore in various chapters of this book, an ethical approach to research is not just about how we approach the far right, but also how we talk about the far right and who and what our research impacts.[1] At particular times, certain terms are preferred over others, and it is not always clear whether researchers carefully consider the impact of their choice of terminology (Hunger and Paxton 2022; Mondon 2022). For example, terms such as 'racism' and 'fascism' are rarely used by mainstream researchers and 'counter-extremism' think tanks and initiatives, while terms that blur the distinction between the left and right, like 'populism', 'radicalisation', and an ever-evolving plethora of buzzwords (coalitional accelerationism, cumulative extremism, salad bar extremism) have become widespread (e.g., Hughes and Miller-Idriss 2021; Tiflati 2022). Similarly, a process of exceptionalisation is often at play where the far and extreme right are portrayed as outside of the norm, rather than as sharing porous and movable borders. The recent focus on 'polarisation' in academic and popular discourse alike has meant that the threat of the far right is often analysed merely in terms of its danger to national security and the status quo, and Nazis are casually lumped in with leftist activists, Muslims (as a racialised and homogenised community), and others as all being equally 'extremist' or 'illiberal'.

These approaches emphasise stopping 'terrorism' – understood as illegal violent incidents, and excluding the daily terror experienced by many members of marginalised or targeted communities, including at the hands of the very state authorities tasked with the prevention of terrorism (Meier 2022; Morrison et al. 2021). Some studies euphemise the racism that is core to far-right campaigns by these parties, movements, and their supporters as the 'legitimate grievances' of those 'left behind' by immigration or cultural or social change (see Mondon and Winter 2020 for an overview). Such euphemisation directly contributes to white supremacist narratives like 'white genocide' and the 'great replacement'. Others suggest that the only way to fight the far right is through kind outreach to those who have fallen into its web, ignoring the danger this may pose and the ways in which it may provide new platforms for hate (see Braune's chapter on the 'compassion narrative').

The mainstreaming of the far right has been accompanied by calls to 'debate' (that is, platform) far-right speakers in academic settings. In the UK and the US, a moral panic about 'cancel culture' on campus has presented difficulties for anti-fascist academics who argue that all research is political. We contend that uncritical demands for empathy with the far right and pressure to form positive relationships with proponents of far-right politics inflict harm, render communities less safe, and neglect the obligation we have towards victims of such politics. In short, the chapters in this book do not simply describe ethical research practices – rather, we are issuing a call to engage in ethical research at a time when our research can either help or hinder the far right. Unethical research can cause real harm: harm to those at the sharp end of such politics, harm to researchers, harm to participants, and harm to the possibility of real democratic participation and human flourishing.

Some of the chapters in this book could be found in more conventional compendiums of research on the far right. However, this book is first and foremost an intervention into the mainstream discourse on the far right and how to fight it. We seek to move away from traditional approaches based on 'post-racial' fantasies which build on the idea that racism is 'frozen'

(Lentin 2020) and only present under exceptional circumstances at the margins of society where it can simply be surveilled and policed. Instead, we begin with the assumption that racism as an ideology evolves constantly and remains present within mainstream structures. As such, this book is grounded in Critical Race Theory (see Ray 2022) and draws from feminist theory and other approaches which have sought to stress the necessity of engaging with the question of power more generally, rather than simply seeing the far right as an aberration and the sole agent in its current success (or even failures).

One of the core strengths of our collection is, therefore, its critical and reflective approach. This is enriched by the range of contributors, from established scholars who have long navigated the challenges such research demands to early career researchers currently facing the most pressing ethical dilemmas and developing innovative strategies to address them. Equally, contributors to this volume describe a range of approaches to ethical research, whether by grappling with the politics themselves, their impact, or the bureaucracy that ethics sometimes involves. As such, we hope this book becomes a valuable resource for undergraduate and postgraduate students interested in the topic, as well as for early career researchers grappling with these very issues. We also hope that it will prove of interest to established scholars and those approaching research on the far right from a less critical perspective to provoke reflection on developed practices. Finally, while the book is written primarily by academics, we hope it will also speak to researchers outside the academy engaged in the work of understanding the far right to counter it, including journalists, antifascists, those working with NGOs countering hate, and others. As editors, along with many of the contributors, we see our scholarship as public and engaged, and we support activist struggles against oppression and for racial and economic justice alongside our scholarship. We hope to see new experiments, discussions, and progress in ethical practice as a result of this book.

This book should also be understood for the critical challenge it poses to mainstream studies of the far right. This volume is more of a starting point for a wider public discussion than a definitive handbook on how to research the far right ethically. Building on the workshops organised by the EthEx Network,[2] we were overwhelmed by the positive response to our call for papers. Thus, in the hope of creating space for a large and wide-ranging number of voices, we invited contributors to submit shorter, reflective contributions rather than traditional, academic chapters. We believe this is a strength of this book, as it has enabled our contributors to highlight challenging and complex issues that frequently are omitted from more traditional formats and centre reflection and criticality. While the answers to key ethical dilemmas remain, at times, elusive, we believe that starting those conversations is absolutely essential, not simply in the ethical journey any scholar must undertake, but particularly at a time when the far right is a very direct threat to so many.

Based on the topics covered and issues discussed during the EthEx workshops, and following discussions within the editorial teams, we crafted a call for papers around core questions which we believe require urgent answers. Following the many excellent submissions, we found six core themes and grouped the chapters into six parts according to these themes.

The first part, "What's in a name", engages with key terminological debates which have been core to the discipline for decades but seeks to push traditional discussions further by weighing the impact of our choice of words. While the chapters offer some leads and suggestions regarding definitions, the objective here is not to police the field and terminology used by scholars, but to highlight that choices are never neutral and always have consequences. As such, this part seeks to highlight the importance of engaging critically with the words we use to carry meaning and the need to reflect on the role our research plays in helping or hindering others in their attempt to make sense of the world we live in. Omran Shroufi's intervention comes first to discuss what the far right is and isn't, but more precisely common oversights which occur in the field when choosing terminology. Building on Omran's contribution, Kurt Sengul develops an urgent plea for scholars in far right studies to take race seriously, noting that "in the absence of race critical analysis, [we] risk (re)producing individualistic and inadequate accounts of racism by focusing exclusively on the rhetoric of racist far-right political actors". This is further developed by George Newth who explores his own trajectory to understand further how race and racism have been neglected in far right studies. Moving away from the topic of racism, Ryan Switzer explores similar tensions regarding the concept of violence and the necessity for "a repertoires of violence approach to understanding how power circulates between state, social movement, and society". Finally, Miranda Jeanne Marie Iossifidis tackles a particularly timely issue, arguing the necessity to account for the inter-relation of white supremacist ideology, racial capitalism, and heteropatriarchy when researching the rise of ecofascism.

Part II, "Positionality, standpoint, and intersectionality", focuses on how the positionality and standpoint of researchers can impact not only on the field but on wider society. Challenging some positivist approaches which have placed the researcher above their research, as if social sciences could be conducted in the same manner as hard sciences, the chapters here argue that our striving to conduct impartial research must start with a clear engagement with our own positionality, but also take into account the wider state of play and norms which may invisibilise certain patterns and structures of oppression. Aurelien Mondon's chapter links this part to the previous one, providing a survey of articles published in the field. Through an analysis of the preferred terms in abstracts and titles, the chapter highlights the ways in which our choices may impact our findings and how the lack of diversity in the field may obscure certain elements and engagement with more critical approaches in terms of race and racism in particular. Some of the chapters are self-reflective contributions, highlighting the impact of doing research on the far right when being at the sharp end of such politics. Ethnographies have proven a popular approach to studying the far right and yet one that is replete with pitfalls and bad practices. As such, we made a conscious decision to provide space for ethnographers to explore such dilemmas, in this part as well as others. Based on her experience conducting ethnographic research in gaming, Imo Kaufman seeks to reconcile with the impossibility at times of disentangling "ideological, ethical, and methodological knots". Balša Lubarda's chapter also explores the dilemmas raised by ethnographic research, the opportunities his own identity and position opened up for him, and the considerations which resulted from this. Catherine Tebaldi and Rae Jereza's chapter adds more to the necessity of engaging critically with the field, exploring "the institutional reproduction of the colonial ethnographer as default and assert[ing] the importance of utilizing anti-colonial, feminist approaches to counter this tendency". This leads us to Elsa Bengtsson Meuller's chapter which draws on decolonial and Black feminist thought to reflect on the risks of enhancing the messages of antifeminist and male supremacist (extremist) ideologies through our role as academics and producers of knowledge. Finally, Aaron Winter reflects on his research experience and decisions about how to engage with the far right as part of a wider examination of the racial politics of research on the far right.

In the third part, "The haunting past: memory and far right studies", contributors consider how collective memory and heritage are appropriated and mobilised by the far right in order to project their ideologies across history. They reflect, further, on the ethical obligation of archaeologists, historians, social scientists, and heritage workers to recognise the political nature of their research, to debunk the far right's narratives of past and present, and to condemn white supremacy across history. At a time when research in the field is increasingly presentist, the chapters in this section demonstrate that we must absolutely engage with wider historical contexts if we are to understand the current resurgence of far-right movements and parties. In the opening chapter, David Farrell-Banks and Lorna-Jane Richardson point out that whilst academic archaeologists increasingly acknowledge the far right's appropriation of the past, frequently, heritage and archaeological discourse echoes these same far-right tropes. Within this context, Farrell-Banks and

Richardson reflect on their experience of archaeology and heritage studies, questioning how popular representations of the past might feed the rhetoric of the far right and how this might be countered within their respective fields. Next, Andrew Fergus Wilson outlines how the far right imposes spiritual, cultural, and folkloric meanings on the landscape and how these movements use the rhetoric of indigeneity. He argues that this requires an active, targeted response and considers how far-right narratives of land can be countered and vanquished. In the next chapter, Meghan Tinsley, Ruth Ramsden-Karelse, Chloe Peacock, and Sadia Habib reflect on their experiences of researching cultural activism in the thick of a right-wing 'culture war'. Drawing from interviews with cultural activists as well as their own experiences of scrutiny and surveillance, the authors argue that amidst its newfound visibility, research on cultural heritage is inherently political. As such, declining to call for change, or promoting a 'balanced' view of history, is an endorsement of imperial amnesia and nostalgia. Further, amidst the prevalence of media and government accusations of 'erasing history', we argue for the importance of providing a counter-narrative, grounded in histories of empire and slavery as well as the literature on power and public space. The following chapter, by Daniel Jones, focuses on the role of archivists in curating and safeguarding far-right paraphernalia. He discusses the obligation of archivists to support the deep decolonisation of the curriculum in relation to British Studies, ensuring a change of content focus is met with a broader base of sources that reflect the experiences of diverse communities. Finally, the chapter by Jean Beaman links collective memory and national identity. Drawing from the author's experiences of researching race and racism in France, Beaman argues that it is crucial to centre individuals' lived experiences and to contextualise these within national and transnational histories.

The fourth part, "Care and safety", centres considerations of harm, risk, and the ethics of care when researching a topic that is inherently harmful. Contributing to the burgeoning literature on researcher safety, the contributors in this section consider harm, risk, and care in reference to the researchers themselves, the community, the participants, and the academy more broadly. Several of the chapters incorporate lived experience and offer practical advice, whilst the others reflect on how environmental and theoretical implications impact risk and harm. With positionality substantially mediating vulnerability to, and experiences of, harm, it is critical to interrogate the presence and availability of care and experiences of safety. Alice Sibley opens the section with a practical reflection detailing their experience of harassment whilst collecting data online and the steps they took to protect themselves. Following that, Kayla Preston addresses the challenges of individualising self-care by emphasising the importance of community for scholars and calls for community-based care and support. In critiquing the measurements of success in academia, Antonia Vaughan's chapter highlights how individualising responsibility for safety has implications for experiences of harm and who stays in academia. Shifting in focus towards institutional understandings of risk, Jackson Wood critiques the securitised ideation of research on the far right, its presence in institutional evaluations of harm, and the end result of 'red zoning' such research. Moving away from harm to the researcher, Luc S. Cousineau's chapter considers and reconciles practising a feminist ethic of care when studying a topic where the participants are so explicitly willingly and actively harmful and how this manifests in the dissemination of research. Collectively, the chapters seek to interrogate practices of care and safety throughout the lifetime of research and the particular structures of evaluating and managing harm, whether that be individual (Sibley), community (Preston), environmental (Vaughan), institutional (Wood), or as a researcher (Cousineau).

Part V, "Complications of engaging far-right participants and formers", concerns the difficult dance involved in research on far-right or former far-right participants: a dance between the seemingly opposed poles of *connection* (understanding, empathetic curiosity, and holding the humanity and complexity of research participants) and *distance* (personal and community safety, emotional boundaries, rejecting and challenging unacceptable views). One theme that emerges in the first three chapters of this part is the need to be deeply reflective about stories, including observing how they can "seduce" us (Tautter) or be deceptively "heart-warming" (Braune), as well as attending to feelings of identification or disidentification with research participants' narratives (Yoshida). Vanessa Tautter's chapter on the ethics of listening shows that there is a form of empathetic listening that nevertheless avoids complicity and wards off the "seduction" to agree or condone. Joan Braune's chapter warns of the potential harms of stories told by former members of hate groups, urging centring and empowering their victims instead. Next, Yutaka Yoshida's chapter reflecting psychoanalytically on an interview with a Japanese far-right activist shows the need for interviewers to reflect on feelings of commonality with the interviewee, while maintaining necessary emotional boundaries. Yoshida's interviewee's perception of the interviewer as an authority figure leads the interviewee to both flatter and resent him, wanting Yoshida to excuse and absolve him at times and viewing him as an oppressive "boss" figure at others. Yoshida's reflexive approach shows both distance and concern for avoiding dehumanising or oversimplifying. Other ways of walking the thin line of connection and distance are addressed in the final two chapters of this part. Katherine Williams engages a feminist research method and seeks to understand participants in the Alternative for Germany party, reflecting on the need to report accurately on research participants while avoiding the appearance of condoning far-right views. In the final chapter in the section, by Carina Hoerst and John Drury, Hoerst reflects on how her research online requires a challenging balancing act with regard to matters of privacy and personal safety as well as the challenges of laws and ethics guidelines requiring "informed consent" when this may not be fully possible.

The sixth and final part of the book, "Activism and dissemination", turns outward as it reflects critically on the ideal relationship between research and activism. In particular, it encourages readers to think more deeply about their role at a time when the resurgence of the far right is putting many communities at risk. The chapter by Richard McNeil-Willson, Michael Vaughan, and Michael C. Zeller examines the ethics of engaging with policymakers within the context of racialised and Islamophobic approaches to Countering Violent Extremism (CVE). Next, Anna A. Meier draws from her interviews with policy elites to consider what it means to be a white researcher in white-dominated spaces researching topics deeply entangled with whiteness. In the following chapter, Remi Joseph-Salisbury, Laura Connelly, and Aurelien Mondon discuss how the principle of working in service can guide the praxes of those researching both anti-racist scholar-activism and the mainstreaming of the far right. The chapter by Isis Giraldo uses the case study of Colombia to call for rethinking the terminology of far right studies and decolonising the field. Gary Younge, reflecting on his experience as a journalist and editor, considers the ethics of interviewing far-right supporters. In the final chapter, Katy Brown argues that we must centralise the ethics of talking 'about' in our understanding of mainstreaming, particularly its relationship to talking 'with', in order to develop a consciousness of the role academia can play in this process. Failing to do so only contributes to the normalisation of far-right discourse.

There are a number of absences in this book which speak to the need for more research on the ethics of researching the far right. First, while we have tried to ensure that our contributors hail from a range of backgrounds, the whiteness and Eurocentrism of the field are such that it is perhaps not as diverse as we had hoped. This may suggest that we need to change the way that research on the far right is done, including shifting which questions are considered most relevant, what concepts and terms are highlighted, and how safety and solidarity are generated, in order to bring in a greater diversity of scholars. While we recognise we have more work to do to connect with a greater diversity of researchers and build more solidarity, we hope some of the ethical changes suggested in this volume will help to change and challenge the field in the direction of greater inclusion and solidarity. Getting more diverse involvement is also made difficult by the very nature of the research, including its particular dangers to those in targeted groups and the emotional toll that working with frightening and dehumanising material can take. As editors, we tried our hardest to mitigate any occurrence of undue harm. This meant planning for a loose timeline and providing tailored deadlines. At times, it meant accepting that contributors would not submit and being grateful for their engagement nevertheless as this was for some a brave undertaking.

Second, we noted a lack of interest in the call for papers from academics from more mainstream and in particular positivist backgrounds. The critical nature of our call for papers always meant that this was to be expected, but it is telling that the need to reflect on our practice in researching the far right is not taken seriously yet in most scholarship on the topic. While it is hoped this book will be read by colleagues with different approaches, we fear that the rejection of considering ethical issues involved in researching such politics is not an oversight, but core to an academic practice which sees objectivity as requiring neutrality and disengagement as well as detachment from considerations regarding positionality or accountability.

The themes of the book are far from exhaustive, exemplified by the events and publications produced since the project was initiated. However, in this book, we are contributing a broad provocation and series of starting points which we hope will be built on. Throughout the book, we consistently reject the claim that research on the far right can or should be 'apolitical', 'objective' or 'neutral'. Rather, in considering ethics reflectively across disciplines, topics, and methods, the chapters make explicit that research on the far right is always political and that it always carries political implications. A number of the chapters contain practical advice, questions for further research, and calls to action. We hope these will be fruitful in moving the field forward and in working together for greater equality and justice, eventually ending the threats posed by far-right political movements.

Notes

1 It is worth noting here that we will use 'far right' for nouns and 'far-right' for adjectives, unless we refer to researchers or studies of the far right which will be written as far right researcher/studies.

2 The EthEx Network (or the Network for Critical Research on the Ethics of Researching the Extreme and Far Right) was created in the summer of 2020 by Meghan Tinsley, Neema Begum, Katy Brown, Natalie-Anne Hall, Aurelien Mondon, Antonia Vaughan, and Yutaka Yoshida.

References

Ashe, S., Busher, J., Macklin, G. and Winter, A. (eds). 2020. *Researching the Far Right: Theory, Method and Practice*. New York: Routledge.

Conway, M. 2021. 'Online Extremism and Terrorism Research Ethics: Researcher Safety, Informed Consent, and the Need for Tailored Guidelines', *Terrorism and Political Violence*, 33(2), 367–380.

Eatwell, R. 2006. 'Community Cohesion and Cumulative Extremism in Contemporary Britain', *The Political Quarterly*, 77(2), April–June 2006, 204–216.

Hughes, B. and Miller-Idriss, C. 2021. 'Uniting for Total Collapse: The January 6 Boost to Accelerationism', Combating Terrorism Center at West Point, *CTC Sentinel*, 14/4, April–May 2021. https://ctc.westpoint.edu/uniting-for-total-collapse-the-january-6-boost-to-accelerationism/ (accessed 12 October 2022).

Hunger, S. and Paxton, F. 2022. 'What's in a Buzzword? A Systematic Review of the State of Populism Research in Political Science', *Political Science Research and Methods*, 10(3), 617–633.

Lentin, A. 2020. *Why Race Still Matters*. Medford, MA: Polity Press.

Meier, A. A. 2022. 'Terror as Justice, Justice as Terror: Counterterrorism and Anti-Black Racism in the United States', *Critical Studies on Terrorism*, 15(1), 83–101.

Mondon, A. 2022. 'Epistemologies of Ignorance in Far Right Studies: The Invisibilisation of Racism and Whiteness in Times of Populist Hype', *Acta Politica*, 58, 876–894.

Mondon, A. and Winter, A. 2020. *Reactionary Democracy: How Racism and the Populist Far Right Became Mainstream*. London: Verso.

Morrison, J., Silke, A. and Bont, E. 2021. 'The Development of the Framework for Research Ethics in Terrorism Studies (FRETS)', *Terrorism and Political Violence*, 33(2), 271–289.

Ray, V. 2022. *On Critical Race Theory: Why It Matters and Why You Should Care*. New York: Random House.

Tiflati, H. 2022. 'The Extremism Market and Salad Bar Ideology', *European Eye on Radicalization*. https://eeradicalization.com/the-extremism-market-and-salad-bar-ideology/ (accessed 12 October 2022).

Part I

What's in a name

1

What the far right is(n't)

Omran Shroufi

This chapter aims to delineate some borders of what the far right is – and isn't – to consolidate existing critique of the trajectory of far right studies (Castelli Gattinara 2020; Mondon and Winter 2020; Brown, Mondon and Winter 2021) and provide a 'checklist' to reflect upon before conducting research. In particular, the chapter focuses on four key potential misconceptions:

1. Far-right politics is not just far-right party politics – often taken as pars pro toto, far-right parties are in fact only part of the picture. They operate alongside far-right writers, academics, think tanks, and non-parliamentary organisations;
2. There is no essential good/bad, far right/non-far right dichotomy – the contemporary far right is not necessarily the single biggest or a uniquely dangerous threat to democracy. Furthermore, the borders between the far right and non-far right are fluid and permeable;
3. The 'us' and 'them' of the far right are contingent – far-right forces may look to defend 'the nation', but some depict whole continents or even 'civilisations' as 'us'. Similarly, demonised 'others' may become sought-after constituents, even just out of strategic calculation, as the far right turns its gaze elsewhere;
4. The far right is not uniform – far-right parties and organisations differ in significant ways, both within and across countries, with some more or less extreme, racist, (neo)liberal, or protectionist.

Far-right politics is not just far-right party politics

Recent media interest has established a strong link between far-right parties and far-right politics, often seen as one and the same thing. Also, within academia, there has been a strong focus on electoral politics and voter preference, both of which are easily measurable and quantifiable, reflective of the dominance of positivist and rationalist approaches in the field. Yet, this overfocus on 'electoralism' (Castelli Gattinara 2020) comes at a cost (Brown, Mondon and Winter 2021), presenting as it does only part of the picture

(Göpffarth 2020; Shroufi and De Cleen 2022). The 'right to difference', for instance, a doctrine that replaced ideas of racial hierarchy with the notion of unique and 'incompatible' cultures (Rueda 2021: 222; Spektorowski 2003) – and which was later picked up by many far-right parties (Copsey 2018; Rueda 2021: 228–233; Rydgren 2005) – was developed by French far-right intellectuals (known as the *Nouvelle Droite*) largely operating outside the realm of party politics.

Focusing too narrowly on parties also overlooks the fact that "the far right is increasingly active in the street" (Castelli Gattinara 2020: 315). Consider for instance 'the Identitarians', the far-right pan-European movement that has taken to the streets to 'defend' Europe from a supposed influx of mass migration; PEGIDA (*Patriotische Europäer gegen die Islamisierung des Abendlandes* – Patriotic Europeans against the Islamisation of the Occident), which organised weekly protests in the East German city of Dresden to oppose (Muslim) immigration and demand more direct democracy; or the anti-Muslim English Defence League (EDL), set up in 2009 as a protest movement to fight the supposed Islamisation of England and defend English identity (Braouezec 2016: 638–639). While these non-parliamentary groups and movements can help shape the political agenda through attention-grabbing events, their success cannot be directly measured at the ballot box – although a symbiotic relationship does exist between these movements and far-right parties (see for instance Göpffarth 2020). The far right is equally active in organising and committing acts of terrorism. Indeed, according to Miller-Idriss (2021: 60), North America, West Europe, Australia, and New Zealand have seen a huge increase in far-right terrorism in recent years, up from one recorded far-right terrorist attack in 2010 to forty-nine recorded far-right terrorist attacks in 2019 – accounting for 82 per cent of all terrorism-related deaths in those countries.

(Mis)interpreting the strength of the far right only through the prism of electoral success similarly risks a situation in which the success or failure of far-right parties is used as a weathervane for the risk posed by extremist, divisive, and exclusionary ideas as such. However, far-right ideas can prosper without a successful far-right party. Even in a country like Germany, which was long considered immune to far-right success, it would be a mistake to see the *Alternative für Deutschland* (AfD) as a turning point. Germany had long been home to an extreme-right subculture that had developed largely independently of a successful far-right party (Backes and Mudde 2000). And, as the mainstreaming of the far-right functions in both directions and is more than just "a one-way process in which the far right moves closer to the mainstream" (Mondon and Winter 2020: 112), a far-right party, as is discussed in detail below, may have little electoral success while its ideas prosper in a new guise (see also Kallis 2013).

There is no black/white dichotomy

Nobody writing about or discussing politics is free from judgement, and nor should they be. It is perfectly reasonable for those concerned about hard-won civil liberties, freedom and equality, or the legacy of fascism to be concerned about the gains far-right parties continue to make. But, as Mondon and Winter point out (2020), it is equally important not to depict the far right as a uniquely dangerous threat to 'our way of life'.

The (undoubtedly well-intended) relief shown when far-right parties lose electoral support is often typical of such a misconception. During the 2019 UK elections, for example, the anti-racist organisation 'Hope not hate' dedicated much of its resources to attacking Nigel Farage's Brexit Party, later celebrating its apparent success in stopping the party from gaining any seats (McGregor 2019). As the organisation's campaign director Matthew McGregor wrote (2019): "We decided to take on Nigel Farage's party because it posed a threat. By winning seats, it would give voice to some really poisonous politics, pull the other parties to the right and create a bridgehead for populism in Parliament." Yet, there was little prospect of the party making significant electoral gains and, as Hope not hate also acknowledged, "[t]he Tories took on the mantle of the hardline pro-Brexit party, coalescing a lot of the Brexit Party's vote behind them" (McGregor 2019). If the designated 'far-right party' loses but its ideas win under a new, and more acceptable, guise, is it not something of a hollow victory? Similarly, during the 2021 state elections in the East German state of Saxony-Anhalt, the prospect of the AfD becoming the biggest party led many to fear the worst. With parts of the media framing the election as 'AfD versus democracy', the ruling centre-right *Christlich Demokratische Union Deutschlands* (CDU) in fact managed to increase its vote by over 7 per cent, while the AfD lost more than 3 per cent. After the election, the then co-leader of the *Sozialdemokratische Partei Deutschlands* (SPD), Norbert Walter-Borjans, while disappointed his party had lost votes, took comfort that "the democratic forces have won overall, the AfD has lost, that is a very important signal" (Haferkamp 2021). Yet, by framing the debate in such binary ways, the goal becomes little more than stopping the far right, rather than generating new political ideas or offering alternatives to the status quo. The far right can legitimately claim to be the only real alternative to business as usual (Mondon and Winter 2020: 5), whilst the 'non-far right', under the pretext the mainstream inherently poses less danger, can get away more easily with promoting racist or exclusionary policies.

A rigid black-white schema essentially overlooks how the borders between the mainstream and far right are "contingent and fluid [...] What is mainstream or extreme at one point in time does not have to be, nor remain, so"

(Brown, Mondon and Winter 2021: 5). Far-right politics does not always come with a clearly marked label, and it would be naïve to think that only far-right politicians – clearly designated as such – are guilty of propagating a far-right worldview. The former Austrian Chancellor Sebastian Kurz, for instance, shortly after agreeing on a coalition agreement with the Austrian Green party, depicted immigration and climate change as equivalent threats to the future of Europe in an interview with the *Financial Times* (Jones 2020). And the writers, thinkers, and commentators who publish articles and books promoting white supremacy or legitimise doomsday theories of an Arab/Muslim takeover of Europe do not always work for organisations clearly designated as 'far right'. For example, Thilo Sarrazin, whose best-selling book *Germany is abolishing itself* (*Deutschland schafft sich ab*) played a key role in stigmatising Arab and Turkish migrants in Germany and breaking taboos on the supposed links between ethnicity and intelligence, was a former board member of German Federal Bank.

The 'us' and 'them' of the far right are not fixed

Far-right politics will not always manifest itself in hatred towards one and the same designated 'other'. Far-right actors will focus their gaze on a variety of different 'others', but also those belonging to 'us' changes as far-right forces shift and swap allegiances. Furthermore, the far right's cherished territorial unit will not always correspond to its respective nation-state.

Whilst Jews had long been the 'special enemy' of the European far right (Bunzl 2007; Mudde 2007: 78–79), most successful 'modern' far-right parties have abandoned crude and explicit notions of antisemitism in their public rhetoric (Bunzl 2007: 29; Mudde 2007: 80). Today, it is much more common to hear the European far right target Muslims in their public discourse and proposed policies (Betz 2013; Kallis 2018; Zúquete 2008), whether through calls to ban the Quran (Geert Wilders), prevent women from wearing the Hijab in public (Marine Le Pen), or restrict the building of minarets (*Schweizerische Volkspartei* – SVP).

Some European far-right actors have even sought to reach out to Jewish communities (Wertheim 2017; Williams 2010) who are now considered a fundamental part of 'our Judeo-Christian Europe'. Not only is the history of Islam in Europe erased, but hundreds of years of Jewish persecution are glossed over and euphemistically repackaged as peaceful co-existence (Kübler 2008: 45). Indeed, it is now not uncommon to hear far-right politicians such as Geert Wilders (*Partij voor de Vrijheid* – PVV) or Marine Le Pen (*Rassemblement National* – RN) claim they are their country's biggest opponent of antisemitism, increasingly depicted as an imported phenomenon from Muslim-majority countries which no longer exists amongst 'indigenous' Europeans (Primor 2011) – a narrative also uncritically replicated in mainstream political debates (see Özyürek 2016). Even a party dogged by accusations of antisemitism and historical revisionism such as the Austrian FPÖ (Wodak 2018) organised an event in November 2016 with the title 'Have we learnt from history? The new antisemitism in Europe', during which ex-leader Heinz-Christian Strache singled out "left-wing parties" for enabling the "import of Islamist anti-Semitism into Europe" (FPÖ 2016).

While questions have been asked about the sincerity of the far right's supposed disavowal of antisemitism (Wodak 2018), the far right's embrace of Zionism and vehement support for Israel is undisputable (Shroufi 2015; Wertheim 2017) – and far-right leaders such as the Lega's Matteo Salvini have been welcomed in Israel with open arms (Trew 2018). To make sense of this development, it is important to understand how many far-right movements now depict a world in which 'we' are locked in a global battle with Islam, with Israel supposedly at the forefront of this conflict. What this shows is that the far right's 'us' is not limited to the respective nation but can extend to Europe, 'the West', or even 'Western civilisation' (Brubaker 2017; Bunzl 2007; Zúquete 2008). It is now not only a case of 'France for the French' but also 'Europe for the Europeans' (Liang Schori 2007). And whilst religion was previously of little importance to many far-right actors, some are now 'rediscovering' their Christian roots (Betz and Meret 2009; Zúquete 2008: 324–329) and have adopted Christianity as a cultural marker of difference and belonging (Brubaker 2017; Hadj-Abdou 2016; Minkenberg 2018), essentially to emphasise their opposition to Islam.

As Mudde (2019: 46) writes, "[a]ll far-right ideologies are built around a strict us-versus-them opposition, but both the us and the them can change over time". Taking a cue from De Cleen et al.'s (2018) critical reflections on populism, when engaging with far-right politics, it is important to pay attention to how far-right politics designates different groups 'us' and 'them' depending on the respective context of national history, political sensibilities, as well as demographic makeup of the state, continent, or (supra-)national organisation in question (see also Betz 2003).

The far right is not uniform

While it is common to speak of *the* far right, what we are dealing with is a relatively diverse range of parties, organisations, and ideas. There are differences between different far-right actors, which are also themselves often internally disunited. Moreover, far-right actors and organisations sometimes attack each other for their lack of 'true' far-right credentials.

A common distinction in much of the literature draws a line between the 'radical' and 'extreme' right. According to this conceptualisation, radical right parties largely operate in line with the civic and democratic norms that have become a cornerstone of West European polities in the post-war era (Halikiopoulou et al. 2013; Rydgren 2018: 1–2), while extreme right parties are wedded to a 'classic' repertoire of far-right ideas, including notions of biological superiority and a hierarchy of races. Even if the line between these two 'types' of parties is hard to distinguish in practice (Copsey 2018; Rydgren 2018: 3), this framework nonetheless helps to highlight the variation that exists within the far right. Not every far-right organisation looks like a group of racist skinheads; in fact, many successful far-right parties have made a conscious effort to appear much more presentable (Berezin 2007; Williams 2010). There is similarly a variety of positions on family values, gay marriage, taxation, or the environment, with some far-right actors more or less secular and others more or less neoliberal.

Also, consider the internal variation that exists within individual far-right movements or parties that are more than just the figureheads seen on television. Far-right parties consist of different factions, often with little in common, with more 'moderate' actors willing to compromise to reach public office, whilst others warn against becoming part of the very elite they set out to challenge. Ever since it was founded in 2013, the German AfD, for instance, has been plagued by infighting over the direction of the party (Havertz 2021: 37–51), with a decidedly more radical and *völkisch* wing dominant in the East. There are also intra-far-right divisions, with some far-right actors highly critical of the path others have chosen. The French MEP Jérôme Rivière left Marine Le Pen's RN in 2022 to join forces with the far-right polemicist Eric Zemmour after complaining that Le Pen had become too soft and was "unable to acknowledge obvious things such as the Great Replacement" (as cited in Darmanin 2022). In the UK, Nick Griffin, ex-leader of the neo-fascist British National Party (BNP), attacked the far-right anti-Muslim street movement EDL for being "a neo-con operation [...] a Zionist false flag operation, designed to create a real clash of civilisations right here on our streets between Islam and the rest of us" (as cited in Richardson 2013: 115).

Writing about the variation on the far right is nonetheless a balancing act. It is important not to lose sight of that which unites far-right parties, movements, and writers at a deeper, ideological level. While this is no easy task, an approach is needed that pays attention to both the variation and the core ideas which unite far-right actors. The radical/extreme distinction is no doubt useful as a heuristic device to help categorise notable differences, but we also need to avoid "becoming overly preoccupied with 'fundamental' or 'essential' ideological differences" (Copsey 2018: 117) between and within far-right parties and movements.

Conclusion

This chapter has been an attempt to consolidate and present several critical reflections on the study of the far right. While this overview is not exhaustive, I believe we have much to gain by reflecting on the following when writing and talking about the far right. First, while party politics are clearly important, other far-right actors and movements exist, and far-right politics can prosper without parties designated as such. Second, the far right is not the only actor pushing divisive or exclusionary politics, and we need to avoid creating a binary choice between a supposedly sensible and rational mainstream and a uniquely dangerous alternative. Third, how the far right operates is not static but shifts and changes. Far-right parties will not always sound 'far right', and they may even claim to defend previously demonised 'others'. And finally, although we often talk about *the* far right, there is a relatively great deal of variation between and within far-right movements, which often do not see eye to eye with one another.

In essence, this chapter argues that reflective and critical research on the far right needs to highlight what is unique and particular about the far right without overlooking similarities with other groups and ideas across the political spectrum. We need to be aware of variation within the far right without losing sight of that which unites it. Furthermore, we should be attentive that history will not always repeat itself identically and that far-right actors may even represent or work for 'non-far right' parties and organisations.

References

Backes, U. and Mudde, C. 2000. 'Germany: Extremism without Successful Parties', *Parliamentary Affairs*, 53(3), 457–468.

Berezin, M. 2007. 'Revisiting the French National Front', *Journal of Contemporary Ethnography*, 36(2), 129–146.

Betz, H.-G. 2003. 'The Growing Threat of the Radical Right'. In: Merkl, P. and Weinberg, L. (eds). *Right-Wing Extremism in the Twenty-First Century*. London: Frank Cass, 74–93.

Betz, H.-G. 2013. 'Mosques, Minarets, Burqas and Other Essential Threats: The Populist Right's Campaign against Islam in Western Europe'. In: Wodak, R., KhosraviNik, M., and Mral, B. (eds). *Right Wing Populism in Europe: Politics and Discourse*. London: Bloomsbury, 71–88.

Betz, H.-G. and Meret, S. 2009. 'Revisiting Lepanto: The Political Mobilization against Islam in Contemporary Western Europe', *Patterns of Prejudice*, 43(3–4), 313–334.

Braouezec, K. 2016. 'Identifying Common Patterns of Discourse and Strategy among the New Extremist Movements in Europe: The Case of the English Defence League and the Bloc Identitaire', *Journal of Intercultural Studies*, 37(6), 637–648.

Brown, K., Mondon, A. and Winter, A. 2021. 'The Far Right, the Mainstream and Mainstreaming: Towards a Heuristic Framework', *Journal of Political Ideologies*, online first, 1–18.

Brubaker, R. 2017. 'Between Nationalism and Civilizationism: The European Populist Moment in Comparative Perspective', *Ethnic and Racial Studies*, 40(8), 1191–1226.

Bunzl, M. 2007. *Anti-Semitism and Islamophobia: Hatreds Old and New in Europe.* Chicago, IL: Prickly Paradigm Press.

Castelli Gattinara, P. 2020. 'The Study of the Far Right and Its Three E's: Why Scholarship Must Go beyond Eurocentrism, Electoralism and Externalism', *French Politics*, 18(3), 314–333.

Copsey, N. 2018. 'The Radical Right and Fascism'. In: Rydgren, J. (ed.). *The Oxford Handbook of the Radical Right.* Oxford: Oxford University Press, 105–121.

Darmanin, J. 2022. 'Marine Le Pen's Top MEP Defects to Eric Zemmour's Campaign', *POLITICO* [Online], 20 January 2022. Available at: https://www .politico.eu/article/marine-le-pen-top-mep-jerome-riviere-defect-eric-zemmour -campaign/ (accessed 7 April 2022).

De Cleen, B., Glynos, J. and Mondon, A. 2018. 'Critical Research on Populism: Nine Rules of Engagement', *Organization*, 25(5), 649–661.

FPÖ. 2016. 'HC Strache: "Antisemitismus stellt ein Verbrechen gegen die Menschlichkeit dar"', www.fpoe.at [Online]. Available at: https://www.fpoe.at/ artikel/hc-strache-antisemitismus-stellt-ein-verbrechen-gegen-die-menschlichkeit -dar/ (accessed 2 June 2018).

Göpffarth, J. 2020. 'Rethinking the German Nation as German Dasein: Intellectuals and Heidegger's Philosophy in Contemporary German New Right Nationalism', *Journal of Political Ideologies*, 25(3), 248–273.

Hadj-Abdou, L. 2016. 'The "Religious Conversion" of the Austrian Freedom Party'. In: Marzouki, N., McDonnell, D., and Roy, O. (eds). *Saving the People: How Populists Hijack Religion.* London: Hurst & Company, 29–46.

Haferkamp, L. 2021. 'Wahl in Sachsen-Anhalt: CDU klar vor AfD, Verluste für die SPD', Vorwaerts [Online], 6 June 2021. Available at: https://www.vorwaerts.de /artikel/wahl-sachsen-anhalt-cdu-klar-afd-verluste-spd (accessed 6 April 2022).

Halikiopoulou, D., Mock, S. and Vasilopoulou, S. 2013. 'The Civic Zeitgeist: Nationalism and Liberal Values in the European Radical Right', *Nations and Nationalism*, 19(1), 107–127.

Havertz, R. 2021. *Radical Right Populism in Germany: AfD, Pegida, and the Identitarian Movement.* London: Routledge.

Jones, S. 2020. 'Austria's Leader Says Immigration as Much a Risk as Climate Change', *Financial Times* [Online], 13 January 2020. Available at: https://www.ft .com/content/e8435d86-3533-11ea-a6d3-9a26f8c3cba4 (accessed 6 April 2022).

Kallis, A. 2013. 'Far-Right "Contagion" or a Failing "Mainstream"? How Dangerous Ideas Cross Borders and Blur Boundaries', *Democracy and Security*, 9(3), 221–246.

Kallis, A. 2018. 'The Radical Right and Islamophobia'. In: Rydgren, J. (ed.). *The Oxford Handbook of the Radical Right.* Oxford: Oxford University Press, 42–60.

Kübler, E. 2008. '"Des Juden laue Verteidiger": Antisemitismus, Philosemitismus und Pluralismus im demokratischen Europa'. In: Bunzl, J. and Senfft, A. (eds). *Zwischen Antisemitismus und Islamophobie: Vorurteile und Projektionen in Europa und Nahost*. Hamburg: VSA-Verlag, 33–52.

McGregor, M. 2019. 'How We Undid the Brexit Party Threat at the Election'. Hope Not Hate [Online]. Available at: https://hopenothate.org.uk/magazine/in-search-of-hope/zero-seats/ (accessed 6 April 2022).

Miller-Idriss, C. 2021. 'From 9/11 to 1/6: The War on Terror Supercharged the Far Right', *Foreign Affairs*, 100(5), 54–65.

Minkenberg, M. 2018. 'Religion and the Radical Right'. In: Rydgren, J. (ed.). *The Oxford Handbook of the Radical Right*. Oxford: Oxford University Press, 366–393.

Mondon, A. and Winter, A. 2020. *Reactionary Democracy: How Racism and the Populist Far Right Became Mainstream*. London: Verso Books.

Mudde, C. 2019. *The Far Right Today*. Cambridge: Polity.

Mudde, C. 2007. *Populist Radical Right Parties in Europe*. Cambridge: Cambridge University Press.

Özyürek, E. 2016. 'Export-Import Theory and the Racialization of Anti-Semitism: Turkish- and Arab-Only Prevention Programs in Germany', *Comparative Studies in Society and History*, 58(1), 40–65.

Primor, A. 2011. 'The Daughter as De-Demonizer', *Haaretz* [Online]. 7 January 2011. Available at: https://www.haaretz.com/1.5104970 (accessed 15 October 2019).

Richardson, J. E. 2013. 'Ploughing the Same Furrow? Continuity and Change on Britain's Extreme Right Fringe'. In Wodak, R., KhosraviNik, M., and Mral, B. (eds). *Right-Wing Populism in Europe*. London: Bloomsbury, 105–119.

Rueda, D. 2021. 'Alain de Benoist, Ethnopluralism and the Cultural Turn in Racism', *Patterns of Prejudice*, 55(3), 213–235.

Rydgren, J. 2005. 'Is Extreme Right-Wing Populism Contagious? Explaining the Emergence of a New Party Family', *European Journal of Political Research*, 44(3), 413–437.

Rydgren, J. 2018. 'The Radical Right: An Introduction'. In: Rydgren, J. (ed.). *The Oxford Handbook of the Radical Right*. Oxford: Oxford University Press, 1–13.

Schori Liang, C. 2007. 'Europe for the Europeans: The Foreign and Security Policy of the Populist Radical Right'. In: Schori Liang, C. (ed.). *Europe for the Europeans: The Foreign and Security Policy of the Populist Radical Right*. Hampshire: Ashgate, 1–32.

Shroufi, O. 2015. 'The Gates of Jerusalem: European Revisionism and the Populist Radical Right', *Race & Class*, 57(2), 24–42.

Shroufi, O. and De Cleen, B. 2022. 'Far-Right Intellectual Discourse about Populism: The Case of the German Institut für Staatspolitik', *Journal of Political Ideologies*, online first, 1–22.

Spektorowski, A. 2003. 'The New Right: Ethno-Regionalism, Ethno-Pluralism and the Emergence of a Neo-Fascist "Third Way"', *Journal of Political Ideologies*, 8(1), 111–130.

Trew, B. 2018. 'Netanyahu Sparks Backlash by Hailing Italy's Far-Right Salvini as "Great Friend of Israel" during Two-Day Trip', *The Independent* [Online]. 12 December. Available at: https://www.independent.co.uk/news/world/middle-east/israel-netanyahu-matteo-salvini-italy-far-right-immigration-hezbollah-tunnels-lebanon-terror-a8679791.html (accessed 27 November 2019).

Wertheim, D. J. 2017. 'Geert Wilders and the Nationalist-Populist Turn Toward the Jews in Europe'. In Wertheim, D. J. (ed.). *The Jew as Legitimation, Jewish-Gentile Relations Beyond Antisemitism and Philosemitism*. London: Palgrave Macmillan, 275–290.

Williams, M. H. 2010. 'Can Leopards Change Their Spots? Between Xenophobia and Trans-Ethnic Populism among West European Far Right Parties', *Nationalism and Ethnic Politics*, 16(1), 111–134.

Wodak, R. 2018. 'The Radical Right and Anti-Semitism'. In: Rydgren, J. (ed.). *The Oxford Handbook of the Radical Right*, Oxford: Oxford University Press, 61–85.

Zúquete, J. P. 2008. 'The European Extreme-Right and Islam: New Directions?', *Journal of Political Ideologies*, 13(3), 321–344.

2

Race, racism, and the far right: critical reflections for the field

Kurt Sengul

The resurgence of an emboldened and increasingly violent global far right has fuelled academic and public interest in the phenomenon within the last decade, resulting in a proliferation of scholarship under what can broadly be considered far right and populism studies (Castelli Gattinara 2020). As highlighted by Brown, Mondon, and Winter, "discussion and debate about the far right, its rise, origins and impact have become ubiquitous in academic research, political strategy and media coverage in recent years" (2021: 1). This explosion of scholarly attention on the global far right has been vast, attracting scholars with a diverse range of disciplinary and methodological expertise. As Ashe, Busher, Macklin, and Winter note, "in recent years, concerns have intensified about the growing influence of the far right, whether at the ballot box or in terms of its wider cultural influence and the attendant threats to peace, societal cohesion and security" (2020: 1). However, owing to the "Atlantic Bias" (Moffitt 2015) afflicting populism and far right studies, research in this area has frequently centred around North American and European contexts. This was particularly evident in the wake of the 2016 Brexit Referendum, the 2016 election of Donald Trump, the 2017 Unite the Right Rally in Charlottesville, Virginia, and the 6 January 2021 storming of the US Capitol Building. Yet extending well beyond Europe and North America, the rise of the far right is very much an international phenomenon (Miller-Idriss 2020). Indeed, in the Australian context, a range of heterogeneous far-right white supremacist parties, organisations, and groups emerged throughout the twenty-first century, typically defined by their anti-Muslim racism. While varying from *radical* to *extreme*, the contemporary far right in Australia is now considered a notable security threat (Allchorn 2021). Moreover, and with the caveat that police propaganda should be treated with scepticism, the Australian Security Intelligence Organisation (ASIO) revealed in 2020 that far-right violent extremism now constitutes up to 40 per cent of the organisation's counter-terrorism caseload, an increase from 10 per cent prior to 2016 (Karp 2020). This proliferation of far-right extremism most violently manifested in the 2019 Christchurch Massacre, where fifty-one Muslim people were murdered during their Friday prayers by Australian white supremacist terrorist Brenton Tarrant. Most recently, a group of thirty neo-Nazis rallied outside the Victorian parliament in March 2023, performing the Nazi salute in support of a transphobic speaking event. These events underscore the very real threat posed by the contemporary far right, "particularly [for] those at the sharp end of their racism" (Mondon and Winter 2021: 371). The study, therefore, of the various manifestations of the far right is vital in not only understanding the dangers they pose but in resisting and challenging them. This suggests that the growing scholarly interest in the contemporary global far right is justified.

However, notwithstanding the many positive contributions to the literature in recent times, several ethical considerations and blind spots have emerged from this increased volume of scholarship, many of which will be explored in this edited edition. One key area of concern identified by critical scholars and activists has been the haphazard treatment of race and racism in the study of the contemporary far right (e.g., Mondon and Winter 2020). Indeed, in addition to the heightened attention given to populism and the far right has been the increasing recognition of race critical scholarship, such as critical race theory (CRT) (Delgado and Stefancic 2017). This work – which has come under increasing attack by the far right in recent times – has implored us to conceptualise racism as structural, systematic, and ordinary rather than aberrational and attitudinal. Yet, this vital body of literature has hitherto received only marginal recognition by the field of far right and populism studies. In this context, this chapter aims to present a critical and reflexive account of my experience of writing a PhD thesis on Australia's most prominent far-right political actor, Pauline Hanson. Specifically, my chapter will focus on the implications of researching a far-right political actor within a white settler colonial context where racism is structural, mainstream, and institutionalised.

Drawing on my research experiences from 2017 to 2021, the argument I advance in this chapter is that in the absence of race critical analysis, scholars risk (re)producing individualistic and inadequate accounts of racism by focusing exclusively on the rhetoric of racist far-right political actors. Moreover, I argue that the effect of this is providing our audiences and readers with a 'safe space' to avoid broader discussions of systematic racism, whiteness, and mainstream culpability. The goal of this chapter is not to simply engage in an exercise in navel-gazing which is often the charge of whiteness studies, but rather to offer a set of critical provocations for scholars engaging in the ethical study of the contemporary far right, particularly within colonial and settler colonial contexts like Australia, Canada, and the United States. I conclude by arguing that anything less than conceptualising the far right within a broader system of race, colonialism, and white supremacism risks the field becoming an obstacle to the project of their dismantlement.

The 'resurgence' of racism in Australia

Although overshadowed by more high-profile far-right and populist figures such as Donald Trump and Rodrigo Duterte, the so-called *populist wave* of 2016 also witnessed the return of Australia's most prominent far-right populist actor Pauline Hanson to federal politics after eighteen years. The return of Hanson and the One Nation political party that bears her name also signalled the return of the far right to Australian electoral politics after largely being absent throughout the twenty-first century. While the success of Pauline Hanson's One Nation (PHON) party has been intermittent and understated at the electoral level in Australia, there is little doubt that Hanson and her party's influence has extended far beyond their electoral presence (Sengul 2022a). Hanson first emerged onto the Australian political landscape in 1996, elected as an independent member for the Queensland seat of Oxley. Hanson was originally preselected as the Liberal candidate for Oxley but was subsequently disendorsed by the party after writing a racist letter to a Queensland newspaper which lamented so-called 'reverse racism' and the alleged 'preferential' treatment afforded to First Nations peoples. Hanson's maiden speech to the House of Representatives set the tone for her overtly nativist and racist brand of populist politics, condemning 'reverse racism', political correctness, Indigenous rights, immigration, and multiculturalism. However, a series of personal and financial scandals, poor party management, and fractured leadership saw the fortunes of Hanson and One Nation quickly deteriorate (Curran 2004). Hanson made several unsuccessful political attempts throughout the 2000s at state and federal levels. It was during this time that Hanson made the transition from political figure to national celebrity, maintaining a constant media presence on reality television and breakfast news programmes. Indeed, the media played a central role in mainstreaming and normalising Hanson throughout the twenty-first century, laying the groundwork for her successful return to politics in 2016 (Bromfield et al. 2021; Sengul 2022b).

The return of Pauline Hanson and One Nation to Australian representative politics was the culmination of a growing anti-Islamic movement in Australia, manifesting in several heterogeneous Islamophobic groups that emerged in opposition to the so-called 'creep' of Sharia law, Halal certification, and the development of mosques and Islamic schools (Sengul 2022c). Indeed, whereas First Nations peoples, Asian Australians, and migrants were the primary targets of Hanson's racism throughout the 1990s, Muslims had become the defining prejudice of One Nation in the twenty-first century. Hanson's 2016 maiden Senate speech warned that Australia was "now in danger of being swamped by Muslims, who bear a culture and ideology that is incompatible with our own" (Hanson 2016). With an overtly

Islamophobic agenda, the contemporary iteration of One Nation called for a ban on Muslim immigration, a Royal Commission into Islam, and the 'banning of the burqa' (Sengul 2021).

It was within this context of an emboldened domestic and international populist far right that I commenced my PhD research in 2017. As a communication and critical discourse scholar, I was particularly interested in the strategic use of language employed by the far right and their extensive use of communicative and performative strategies in the contemporary mediascape. As a critical scholar, I wanted to interrogate how language and discourse were used strategically by the far right in Australia to achieve their discriminatory and exclusionary goals. Given that Pauline Hanson represented Australia's most successful and prominent populist far-right figure, I took the decision to undertake a critical discourse analysis of her political speeches during the Forty-Fifth Parliament of Australia (2016–2019).

The experience of presenting and disseminating my preliminary findings throughout 2017 and 2018 was a particularly transformative process in shaping my thinking around race and the far right in Australia. Presenting my work in conferences and seminars in the first few months of my thesis exposed me to how predominately white liberal audiences perceived racism in Australia. The presentations would invariably go very well, which is not a statement on the quality of my work, but rather that audiences were very receptive and engaged with the subject matter. Everybody had an opinion on Pauline Hanson and seemed to *enjoy* listening to – and participating in – discussions about her return to Australian politics. Audiences *revelled* in their collective disgust of Hanson and expressed horror at the thought of the return of One Nation to Australian political life. This response was understandable given that the audiences tended to be full of 'good' liberals who have disliked Hanson from the outset of her political career in the 1990s. Nevertheless, despite their personal derision of Hanson, audiences appeared *comfortable* listening to the presentations and engaging with the topic. Indeed, there appeared to be a sense of catharsis on the part of audience members in mocking Pauline Hanson and her One Nation senators. Eliciting feelings of comfort and enjoyment from audiences was unsettling given the violent and racist rhetoric being discussed, yet at the time I lacked the concepts, theories, and language to comprehend and articulate what was occurring.

What became clear from these discussions is that for many observers, Hanson's election represented the *resurgence of racism* in Australia and a return to the ugly race politics of the 1990s. For many, racism had reared its ugly head in Australian politics for the first time in almost two decades. Indeed, these sentiments were explicitly articulated by colleagues and audience members in these discussions. In 2018 for example, the Australian Race

Discrimination Commissioner delivered a lecture entitled 'Confronting the Return of Race Politics' in which he warned that "we must remain vigilant because race politics is back" (Soutphommasane 2018: np). I could immediately see parallels with the discourse surrounding other far-right populist figures like Donald Trump and Jair Bolsonaro who were often positioned as something *novel* and *abnormal*. It was the idea that Hanson represented the 'return' of race politics to Australia that was particularly confounding given that Hanson had been absent from electoral politics since the late 1990s.

In fact, prior to 2016, there had not been a meaningful far-right presence at a state or federal level in Australia since One Nation held eleven seats in the Queensland parliament from 1998 to 2001. This highlights that in the absence of an electorally significant far right, all of the racist policies, practices, and political rhetoric enacted throughout the twenty-first century were done so via the mainstream political parties. In fact, a strong argument can be made that voters looking for nativist far-right politics have been well served by both major political parties and dominant media outlets in Australia. This can be seen with the disproportionate incarceration and state violence perpetrated against First Nations peoples to the punitive regime of mandatory detention of refugees and asylum seekers, both of which maintain bipartisan political support. Moreover, the mainstreaming of Islamophobia in Australia in the wake of the 9/11 terrorist attacks has been well documented in the literature (Abdel-Fattah 2018). For example, Poynting and Briskman note that "Islamophobia has progressed from a fringe element in Australian society to a position of respectability through its institutionalisation in public and private spheres" (2018: 5). Moreover, it is widely accepted that conservative prime minister John Howard effectively made the far right redundant throughout the 2000s by appropriating their signature policy issues around immigration, refugees, and asylum seekers (Curran 2004). This reality is neatly captured by comments made by a former One Nation voter to the *Weekend Australian* newspaper in 2002:

> I thought she [Hanson] was on the right track wanting to keep all these Asians out of the place … Then I was pleased to see the Liberals come to their senses and pick up part of her platform by getting rid of these so-called political refugees … So good on you Johnny Howard, I say. (cited in Curran 2002: 43)

In this context, the far right should be considered a marginal actor in discussions of racism in Australia when compared with the mainstream parties. Yet, this was clearly not reflected in the experiences of my PhD research in which racism was firmly viewed as synonymous with Pauline Hanson. What became clear was that my intention of interrogating the mechanics and discursive structures of Hanson's political communication was doing more harm than good by facilitating a 'safe space' to avoid critical discussions of how race *actually* works in Australia. It was not until I started to engage more broadly with race critical scholarship that I was able to make sense of the phenomenon at play here, as well as identify deficiencies in populism and far right studies.

Whiteness, innocence, and the racial project

Engaging with race critical literature in the latter half of my PhD revealed that the complexity of researching the far right within a settler colonial context like Australia could not be sufficiently reconciled through the theories, definitions, and concepts associated with extant populism and far right scholarship. Scholars and activists working within *critical race theory*, *whiteness studies*, *critical Indigenous studies*, and *settler colonial studies* have implored us to think of racism in terms of systems and structures as opposed to attitudes and beliefs. From this perspective, racism should not be seen as the errant beliefs of a few 'bad apples' but rather as woven into the very fabric of society at an institutional and structural level (Meghji 2022). Yet, as noted by Watego, Singh and Macoun, the view that racism is "related to racial hatred or to racial prejudices held by an individual or group ... remains influential both popularly and academically" (2021: 5). The implication of viewing racism at the individual and attitudinal level is that "the more structural, institutional or mainstream forms of hate, inequality and scapegoating" (Mondon and Winter 2021: 371) are ignored. Following Alana Lentin, I understand race as "a technology for the management of human difference, the main goal of which is the production, reproduction, and maintenance of white supremacy" (2020: 5). Moreover, that race is, "above all else, a project of colonial distinction and a system for legitimation to justify oppressive and discriminatory practices" (Lentin 2020: 7). This colonial project of distinction is at the heart of white settler colonial states such as Australia which are defined by their *ongoing* violent dispossession of Indigenous lands and sovereignty (see e.g., Wolfe 2006). Within this racial state, those who are racialised as white benefit from a set of "unearned invisible assets that benefit white people in their everyday lives; they are possessions" (Moreton-Robinson 2015: 97). As further noted by Aileen Moreton-Robinson (2015), this system of *whiteness* inherent to settler colonies is hegemonic across the economic, political, and cultural sectors in Australia. Indeed, these racial logics are embedded in all spheres of Australian society, including the media, the arts, the legal and criminal justice system, the bureaucracy, sport, business, and politics. This was vividly revealed in Debbie Bargallie's (2020) ground-breaking research exposing the structural racism directed towards Indigenous employees within the Australian Public Service (APS). The APS serves as a useful example of an institution that has been relatively untouched by the far right in Australia which has exerted minimal influence over its culture, practices, and policies, and yet is nevertheless a site of systemic racism. The point to make here is that Australia's colonial and racial project is held together through a patchwork of assemblages that *we* – meaning those who derive benefit from whiteness and the dispossession of Indigenous lands and sovereignty – contribute to maintaining.

To apply this race critical frame to the experiences of my PhD research, it is clear that reducing racism in Australia to a few 'bad apples' like Pauline Hanson presents white and settler Australians with a convenient way of ignoring the role we all play in maintaining the colonial project of race. In many ways, this reflects Gloria Wekker's (2016) notion of *white innocence* and what Eduardo Bonilla-Silva (2014) refers to as *colour-blindness* to explain the flawed but dominant idea that Australia is essentially a harmonious, multicultural, and tolerant post-racial society, save for a small group of ignorant individuals. Indeed, this sentiment is captured by Ghassan Hage who argues that "white Australians have an interest in someone else perceived as 'irrational and/or immature … by distinguishing themselves from the 'extremists'" (2000: 246). Hage's prescient point about white Australians can readily be applied to the reaction to other far-right populist leaders such as Donald Trump and Marine Le Pen.

The purpose of this analysis is not to critique individual audience members for their responses, but rather to critically reflect on how my own research reinforces and perpetuates a 'bad apple' view of racism. This question is one that confronts all scholars researching the far right in countries like Australia, Canada, New Zealand, the United Kingdom, and the United States where the far right has played a secondary role in the subjugation of negatively racialised peoples yet has often dominated discussions of racism in these places. The question then turns to how we can ethically and effectively research the far right within colonial and settler colonial contexts without reinforcing the violent narratives of whiteness.

Race, racism, and the far right

With notable exceptions, the far right and populism literature has been unable to adequately reconcile with the racism of the contemporary far right in a meaningful way. In many cases, racism is seldom mentioned in analyses of the far right, with scholars opting for terms such as 'nativism' or turning to euphemisms such as 'populism' (Brown and Mondon 2021). This surprising omission from mainstream far right scholarship has been noted by Mondon and Winter who suggest that "It is fascinating to see how the 'term' racism has become almost absent from studies of the far right in political science" (2021: 108). When racism does get mentioned, it is most often discussed from a narrow attitudinal and individualistic perspective. As scholars of the far right, we necessarily find ourselves researching the most extreme manifestations of racist politics. In many respects, our research centres on the ultimate 'bad apples' in society, so it should be somewhat unsurprising that the literature has tended to reflect this. I suggest that there are several reasons why the field has been unable to meaningfully address the racism of the far right: the first relates to the aforementioned absence of a structural understanding of racism within the field. Indeed, without a race critical framework, it is entirely logical to view far-right actors like Pauline Hanson and Donald Trump as the key sources of racism in society given the overt nature of their racial politics.

The second reason relates to how the far right has tended to express its racism in recent times. It is commonly accepted that contemporary iterations of the far right – and particularly the populist radical right – have tended to move away from so-called 'biological racism' to a focus on the alleged cultural deficiencies of negatively racialised peoples (Wodak 2021). This focus on culture, rather than biology, has granted the modern far right more mainstream acceptability and exposed outmoded understandings of racism from within the field of populism and far right studies. This is reflected in Cas Mudde's highly influential conceptualisation of the *populist radical right* in which he argues that "while nativism could include racist arguments, it can also be nonracist (including and excluding on the basis of culture or even religion)" (2007: 19). While I would strongly challenge the notion that using cultural categories to distinguish between ingroups and outgroups can ever be 'nonracist', Mudde's view provides a plausible explanation for why mainstream political science has been so hesitant to use the term racism. It may be that, however misguided, many scholars within the field simply do not consider cultural constructions of human difference to be racist. This is akin to what Alana Lentin refers to as 'frozen' understandings of racism by which "'real racism' is frozen in past examples that float free from the wider context within which they can be fully understood" (2020: 64). From this perspective racism is firmly rooted in biology, and colonialism is viewed as a historical event, rather than an ongoing process (Wolfe 2006).

The final reason relates to the positivist epistemological underpinnings of disciplines like political science which strive for so-called objective, value-free research. From this dominant paradigm, scholars see themselves as *neutral* observers of the far right, rather than participants in the struggle against it. This puts it at odds with the politically informed nature of critical scholarship which explicitly and unashamedly adopts a stance against racism and other forms of discrimination such as homophobia, transphobia, classism, and ableism. As many critical scholars encounter when engaging in academic publishing and public-facing activities such as writing for the media, there is strong resistance to even using the term 'racism' in our writing, let alone adopting an oppositional position against it.

Taken together, we can see a field that is largely ill-equipped to adequately deal with the racism associated with the contemporary far right, nor has the capacity to understand "racism's shameless, chameleon-like capacity to 'morph' and adapt whenever it sets its gaze on a new object of resentment" (Abdel-Fattah 2021: 2). In the following section I advance a set of reflections for how the field should conceptualise the far right within colonial and settler colonial contexts.

Conclusion and critical reflections for the field

Recent events have reinforced the vital need for research examining the heterogeneous manifestations of the contemporary global far right. For the most part, the increase in scholarship witnessed over the past five years has been a welcome development for the field, leading to a more sophisticated and holistic understanding of the far right. Yet, it is also imperative for those working in the field to critically reflect on some of the ethical considerations and issues that have arisen from this burgeoning scholarship. Drawing on my experience of conducting a PhD on the Australian far right, the purpose of this chapter was to critically explore the complexity of researching the far right within a settler colonial context where racism is structural, systemic, and mainstream. While these experiences are very much my own, the themes discussed in this chapter are likely to resonate with colleagues abroad. What became clear from my research process and through observing the reactions to other far-right leaders such as Donald Trump was an impetus to position these political actors as a few 'bad apples' disrupting the civility of *politics as usual*. Often framed through a *lone wolf* discourse, these individuals were presented as novel aberrations, rather than an interconnected network of actors in the pursuit of global white supremacism. What was also evident is that many white Australians have a strong incentive to frame right-wing actors like Pauline Hanson as extreme outliers as it provides a useful distraction from mainstream culpability.

The question for scholars of the far right is whether our research is having the deleterious effect of reinforcing and entrenching inadequate and harmful understandings of racism as the intolerant beliefs and attitudes of

a small number of ignorant individuals. At a time when race critical theorists and global activist movements such as Black Lives Matter are making
headway in exposing the structural nature of racism, it would be egregious
for the field of populism and far right studies to undermine this vital project
through our work. Indeed, as has been argued here and elsewhere (e.g.,
Mondon and Winter 2020), far right scholarship in the main has struggled
to reconcile with the racism of the twenty-first-century far right. My argument is that through bridging far right and race critical scholarship, a far
richer understanding of the contemporary far right is possible.

From this perspective, far-right actors should not be thought of as 'bad
apples' in an otherwise tolerant and harmonious system, but rather as direct
products of their colonial and racial contexts. Importantly, the far right
must be conceptualised as playing one particular role, among many, in
maintaining the larger projects of race, white supremacy, and settler colonialism. While the role they play in maintaining these systems is particularly
overt, sinister, and violent, in many contexts it will be secondary to the role
of mainstream actors. By understanding the far right as part of a broader
system of race and white supremacy, we are better able to understand how
these systems and structures are maintained, reproduced, and reinvented.
Indeed, white supremacist systems cannot be maintained by the far right
alone. This is where analysing the far right in the absence of a race critical
framework absolves the many other actors who work to maintain racialised
structures. For example, a race critical lens allows us to critically interrogate the role of the media in platforming and normalising the far right, as
well as the mainstream political parties who have adopted their policy positions on issues like immigration and the treatment of asylum seekers. In the
Australian context, for example, Pauline Hanson was elevated to the status
of celebrity by a media who craved her 'controversial' viewpoints, while her
signature policies have largely been implemented by both centre-left and
right parties (Sengul 2023).

As rightly put by Ali Meghji, the elections of far-right populists like
Pauline Hanson and Donald Trump "were not a radical break with the past,
but rather ... they emerged from racial ideologies and emotions that were
deeply entrenched in the racialized social system" (2022: 138). While it may
be tempting to view these figures as aberrations, they are very much products
of the systems that produced them and facilitated their rise. Moreover, a race
critical perspective would help to ensure that our solutions to challenging the
far right are attuned to the people directly impacted by them. For example,
scholars will often turn to carceral and state-based solutions in response to
the far right which often runs counter to the interests and wishes of over-
policed marginalised and racialised communities.

At the same time, our focus on systems and structures should not mini-mise the threat of the far right, nor does it make its study redundant. There are important distinctions between the far right and the mainstream, and we must not lose sight of their violent defence of whiteness and its asso-ciated privileges. As Ghassan Hage notes on the rise of Pauline Hanson, "the *Hansonisation* of our souls and our national culture … is not a threat which can be taken lightly. It has the potential to poison the very texture of our daily lives. Indeed, it has begun to do so" (2000: 5, emphasis added). Far-right actors like Pauline Hanson have had corrosive influences over the political, social, and cultural contexts in which they exist. Their presence in political life has played a key role in the normalisation and mainstream-ing of racist policies and rhetoric. Thus, scholars of the far right do have an important role to play in our understanding of how race operates. Yet, *Hansonism*, *Orbanism*, and *Trumpism* did not occur in a vacuum. In the absence of the wholesale dismantling of white supremacy, colonialism, and systemic racism, efforts to challenge and resist the far right are ultimately doomed to fail. A social system structured by race will always have people willing to violently defend it. It is no longer tenable for scholars of the far right to be disinterested neutral observers of the growing creep of violent racist right-wing politics. To quote Alana Lentin, "racist ideas, practices, and policies do not always result in violence and death, but they are never very far away" (2020: 3).

References

Adbel-Fattah, R. 2018. *Islamophobia and Everyday Multiculturalism in Australia.* New York: Routledge, Taylor & Francis.

Abdel-Fattah, R. 2021. *Coming of Age in the War on Terror.* Sydney, NSW: NewSouth.

Allchorn, W. 2021. 'Australian Radical Right Narratives and Counter-Narratives in an Age of Terrorism', Centre for Analysis of the Radical Right. https://hedayah .com/app/uploads/2021/09/002_Final_CARR-Hedayah_Australia-Country -Report_2021JAN26.pdf (accessed 2 September 2022).

Ashe, S., Busher, J., Macklin, G., and Winter, A. (eds). 2020. *Researching the Far Right: Theory, Method and Practice. Fascism and the Far Right.* Abingdon and New York: Routledge.

Bargallie, D. 2020. *Unmasking the Racial Contract: Indigenous Voices on Racism in the Australian Public Service.* Canberra, ACT: Aboriginal Studies Press.

Bonilla-Silva, E. 2014. *Racism without Racists: Color-Blind Racism and the Persistence of Racial Inequality in America.* 4th ed. Lanham, MD: Rowman & Littlefield Publishers.

Bromfield, N., Page, A., and Sengul, K. 2021. 'Rhetoric, Culture, and Climate Wars: A Discursive Analysis of Australian Political Leaders' Responses to the Black Summer Bushfire Crisis'. In: Feldman, F. (ed.). *When Politicians Talk*. Singapore: Springer Singapore, 149–167.

Brown, K., Mondon, A., and Winter, A. 2021. 'The Far Right, the Mainstream and Mainstreaming: Towards a Heuristic Framework', *Journal of Political Ideologies*, online first.

Brown, K. and Mondon, A. 2021. 'Populism, the Media, and the Mainstreaming of the Far Right: The Guardian's Coverage of Populism as a Case Study', *Politics*, 41(3), 279–295.

Castelli Gattinara, P. 2020. 'The Study of the Far Right and Its Three E's: Why Scholarship Must Go beyond Eurocentrism, Electoralism and Externalism', *French Politics*, 18(3), 314–333.

Curran, G. 2004. 'Mainstreaming Populist Discourse: The Race-Conscious Legacy of Neo-Populist Parties in Australia and Italy', *Patterns of Prejudice*, 38(1), 37–55.

Delgado, R., and Stefancic, J. 2017. *Critical Race Theory: An Introduction*. 3rd ed. New York: New York University Press.

Hage, G. 2000. *White Nation: Fantasies of White Supremacy in a Multicultural Society*. New York: Routledge.

Hanson, P. 1996. 'Parliament of Australia, House of Representatives', Hansard, 10 September, 3859–3862. https://parlinfo.aph.gov.au/parlInfo/search/display /display.w3p;adv=yes;orderBy=_fragment_number,doc_date-rev;page=2;query =Dataset%3Ahansardr,hansardr80%20Decade%3A%221990s%22%20Year %3A%221996%22;rec=3;resCount=Default (accessed 12 October 2022).

Hanson, P. 2016. 'Parliament of Australia, Senate', *Hansard*, 14 September, 937–941. https://parlinfo.aph.gov.au/parlInfo/search/display/display.w3p;db=CHAMBER ;id=chamber%2Fhansards%2F16daad94-5c74-4641-a730-7f6d74312148 %2F0140;query=Id%3A%22chamber%2Fhansards%2F16daad94-5c74-4641 -a730-7f6d74312148%2F0000%22 (accessed 12 October 2022).

Karp, P. 2020. 'Asio Reveals up to 40% of Its Counter-Terrorism Cases Involve Far-Right Violent Extremism', *The Guardian*, 22 September, www.theguardian.com /australia-news/2020/sep/22/asio-reveals-up-to-40-of-its-counter-terrorism-cases -involve-far-right-violent-extremism (accessed 15 September 2022).

Lentin, A. 2020. *Why Race Still Matters*. Cambridge and Medford, MA: Polity Press.

Meghji, A. 2022. *The Racialized Social System: Critical Race Theory as Social Theory*. Medford, MA: Polity Press.

Miller-Idriss, C. 2020. *Hate in the Homeland: The New Global Far Right*. Princeton, NJ: Princeton University Press.

Moffitt, B. 2015. 'Contemporary Populism and "The People" in the Asia-Pacific Region'. In: de la Torre, C. (ed.). *The Promise and Perils of Populism*. Lexington, KY: University of Kentucky Press, 293–316.

Mondon, A. and Winter, A. 2020. *Reactionary Democracy: How Racism and the Populist Far Right Became Mainstream*. Brooklyn, NY: Verso Books.

Mondon, A. and Winter, A. 2021. 'From Demonization to Normalization: Reflecting on Far Right Research'. In: Ashe, S., Busher, J., Macklin, G., and Winter A. (eds).

Researching the Far Right: *Theory, Method and Practice*. Abingdon: Routledge, 370–382.

Moreton-Robinson, A. 2015. *The White Possessive: Property, Power, and Indigenous Sovereignty. Indigenous Americas*. Minneapolis, MN: University of Minnesota Press.

Mudde, C. 2007. *Populist Radical Right Parties in Europe*. Cambridge: Cambridge University Press.

Poynting, S. and Briskman, L. 2018. 'Islamophobia in Australia: From Far-Right Deplorables to Respectable Liberals', *Social Sciences*, 7(11), 213.

Sengul, K. 2021. '"It's OK to Be White": The Discursive Construction of Victimhood, "Anti-White Racism" and Calculated Ambivalence in Australia', *Critical Discourse Studies*, online first.

Sengul, K. 2022a. '"I Cop This Shit All the Time and I'm Sick of It": Pauline Hanson, The Far-Right and the Politics of Victimhood in Australia'. In: Smith, E., Persian, J., and Fox, V. J. (eds). *Histories of Fascism and Anti-Fascism in Australia*. London: Routledge, 199–217.

Sengul, K. 2022b. 'Performing Islamophobia in the Australian Parliament: The Role of Populism and Performance in Pauline Hanson's "Burqa Stunt"', *Media International Australia*, 184(1), 49–62.

Sengul, K. 2022c. 'The Role of Political Interviews in Mainstreaming and Normalizing the Far-Right: A View from Australia'. In: Fledman, O. (ed.). *Adversarial Political Interviewing: Worldwide Perspectives During Polarized Times*. Singapore: Springer Nature Singapore, 357–375.

Sengul, K. 2023. 'The Shameless Normalization of Debasement Performance: A Critical Discourse Analysis of Pauline Hanson's Australian, Far-Right, Populist Communication'. In: Feldman, O. (ed.). *Debasing Political Rhetoric: Dissing Opponents, Journalists, and Minorities in Populist Leadership Communication*. Singapore: Springer, 1–17.

Soutphommasane, T. 2018. 'Confronting the Return of Race Politics'. *Lecture to the Whitlam Institute*, Western Sydney University. https://humanrights.gov.au/about/news/speeches/confronting-return-race-politics (accessed 9 June 2022).

Watego, C., Singh, D., and Macoun, A. 2021. 'Partnership for Justice in Health: Scoping Paper on Race, Racism and the Australian Health System, Discussion Paper'. Melbourne: The Lowitja Institute. www.lowitja.org.au/page/services/resources/Cultural-and-social-determinants/justice/partnership-for-justice-in-health-scoping-paper-on-race-racism-and-the-australian-health-system (accessed 6 October 2022).

Wekker, G. 2016. *White Innocence: Paradoxes of Colonialism and Race*. Durham, NC: Duke University Press.

Wodak, R. 2021. *The Politics of Fear: The Shameless Normalization of Far-Right Discourse*. 2nd ed. Thousand Oak, CAs: Sage.

Wolfe, P. 2006. 'Settler Colonialism and the Elimination of the Native', *Journal of Genocide Research*, 8(4), 387–409.

3

When racism seems to be the hardest word: critical reflections from studying the Lega (Nord)

George Newth

In 2014, Matteo Salvini, leader of the Italian far-right party, the Lega,[1] tweeted a photo of himself wearing a t-shirt which read "I am a populist!" (Salvini 2014). Having often stated his fondness for the term populist/populism, Salvini has threatened to sue those who call him racist (Salvini 2016). This is part of a wider trend in far/extreme right politics with both Marine Le Pen (*The Local* 2013) and Nigel Farage (Peck 2020; Read 2019) similarly claiming to be populists, while bristling at accusations of being racist. In the meantime, populism has become the most frequently used term in scholarly research on the Lega in the field of political science, while racism remains amongst the least frequently used terms.[2] This raises a pressing ethical issue for the study of the far and extreme right: the need to move away from paradigms and approaches which euphemise racist ideology. In this chapter, I draw on my experience researching the Lega and reflect on why racism has been largely absent in political science analyses of this party.[3]

In this chapter, I define the Lega as populist far right. While far right can be used as an umbrella term for extreme and radical right actors (Pirro 2022), here it is used as an analytical concept in and of itself. Far right refers to parties or individuals that espouse a racist ideology, albeit articulated "often in an indirect, coded [and] covert manner, notably by focusing on culture and/or occupying the space between [...] the extreme and the mainstream" (Mondon and Winter 2020: 19). Racism is an ideology "in which the human race is divisible into distinct 'races', each with specific natural characteristics derived from culture, physical appearance or both" (Garner and Selod 2015: 11). Meanwhile, populism refers to a discourse which constructs "the people" as "a large powerless group" in juxtaposition to an "elite" conceived as a "small and illegitimately powerful group" (De Cleen and Stavrakakis 2017: 310). The Lega is far right insofar as it has espoused a racist ideology, albeit alongside its regionalist/nationalist ideology. Formed in 1991 under Umberto Bossi, as a merger of North Italian regionalist movements, the Lega campaigned for some form of autonomy for the North until Bossi's resignation in 2012. Under his successor, Matteo Salvini, the party underwent a gradual yet steady transformation from a regionalist to a nationalist party between 2013 and 2017 (Albertazzi et al. 2018). The Lega has consistently defined the region and nation in ethnic and racial terms, leading to the (cultural and physical) racialisation of a series of 'out-groups' (Maccaferri and Newth 2022). The prefix 'populist' refers to the party's discourse which has juxtaposed 'the (North) Italian people' against a series of elites (Maccaferri and Newth 2022).

Following this introduction, the chapter is divided into two sections. The first section poses three reflections on my experience of studying the Lega. The second section then offers three suggestions for critical and ethical engagement with the far right.

Reflections from studying the Lega (Nord)

Political science, positionality, and whiteness

While subject to analyses from several disciplines, the Lega has nevertheless predominantly been placed under the lens of political science. The whiteness of this discipline has contributed to the absence of racism as an analytical category (Mondon 2022; Zuberi and Bonilla-Silva 2008). Much scholarly work has examined the role of the Lega in government and its core campaign issues (Albertazzi et al. 2018; Fella and Ruzza 2009; Albertazzi and McDonnell 2010; Cento Bull 2010), the construction of a 'Northern Question' in Italian politics (Diamanti 1996; Biorcio 1997; Cento Bull and Gilbert 2001) well as the geographical spread of the party's vote (Diamanti 1996; Giordano 2000; Albertazzi and Vampa 2021). While undoubtedly important in understanding the party's "fluctuating fortunes" (Cento Bull 2015), such approaches neglect an examination of how racism and far-right ideology are articulated and how this relates to the mainstream (Brown 2019, 2023; Maccaferri and Newth 2022).

My latest thinking on the Lega is different from my initial research which eschewed racism for terms such as nativism (Newth 2018). This was due to two factors. First, to meet the demands of gatekeepers, I used existing paradigms without feeling able to question their accuracy, precision, and/ or 'whiteness' in methodological terms.[4] This raises the question of how difficult it can be for early career researchers to challenge dominant paradigms. Second, my approach was rooted in two disciplines which have been dominated by white academics, Italian studies (Zhang 2021) and political science (Mondon 2022). As a white cis male researcher, I have not been at the sharp end of the Lega's racist discourse and ideology. Indeed, I have been the beneficiary of what Charles W. Mills has termed "the racial contract", a form of white supremacy which entails that

> standard textbooks and courses have for the most part been written and designed by whites, who take their racial privilege so much for granted that they do not even see it as political, as a form of domination. (Mills 1997: 1)

My research questions for my PhD research, for example, did not contain the words 'race' or 'racism', and focused predominantly on regionalism, nationalism, and populism. This relates to a wider issue regarding temporal factors to which this chapter now turns.

'Right-wing turns'

Since its formation, the Lega has consistently espoused a far-right form of ideology, either in its regionalist or nationalist form (Barcella 2022). However, interpretations of the Lega's nationalist projects as 'right-wing turns' have risked regionalism becoming a proxy term for racism (Cento Bull 2001; Albertazzi et al. 2018).⁵ The first of these projects was when the Lega campaigned for an independent 'Padania' (an imaginary nation-state north of the River Po) between 1996 and 1999. Prior to secessionism, the Lega held more "idiosyncratic positions" on "European co-operation and federal ideals of self-determination" (Cento Bull 2011). The party's "performative anti-fascism" also depicted its regionalist project as "anti-fascist" and "beyond left and right" (Newth and Maccaferri 2022). A shift to Padanian nationalism brought the Lega more in step with other far-right parties in Europe with greater emphasis on defending 'national' borders (Passarelli and Tuorto 2022; Albertazzi et al. 2018; Woods 2010), a pivot towards Euroscepticism (following Italy's acceptance into the EMU in 1998), a growing 'clash of civilisations' discourse, particularly following 9/11, and decline in performative anti-fascism. However, prior to secessionism, the Lega promoted hard regional borders (Newth 2019), fomented racist moral panics (Newth 2023a), and engaged in 'Great Replacement' theories (Bossi 1992). Meanwhile, performative anti-fascism was an attempt to legitimise racism against southern Italians, with its ahistorical view that "neo-fascism was […] part of the Southern *ethnie*" (Levy 2015).

While secessionism, as a policy, was abandoned in 1999, Padanian imagery continued to play a key role in Lega identity until the end of 2017 when Salvini abandoned his party's historic cause of regionalism for nationalism, arguably cementing the Lega's far-right identity (Brunazzo and Gilbert 2017; Albertazzi et al. 2018; Passarelli and Tuorto 2018). Strengthening the

Lega's relations with neo-fascist organisations, Salvini dropped any pretence of the Lega having an anti-fascist heritage (Rapisarda 2015), claiming that fascism and anti-fascism no longer exist. However, Bossi had begun forming connections with the far and extreme right in Europe sometime before Salvini (Ignazi 2005; La Repubblica 1993; Mammone 2009). Furthermore, Salvini's false equivalence between fascism and anti-fascism stems from Bossi's "performative anti-fascist" claim to be post-ideological (Newth and Maccaferri 2022).

Considering both nationalist projects as 'right-wing turns' neglects how regionalism and nationalism *both* form part of the far right when articulated alongside racism. When the Lega has been described as extreme right (Passarelli and Tuorto 2012; 2018), far right (Cento Bull and Gilbert 2001), and populist radical right (Albertazzi et al. 2018), these paradigms have either been ill-defined or used alongside other terms.[6] This can contribute to a blurring of conceptual boundaries which can euphemise racist ideology, to which this chapter now turns.

The overuse (and misuse) of populism and nativism

Populism and nativism have both been used as proxy terms for racism when defining the Lega. While populist discourse has been a consistent feature of the party's communication (Biorcio 1991; Albertazzi and McDonnell 2005; 2010), warnings regarding semantic precision have often been neglected (Mudde 2007; Glynos and Mondon 2016).

Recent work on the Lega has asserted that populism is *the* defining feature of the Lega (Albertazzi and Vampa 2021; Albertazzi et al. 2021; Albertazzi and Zulianello 2021). This represents how years of considering populism as a core ideology have obscured and euphemised the party's racist politics (Zaslove 2007; McDonnell 2006; Fella and Ruzza 2009; Albertazzi and McDonnell 2015). Contemporary research on Salvini's social media activity has contributed to a proliferation of terms such as 'ethno-regionalist populism' and 'right wing populism' (Berti 2021; Bobba 2019) which make populism the core term, while decentring exclusionary ideologies and discourses such as racism and nativism.

Scholarship on the Lega reflects a damaging trend in current understandings of nativism which considers it 'non-racist' (Mudde 2007) or 'race neutral' (Bosniak 1997), thus underestimating the process of racialisation which juxtaposes 'the native' against the 'non-native'. Nativism is also often conflated with populism (Newth 2023b). Indeed, the fact that the Lega's ideology has been at times defined as 'nativist populist' (Woods 2021) or 'nativist nationalist' (Albertazzi et al. 2018) reflects a muddying of the waters of different discourses and ideologies (Albertazzi et al. 2018; Passarelli and Tuorto 2022). As a result, like populism, nativism has itself at times become a 'fuzzy' word for the Lega's racism and Islamophobia (Newth 2019; Betz 2019) and served to euphemise and mainstream the Lega's far-right ideology and discourse.

Rules of engagement

Drawing from the reflections above, what follows are three tentative, non-prescriptive guidelines to encourage reflexivity and a less euphemising way of referring to the far and extreme right.

Defining, not euphemising

Accurate definitions of the far right should endeavour to highlight its damaging ideology and discourse. This requires a reflection on how we interpret concepts and a critical examination of the euphemistic qualities of terms such as 'nativist' and 'populist'. This does not mean discarding these terms, but rather being clear about their role in politics (Glynos and Mondon 2016; Bice and Maiguashca; Mudde 2007; De Cleen and Glynos 2021; Newth 2024). To paraphrase Zaslove (2011: 74), it is not always possible, nor necessary, to distinguish between regionalist and far-right ideologies; these ideologies may at times overlap and influence one another. Racialisation along cultural lines, for example, can take place just as easily through a regionalist ideology as a nationalist ideology, if the region is viewed in ethnic and exclusionary terms (Newth 2024). Paradigms examining the far right should, therefore, strive to be anti-racist and actively combat the far right as well as define it. Such an approach recognises "the importance of rejecting neutrality in favour of taking the side of oppressed communities" (Joseph-Salisbury and Connelly 2021). Clearly defining the components of the frameworks we are using so that they illustrate the ideological and/ or discursive features of the parties/individuals being examined is key to avoiding euphemistic definitions. For more anti-racist paradigms to gain space and readership in academic journals, however, gatekeepers must become more open to critical and experimental approaches from (early career) colleagues who challenge hegemonic definitions.

Reflexivity, positionality, interdisciplinarity

Reflexivity, defined here as a process of "learning to reflect on your behaviour and thoughts, as well as on the phenomenon under study" is a key element of any academic discipline (Watt 2007). Reflexivity entails viewing race, gender, and class not just as empirical subjects but as structural factors which influence our scientific gaze (Maxey 1999; Zuberi and Bonilla Silva 2008). This involves reflecting on positionality, i.e. how our identities may impact our production of knowledge. As researchers of the far right, this may involve reflecting on white privilege (Diangelo 2018), whiteness, and white logic (Zuberi and Bonilla Silva 2008) to debunk the notion of political science as a 'value-free' discipline.

Expanding beyond the boundaries of political science can "allow researchers to operationalise a new criticality in their work" (Warleigh-Lack and Cini 2009). While still an overwhelmingly white discipline (Zuberi and Bonilla Silva 2008: 14), the fact that sociology "holds a wide and sophisticated literature on racism" should encourage political science scholars to engage more closely with sociological concepts (Mondon 2022). Sociological approaches have contributed to recognising processes of racialisation and reinforcement of white supremacy (Sivanandan 2001; Garner and Selod 2015; Rzepnikowska 2019). This involves "real dialogue with scholars from other disciplines" and preparation "to sacrifice our disciplinary identity where it is no longer helpful" (Warleigh-Lack and Cini 2009). An important example of reaching out beyond disciplinary confines to enrich understanding of the political is that of the continuous dialogue with the study of ideologies and discourses (Freeden 2021).

Discourse, the mainstream, and mainstreaming

Bringing racism into sharper focus in studies of far-right ideology entails an examination of discourse and discursive processes and how this relates to the mainstream (Brown 2023; Brown et al. 2021; Krzyżanowski 2020). Indeed, the fields of critical discourse studies (CDS) and discourse theory (DT) have long recognised the importance of discourse in maintaining, replicating, and recontextualising racist and racialised structures in society (Wodak 2015; Reisigl and Wodak 2009). While CDS arguably has not engaged thoroughly enough with its own use of terminology (such as populism and right-wing populism), it can provide examples of how the far right discursively constructs its ideology (Richardson and Wodak 2009). We must pay more attention to *how* political actors formulate and disseminate ideology (De Cleen and Stavrakakis 2017), not just what they say, and examine also how far-right parties refute accusations of racism (Brown et al. 2021; Brown 2023). Matteo Salvini presenting reactionary ideology as "simple common sense" is a case in point (Newth 2024; Newth and Maccaferri 2022). Furthermore, the embeddedness of far-right actors such as Salvini in the mainstream means that we should continue to engage with how the mainstream continues to provide a platform for reactionary ideas (Brown et al. 2020; Forchtner et al. 2013). By critically examining how far-right ideology is shaped and constructed discursively, we can address inconsistencies within existing paradigms and emphasise racism as a key defining feature of the far right.

Conclusion

Political science's neglect of racism as an analytical tool not only limits our understanding of far- and extreme-right actors but also potentially trivialises the experiences of those at the sharp end of their ideology. This chapter has highlighted some of the contributing factors behind this key ethical issue and, in turn, provided tentative suggestions for how to tackle it. First is the use of definitions that recognise the insidious nature of racism and how it might blend with/be articulated alongside other ideologies. This also, however, requires a contribution on the part of gatekeepers to encourage and nurture research and approaches from early to mid-career scholars which challenge existing paradigms. Second is a reflexive approach that invites dialogue with other disciplines and recognises the willingness to engage with new paradigms and definitions as a virtue, rather than a weakness. Finally, there must be continuous engagement with discursive approaches that encourage a clearer distinction between far-right ideology and populist and/ or nativist discourses. In line with these reflections, it is my hope that this chapter will encourage dialogue between scholars and students alike and the pursuit of anti-racist paradigms to examine far and extreme right actors.

Notes

1 As an amalgamation of autonomist regionalist 'leagues', in 1991, the original party name was Lega Nord (Northern League), and from 1996 onwards Lega Nord per l'Indipendenza della Padania (Northern League for the Independence of Padania). In 2018, the party rebranded as the Lega, which includes sister organisations Lega per Salvini Premier and Noi con Salvini. As of 3 August 2020, Lega per Salvini Premier has superseded all other denominations. For convenience, this chapter refers to the party of both the Bossi and Salvini era as 'the Lega'.

2 This data is drawn from ongoing research on the Lega and the French National Front/National Rally on webofscience (Newth and Mondon, forthcoming). The parameters of the research are Lega – 1990 to 25 October 2021 – articles only – limited relevant categories. AB = (Lega) OR TI = (Lega). 122 entries.

3 Racism, as an analytical tool, has not been entirely absent in approaches to the Lega. See, amongst others, Cento Bull (1996), De Matteo (2011), Huysseune (2006), Levy (2015), and Garau (2010). Such engagement with sociology and cultural studies, however, has been the exception rather than the rule.

4 While my monograph (Newth 2023a) also uses the terms populist regionalism and populist nationalism, these are used under an umbrella term of populist far right which clearly defines of the role of racism.

5 I do not intend to diminish the important debates regarding whether the Lega's ethno-regionalist identity should be considered as part of New Right ideology, which have helped understand the Lega's early project of delegitimising and dismantling the Italian state. See, for example, Cento Bull (2003, 2011) and Spektorowski (2003).

6 In Passarelli and Tuorto's (2018) analysis of Salvini's Lega, for example, no fewer than six terms are used, including 'New Extreme Right', 'National Neo-Fascists', 'New Right', 'New European Right', 'Radical Right', and 'Populist'.

References

Albertazzi, D., Giovannini, A. and Seddone, D. 2018. 'No Regionalism Please, We Are *Leghisti*! The Transformation of the Italian Lega Nord under the Leadership of Matteo Salvini', *Regional and Federal Studies*, 28(5), 645–671.

Albertazzi, D. and McDonnell, D. 2005. 'The Lega Nord in the Second Berlusconi Government. In a League of Its Own', *West European Politics*, 28(5), 952–972.

Albertazzi, D. and McDonnell, D. 2010. 'The Lega Nord back in government', *West European Politics*, 33(6), 1318–1340.

Albertazzi, D. and McDonnell, D. 2015. *Populists in Power*. London and New York: Routledge.

Albertazzi, D. and Vampa, D. 2021. *Populism in Europe: Lessons from Umberto Bossi's Northern League*. Manchester: Manchester University Press.

Albertazzi, D. and Zulianello, D. 2021. 'Populist Electoral Competition in Italy: The Impact of Sub-National Contextual Factors', *Contemporary Italian Politics*, 13(1), 4–30.

Barcella, P. 2022. *La Lega: Una Storia*. Rome: Carocci Editore.

Berti, C. 2021. 'Right-Wing Populism and the Criminalization of Sea-Rescue NGOs: The "Sea-Watch 3" Case in Italy, and Matteo Salvini's Communication on Facebook', *Media, Culture & Society*, 43(3), 532–550.

Betz, H. G. 2019. 'Facets of Nativism: A Heuristic Exploration', *Patterns of Prejudice*, 53(2), 111–135.

Biorcio, R. 1991. 'La Lega Come Attore Politico: Dal Federalismo al Populismo Regionalista'. In: Mannheimer, R. (ed.). *La Lega Lombarda*. Milan: Feltrinelli, 34–82.

Biorcio, R. 1997. *Le Storia, le idee, e la logica d'azione della Lega Nord*. Rome: il Saggiatore.

Bobba, G. 2019. 'Social Media Populism: Features and "Likeability" of Lega Nord Communication on Facebook', *Eur Polit Sci*, 18, 11–23.

Bosniak, L. S. 1997. '"Nativism" the Concept: Some Reflections'. In:Perea,J. F. (ed.). *Immigrants Out! The New Nativism and the Anti-Immigrant Impulse in the United States*. New York and London: University of New York Press, 279–299.

Bossi, U. 1992. 'L'islam in casa e Roma costruisce moschee', *Lombardia Autonomista*, 18 January.

Brown, K. 2019. 'When Eurosceptics Become Europhiles: Far-Right Opposition to Turkish Involvement in the European Union', *Identities*, 27(6), 633–654.

Brown, K. 2023. *Talking 'With' and 'About' the Far Right: Putting the Mainstream in Mainstreaming*. PhD thesis, Bath: University of Bath.

Brown, K. and Mondon, A. 2020. 'Populism, the Media and the Mainstreaming of the Far Right: *The Guardian*'s Coverage of Populism as a Case Study', *Politics*, 41(3), 279–295.

Brown, K., Mondon, A. and Winter, A. 2021. 'The Far Right, the Mainstream and Mainstreaming: Towards a Heuristic Framework', *Journal of Political Ideologies*, online first.

Brunazzo, M. and Gilbert, M. 2017. 'Insurgents against Brussels: Euroscepticism and the Right-Wing Populist Turn of the Lega Nord since 2013', *Journal of Modern Italian Studies*, 22(5), 624–641.

Cento Bull, A. 1996. 'Ethnicity, Racism and the Northern League'. In: Levy, C. (ed.). *Italian Regionalism*. Oxford: Berg, 171–189.

Cento Bull, A. 2010. 'Addressing Contradictory Needs: The Lega Nord and Italian Immigration Policy', *Patterns of Prejudice*, 44(5), 411–431.

Cento Bull, A. 2011. 'Breaking Up the Post-War Consensus: The Ideology of the Lega in the Early 1990s', *The Italianist*, 31(1), 112–122.

Cento Bull, A. 2015. 'The Fluctuating Fortunes of the Lega Nord'. In: Mammone, A., Giap Parini, E. and Veltri, G. A. (eds). *The Routledge Handbook of Contemporary Italy, History, Politics and Society*. New York: Routledge, 204–214.

Cento Bull, A. and Gilbert, M. 2001. *The Lega Nord and the Northern Question in Italian Politics*. Basingstoke: Palgrave Macmillan.

De Cleen, B. and Glynos, J. 2021. 'Beyond Populism Studies', *Journal of Language and Politics*, 20(1), 178–195.

De Cleen, B., Glynos, J. and Mondon, A. 2018. 'Critical Research on Populism: Nine Rules of Engagement', *Organization*, 25(5), 649–661.

De Cleen, B. and Stavrakakis, Y. 2017. 'Distinctions and Articulations: A Discourse Theoretical Framework for the Study of Populism and Nationalism', *Javnost – The Public*, 24(4), 301–319.

DeMatteo, L. 2011. *L'idiota in Politica. Antrolpologia della Lega Nord*. Milan: Feltrinelli.

Diamanti, I. 1996. *Il Male del Nord, Lega Localismo, Secessione*. Rome: Donzelli.

DiAngelo, R. 2018. *White Fragility: Why It's So Hard for White People to Talk About Racism*. London: Allen Lane.

Fella, S. and Ruzza, C. 2009. *Reinventing the Italian Right*. London and New York: Routledge.

Forchtner, B., Krzyżanowski, M. and Wodak, R. 2013. 'Mediatization, Right-Wing Populism and Political Campaigning: The Case of the Austrian Freedom Party'.

In: Ekström, M. and Tolson, A. (eds). *Media Talk and Political Elections in Europe and America*. London: Palgrave Macmillan, 205–228.

Freeden, M. 2021. 'Discourse, Concepts, Ideologies: Pausing for Thought', *Journal of Language and Politics*, 20(1), 47–61.

Garau, E. 2010. *The Politics of National Identity in Italy: Immigration and Italianità*. London: Routledge.

Garner, S. and Selod, S. 2015. 'The Racialization of Muslims: Empirical Studies of Islamophobia', *Critical Sociology*, 41(1), 9–19.

Giordano, B. 2000. 'Italian Regionalism or "Padanian" Nationalism – The Political Project of the Lega Nord in Italian Politics', *Political Geography*, 19(4), 445–471.

Glynos, J. and Mondon, A. 2016. 'The Political Logic of Populist Hype: The Case of Right-Wing Populism's "Meteoric Rise" and Its Relation to the Status Quo', Populismus Working Paper Series, No. 4.

Huysseune, M. 2006. *Modernity and Secession: The Social Sciences and the Political Discourse of the Lega Nord in Italy*. New York and Oxford: Berghahn Books.

Ignazi, P. 2005. 'Legitimation and Evolution on the Italian Right Wing: Social and Ideological Repositioning of *Alleanza Nazionale* and the *Lega Nord*', *South European Society and Politics*, 10(2), 333–349.

Joseph-Salisbury, R. and Connelly, L. 2021. *Anti-Racist Scholar Activism*. Manchester: Manchester University Press.

Krzyżanowski, M. 2020. 'Normalization and the Discursive Construction of "New" Norms and "New" Normality: Discourse in the Paradoxes of Populism and Neoliberalism', *Social Semiotics*, 30(4), 431–448.

La Repubblica. 1993. 'Quei Tre Leghisti con l'anima nera', *La Republicca*, Available from: https://ricerca.repubblica.it/repubblica/archivio/repubblica/1993/11/19/quei-tre-leghisti-con-anima.html (accessed 1 July 2020).

Levy, C. 2015. 'Racism, Immigration and New Identities in Italy'. In: Mammone, A., Giap Parini, E. and Veltri, G. A. (eds). *The Routledge Handbook of Contemporary Italy, History, Politics and Society*. New York: Routledge, 49–64.

The Local. 2013. 'We Are Not Extreme Right: France's National Front', *The Local*. https://www.thelocal.fr/20131003/we-are-not-extreme-right-national-front/ (accessed 25 January 2023).

Maccaferri, M. and Newth, G. 2022. 'The Delegitimisation of Europe in a Pro-European Country: "Sovereignism" and Populism in the Political Discourse of Matteo Salvini's Lega', *Journal of Language and Politics*, 21(2), 277–299.

Mammone, A. 2009. 'The Eternal Return? Faux Populism and Contemporarization of Neo-Fascism across Britain, France and Italy', *Journal of Contemporary European Studies*, 17(2), 171–192.

Maxey, I. 1999. 'Beyond Boundaries? Activism, Academia, Reflexivity and Research', *Area*, 31(3), 199–208.

McDonnell, D. 2006. 'A Weekend in Padania: Regionalist Populism and the Lega', *Politics*, 26(2), 126–127.

Mills, C. W. 1997. *The Racial Contract*. Cornell, NY: Cornell University Press.

Mondon, A. 2022. 'Epistemologies of Ignorance in Far Right Studies: The Invisibilisation of Racism and Whiteness in Times of Populist Hype', *Acta Politica*, online first.

Mondon, A. and Winter, A. 2020. *Reactionary Democracy: How Racism and the Populist Far-Right Became Mainstream*. London: Verso.

Mudde, C. 2007. *Populist Radical Right Parties in Europe*. Cambridge: Cambridge University Press.

Newth, G. 2018. *Fathers of the Lega Nord*. PhD thesis, University of Bath.

Newth, G. 2019. 'The Roots of the Lega Nord's Populist Regionalism', *Patterns of Prejudice*, 53(4), 384–406.

Newth, G. 2023a. *Fathers of the Lega: Populist Regionalism and Populist Nationalism in Historical Perspective*. Abingdon: Routledge.

Newth, G. 2023b. 'Rethinking "Nativism": Beyond the Ideational Approach', *Identities*, 30(2), 161–180.

Newth, G. 2024. 'Talking about the Far Right and Common Sense: A Case Study of Matteo Salvini's Lega (2018–2023)', *Acta Politica*.

Newth, G. and Maccaferri, M. 2022. 'From Performative Anti-Fascism to Post-Fascism: The Lega (Nord)'s Political Discourse in Historical Context', *Journal of Political Ideologies*, online first.

Newth, G. and Mondon, A. 2023. 'What's in a Name? A Critical Study of Terminology in Research on the Lega (Nord) and Front/Rassemblement National'. Ongoing research.

Passarelli, G. and Tuorto, D. 2012. *Lega & Padania*. Bologna: Il Mulino.

Passarelli, G. and Tuorto, D. 2018. *La Lega di Salvini: Estrema Destra di Governo*. Bologna: Il Mulino.

Passarelli, G. and Tuorto, D. 2022. 'From the Lega Nord to Salvini's League: Changing Everything to Change Nothing?', *Journal of Modern Italian Studies*, 27(3), 400–415.

Peck, T. 2020. 'Nigel Farage Raved about Populism to EU Parliament – Right after an Auschwitz Survivor Spoke', *The Independent*. www.independent.co.uk/voices/nigel-farage-brexit-auschwitz-survivor-eu-parliament-auld-lang-syne-a9308816.html (accessed 25 February 2023).

Pirro, A. 2022. 'Far Right: The Significance of an Umbrella Concept', *Nations and Nationalism*, online first.

Rapisarda, A. 2015. *All'armi siam leghisti: Come e perché Matteo Salvini ha conquistato la Destra*. Reggio Emilia: Compagnia Editoriale Aliberti.

Read, J. 2019. '"You'd Struggle to Find Anything Racist about Me" – Nigel Farage in Hysterical Rant at Piers Morgan', *The New European*. https://www.theneweuropean.co.uk/brexit-news-nigel-farage-snaps-at-piers-morgan-life-stories-52992/ (accessed 26 March 2022).

Reisigl, M. and Wodak, R. 2009. 'The Discourse-Historical Approach (DHA)'. In: Wodak, R. and Meyer, M. (eds). *Methods of Critical Discourse Studies*. London: SAGE Publishing, 87–121.

Richardson, J. E. and Wodak, R. 2009. 'Recontextualising Fascist Ideologies of the Past: Right-Wing Discourses on Employment and Nativism in Austria and the United Kingdom', *Critical Discourse Studies*, 6(4), 251–267.

Rzepnikowska, A. 2019. 'Racism and Xenophobia Experienced by Polish Migrants in the UK before and after the Brexit Vote', *Journal of Ethnic and Migration Studies*, 45(1), 61–77.

Salvini, M. 2014. Tweet available from: https://twitter.com/matteosalvinimi/status/471311146700779522 (accessed 14 April 2022).

Salvini, M. 2016. *Secondo Matteo: Follia e corraggio per cambiare il paese*. Milan: Rizzoli.

Sivanandan, A. 2001. 'Poverty is the New Black', *Race & Class*, 43(2), 1–5.

Spektorowski, A. 2003. 'Ethnoregionalism: The Intellectual New Right and the Lega Nord', *The Global Review of Ethnopolitics*, 2(3), 55–70.

Warleigh-Lack, A. and Cini, M. 2009. 'Interdisciplinarity and the Study of Politics', *European Political Science*, 8, 4–15.

Watt, D. 2007. 'On Becoming a Qualitative Researcher: The Value of Reflexivity', *The Qualitative Report*, 12(1), 82–101.

Wodak, R. 2015. *The Politics of Fear: What Right-Wing Populist Discourses Mean*. London: SAGE Publishing.

Woods, D. 2010. 'A Critical Analysis of the Northern League's Ideographical Profiling', *Journal of Political Ideologies*, 15(2), 189–219.

Woods, D. 2021. 'A Boat Load Too Many: How the League Uses Global Migration Crisis to Undermine Liberal Democracy in Italy', *Chinese Political Science Review*, 7, 305–320.

Zaslove, A. 2007. 'Alpine Populism, Padania and Beyond: A Response to Duncan McDonnell', *Politics*, 27(1), 64–68.

Zaslove, A. 2011. *The Re-invention of the European Radical Right: Populism, Regionalism and the Italian Lega Nord*.Montreal and Kingston, QC: McGill-Queen's University Press.

Zhang, G. 2021. 'Diversity and Decolonization in Italian Studies' Blog Post. The University of British Colombia. https://fhis.ubc.ca/news/diversity-and-decolonization-in-italian-studies/ (accessed 17 May 2022).

Zuberi, T. and Bonilla-Silva, E. 2008. *White Logic, White Methods: Racism and Methodology*. Lanham, MD: Rowman and Littlefield.

4

When the far right experiences violence: our ethical duty to the othered

Ryan Switzer

Research on the far right should be conducted with the utmost ethical sensitivity to those at the sharp end of far-right violence. In this chapter, I argue that this sensitivity requires critical, at times uncomfortable examinations of the violence experienced by far-right activists themselves. Throughout my own fieldwork in Sweden's far-right scene, violent narratives of victimisation and stigmatisation have emerged as central to activists' understandings of their political selves. An expanded theoretical understanding of violence, beyond positivism, can better illuminate the circulation of violence in our societies. This piece then has two interconnected goals. First, I provide a note on how to begin broadening our understanding of far-right violence. And second, I explore the ethical dilemmas this expansion reveals based on my own experiences in the field. I draw on the work of ethnographers engaged in this debate over how to handle the possibilities of reproducing far-right violence and provide examples from my own fieldwork.

Violence has multiple competing definitions across disciplines. But any conceptual murk surrounding violence is more suggestive of a modernity with multiple, overlapping avenues for violence rather than some scholarly shortcoming in consensus. Sociology, anthropology, and social theory have long recognised forms of violence beyond immediate physical acts, including symbolic violence (Bourdieu 1989), divine violence (Benjamin 1921), structural violence (Farmer 2004), racialised violence (Butler 2020), and state violence (Ron 1997). The study of far-right violence has yet to follow suit and incorporate these nuanced conceptualisations of violence into analyses. Very crudely, debates over violence's definition could be divided into those which prioritise physical violence (to strike and be struck) versus those slower forms, which stigmatise and inhibit agency and the freedom of movement (Menjívar and Abrego 2012). I take the latter approach to explore where an expansion of violence's definition takes our research practices and ethics.

There is much at stake in who gets to define violence's parameters (Butler 2021). Where outright, physical violence is cause for democratic disqualification in electoral systems (Rydgren 2007) followers of far-right ideology, built on "exclusionary, hierarchal, and dehumanizing ideals that prioritise and seek to preserve the superiority and dominance of some groups over others" (Miller-Idriss 2022: 8), must find means of social control which straddle the boundary of legality to be democratically compliant. Violence as a diverse repertoire does involve harassment, mental duress, detention, and the inhibition of agency (see Evans and Lennard 2018). The revolutionary right's turn from bombs to metapolitical books (Ravndal 2021) suggests violence and its preparation do not always fit rigid categorisation.

A reconsideration of far-right violence more faithfully reflects the reality of the interaction between symbolic, verbal, and physical violence (Pontiki et al. 2022). It also, especially when considered from an ethnographic perspective, speaks to ongoing ethical dilemmas when conducting up-close research on these movements. It would be intellectually dishonest for a critical turn in the field's understanding of violence to be myopic. When I say myopic, I mean we cannot ignore the violence inflicted on right-wing activists as well – following the interpretivist sociological dictum to not adjudicate what *is* true but to interrogate what an informant understands (and may even *know*) to be true.

Conceptualising violence

What is far-right violence? Leading researchers of far-right violence define violence in a recent edited volume on research methods as "exclusively … the intentional use of *physical force* with the potential for causing death, disability, injury, or harm" (Ravndal and Jupskås 2020: 133). The authors justify their analytical distinction between their violence and other forms of violence which they recognise ("threats, hate speech, or symbolic acts") as the "threshold for committing physical attacks against other human beings is considerably higher than for making threats or hateful remarks" (2020: 133–134). Similarly, the *Oxford Handbook of the Radical Right*'s entry on "Political Violence and the Radical Right" operationalises a positivistic understanding of violence. The authors typologise 'radical right' violence as either rioting, lone-wolf attacks, terrorist attacks, or parties' youth wings' attacks on minorities (Weinberg and Assoudeh 2018: 592). These definitions reflect their architects' goals: to empirically measure the forms and consistency of violence committed in the name of extremist nativism. Answers to these questions have serious implications for counter-terrorism work and deradicalisation efforts. However, important features of the field of violence are neglected and misunderstood by this narrow, empiricist conceptualisation.

Treating violence as a culturally dependent repertoire opens up an understanding of a far-right violence which is mutually inclusively physical, verbal, and symbolic. Consider a resolution by House Republicans following the far-right riot at the US Capitol in 2021. Eight people died as a result of the event, one trampled under the feet of their allies and one shot by a police officer. In their censure of party members who had defected to aid Democrats in investigating the uprising, the Republican National Committee declared: "Representatives Cheney and Kinzinger are participating in a Democrat-led persecution of ordinary citizens engaged in legitimate political discourse" (Republican National Committee 2021). Democrats decried Republicans' conflation of the rioters and political speech, reinforcing the binary between a valorised discourse and illegitimate violence. But what House Republicans unknowingly capture is a more genuine representation of the inextricable union between language and violence. Any movement banding together to protest their conditions begins by constructing an imaginary in some way rooted in their reality: 'immigrant ghetto', 'globalists', 'stolen election'. "So precisely when we are dealing with the scene of a furious crowd, attacking and burning buildings and cars, lynching people, etc., we should never forget the placards they are carrying and the words that sustain and justify their acts" (Žižek 2009: 57). Insofar as critics of the Republicans' censure hinge their critique on the word 'legitimate', one should ask why the boundary of legitimacy/illegitimacy hinges on an act of physicality. In English common law, 'assault', a word etymologically linked to corporality ('to leap' in Old French), has been understood as speech acts since the sixteenth century. Kevin Greeson died in the Capitol Riot of a heart attack and, according to a statement by his family, never participated in any hand-to-hand combat with Capitol police himself. But in the days leading to the riot, he wrote on social media: "Let's take this fucking Country BACK!! Load your guns and take to the streets!" (Associated Press 2021). Symbols begot by words are the building blocks of physically violent political action. Starting at the conceptual level then, the foundation of our work, academics can employ concepts which reveal the dynamics of violence instead of hiding them. What (some could argue) we may lose in conceptual precision, we redeem in our more faithful recounting of a social movement's representations of reality.

The violence of dehumanisation/to humanise the violent

As academics of the far right, we collect data on violent events which may anger us, we process them with dispassion, and incorporate them into our work. An instructive passage from a pioneer of the sociology of the extreme right, Kathleen Blee, goes: "Earlier feminist dictums to respect the truth of individual experiences, preserve the integrity of ordinary people's lives, and seek what Judith Stacey calls 'an egalitarian research process characterised by authenticity, reciprocity, and intersubjectivity between the researcher and her subjects' provide little guidance for studying those we loath or fear" (2017: 18). Recent ethnographies of the far right have recognised their work's potential for making one a conduit of verbal or symbolic violence (Teitelbaum 2019: 21; Pilkington 2016: 28). In multiple troubling cases, academics have experienced that violence themselves (see Thorleifsson 2022). Increasing calls to engage in these ethnographic studies of the far right – accepting this work's complicated moral and psychic challenges (Castelli Gattinara 2020) while committing to a scholarship which prioritises dignity and human rights (Thorleifsson 2022) – has only heightened the necessity of a research ethics which takes the wide range of potential violence seriously.

Throughout 2022, I attempted to walk this tightrope myself, regularly attending events hosted by the far-right movement party, Alternative for Sweden (*Alternativ för Sverige* – AfS). AfS bills itself as Sweden's only 'återvandring' or 'return migration' party. This is their core principle: that at least one million people – non-ethnically Swedish citizen criminals, the undocumented, and those who fail to integrate – should be deported in order to protect the Swedish welfare state and national heritage. Entering into that field recognising that "In such cases, showing solidarity with those we study may make us accomplices to acts of symbolic or real violence" (Teitelbaum 2019: 21) has yielded some unexpected ethical questions.

Over the course of one tense morning, an informant[1] and I exchanged several messages about the political intentions of my work. I had asked a clarifying question about one of the informant's social media accounts. The informant answered and then added that he already knew what the conclusions of my dissertation would be. Though I was mentally prepared to be Googled, I still was jarred to receive several links to left-wing magazines I had written for in the past and a page citing my affiliation to the George Soros–founded Central European University. With these links as evidence, the informant told me that I would write that his activism was incompatible with liberal democracy and had to be stopped. He told me I would ignore left-wing activists' violence against him and their use of strategies similar to his own. I don't have much sympathy for this informant's calls for recognition. He participates in Sweden's right-wing doxxing apparatus. Spread out over several social media channels, he helps publish the addresses and personal information of political opponents. In our conversations, he has consistently said that this is a tactic he adopted from left-wing movements – which have previously targeted him with physical violence, according to widely shared video evidence. These narratives of victimisation and stigmatisation, employed in the justification of activism and anger at 'the system', emerged as some of the most consistent features of my interviews with activists. One activist described to me how some of his family had cut him off since he joined a white supremacist organisation:

> They just say your evil your evil your evil your evil your evil [*sic*]. We'll have anything more to do with you. Which is to say, excuse my language, is fucking sick. These are my sisters. We loved each other we were really really close. And suddenly just because I have a different opinion about the amount of immigration Sweden should have I am cut off forever probably. And I mean you are kind of used to this if you take a step back and you take a look at this it's just sick. Blood! Blood! Family! But I'm sure this is because of the propaganda. Because media tells everyone if you don't like immigrants you are evil and you should not have anything to do with evil people.

In their cross-national study of far-right activists in Europe, Bert Klandermans and Nonna Mayer concluded that the stigmatisation of these actors is experienced widely across Europe, making these stories of excommunication or the loss of work common (2005). In a recent large-scale survey of Sweden Democrats (SD) supporters (now very much a mainstream party), a majority reported being stigmatised for their views. All in an accompanying interview reported some kind of personal, negative effect from their membership in SD (Ammassari 2022).

Where I had initially planned to write this piece solely on the discrete violence experienced by minorities racialised by the far right, the conversation with my informant confronted me with violence's various interpretational frameworks. It pushed my understanding of repertoires of violence to incorporate dynamics of violence between oppositional actors. When not claiming to be the Silent Majority, far-right activists often position themselves as a minority oppressed by the EU, criminal immigrants, feminists, or politically correct institutions. And though they deny many of the post-1968 struggles of the New Left and the political correctness adopted to reinforce the recognition of those identities, I have spoken to several activists on the Swedish far-right scene who adopt the language of those movements of recognition. For example, several activists have used the metaphor of 'coming out' as openly far right (Informant David 2022; Informant Michael 2022), a phrase adopted by the gay community from debutante balls in the 1930s. Secrecy and internal suppression protect them from the potential of being cut off from their families, losing their jobs, intimidation, or being targeted by the state. Far-right movements, who often advocate more minimalist definitions of violence and punitive law and order policies, claim those narratives in portraying themselves as the truly, legitimately victimised. The humanising act of recognising the affective impact of being painfully cut off from a familial support system or the solidarity built after being targeted by antifascists opens pathways for understanding the attraction of dehumanising, violent ideologies. Cathrine Thorleifsson, in her proposition of a "moral anthropology", points towards exactly this: the sometimes-painful humanisation of the dehumaniser as a way to reclaim the humanity of the dehumanised (2022).

Conclusion – handling violence ethically

So how do we balance our duties to the violently othered: the doxxed, the humiliated, the provoked, the imprisoned? What about when any of those ascriptions have 'far right' attached to them? It begins with the recognition that we live in a "public sphere where semantic confusion has been sown about what is and is not violent" (Butler 2021: 5). Recent left-wing social movements have pushed to publicise the wide-ranging effects of systematic violence on religious, sexual, and ethnic minorities. Meanwhile, oppositional movements vie for the monopoly on violence's naming practice by offering a more minimalist definition while claiming those protections for themselves.

According to this year's Center for Research on Extremism's *Right-Wing Terrorism and Violence Report* (Ravndal et al. 2022), "2021 was the third least violent year since 2015 when counting all attacks (fatal and non-fatal); it was among the three least violent years since 1990 when counting fatal attacks only; and it was among the two least deadly years since 1990 in terms of fatalities" (Ravndal et al. 2022: 1). This should not take academics' attention away from the potentials of violence, of course. It only means that the parliamentary far right works through democratically legitimate paths to reshape democracy in its own nativism, populist, authoritarian image, an image based on forced exclusion and dehumanisation (Mudde 2007). Today, many on the so-called radical right lean more and more on the state to inflict violence on its targets (Switzer and Beauduin 2022) or reproduce images and language which validate violence against others (Wahlström et al. 2021). Again, to give the example of Sweden, a recent drop in physical meetings of far-right activists has been paired with an explosion of alternative media outlets which produce in bulk racialising stories of immigrant crime and white victimisation (Expo 2022). This activism is crucial in contributing to nationalists' feelings of violence done to them, narratives of imperilment that then go on to justify acts of material violence (Marcks and Pawelz 2022). A nebulous definition of violence exposes this relationship but certainly introduces tests for our research ethics.

In Sweden, the determination of ethical research is made through a rationalist cost/benefit analysis of 'legitimate interests' in research: quest for knowledge, individual privacy, and risk of harm being a few (Swedish

Research Council 2017). When we begin to see the risk of violent harm within every interaction, immediately we can visualise the hundreds of ways such extensive considerations could stretch ethical demands of academic work until they tear, particularly in an era of increasingly centralised ethical review boards and public scrutiny of research.

Critical scholars have developed guidance on handling the violence of the researcher/informant dynamic when the informant is from a marginalised group (see Grimaldi et al. 2015) which is, in part, applicable to our case. I share these authors' recognition that fieldwork is a 'confrontational space'

> Characterized by disruption of other people's lives, violence, exploitation and betrayal (Rabinow 1977) that can (and often do) occur as a result of the intertwining between "micropolitics of personal relations" and the wider discursive and structural dynamics of social reproduction and control (Thomas 2003). (works cited in Grimaldi et al. 2015: 2)

We can begin to approach the ethical handling of our data by exploring the idea that affect powers anxieties of invasion, replacement, and betrayal. If this is where the seeds of physical violence in individuals are planted, then in our processing of this data, where the ethnographic interpretation begins, we must first take these ideas as worthy of inquiry and not eject them. But instead of capturing any objective reality of, for example, 'non-Westerners' incompatibility with democracy', we have to remind ourselves that these scenes are filtered through the lens of an ideological camera, framing these events in ways that are productive for movement goals (Doerr et al. 2013). A balance has to be struck between analysing those goals and furthering them. Yes, all possible steps should be taken to avoid the uncritical reproduction and dissemination of propaganda. But the anxiety over handling far-right activists' deeply held senses of victimisation must be challenged too. The attempted theorisation of violence's circulation is not a zero-sum game. Comprehending the circulation of violence between symbol, speech, and act (particularly if an academic's goal is to protect racialised minorities from far-right violence) requires exploring the individual logics of violent victimisation – instead of just automatically disregarding feelings as myth, imaginary, fever dream, or fantasy.

Note

1 All informants provided informed consent. The fieldwork I reference in this piece has been approved by the Swedish Ethics Review Authority, case number: 2021–05872–01.

References

Ammassari, S. 2022. 'It Depends on Personal Networks: Feelings of Stigmatisation among Populist Radical Right Party Members', *European Journal of Political Research*, online first.

Associated Press. 2021. 20 April. 'Veterans on Each Side of the Divide among Capitol Mob Dead'. AP News. https://apnews.com/article/capitol-siege-veterans -coronavirus-pandemic-75d1c219024e5702e6876766340d4447 (accessed 17 October 2023).

Benjamin, W. 1921 [2007]. 'Critique of Violence'. In: Lawrence, B. B. and Karim, A. (eds). *On Violence*. Durham, NC: Duke University Press.

Blee, K. M. 2017. *Understanding Racist Activism: Theory, Methods, and Research*. Abingdon: Routledge.

Bourdieu, P. 1989. 'Social Space and Symbolic Power', *Sociological Theory*, 7(1), 14.

Butler, J. 2020. *The Force of Nonviolence: An Ethico-Political Bind*. London: Verso Books.

Castelli Gattinara, P. 2020. 'The Study of the Far Right and Its Three E's: Why Scholarship Must Go beyond Eurocentrism, Electoralism and Externalism', *French Politics*, 13(3), 314–333.

Doerr, N., Mattoni, A. and Teune, S. 2013. 'Towards a Visual Analysis of Social Movements, Conflict, and Political Mobilization'. In: Doerr, N., Mattoni, A., and Teune, S. (eds). *Advances in the Visual Analysis of Social Movements*. Bingley: Emerald Group Publishing Limited, xi–xxvi.

Evans, B. and Lennard, N. 2018. *Violence: Humans in Dark Times*. New York: City Lights Books.

Expo. 2022. Svensk rasideologisk miljö 2021: Fakta, analys, och trender. https:// expo.se/tidskriften/svensk-rasideologisk-milj%C3%B6–2021 (accessed 17 October 2023).

Farmer, P. 2004. 'An Anthropology of Structural Violence', *Current Anthropology*, 45(3), 305–325.

Grimaldi, E. M., Serpieri, R., and Spanò, E. 2015. 'Positionality, Symbolic Violence and Reflexivity: Researching the Educational Strategies of Marginalised Groups'. In: Bhopal, K. and Deuchar, R. (eds). *Researching Marginalized Groups*. Abingdon: Routledge, 134–148.

Klandermans, B. and Mayer, N. 2005. *Extreme Right Activists in Europe: Through the Magnifying Glass*. Abingdon: Routledge.

Marcks, H. and Pawelz, J. 2022. 'From Myths of Victimhood to Fantasies of Violence: How Far-Right Narratives of Imperilment Work', *Terrorism and Political Violence*, 34(7), 1415–1432.

Menjívar, C. and Abrego, L. J. 2012. 'Legal Violence: Immigration Law and the Lives of Central American Immigrants', *American Journal of Sociology*, 117(5), 1380–1421.

Miller-Idriss, C. 2022. 'Hate in the Homeland'. In: *Hate in the Homeland*. Princeton, NJ: Princeton University Press.

Mudde, C. 2007. *Populist Radical Right Parties in Europe*. Cambridge: Cambridge University Press.

Pilkington, H. 2016. *Loud and Proud: Passion and Politics in the English Defence League*. Manchester: Manchester University Press.

Pontiki, M., Saridakis, N., Gkoumas, D., and Gavriilidou, M. 2022. '# le_petit_koulis and# tsipras_the _traitor: Verbal Aggression as an Aspect of Political Violence on Greek Twitter', *Journal of Modern Greek Studies*, 40(1), 63–93.

Ravndal, J. A. 2021. 'From Bombs to Books, and Back Again? Mapping Strategies of Right-Wing Revolutionary Resistance', *Studies in Conflict & Terrorism*, online first.

Ravndal, J. A. and Jupskås, A. R. 2020. 'Methods for Mapping Far Right Violence'. In: Ashe, S., Busher, J., Macklin, G., and Winter, A. (eds). *Researching the Far Right: Theory, Method and Practice*. Abingdon: Routledge.

Ravndal, J. A., Tandberg, C., Jupskås, A. R. and Thorstensen, M. 2022. 'RTV Trend Report 2022: Right-Wing Terrorism and Violence in Western Europe, 1990–2021', *CREX*. www.sv.uio.no/c-rex/english/publications/c-rex-reports/2022/rtv_trend_report_2022.pdf (accessed 17 October 2023).

Republican National Committee. 2021. 'Resolution to Formally Censure Liz Cheney and Adam Kinzinger and to No Longer Support Them as Members of the Republican Party', *New York Times*. https://int.nyt.com/data/documenttools/rnc-censure-resolution/58226d40412e4f18/full.pdf (accessed 17 October 2023).

Ron, J. 1997. 'Varying Methods of State Violence', *International Organization*, 51(2), 275–300.

Rydgren, J. 2007. 'The Sociology of the Radical Right', *Annual Review of Sociology*, 33(1), 241–262.

Swedish Research Council. 2017. *Good Research Practice*. Vetenskapsrådet.

Switzer, R. and Beauduin, A. 2022. 'Embodied Nativism in Denmark: Rethinking Violence and the Far Right', *Ethnic and Racial Studies*, online first.

Teitelbaum, B. R. 2019. 'Collaborating with the Radical Right: Scholar-Informant Solidarity and the Case for an Immoral Anthropology', *Current Anthropology*, 60(3), 414–435.

Thorleifsson, C. 2022. 'Understanding Dehumanization: How Scholarship Can Defend the Human in an Era of Illiberal Nationalism'. In: Lothe, J. (ed.). *Research and Human Rights*. Oslo: Novus forlag.

Wahlström, M., Törnberg, A., and Ekbrand, H. 2021. 'Dynamics of Violent and Dehumanizing Rhetoric in Far-Right Social Media', *New Media & Society*, 23(11), 3290–3311.

Weinberg, L. and Assoudeh, E. 2018. *Political Violence and the Radical Right*. Oxford: Oxford University Press.

Žižek, S. 2009. *Violence: Six Sideways Reflections*. London: Profile Books.

5

Ecofascism, far-right ecologism, and neo-Malthusianism

Miranda Jeanne Marie Iossifidis

The climate crisis is "inherently a racist crisis globally" (Sultana 2022: 5) and the impacts of climate change are uneven and unfairly distributed, "intensified by the unequal distribution of wealth and resources" (Sealy-Huggins 2018: 101). The relationship between racial capitalism (Robinson 1983; Vergès 2019) and climate change can be approached through what Bhambra (2007) terms our frequently forgotten global 'connected histories' which emphasises the centrality of colonialism, exploitation, and capital accumulation to modernity (see Yusoff 2018) and Sultana notes the link between climate change, colonialism and exploitation being made as early as 1991 (Agarwal and Narain 2012; Williams 2021 in Sultana 2022: 5). Whilst global climate and environmental justice movements have burgeoned, far-right environmental ideas have become more mainstream in recent years. In particular, the supposed relationship between 'overpopulation' and migration with environmental crisis and degradation (Bhatia et al. 2020; Strathern et al. 2019; Lewis 2017). In response to the editors of this book calling for discussion of terminology in researching the far right, this chapter focuses on far-right responses to the climate crisis, rather than scepticism or denialism, and the ways in which interdisciplinary scholars, writers, and activists work with concepts of ecofascism, far-right ecologism, green nationalism, and neo-Malthusianism. In it I argue that the inter-relation of white supremacist ideology, racial capitalism, and heteropatriarchy must be central to our analysis and that we must take ecofascism seriously – in spite of its diverse usage – as a political myth which is increasingly evident in mainstream political discourse. Political myths take the kernels of historical narratives, and ground them in contemporary significance, containing within them a determination to act on the present (Bottici 2007). In other words, political myths have concrete cultural and material effects. As Moore and Roberts note, the far right cannot be treated "as an aberrant force external to and preying on wider society, but as the most extreme part of a distribution, involved in a complicated dance with the rest of society" (2022: 5).

Focusing on ecofascism as political myth-making helps us to identify and analyse the ways in which environmental narratives are mobilised by varied actors to provide contemporary significance to far-right concerns. It also speaks to and names antifascist eco-anxieties around climate present(s) and futures. We must remain attentive to how, as a term that coalesces a cluster of discourses, ecofascism can help us identify specific tropes of far-right ecologism and their mainstreaming within right-wing and liberal environmentalism in diverse cultural, political, and social settings (see Brown et al. 2021).[1] This resonates with Anson and Banerjee's exploration of ecofascism as an "ongoing, metamorphosing politics of proximity in the places and practices of everyday life" (2023: 143), which entails rescaling it from a "hypervisible series of unthinkable acts into a *method* and *practice* for negotiating a planetary eschaton of degradation and extinction" (2023: 144). Being attentive to ecofascist political myth-making requires an anti-fascist, anti-racist, anti-neo-Malthusian, intersectional feminist approach that centres reproductive, environmental, and climate justice.

The chapter first outlines current conceptualisation of ecofascism and far-right ecologism, before moving on to a discussion of the centrality of neo-Malthusianist images and tropes in contemporary far-right ecological discourses as well as liberal environmentalism, focusing specifically on populationisms and bordering practices.

Ecofascism and far-right ecologism

The Out of the Woods collective define ecofascism as the use of "ecological crisis" by the far right "to justify actions of extreme violence, necropolitics [and] racial cleansing" (2020: 21). We can draw on Moore and Roberts' approach, from their recent book, *The Rise of Ecofascism, Climate Change and the Far-Right* (2022); they consider contemporary far-right configurations as a spectrum, which includes political parties and emerging environmental authoritarianism, as well as young far-right and fascist movements and "ecofascist" terrorists (2022: 5).[2] For Forchtner and Lubarda, ecofascism as a term does not allow for discussion of the complexity and breadth of the intersection of the far right and the environment, identifying far-right ecologism as a more useful lens (see Forchtner 2019a–d; 2020; Lubarda 2020; and Forchtner and Lubarda 2022).[3] If we use Moore and Roberts' spectrum, regardless of terminology, what matters for both far-right ecologists and ecofascists in a given ecology is "particular racial blood ties, under whose spell all forms of domination and solidarity must work" (Moore and Roberts 2022: 136).

In recent years we have seen ecofascism discussed more widely across different media and works that straddle academic, activist, and accessible formats. A recent interactive comic by the Anti-Creep Climate Initiative

Collective, *Against the Ecofascist Creep, Debunking Ecofascist Myths* (2022), engages with mainstream popular media (including the *Avengers* films with ecofascist villain Thanos) and details six "everyday ecofascist myths" with accompanying discussion topics, tactics and strategies. This speaks to what Moore and Roberts call the "ecofascist hypothesis" which is "the widespread anxiety that our political future might be 'ecofascism'" (2022: 5). Taking climate anxiety (Verlie 2022) and speculative ecofascist futures seriously, I extend this argument to consider ecofascism as political myth (Bottici 2007, 2011).[4] This focus on ecofascist political myth-making as an ongoing process comprised of images, figures, and characters is useful both in terms of describing the politics of climate anxieties about speculative futures and for anti-fascist research that can identify necropolitical, violent, racist action and discourse deployed in the name of ecological crisis.

Crucial to our contemporary understanding of far-right mobilisation of the climate crisis is Janet Biehl and Peter Staudenmaier's book *Ecofascism Revisited: Lessons from the German Experience* (2011). Staudenmaier's tracing of ecofascism's antecedents details the "peculiar synthesis of naturalism and nationalism forged under the influence of the Romantic tradition's anti-Enlightenment irrationalism", through two nineteenth-century figures: Ernst Moritz Arndt and Willhelm Heinrich Riel ([1995] 2011: 15). Arndt and Riel's antisemitism, focus on racial purity, arguments against miscegenation, and glorification of rural peasant values influenced the *völkisch* movement, uniting "ethnocentric populism with nature mysticism" (2011: 17). Staudenmaier argues that the *völkisch* movement "pointedly refused to locate the sources of alienation, rootlessness and environmental destruction in social structures, laying the blame instead to the rationalism, cosmopolitanism, and urban civilisation", and thus reformulated "traditional German antisemitism into nature-friendly terms" (2011: 17; see also Varco 2023). Arndt, an early 'modern' ecological thinker, wrote in 1815 of the inter-connectedness of all creatures, be they shrub, worm, or human as "all one single unity" (in Staudenmaier 2011: 16), an environmentalism bound up with antisemitism and xenophobic nationalism: his concerns couched in terms of the well-being of *German* soil and the *German* people (Staudenmaier 2011: 16). The *völkisch* movement coalesced violent and romantic nineteenth-century concerns; the emergence of modern ecology brought together "aggressive nationalism, mystically charged racism and environmental concerns" (Staudenmaier 2011: 19).

From its very beginning, ecology has been bound up in a reactionary political framework; German zoologist Ernst Haeckel, an enthusiastic supporter of eugenicism, coined the term 'ecology' in 1867, and was the chief populariser of Darwin and evolutionary theory in the German-speaking world (Staudenmaier 2011). Here we see anti-humanist notions of 'natural order', which have long been central to right-wing environmental thought, develop and mix with *völkisch* anti-industrialism, anti-urbanism, antisemitism, and pseudo-scientific racism, a crucial conflation of biological and social categories (Staudenmaier 2011: 19) which is threaded through contemporary far-right ecological discourses. As such, the relationship between spirituality, organicism, and naturalism, epitomised in ecofascist discourse (Lubarda 2020) by Richard Walther Darré's infamous proclamation (and popularisation) of the slogan "blood and soil" (*blut und boden*), has an even longer history, circulating in *völkisch* circles since the Romantic era (Staudenmaier 2011: 31). However, the contradictions at the core of such stances are evident: citing Darré's zest for modern roads and airships, characteristic of Nazism, Malm and the Zetkin Collective note that "not even the Nazi theorist with the greenest reputation could avoid flipping brown naturalism into a project for actual domination of nature" (Malm and the Zetkin Collective 2021: 607). Indeed, for Malm and the Zetkin Collective, historiography "refutes the myth of green Nazism", acknowledging that "what did exist was a measure of nature-related *rhetoric*" (2021: 615). They argue that Biehl and Staudenmaier's interest in "bestowing green diplomas on Nazism" stems from their fight to drive reactionaries out of the environmental movement in the 1980s and 1990s (Malm and the Zetkin Collective 2021: 614).

These historical and conceptual foundations of ecofascism nonetheless remain important for any contemporary analysis of far-right ecologism, as they form part of a lexicon which continues to offer intellectual sustenance to both far-right and liberal environmentalism (see Tilley and Ajl 2023). Indeed, for Lubarda, ecofascism "may be inadequate to capture the breadth of discourses on the natural environment coming from the far-right actors" (2020: 714), and he therefore sets out a framework to explore the nexus of far-right ecologism for prospective empirical research. This builds on methodological and conceptual concerns around the "unacceptable lack of precision which makes ecofascism an 'embittered taunt'" (Griffin 1991: 2 in Lubarda 2020: 714). His morphology of far-right ecologism brings together naturalism, spirituality and mysticism, organicism and autarky, authority, nostalgia, and Manicheanism. Lubarda argues that while "invoking 'ecofascism' might seem conducive to preventing the proponents of such worldviews from permeating the mainstream ... contemporary far-right ecological values are too complex and elusive to be reduced to (neo)fascism" (2020: 716).

This is an important point. However, rather than reducing the complexities of far-right ecologism to ecofascism, I want to propose an understanding of ecofascism as a collection of images, tropes, and motifs that form part of political myth-making. Ecofascist political myth-making is composed of these kernels of narratives that are found in a diversity of settings. This approach entails engaging with antifascist research and activism and a "portable concept of fascism that makes these dangers legible" (Eley 2013: 217) so that the term as it is used *in situ* goes towards helping us identify distinct formulations of the far right's usage of climate crisis for violent and racist ends. Here I am drawing on Paxton's (1998) conceptualisation of fascism that emphasises temporal processes and social relations, as well as Eley's proclamation that "we should concern ourselves with the production of fascist potentials" and be alert to "the kind of crisis where a politics that begins to look like fascism can coalesce" (Eley 2013: 123–124). One crucial way in which the far right has long sought to use ecological crisis as a means for necropolitical ends is through the notion of 'population', which is inseparable from neo-Malthusianism. I'll now focus on speculative ecofascist presents and futures which hold neo-Malthusianism at their core.

Neo-Malthusianism and populationism

All of our environmental problems become easier to solve with fewer people, and harder – and ultimately impossible – to solve with ever more people. (David Attenborough in Population Matters 2023)

In the context of imperial expansion and proto-social Darwinian views of race and eugenics, British theologian and economist Thomas R. Malthus posited a particular political-theoretical 'principle of population' at the end of the eighteenth century, a calculative approach to resources and humanity that sees all social, political, economic, and environmental crises as derived from 'overpopulation' (see Murphy 2017). Neo-Malthusianism refers to movements developed in the nineteenth century "which referred to Malthus in their crisis diagnosis but differed in the means proposed to cope with 'overpopulation'" (Schulz 2021: 14). Contemporarily, we can see "various populationisms" being mobilised in myriad ways which "render humanity abstract and relative by placing it in opposition to nature or the economy" (Bhatia et al. 2020: 336). For Bhatia et al., these binaries "identify problems of surplus or scarcity that provide a logic of remediation, a rationale for intervening in ways that conceal and reinforce systems of power and inequality" (2020: 336). This is evident in what Sultana calls "the homogenizing tendencies of an undifferentiated 'we' in common climate discourse", whereby "those experiencing climate impacts more violently are also often rendered 'less than human'" (Sultana 2022: 5).

The revival of neo-Malthusianism in the mid-to-late twentieth century is well-documented: white nationalists re-articulated 'population' with 'environment' in key formative publications in environmental studies (Tilley and Ajl 2023: 202). Popular neo-Malthusian texts, such as Paul Ehrlich's 1968 bestseller *The Population Bomb*, were intrinsically tied to the burgeoning environmental movement (Robertson 2012 in Malm and the Zetkin Collective 2021: 198–199). Garrett Hardin's *The Tragedy of the Commons* infamously argued that "to couple the concept of the freedom to breed with the belief that everyone born has an equal right to the commons is to lock the world into a tragic course of action" (Hardin 1968: 1246). Deep ecologists (or as Bookchin [1987] called them, 'Deep Malthusians' – "the fast food of quasi-radical environmentalists") advocated for the Rwandan famine and AIDS crisis helping the 'balance of nature' and over-population (Morris 1993: 37). Indeed, Sir David Attenborough, patron of Population Matters, has spoken about the relationship between the "natural world", famine, and "overpopulation" in several interviews (Furness 2013; Jones 2013).

Feminists have long understood populationism as being embedded in a "depoliticising statistical knowledge production" and inextricably tied to the social-Darwinist, colonial racist rationalities and histories (Schulz 2021) briefly detailed earlier. Whilst the trope of the population bomb may be diminishing, Bhatia et al. note that shifts in language around population control and policy began around the International Conference on Population and Development in Cairo in 1994, whereby the language, assumptions, and norms supporting population control were supplanted by those supporting reproductive rights and health (Eager 2004: 2 in Bhatia et al. 2020: 334). Since the 2010s, there has been a resurgence of feminist thought and activism focused on reproduction in relation to climate crisis. Schulz (2021) identifies the troubling contemporary embeddedness – with very different attachments – of 'population' in different settings, as does Sasser in her work on the intersection of populationism, reproductive rights, and climate change politics (2018). Here, neo-Malthusianism as a kernel of ecofascism can help us to identify racist, violent, necropolitical rationalities and narratives that are pernicious. These populationisms can be found not only in "the explicitly racist version or right-wing ecofascism, but also permeates apparently unpolitical mainstream technocratic environmental data politics", as well as birth strike climate activism and posthumanist feminist agendas (Schulz 2021: 13). Indeed, Haraway's work, the call to 'Make Kin Not Babies!' is part of a desired future in which "human people of this planet can again be numbered two or three billion" (2016: 162, see Strathern et al. 2019). These desires, aired semi-frequently in *The Guardian* and by UK charity Population Matters, closely aligned with white supremacist genocidal desires, also plagued the brief UK birth strike campaign group. Former organiser and co-founder Jessica Gaitán Johannesson describes in *gal-dem* how their calls for a labour strike were understood in terms of overpopulation and details their experience of racism and reproductive coercion, with their Facebook group inundated with populationist content, which "led many, particularly people of colour, to feel uncomfortable and even unsafe" (2023). Indeed, Bhatia et al. caution us that "scholarship that secures population control within a closed narrative of the past forecloses the possibility of recognising how populationist thinking and interventions persist" and point towards three new forms of populationism which focus on optimising numbers (demo), spaces (geo), and life itself (bio) that have emerged in response to the anticipated effects of climate change and unsustainable development (2020: 344).

Racism is central to the construction of 'overpopulation' as an environmental problem, and to the white supremacist notions of extinction and replacement (see Lentin 2020). In the late twentieth century, scientists' use of race as a language to describe biological grouping was replaced with population, "a term seemingly devoid of claims to racial difference" (Murphy 2017: 135). And yet, as Murphy argues, "figures of massified life, in the forms of multitudes, crowds, and overpopulation, have been persistently racializing figures. Race is the grammar and ghost of population" (2017: 135). As such, notions of 'overpopulation' have remained central not only to the right and far right (Macklin 2022; Taylor 2020) but, as Tilley and Ajl argue, to liberal environmentalism, as the arena for effectively laundering white nationalist priorities into policy-oriented analyses and proposed solutions in response to the urgency of climate change (2023; see also Dyett and Thomas 2019). These concerns of population are tied to violent bordering practices, which I will now turn to.

Soil, land, and ecobordering

The best ally of ecology is the border. (Jordan Bardella, Rassemblement National in Landrieu 2019)

Nationalism and environmentalism go hand in hand: it is a pride in your people, pride in your nation and pride in the very soil of the land. (UKIP 2017, in Turner-Graham 2020: 66)

The racialised, gendered, and class dynamics of colonialism are fundamental to any contemporary understanding of 'nature' and 'environment' (Bhandar 2018) as well as any form of green nationalism, whereby protection of the white nation is protection of nature, and the "ecological crisis is not denied but enlisted as a reason to fortify borders and keep aliens out" (Malm and the Zetkin Collective 2021: 218). Here, neo-Malthusianism and the mysticism of national nature (as previously detailed) come together in the form of contemporary green nationalism (Malm and the Zetkin Collective

2021: 219). However, Malm and the Zetkin Collective note that the parties espousing it in the 2010s were "unable to hit any target other than innocents or victims", and "made no efforts to cut any actual emissions" (2021: 242). Nevertheless, the far-right ecological lineage of Haeckel and Darré continues to find a contemporary home in a "synthesis of naturalism and nationalism", which "takes the form of yearning for 'natural' borders" and long-lost territories (Lubarda 2020: 723–724).

This intersection of soil, land, colonialism, and nationalism takes on particular contours in the UK context. In the interwar period an "organo-fascist vision of a culturally homogeneous nation or race" emerged, "dependent on the soil and deriving identity from it" (Stone 2004: 183). Emily Turner-Graham notes that 'degeneration' was a key concept for ruralists, which entailed "the deterioration of the English race and its national values, resulting in the decline of the British empire" (Dietz 2008: 810 in Turner-Graham 2020: 62). Organisations such as the Soil Association were formed, comprised of prominent fascists such as Rolf Gardiner, Harold John Massingham, Viscount Lymington, and Jorian Jenks, who had a "quasi-mystical reverence for the soil" (2020: 62–63). Jenks advised the British Union of Fascists on agricultural issues and wrote their post-war agricultural policy, which sought to rid the countryside of pests and disease (Coupland 2017).

Protecting 'national biodiversity' tied to racism is a common recurring thread. In the 1980s and 1990s, the National Front adopted environmentalism and criticised existing green parties for not discussing causes like the "endangerment of white Britons" (Coates 1993) with an ecologism understood explicitly through the frame of race (Moore and Roberts 2022: 37). In the mid to late 2010s, the BNP claimed to be Britain's "only true Green party" due to the neo-Malthusian logic that they alone "recognise that overpopulation – whose primary driver is immigration ... is the cause of the destruction of our environment" (BNP 2019 in Turner and Bailey 2022: 118–119; see also Forchtner and Kølvraa 2015). UKIP's former leader Nigel Farage also drew explicitly on discourses of overpopulation during his tenure (Turner-Graham 2020: 65), with their environmental policy statement updated by their spokesperson for the environment in 2017 to "protect this green and pleasant land" (Turner-Graham 2020: 64) and emphasise the relationship between the environment, EU, and Brexit, and calling for protection of "our precious countryside for future generations" (UKIP 2017: 52) – a trend seen across Europe. More recently, the white supremacist ethnonationalist far-right party Patriotic Alternative, founded in 2019, has risen to prominence through 'community building' involving camping and hiking in the countryside, rather than through the sort of large-scale demonstrations pursued by street movements in the 2010s (see Childs 2023; Red Flare with Moore and Roberts 2022).[5]

At a European level, in response to growing environmental concerns, Forchtner argues that many European right-wing parties have focused anew on climate change, turning away from previous scepticism and denialism (2019a). Here we see some contemporary formulations of ecofascist, neo-Malthusian, and colonial discourses. Turner and Bailey have identified what they consider a new environmental discourse emerging from European far-right parties, which they conceptualise as 'ecobordering' (2022). Amplifying nationalist concerns at a European scale, they argue that ecobordering engenders fears about the "supposedly active threat of immigration to previously 'pure' and 'sustainable' spaces of national nature, and thus presents borders as forms of environmental protection" (Turner and Bailey 2022: 126). They identify two major expressions of ecobordering discourse: "migration as environmental plunder" which "highlights the impacts of migration on national environmental resources and emphasises the link between immigration and population growth, in order to stoke fears of depleting resources and the exacerbation of local environmental issues" (2022: 118). The second expression, the "migrant as environmental vandal", personifies environmental degradation, tied to notions of rootlessness, and lack of belonging, in contrast to white European 'natives' as "responsible custodians predisposed to the careful management of natural resources" (2022: 118). Here we can see the traces of various European far-right movements, as detailed by Malm and the Zetkin Collective (2021: 190–249).

Fortress Europe, with ever more technologically sophisticated and securitised borders (see Marino 2021; Walia 2021), becomes a calculative response designed to both cultivate and supposedly soothe climate anxieties knotted to mystical formulations of blood and soil, ethno-nationalism, and neo-Malthusianism. In Turner and Bailey's analysis, ecobordering is the sanitisation and reworking of ecofascist and colonial logics of race, a means of obscuring capitalist processes underpinning ecological crisis and degradation precisely to "formulate a discourse designed to engender fears around human mobility" (2022: 113). Despite the indelible connection between climate crisis, racial capitalism and colonialism, white supremacist fears of 'white genocide' and 'replacement' will continue to be deployed against climate refugees; the United Nations Refugee Convention still does not cover persons subject to climate change–induced displacement as a reason for claiming refugee status (see Askland et al. 2022; Fornalé and Doebbler 2017).[6]

Conclusion

Ecofascism is a slippery idea. What we do know is that ecofascist myths fuel white supremacy, ultra-nationalism, patriarchy, ableism, authoritarianism, and mass murder. They are also common misconceptions or deliberate misunderstandings about the world. Ecofascist myths can creep into actual environmentalists' rhetoric and efforts – and doom a real chance at a just, sustainable future. Our goal is to work together to recognize and remove ecofascist ideas from the way we think and talk about the world. (Anti-Creep Climate Initiative 2022: 12)

Speculative ecofascist present(s) and futures are important to engage with – despite or perhaps because of sensationalist media coverage giving fascists more airtime – precisely because ecological anxieties and political myths have cultural and material effects. The different kernels that I have briefly engaged with here interlink and cluster in the form of narratives and discourses that provide meaning and significance for diverse actors, forming dangerous and violent constellations in the name of urgent climate crisis. As such, we need to be attentive to these pernicious ideas as they emerge in diverse settings, including "aesthetic forms and performative practices", which are "fertile breeding grounds for cultural imaginations and political imaginaries that can provide both insights and interruptions to its [ecofascism] alarming naturalization across the globe" (Anson and Banerjee 2023: 144).

The far right will take continue to advantage of the deepening of the climate crisis globally and everyday climate anxiety. As such we can anticipate the amplification of violent, racist, and necropolitical concerns coalescing around the intersection of reproduction, population, borders, and migration all in the name of the environment. Whatever conceptual terminology we use, we have to be able to identify, critique, and contest ecofascist, far-right, and neo-Malthusian expressions and the mobilisation of these discursive tropes wherever they emerge. This entails stating our antagonists clearly (cf Moore and Roberts 2022). Creating and sharing accessible resources, such as those made by the Anti-Creep Climate Initiative, are key to responding to these discourses, as is working with anti-fascist, anti-racist, and feminist spaces and groups and learning from and with reproductive, environmental, and climate justice movements (Sze 2020) in order to collectively imagine, create, and act upon different environmental present(s) and future(s).

Notes

1 Taking on Brown et al.'s definition of mainstreaming as a multifaceted and multi-directional "process by which parties/actors, discourses and/or attitudes move from marginal positions on the political spectrum or public sphere to more central ones, shifting what is deemed to be acceptable or legitimate in political, media and public circles and contexts" (2021: 9).

2 For discussion of ecofascist terrorist attacks and manifestos, see Malm and the Zetkin Collective (2021), Reid Ross and Bevensee (2020), Forchtner (2019b), and many others.

3 For a very recent mapping of existing scholarship on the far right and the environment, see Lubarda and Forchtner (2022).

4 A crucial aspect to understanding the specificity of the narratives of political myth is that they form a process and that this process is inherently plural. Bottici builds on Blumenberg's (1985) theory of myth as "work on myth", which posits myth as a *process of the continual reworking of a basic narrative core or mythologem*, rather than as a product that is given once and for all. She notes that myth is "made of images, figures, and characters" (Bottici 2007: 106) which is useful for us in identifying the different components of far-right ecologism and their contemporary significance.

5 Patriotic Alternative has of April 2023 split, with a large faction forming a new party, Homeland, whose inaugural meeting was on 20 April (Hitler's birthday). See Red Flare (2023).

6 It is worth noting that in December 2020, a Bangladeshi man was granted refugee status by the appeals court for the Administrative Court of Bordeaux due to air pollution, the "first time a court has taken into account environmental criterion to justify a person benefitting from the status of a sick foreigner" in France. See Louarn (2021).

References

Agarwal, A. and Narain, S. 2012. 'Global Warming in an Unequal World: A Case of Environmental Colonialism'. In: Dubash, N. K. (ed.). *Handbook of Climate Change and India*. Abingdon: Routledge, 105–112.

Ansen, A. and Banerjee, A. 2023. 'Green Walls: Everyday Ecofascism and the Politics of Proximity', *boundary*, 2(50),1.

Anti-Creep Climate Initiative: Anson, A., Galentine, C., Hall, S., Menrisky, A., and Seraphin B. 2022. *Against the Ecofascist Creep, Debunking Ecofascist Myths*. https://www.asle.org/features/stemming-the-creep-of-ecofascism-a-primer/ (accessed 17 October 2023).

Askland, H. H., Shannon, B., Chiong, R., Lockart, N., Maguire, A., Rich, J. and Groizard, J. 2022. 'Beyond Migration: A Critical Review of Climate Change Induced Displacement', *Environmental Sociology*, 8(3), 267–278.

Bhambra, G. 2007. *Rethinking Modernity: Postcolonialism and the Sociological Imagination*. London: Palgrave Macmillan.

Bhandar, B. 2018. *Colonial Lives of Property: Law, Land, and Racial Regimes of Ownership*. Durham, NC: Duke University Press.

Bhatia, R., Sasser, J. S., Ojeda, D., Hendrixson, A., Nadimpally, S., and Foley, E. E. 2020. 'A Feminist Exploration of "Populationism": Engaging Contemporary Forms of Population Control', *Gender, Place & Culture*, 27(3), 333–350.

Blumenberg, H. 1985. *Work on Myth*, trans. R. Wallace. Cambridge, MA: MIT Press.

Bookchin, M. 1987. 'Social Ecology versus Deep Ecology: A Challenge for the Ecology Movement', *Green Perspectives: Newsletter of the Green Program Project*, 4–5.

Bottici, C. 2007. *A Philosophy of Political Myth*. Cambridge: Cambridge University Press.

Bottici, C. 2011. 'Towards a Philosophy of Political Myth', *Iris – European Journal of Philosophy and Public Debate* III, 31–52.

Brown, K., Mondon, A., and Winter, A. 2021. 'The Far Right, the Mainstream and Mainstreaming: Towards a Heuristic Framework', *Journal of Political Ideologies*, 1–18.

Childs, S. 2023. 'The Anti-Fascist Research Group Exposing Britain's Neo-Nazi Threat: The Leader of Patriotic Alternative Congratulates Supporters When They "Welcome White Babies into the World"', *Novara Media*. https://novaramedia .com/2023/01/10/the-anti-fascist-research-group-exposing-britains-neo-nazi -threat/ (accessed 17 October 2023).

Coates, I. 1993. 'Cuckoo in the Nest: The National Front and Green Ideology'. In: Holder, J. et al. (eds). *Perspectives on the Environment: Interdisciplinary Research in Action*. Aldershot: Avebury, 13–23.

Coupland, P. 2017. *Farming, Fascism and Ecology: A Life of Jorian Jenks*. Routledge.

Dyett, J. and Thomas, C. 2019. 'Overpopulation Discourse: Patriarchy, Racism, and the Specter of Ecofascism', *Perspectives on Global Development and Technology*, 18(1–2), 205–224.

Eager, P. W. 2004. *Global Population Policy: From Population Control to Reproductive Rights*. Aldershot: Ashgate.

Ehrlich, P. R. 1971 [1968]. *The Population Bomb*. Cutchogue, NY: Buccaneer Books.

Eley, G. 2013. *Nazism as Fascism: Violence, Ideology, and the Ground of Consent in Germany 1930–1945*. London: Routledge.

Forchtner, B. 2019a. 'Climate Change and the Far-Right', *WiRE's Climate Change*, 10:e604, 1–11.

Forchtner, B. 2019b. 'Eco-Fascism: Justifications of Terrorist Violence in the Christchurch Mosque Shooting and the El Paso Shooting', *Open Democracy*, 13 August. https://www.opendemocracy.net/en/countering-radical-right/eco-fasci sm-justifications-terrorist-violence-christchurch-mosque-shooting -and-el-paso-shooting/ (accessed 17 October 2023).

Forchtner, B. 2019c. 'Nation, Nature, Purity: Extreme-Right Biodiversity', *Patterns of Prejudice*, 53(2), 11–31.

Forchtner, B. 2019d. 'The National Ecosystem: Radical Right and Biodiversity', *Fair Observer*, 14 March. https://www.fairobserver.com/region/europe/radical -right-environmentalism-national-ecosystem-biodiversity-germany-news-19991/ (accessed 17 October 2023).

Forchtner, B. 2020. 'Far-Right Articulations of the Natural Environment: An Introduction'. In: Forchtner, B. (ed.). *The Far-Right and the Environment: Politics, Discourse and Communication*. Oxford: Routledge, 1–18.

Forchtner, B. and Kølvraa, C. 2015. 'The Nature of Nationalism: Populist Radical Right Parties on Countryside and Climate'. *Nature and Culture*, 10(2), 199–224.

Fornalé, E. and Doebbler, C. F. 2017. 'UNHCR and Protection and Assistance for the Victims of Climate Change', *The Geographical Journal*, 183(4), 329–335.

Furness, H. 2013. 'Sir David Attenborough: If We Do Not Control Population, the Natural World Will', *The Telegraph*. https://www.telegraph.co.uk/culture/tvandradio/10316271/Sir-David-Attenborough-If-we-do-not-control-population-the-natural-world-will.html (accessed 17 October 2023).

Gaitán Johannesson, J. 2023. 'Why the "Overpopulation Problem" Is an Issue of White Supremacy', *gal-dem*. https://gal-dem.com/overpopulation-problem-white-supremacy-climate-crisis/ (accessed 17 October 2023).

Griffin, R. 1991. *The Nature of Fascism*. London: Pinters Publisher Limited.

Haraway, D. J. 2016. *Staying with the Trouble: Making Kin in the Chthulucene*. Durham, NC: Duke University Press.

Hardin, G. 1968. 'The Tragedy of the Commons', *Science*, 162(3859), 1243–1248.

Jones, P. 2013. 'David Attenborough: "Humans Are a Plague on the Earth"', *Radio Times*. https://web.archive.org/web/20140808052741/http://www.radiotimes.com/news/2013-01-22/david-attenborough-humans-are-a-plague-on-the-earth (accessed 17 October 2023).

Kølvraa, C. and Forchtner, B. 2019. 'Cultural Imaginaries of the Extreme Right: An Introduction', *Patterns of Prejudice*, 53(3), 227–223.

Landrieu, V. 2019. 'Jordan Bardella: "Le meilleur allié de l'écologie, c'est la frontière', *Les Echos*, 7 April 2019.

Lentin, A. 2020. *Why Race Still Matters*. Cambridge: Polity Press.

Lewis, S. 2017. 'Chthulu Plays No Role for Me', *Viewpoint Magazine*. https://viewpointmag.com/2017/05/08/cthulhu-plays-no-role-for-me/ (accessed 17 October 2023).

Louarn, A.-D. 2021. 'A Bangladeshi Migrant Becomes the First "Environmentally Displaced" Person in France', *Info Migrants*. https://www.infomigrants.net/en/post/29589/a-bangladeshi-migrant-becomes-the-first-environmentally-displaced-person-in-france (accessed 17 October 2023).

Lubarda, B. 2020. 'Beyond Ecofascism? Far-Right Ecologism (FRE) as a Framework for Future Inquiries', *Environmental Values*, 29(6), 713–732.

Lubarda, B. and Forchtner, B. 2022. 'Far Right and Environment: Past-Present-Future'. In: Bruno, V. A. (ed.). *Populism and Far-Right: Trends in Europe*. Milan: EduCATT, 85–113.

Macklin, G. 2022. 'The Extreme Right, Climate Change and Terrorism', *Terrorism and Political Violence*, 34(5), 979–996.

Malm, A. and the Zetkin Collective. 2021. *White Skin, Black Fuel: On the Danger of Fossil Fascism*. London: Verso Books.

Marino, S. 2021. 'The Foundations of Fortress Europe'. In: *Mediating the Refugee Crisis*. Cham: Palgrave Macmillan, 13–39.

Moore, S. and Roberts, A. 2022. *The Rise of Ecofascism: Climate Change and the Far Right*. Cambridge: Polity Press.

Morris, B. 1993. 'Reflections on Deep Ecology'. In: *Deep Ecology and Anarchism, a Polemic*. London: Freedom Press, 37–46.

Murphy, M. 2017. *The Economization of Life*. Durham, NC: Duke University Press.

Out of the Woods. 2020. 'Interview with Out of the Woods', *Journal of Aesthetics and Protest*, 11, 18–22.

Paxton, R. O. 1998. 'The Five Stages of Fascism', *The Journal of Modern History*, 70(1), 1–23.

Population Matters. 2023. 'David Attenborough's Greatest Achievement', *Population Matters*.   https://populationmatters.org/news/2023/05/david-attenboroughs-greatest-achievement/ (accessed 17 October 2023).

Red Flare. 2023. 'Homeland: British Fascism Fractures', 24 April 2023. https://redflare.info/Homeland_British_fascism_fractures-RF.pdf (accessed 17 October 2023).

Red Flare, Moore, S., and Roberts, A. 2022. 'Britain's Growing Far-Right Party is a Serious Threat', *Novara Media*, 6 January 2022.

Reid Ross, A. and Bevensee, E. 2020. *Confronting the Rise of Eco-Fascism Means Grappling with Complex Systems*. CARR Research Insight 2020.3. London: Centre for Analysis of the Radical Right.

Robertson, T. 2012. *The Malthusian Moment: Global Population Growth and the Birth of American Environmentalism*. New Brunswick, NJ: Rutgers University Press.

Robinson, C. 1983 [2000]. *Black Marxism: The Making of the Black Radical Tradition*. Oakland, CA: University of North Carolina Press.

Sasser, J. S. 2018. *On Infertile Ground: Population Control and Women's Rights in the Era of Climate Chang*. New York: New York University Press.

Schultz, S. 2021. 'The Neo-Malthusian Reflex in Climate Politics: Technocratic, Right Wing and Feminist References', *Australian Feminist Studies*, 36, 485–502.

Sealey-Huggins, L. 2018. 'The Climate Crisis is a Racist Crisis: Structural Racism, Inequality and Climate Change'. In: Johnson, A. (ed.). *The Fire Now: Anti-Racist Scholarship in Times of Explicit Racial Violence*. London: Zed Books, 99–113.

Staudenmaier, P. 2011 [1995]. 'Fascist Ecology: The "Green Wing" of the Nazi Party and Its Historical Antecedents'. In: Biehl, J. and Staudenmaier, P. (eds). *Ecofascism Revisited: Lessons from the German Experience*. Norway: New Compass Press, 13–42.

Stone, D. 2004. 'The Far Right and the Back-to-the-Land Movement'. In: Gottlieb, J. V. and Linehan, T. P. (eds). *The Culture of Fascism: Visions of the Far Right in Britain*. London: I.B. Tauris, 182–198.

Strathern, M., Sasser, J. S., Clarke, A., Benjamin, R., Tallbear, K., Murphy, M., Haraway, D., Huang, Y.-L., and Chia-Ling, W. 2019. 'Forum on "Making Kin Not Population: Reconceiving Generations"', *Feminist Studies*, 45(1), 159–172.

Sultana, F. 2022. 'The Unbearable Heaviness of Climate Coloniality', *Political Geography*, 99, 102638, 1–14.

Sze, J. 2020. *Environmental Justice in a Moment of Danger*. Oakland, CA: University of California Press.

Taylor, B. 2020. 'Alt-Right Ecology: Ecofascism and Far-Right Environmentalism in the United States'. In: Forchtner, B. (ed.). *The Far Right and the Environment: Politics, Discourse and Communication*. London: Routledge, 275–292.

Tilley, L. and Ajl, M. 2023. 'Eco-Socialism Will Be Anti-Eugenic or It Will Be Nothing: Towards Equal Exchange and the End of Population', *Politics*, 43(2), 201–218.

Turner, J. and Bailey, D. 2022. '"Ecobordering": Casting Immigration Control as Environmental Protection', *Environmental Politics*, 31(1), 110–131.

Turner-Graham, E. 2020. 'Protecting Our Green and Pleasant Land'. In: Forchtner, B. (ed.). *The Far Right and the Environment: Politics, Discourse and Communication*. London: Routledge.

UKIP. 2017. *UKIP General Election Manifesto 2017*. https://manifesto.deryn.co.uk/ukip-general-election-manifesto-2017/ (accessed 16 October 2023).

Varco, M. 2023. 'Volk Utopia: Racial Futures and Ecological Politics on the German Far-Right', *Geoforum*, 103823.

Vergès, F. 2019. 'Capitalocene, Waste, Race, and Gender', *e-flux journal*, 100.

Verlie, B. 2022. *Learning to Live with Climate Change: From Anxiety to Transformation*. London and New York: Routledge.

Walia, H. 2021. *Border and Rule: Global Migration, Capitalism, and the Rise of Racist Nationalism*. London: Haymarket Books.

Williams, J. 2021. *Climate Change Is Racist: Race, Privilege and the Struggle for Climate Justice*. London: Icon Books.

Yusoff, K. 2018. *A Billion Black Anthropocenes or None*. Minneapolis, MN: University of Minnesota Press.

Part II

Positionality, standpoint, and intersectionality

6

'Far right studies' and the unbearable whiteness of being

Aurelien Mondon

In the ideal polity one seeks to know oneself and to know the world; here such knowledge may be dangerous. (Mills 1997: 98)

The political reverberations of the murder of George Floyd by the police on 25 May 2020 and the resurgence of the Black Lives Matter movement had a deep symbolic impact across society. At first sight, it even appeared to lead to an awakening within academia as to the role academics may have played in supporting structures of oppression, if only through their passive approach to such matters. In political science, this was exemplified by the statement released in June 2020 by the American Political Studies Association (APSA 2020) "condemning systemic racism" and acknowledging that their "own programs, procedures, teaching, and scholarship may be shaped by or contribute to upholding, rather than dismantling, systems of oppression". Yet this welcome introspection was qualified, and perhaps somewhat downplayed, by the claim that "political scientists have long examined the linkages between race, power, governance, social injustice and oppression".

The coalescence of such events and movements with the end of the Trump presidency and the lead-up to the insurrection on 6 January 2021 demonstrates that white supremacy and racism remain part and parcel of politics in the US. Such trends are also witnessed in much of the 'West', and even beyond, as many countries have wrestled with the resurgence of far-right politics as well as the ongoing systemic nature of racism in their societies. As such, the topic is central to understanding not just the threats posed to democracy but the limitations of its current, liberal hegemonic articulation.

'Far right studies', understood here as a loose field of research predominantly located in politics and political science, had not waited for the election of Trump to become a booming field. In fact, publications on these politics have often surpassed those on other party families, including those in government. Yet, for a field that is notorious for its lively definitional debates and a general willingness to evolve and reinvent itself terminologically, it has often appeared unwilling to engage with racism as a concept, particularly its systemic nature, but also slow to react to new developments brought about by societal events.[1]

Instead, there has been a tendency to use and focus on concepts which have either exceptionalised the phenomena studied, diverted attention away from racism, or even euphemised such politics. This can be seen in the use of terms such as nativism and populism (see Newth 2021; Mondon 2023). This is not to say that these terms cannot be useful in understanding the current context but that they have often been chosen instead of more stigmatising, but also precise terms (Collovald 2004). In particular, there appears to have been a reluctance to engage with racism as an evolving concept, despite the sophisticated literature on the matter in sister disciplines such as sociology.[2] As such, it is argued here that far right studies has failed to reckon with the issues which have led not only to the resurgence of the Black Lives Matter movement but also to the mainstreaming of far-right politics: namely that racism remains not only a useful tool to explain our political landscape but one that takes many shapes and is present across the board, from the more extreme forms of politics to mainstream structures of power.

Building on wider research on the topic (Mondon 2022a), this chapter aims to explore and challenge how the field has tended to reinforce assumptions regarding the post-racial status of Western societies in particular, discussing racism only through its illiberal articulations and euphemising or even invisibilising its more liberal and systemic forms as well as obscuring their inherent relationship. This is not to say that there are no valid reasons to focus on the more extreme and illiberal articulations of racism, quite the contrary. Yet, overall, this has not been balanced with similar attention paid to their more mainstream counterparts, and this imbalance has played a role in the process of mainstreaming far- and extreme-right politics.

Populist hype in the post-racial fantasy

The findings that inform this chapter are based on an overall corpus of over 500,000 words, which consists of the titles and abstracts of all academic articles referenced in the Web of Science database between 2016 and 2021 that contained either far right, extreme right, radical right, populist right, or right-wing populis*.[3] In total, 2,543 articles were collected. Data was analysed based on the mixed-methods approach first developed by Katy Brown (2023; Brown and Mondon 2020; see also Mondon 2022a for this particular data).

A key finding in the research is that the full corpus tends to rely more on euphemistic terms, which could potentially divert attention away from the evolving nature of the parties in question and their ideological roots. 'Far right' is the most prominent term, which, while not necessarily euphemistic in and of itself, raises interesting questions as it is perhaps one of the least well-defined terms in the field, particularly when compared to the ones it has replaced such as extreme and radical right or fascism and even populism. Yet, it is 'populism' that demonstrates best the process of euphemisation and diversion as it is the second most used in the full corpus (present in 46.8 per cent of articles). This is striking yet hardly surprising considering the prevalence of what has been described elsewhere as a 'populist hype' in far right studies (see Glynos and Mondon 2019; Maiguashca 2019).

Concerns over the use of the term populism (or more precisely its careless use) are hardly new or underdeveloped (see Collovald 2004; Bale et al. 2011; Glynos and Mondon 2019; De Cleen et al. 2018; Dean and Maiguashca 2020; Hunger and Paxton 2021; De Cleen and Glynos 2021). To be clear, this is not to say that there is no use for the concept of populism in far right studies. The aim is to reflect on how and how much it is used and the impact this has on what is primed and what is ignored, what is highlighted and what is obscured. Tellingly, right-wing populis* appeared in 32.1 per cent, even though this terminology has been widely criticised by both main schools of thought on populism which broadly argue that it should be considered either a discourse or at best a thin ideology rather than a core tenet to understand the politics of such parties (see Katsambekis 2020).

The careless use of populism and its hype is not simply a terminological or conceptual issue but a political one: using it instead of racism, for example, can divert attention away from the exclusionary nature of such politics but also link so-called populist politics to 'the people' qua demos. This not only gives them a veneer of democratic support, which they generally lack, but also places the blame for the rise of such politics squarely on 'the people', as if politics was simply a matter of bottom-up pressure rather than top-down mediation and agenda setting (see Brown et al. 2021; Mondon 2022b). In turn, it removes the agency and responsibility from mainstream elite actors, whether they be in the media, politics, or even academia, regarding the rise of reactionary politics, as if these actors had no power to influence politics, policy, or public discourse. If anything, the fact that many far-right leaders enjoy and even demand being called populist should come as a warning sign to academics.

In contrast, terms that point either to the more extreme and oppressive nature of these parties, movements, and ideologies or to their racism in particular are far less prominent in the full corpus: extreme right, a key descriptor in the 1990s and early 2000s, appears in just 390 articles (15.3 per cent), violence in only 184 (7.2 per cent), authoritarian* in 157 (6.2 per cent), nativis* in eighty-three (3.3 per cent) and supremac* in forty-eight (1.9 per cent). One could argue that authoritarianism and nativism could be implied by radical right if this term is based on Cas Mudde's approach and definition of the populist radical right (2007), but it would still fail to

Figure 6.1 Wordcloud for key terms based on articles (n = 2,543).

explain why populism is so much more prevalent than radical right despite Mudde's warning that radical right is the key descriptor. Finally, and of more direct relevance to this chapter, rac* appears in 285 articles (11.2 per cent), racis* in 175 (6.9 per cent), white* in 141 (5.3 per cent), and whiteness in thirteen (0.5 per cent).

   This is not to say that the use of stronger, more stigmatising (but also often more precise) terms means that the approach is automatically reflective and deals with systemic racism. In fact, many of these articles focus on the more illiberal articulations of racism, which can at times serve, consciously or not, to conceal the more liberal ones, which are not only more mundane but also core to current political structures of oppression (see Mondon and Winter 2020). Illiberal articulations of racism are those more closely associated with traditional forms of racism and often find echoes in the politics of fascism, Nazism, or historic colonialism. Even though they are grounded in the present, they also echo more traditional articulations of racism (based on biology and widely acknowledged to be freakish) and circumscribed events linked to the exceptional actions of individuals threatening *our* post-racial contract. They are therefore posited as belonging to a political world that is not *ours*, based on conceptions of racism which remain 'frozen' in time and place (see Lentin 2020). As such, it limits the qualifier 'racis*' to extreme acts which can be isolated as individualised and extraordinary and "are thus rendered illegible, [and] disparate impact is reduced to merely unfortunate happenstance" (Goldberg 2016). Illiberal racist events are thus widely denounced, even by far-right actors. This affords them a veneer of respectability that is too often taken for granted by mainstream actors, including academics: if they denounce racist acts, how could they be *really* racist themselves?

This not only lends credibility and legitimacy to the far right, taking them at their word that they have changed and accept the rules of the democratic game, but it also obscures liberal articulations of racism and allows many mainstream actors to find comfort in the post-racial fantasy. Liberal articulations of racism are thus constructed in opposition to illiberal ones. Racialisation in this case is justified through the use and perversion of what is generally thought of as liberal and even progressive values such as women's and LGTBQ+ rights or 'free speech' (see Puar 2007 on homo-nationalism; Farris 2012 on femonationalism; Titley 2020 on 'free speech'), but also by the simplistic claim that one cannot be racist if they denounce (illiberal) racism. Needless to say, this does not mean that illiberal articulations should not be denounced or studied, quite the contrary, as they have a serious impact on the lives of many at the sharp end of such politics. Yet denouncing them without acknowledging broader structures of oppression such as systemic racism or patriarchy embedded in our current liberal system only serves to obscure and perpetuate them.

Going back to our corpus, it is particularly striking that out of 141 articles mentioning 'white*', only seven (sixteen occurrences) were published in dedicated political science and international relations journals. Out of these seven articles, one mentions 'white identity', 'white majority', and 'white working-class voters' in uncritical positive terms, and none mention 'whiteness'. This is hardly surprising as the term appeared in only thirteen articles in the whole sample, with fifteen out of the twenty-nine occurrences found in only two articles' titles and abstracts. When the term appeared, it was generally clear in the context that it was taken in a critical manner and aimed to highlight more systemic patterns of racial oppression and advantage.

Racism, anti-racism, and positionality as researchers of the far right

The avoidance of rac*, racis*, or whiteness in the field and the overemphasis on more problematic, less well-defined, or more contentious and

euphemistic concepts such as populism and far right are particularly interesting in the wider political context. There often appears to be a disconnect
between what is seen as important and worthy of support in public and
what is seen as serious enough to warrant consideration in the academic setting. Indeed, many academics will lend public support to anti-racist movements such as Black Lives Matter or be vocal against Trump's racism and
his fuelling of white supremacy and the most extreme right. Yet it is striking
how they often fail to use similar terminology in their academic research or
engage with the more systemic forms of oppression denounced by movements such as BLM which they publicly support. While public interventions can be in part attributed to virtue signalling, it is just as likely many
truly believe in them and in their support for these causes, but fail to link
them up to their own (passive) participation in the structures of oppression
they denounce by simple omission or euphemisation in their work and their
access to privileged modes of public discourse shaping.

Such a disconnect and dissonance between public and academic
personas – where the same person can support movements such as Black
Lives Matter or oppose Trump through their social media persona and
yet refuse to use terms such as racism in 'serious' 'professional' settings or
engage critically in their positionality as white (but also male, cis etc.) – can
be linked to the research undertaken by Perry et al. (2021: 10). Their data,
collected in August 2020, evidences the proliferation of 'anti-racism' and
'anti-racist' language in mainstream discourse and amongst white liberals in
particular. However, it suggests that

> although progressive racial views are strongly associated with self-describing
> as "anti-racist", among the strongest predictors was also identifying as
> "'colorblind' when it comes to race". In fact, color-blindness was an even
> stronger predictor of identifying as "anti-racist" than willingness to confront
> a racist friend or a rejection of old-fashioned racism.

This dissonance could be explained by "progressive whites (not minorities)
self-describing as 'anti-racist', particularly those characterised by a more
'generic liberalism' on racial issues (i.e., a liberalism that affirms any racial
attitudes that seem liberal, rather than explicitly race critical or radical)" and
therefore not seeing the issue as worthy of central and prominent integration
in 'serious', 'sensible' research about politics and liberal democracy (unless it
touches on illiberal forms of racism). Research by Geoffrey T. Wodtke (2016)
suggests that more nefarious behaviours may be at play in this context as

> despite their more favorable views about blacks, greater support for racial
> equality in principle, and great awareness of discrimination, whites with

higher verbal ability are generally no more likely than their counterparts with lower ability to support specific policies designed to realize racial equality in practice. In fact, whites with higher ability are significantly less likely than whites with lower ability to support school busing programs or workplace racial preferences, although the relationship between verbal ability and policy support is not strictly monotonic. (41)[4]

That much of far right studies has been conducted in political science relates to what Charles Mills refers to as epistemology of ignorance.[5] This is often based on the normative belief that one's work is scientific rather than political, as if research in social sciences can be removed not only from the world it seeks to understand, but also from research having an impact on said world and its mediated understanding. It is noteworthy that for this edited collection we received no abstracts from colleagues who choose more positivist approaches despite these occupying a large chunk of the research undertaken on the far right. It is not altogether surprising though as these approaches and methodologies are often used to reinforce white logics, conferring whites "a sense of superiority, a sense that they know things", as well as the 'White man's burden' – the urge so many whites feel to educate and 'civilise' non-whites, which has served historically as the moral and intellectual foundation for colonialism and 'internal colonialism' (Zuberi and Bonilla-Silva 2008: 18). Belief in a scientific aspect of research is key to allowing the researcher to eschew ethical considerations beyond the box-ticking exercise organised by institutions. As Mills (1997: 123) highlighted, it is easy to be

> blinded to realities that we should see, taking for granted as natural what are in fact human-created structures. So we need to see differently, ridding ourselves of class and gender bias, coming to recognize as political what we had previously thought of as apolitical or personal, doing conceptual innovation, reconceiving the familiar, looking with new eyes at the old world around us.

The necessity for critical engagement with racism and whiteness in far right studies is all the more essential at a time when the mainstreaming of far-right politics, whether through electoral victories or discursive hegemonic progress, continues to worsen. Academics cannot afford to study the far right in euphemistic ways, particularly as events across the globe make clear that the far right remains a lethal and powerful force rather than an aberration as we comforted ourselves for too long. We must acknowledge as a starting point that racism continues to be a core structural issue rather than one 'frozen' in the past, outside of *our* current (neo)liberal order. To some extent, the murder of George Floyd in 2020 led to an awakening in consciousness in many that racism is part and parcel of liberal societies and that the idea of the post-racial is indeed a myth. However, such awakening can easily be downplayed and circumscribed through the creation of new 'sincere fictions' (Bonilla-Silva 2006) where one can portray oneself as supportive of the movement, all the while continuing to (passively) uphold the very racist structures denounced by said movement. This could not be clearer than in the APSA statement written following the brutal murder of George Floyd, and yet the lack of reckoning in the discipline since.

A plea for ethical, anti-racist far right studies

While this chapter is critical of the current state of far right studies, it is not about finger-pointing, but rather a plea for more self-reflection and for a more ethical, anti-racist research practice. This is something that I have had to work through myself and continue to do so, learning, repairing mistakes, and correcting course. This is therefore about what should be core to the academic process, that is, trial and error, learning, and reflecting. Admitting mistakes, rectifying them, and challenging one's ignorance is surely a more academically sound approach than denial and grandstanding, whether one is early in their career or already a gatekeeper.

In a context where far-right politics are an ever-growing threat to democracy and minorities, it is essential for academics to challenge normative assumptions and white (but also male, cis, ableist) methods within their academic work or risk becoming part of the problem through epistemic ignorance. This requires therefore not only an in-depth reflection about our positionality as researchers, but a commitment to social justice and anti-racism as core to our practice. As Tukufu Zuberi (2001: 12) notes, "as we study, as we investigate, we must offer solutions that solve, and the world justifiably must demand not a lack of values and convictions, but rather the dedication to justice and an ability to present the truth as we understand it regardless of the challenges it presents". This means that we must do away with the idea that there can be objective, neutral research in social sciences. This could not be clearer than in the field of far right studies, where this 'balance' would suggest that we must stand between fascism and anti-fascism or racism and anti-racism. Instead, we must commit to what Remi Joseph-Salisbury and Laura Connelly (2021) have termed 'anti-racist scholar-activism', which is explored at more length in Chapter 30.

A useful way to engage in this process is to reflect upon the journey one can take as a white researcher, something that is neatly summarised in Barnor Hesse's famous 'eight white identities'.[6] Acknowledging the many subject positions between white supremacy and white abolitionism can help us as researchers build a more nuanced understanding of our positionality, of the wages of whiteness many continue to benefit from, and how a colour-blind approach is not neutral or apolitical but complicit in reaction.

Notes

1 This is not unique and a similar trend is highlighted in fascism studies by Anastasia Kanjere (2022) who highlights the lack of engagement with Critical Race and settler colonial studies. As France Winddance Twine and Charles A. Gallagher (2012: 7) noted, this also matches earlier, wider developments, whereby "throughout much of the twentieth-century mainstream, white social scientists did not focus on the institutions that created, reproduced and normalized white supremacy".
2 While much remains to be done in sociology, most sophisticated understandings of race and racism have emerged in the discipline, including most critical self-introspections (see for example Zuberi and Bonilla-Silva 2008).
3 For more detail on the methodology and corpus, see Mondon (2022).
4 Verbal ability is defined by Wodtke as "the subset of skills related to understanding and analyzing language".
5 On this, see also the edited book by Shannon Sullivan and Nancy Tuana (2007).
6 Hesse's eight white identities are: White Supremacist; White Voyeurism; White Privilege; White Benefit; White Confessional; White Critical; White Traitor; White Abolitionist. For more detail: https://twitter.com/barnor_hesse/status/796784744591724544 (accessed 11 October 2023).

References

APSA. 2020. 'APSA Statement Condemning Systemic Racism', *Political Science Now*, June.

Bale, T., van Kessel, S., and Taggart, P. 2011. 'Thrown Around with Abandon? Popular Understandings of Populism as Conveyed by the Print Media: A UK Case Study', *Acta Politica*, 46, 111–131.

Bonilla-Silva, E. 2006. *Racism without Racists: Color-Blind Racism and the Persistence of Racial Inequality in the United States*. New York: Rowman and Littlefield.

Brown, K. 2019. 'When Eurosceptics Become Europhiles: Far-Right Opposition to Turkish Involvement in the European Union', *Identities*, 27(6), 633–654.

Brown, K. 2023. *Talking 'With' and 'About' the Far Right: Putting the Mainstream in Mainstreaming*. PhD thesis, Bath: University of Bath.

Brown K. and Mondon, A. 2020. 'Populism, the Media and the Mainstreaming of the Far Right: *The Guardian*'s Coverage of Populism as a Case Study', *Politics*, 41(3), 279–295.

Brown, K., Mondon, A., and Winter, A. 2021. 'The Far Right, the Mainstream and Mainstreaming: Towards a Heuristic Framework', *Journal of Political Ideologies*, online first.

Collovald, A. 2004. *Le Populisme Du FN : Un Dangereux Contresens*. Bellecombe-en-Bauges : Ed. du Croquant.

De Cleen, B. and Glynos, J. 2021. 'Beyond Populism Studies', *Journal of Language and Politics*, 20(1), 178–195.

De Cleen, B., Glynos, J. and Mondon, A. 2018. 'Critical Research on Populism: Nine Rules of Engagement', *Organization*, 25(5), 649–661.

Dean, J. and Maiguashca, B. 2020. 'Did Somebody Say Populism? Towards a Renewal and Reorientation of Populism Studies', *Journal of Political Ideologies*, 25(1), 11–27.

Farris, S. 2012. 'Femonationalism and the "Regular" Army of Labor Called Migrant Women', *History of the Present*, 2(2), 184–199.

Gallagher, C. A. and Winddance Twine, F. (eds). 2012. *Retheorizing Race and Whiteness in the 21st Century: Changes and Challenges*. Abingdon: Routledge.

Glynos, J. and Mondon, A. 2019. 'The Political Logic of Populist Hype: The Case of Right Wing Populism's "Meteoric Rise" and Its Relation to the Status Quo'. In: Cossarini, P. and Vallespín, F. (eds). *Populism and Passions: Democratic Legitimacy after Austerity*. Abingdon: Routledge.

Goldberg, D. T. 2016. *Are We All Postracial Yet?* Cambridge: Polity Press.

Hesse, B. n.d. 'The 8 White Identities', https://twitter.com/barnor_hesse/status/796784744591724544 (accessed 11 October 2023).

Hunger, S. and Paxton, F. 2021. 'What's in a Buzzword? A Systematic Review of the State of Populism Research in Political Science', *Political Science Research and Methods*, 1–17.

Joseph-Salisbury, R. and Connelly, L. 2021. *Anti-Racist Scholar-Activism*. Manchester: Manchester University Press.

Kanjere, A. 2022. 'Fascists in and out of Uniform: Situating Street Fascism in the Broader Context of White Supremacy'. In: Smith, E., Persian, J., and Fox, V. J. (eds). *Histories of Fascism and Anti-Fascism in Australia*. Abingdon: Routledge.

Katsambekis, G. 2020. 'Constructing "the People" of Populism: A Critique of the Ideational Approach from a Discursive Perspective', *Journal of Political Ideologies*, online first.

Lentin, A. 2020. *Why Race Still Matters*. Cambridge: Polity Press.

Maiguashca, B. 2019. 'Resisting the "Populist Hype": A Feminist Critique of a Globalising Concept', *Review of International Studies*, 45(5), 768–785.

Mills, C. W. 1997. *The Racial Contract*. Ithaca, NY: Cornell University Press.

Mondon, A. 2022a. 'Epistemologies of Ignorance in Far Right Studies: The Invisibilisation of Racism and Whiteness in Times of Populist Hype', *Acta Politica*, online first.

Mondon, A. 2022b. 'Populism, Public Opinion, and the Mainstreaming of the Far Right: The "Immigration Issue" and the Construction of a Reactionary "People"', *Politics*, online first.

Mondon, A. 2023. 'Populism (Studies) Does Not Exist, But It Still Matters', *Populism Studies*, online first.

Mondon, A. and Winter, A. 2020. *Reactionary Democracy: How Racism and the Populist Far Right Became Mainstream*. London: Verso.

Mudde, C. 2007. *Populist Radical Right Parties in Europe*. Cambridge: Cambridge University Press.

Newth, G. 2021. 'Rethinking "Nativism": Beyond the Ideational Approach', *Identities*, online first.

Perry, S. L., Frantz, K. E., and Grubs, J. B. 2021. 'Who Identifies as Anti-Racist? Racial Identity, Color-Blindness, and Generic Liberalism', *Socius: Sociological Research for a Dynamic World*, 7, 1–12.

Puar, J. 2007. *Terrorist Assemblages: Homonationalism in Queer Times*. Durham, NC and London: Duke University Press.

Sullivan, S. and Tuana, N. 2007. *Race and Epistemologies of Ignorance*. New York: State University of New York Press.

Titley, G. 2020. *Is Free Speech Racist?* London: Polity.

Wodtke, G. T. 2016. 'Are Smart People Less Racist? Verbal Ability, Anti-Black Prejudice, and the Principle-Policy Paradox', *Social Problems*, 63(1), 21–45.

Zuberi, T. 2001. *Thicker Than Blood: How Racial Statistics Lie*. Minneapolis, MN: University of Minnesota Press.

Zuberi, T. and Bonilla-Silva, E. 2008. *White Logic, White Methods: Racism and Methodology*. Lanham, MD: Rowman & Littlefield.

7

Safety and silence: oral history, far right research, and the paradox of the 'vocal minority'

Imo Kaufman

Death to all Jews.

– Text from a banner PewDiePie commissioned in a video
(Mahdawi 2017)

An introduction to the problem

In 2003 a documentary aired on the BBC called *Louis and the Nazis*, in which Louis Theroux visits California to meet with Tom Metzger, the Aryan Resistance, and various skinhead groups (Cabb and Theroux 2003). During the documentary, Louis visits a skinhead called Skip and his family and friends at their house. Depicted in their home are several flags, all Nazi or Confederate. The interview appears to be going well until Louis asks an awkward question:

Louis: So, if I told you if I was Jewish, would that create a problem between us?

Skip: Well, because you've got the camera right now I'd allow you to stay. If not, I'd probably kick your ass and put you in the street somewhere.

Louis: For real?

Skip: Pretty much, because a Jew wouldn't be here on my property. Are you Jewish?

Louis: Do you mind if I don't answer that?

[Skip and the others laugh]

Louis: [laughs] I'm not saying yes or no.

Skip: So you're on the fence? You're on the fence.

Louis: I'll tell you why – I'm not a racist, and I actually think it's wrong to be a racist. And so I feel as though by saying whether I'm Jewish or not I'm kind of in a way acknowledging the premise that it really matters when I think it shouldn't and it doesn't.

I agree with the first half of Louis's statement here; that it should not matter if he is Jewish. It should not matter but, it does. When Louis tells us it (Jewishness) 'doesn't' matter he speaks with a false, or perhaps fantastical, authority; Jewishness can only escape mattering, in this context, in a world without antisemitism. Such a world is unlikely to ever exist. Skip's threat of violence demonstrates the very fact that Jewishness does *matter*, as for him it has violent, and hence material, implications. Important to note, too, is that Louis is protected by the proxy of his camera crew, presumably the BBC's prestige, and the fact that he is not Jewish. Louis's possible Jewishness has no ontological status beyond his proposition to Skip; it is a talking point, a provocation, nothing more.

In my research, I explore a lived, and living, experience of gaming in the UK through interviews. Within the context of my research, and beyond, my Jewishness, unlike Louis's, is very real. When I have brought it up in gaming spaces (the same or similar spaces I research) I have often, if not always, experienced antisemitism. I remember once, acutely, during a shift at CeX (a second-hand videogame and electronics store in the UK) in Holloway, London, my area manager and co-workers doing a Sieg Heil salute. It was funny, you see (or do not see), because I am Jewish.

I often observe passive antisemitism in gaming spaces. I have seen people with profile pictures of Hitler on Steam. I remember in an online game I frequent another player having the name "Gas Chambers". At the start of 2022, Roblox had to remove an experience called "Camp Concentration" created by players which featured "Nazi soldiers, gas chambers, and dead bodies" (Anon 2022). Games themselves can reproduce antisemitic stereotypes, such as the *Dragon Age* series which depicts dwarves as an isolationist, classist, and materialistic race, even giving them golems, whose origination is in Jewish folklore, controlled through scrolls in their mouths (Bioware 2009–2014). The point I am making here is that, even if in moderation or rare occurrence, gaming spaces – social space; online space; games themselves – are saturated with antisemitism. As a Jewish player, I cannot help not only encountering it but noticing it. The choice presented to me, then, is not whether I engage with the far right – as I already unavoidably do, both their ideas and potentially their people – but how I engage, or do not, with them in my research.

As a researcher I am, by not making my Jewishness explicit, in Skip's words, sitting on the fence. The fence is perhaps where the gate of Gamergate resides, a gate I am invested in finding: the point where a door can open between gaming and the far right. But, akin to Louis, I agree it is wrong to be a racist (or antisemitic, if being specific). Surely, then, Louis is not sitting on the fence but standing on the other side. Maybe it is specifically the Jew who sits on the fence, the duplicitous manipulator who is always part of a scheme or conspiracy. Am I secretly orchestrating the destruction of the white race or running the global media? Even if I deny this fact, surely, I, a Jew, *would* – hence I sit on the fence as I cannot prove I am on either side of it. The Jew maintains their threat spatially through the very fact they are impossible to pin down. Skip tells us as much when he says, "a Jew wouldn't be here on my property", but he is still upset at the idea that one *could* be because you can never know, for sure, that there is not.

My postgraduate research requires me to undergo annual reviews. In my first year, my reviewers asked me why I was not interviewing anyone far right. This question surprised me. I explained I was Jewish and that to anyone aware, Kaufman was a dead giveaway. The question was immediately dropped. Not only would my interviewing far-right individuals be difficult to pass through ethics, but it would also be unsafe. I am not Louis Theroux, a successful gentile, white, male documentarian – I cannot say that being Jewish does not matter to me because it does, both in meaning and materiality. My Jewishness is *me*, my body; it is how I *matter*. I do not need to reach out to far-right individuals to record or feel their harm either. PewDiePie, a YouTuber with over 100 million subscribers in 2022, once paid two men to hold a sign that read "Death to all Jews" and to dance in a video (Mahdawi 2017). Whilst it was played off as an absurdist joke, the damage was already done; I saw it, I read it, I felt it. As stated before, I cannot avoid antisemitism in gaming, and it is not just in stolen moments or occasional usernames – it evidently has the potential to go mainstream.

The threat of the far right to me is not abstract but vividly realised and identifiable. Participant 6, a gaming professor, told me that being blocked on Twitter through a mass Social Justice Warrior blacklisting tool was a "career highlight" (Participant 6: 9). There are countless lists of games researchers on 4Chan and Reddit that are damned by their left-wing agendas or feminist approaches; the idea of being on a blocklist (a mass blocking tool) has become a 'highlight', normalised beyond concern. Not only does Participant 6 downplay its severity, but he also unintentionally naturalises the interrelation between game studies and online harassment. And harassment is not the only risk. In 2021, the United Kingdom saw its first instance of gun violence connected to Incel and gaming culture, where five people tragically lost their lives (BBC 2021). And, as a lesbian and female-presenting queer, my other identities are perfectly capable of attracting their own vitriol and abuse. Considering all this, we are presented with a practical question: I, a Jewish person, cannot avoid or escape antisemitism in daily life or in gaming, and (as we will see in the next section) it haunts my research, constantly talked around if not talked about, so – where does this leave me?

The 'vocal minority'

Here are segments from four, out of twelve, of my interviews. Interviews are with participants who are from gaming spaces beyond play alone, such as heritage, research, content creation, and the gaming industry. The interviews explored participants' gaming experiences and opinions. Whilst a lot of participants alluded to a toxic other, four directly used the term 'vocal minority' when discussing an abusive (usually white and male) segment of the gaming community online.

P4: I feel like sometimes the gaming community has been I guess unfairly labelled because of some bad eggs [laughs] and they are very you know the people that are quite vocally bad are loud but I don't think they represent the majority of the community. (Participant 4: 7)

P6: there's a group of people who are just dicks and are just awful people and they were the vocal I wanna say vocal minority I'm maybe being naive in thinking it's a minority but erm they were the vocal minority that really just ruined it for everybody … it's the narrative of Gamergate is is a bunch of largely entitled white male pricks. (Participant 6: 8)

P7: it's straight white man vision that's what that's what it is so it's hard to have conversations outside of that cause you get such push back from what is ultimately a vocal minority of people they're just very vocal and they have a big platform in the space compared to who they are representative of the actual demographic of people that play games these days. (Participant 7: 12)

P8: I think it's the there's er extremely loud but yeah the vocal minority I suppose is the phrase who love to complain whenever they don't [clears throat] ironically don't see themselves represented because they're not playing as a straight white male. (Participant 8: 3)

Both directly and indirectly, we can observe the concept of a 'vocal minority' here across a third of my interview data. Participant 4 does not explicitly say it but refers to 'bad eggs' who are 'vocally loud' and not the 'majority'. She does refer to a 'vocal minority' later in the interview (Participant 4: 8). The vocal minority becomes a majority experience in my interview data; their minoritisation is maintained through characterisation of them as such and nothing more. This vocal minority are connected to Gamergate, to whiteness, to maleness, to issues of representation and online abuse. This minority are ruining, or tainting, gaming for everyone else; this 'minority' is a disruptive force, even if their complaints are unfounded. We can confidently connect expectations of white, male hegemonic representation to far-right ideology and we know these discourses (re)surfaced in Gamergate too (Bezio 2000: 564). The vocal minority are undeniably present in my interviews; talked around, if not talked about; haunting my interviews in a spectral sense – not quite there but also never not. I do not need to speak directly to them, the vocal minority, to record them – they are *already here*.

The consequence of Gamergate and online abuse is, in part, a subjugation of minority players. Part of my investment in the issue of the far right in gaming is to determine how best to approach it, to counteract the harassment and abuse said players face. This means confronting the paradoxical claims of the vocal minority which, in part, perpetuate and undermine the harm actual minorities in gaming spaces experience. There is an irony in trying to uplift an actual vocal minority by challenging the falsity of another. And this irony is one of the clever ways far-right ideologies maintain themselves; by establishing their own fantastical victimhood, they can both operate on the defensive and deny others their genuine grievances (Allan 2016). 'Vocal minority' as a phrase is already contradictory. White men are not a minority in gaming; they are a majority in industry and gaming representation. The 'vocal' proportion of them may well be a minority of the majority, but it implies that they are minoritised. My interview participants, intentionally or not, reproduce their claim through their very adoption of the term 'vocal minority'. The minoritisation is not representational or systematic but performative; these men are minoritising *themselves* through their own words, spoken or written, as part of an intricate (often subconscious) ideological mechanism. And this mechanism is further reproduced as others, even those seemingly outside such ideological structures, echo their language and terminology. Until they, the 'vocal minority', claim victimhood, it does not exist. Just like Louis's Jewishness it exists as a provocation, a means to an end.

In the process of untangling far-right gaming discourses, I hope to help many of the white men who have found themselves enmeshed in these ideological webs, the first step of which is scrutinising how such webs are woven and *how* exactly they are tangled up. Only then can we begin to prise apart the knots. The vocal minority itself exists in a sort of in-between space. They are loud, presumably, because they are unheard. But if I do not hear them, if I turn away from them, how vocal truly are they? Alternatively, if I turn to them to listen, and I listen enough, they stop being the minoritised, ignored community/individual they claim to be. The vocal minority's power, then, sits in an in-between space, as yet another provocation. The concept of a 'vocal minority', of being unheard, is also not neutral but lends itself to ideological far-right mechanisms. Operating on the defensive allows conservative voices to "manufacture crisis", utilising "the tropes of multiculturalism, equality and freedom to maintain an ideological space where racism and repression may appear natural" (Atton 2006: 586; Allan 2016: 37).

Surely, it is only natural to be vocal if you are a minority or if you (or your videogames) are under attack? And feeling unheard, or neglected, is partly what draws individuals to such spaces, even if such supposed discrimination is wholly imagined or bigoted in its foundation (Kimmel 2013: 265). If I do not give them a space at the metaphorical table, do I risk contributing to isolation that makes individuals vulnerable to radicalisation in the first place?

The paradox

The paradox here operates methodologically, ideologically, and personally. My research is qualitative, reflexive, and open in practice (O'Reilly 2004: 43; Flick 2007: 13; Tracy 2010). Yet I cannot be fully open, both in how I present myself (I do not explicitly discuss my Jewishness) or in the reach of my research (my participant demographics). Ideologically it seems dangerous to platform far-right discourses and ideas, but, as discussed in the previous section, feeding into far-right narratives about being ignored, even if unintentionally, can be harmful. I am incredibly curious about far-right individuals who exist in, or emerged from, gaming spaces, but I understand that reaching out to them would risk my own personal safety – and there is no way to align this with my qualitative emphasis on openness. Hence, in my interview practice, I am talking about them without talking to them; I am talking *around* them. The methodological inconsistencies, my research interests being in part eroded by my practice, are maintained by the ideological and the personal.

Perhaps I can justify the ideological contradiction through another example with Louis Theroux. Louis now has three documentaries exploring the lives of the Westboro Baptist Church (Theroux 2007–2019). In the second and third documentaries, Louis is confronted with individuals who are trying to join the church because of his work; in trying to expose their inhumanity, Louis, intentionally or not, advertised their belief systems to the wider world. My research is in collaboration with a national museum and therefore has the potential to be disseminated through exhibitions and public-facing material. The other ideological issue, that I am inadvertently feeding white male narratives of victimhood by bypassing their participation, is harder to resolve. This is, in part, how far-right ideologies flourish. I cannot talk to them without propagating their ideas indirectly, I cannot ignore them without helping to maintain their discourses; I cannot win. This reflects the incredible ability of far-right ideologies to maintain and (re)produce themselves; they are always "contradictory" (Hall 2011: 713).

Some Jewish researchers are open about their Jewishness in their research. Masculinity scholar Kimmel describes informing far-right interview participants he's Jewish, telling us that: "I wasn't going to 'pass', so I didn't even try" (Kimmel 2013: 240). Knowing that I cannot securely pass as gentile in interviews meant I 'didn't even try'. But my not trying took me in the opposite direction; knowing I would not pass meant I did not enter that space. Notably, Kimmel's openness means he has to navigate potential dangers: meeting participants in the daylight, in public, and even parking his car several blocks away (Kimmel 2013: 240–241). Kimmel's book was published in 2013, the year before Gamergate; the landscape and machinations of far-right abuse and harassment have shifted significantly since. In a 2019 interview, Anita Sarkeesian, who was incessantly doxed and harassed during Gamergate, describes still feeling vulnerable walking down the street and avoiding restaurant window seats (Campbell 2019). Whilst Gamergate was mostly online, it had very real impacts on people's material, lived lives and still does. As a researcher in game studies who is concerned with far-right ideologies in gaming, it can only feel like a cautionary tale. And, in a way, far-right intentions from within the Gamergate movement have already won here. I, a Jewish researcher, am allowing fear of abuse or harm to control what and who I research and how I do it. I, unlike Louis, would never have dared venture onto Skip's property in the first place.

Power in paradox

Maybe I do not want to resolve the contradictions here; maybe there is something to be said about paradoxical research, about research that fails to quite make sense. Far-right ideologies are, in part, sustained by paradox – and within this/their system I cannot win, so I must fail. Queer theorist Halberstam tells us that failing against, or outside of, a system can open alternative possibilities of thinking and being (Halberstam 2011). The far right as a problem in gaming is not going away. In my interviews, the fact that far-right communities and discourses come up naturally in almost every one, even if only alluded to, is damning. The problem *is* there, and yet we talk around it – sometimes without knowing it. The far right haunts my interview data – parasitic, a reminder of the threat of harm (potentially even death) and impossible to truly grasp, to *touch*. It (the far-right body and bodies) is ethereal in that it is delicate, always at risk and under attack, but otherworldly and unreachable. The true issue in my interviews is not that I have turned away from the far right, that I have ignored it, but that I cannot even if I wanted to. As queer historian Love tells us so aptly: "the desire to forget may itself be a symptom of haunting" (Love 2009: 1).

I want to pull apart Gamergate, understand where it came from, what it is, and why, in some ways, it is still here. The gate in Gamergate feels significant, especially when we think about Skip's fence – both the metaphorical fence Louis apparently sits on and the fence that presumably surrounds his property (that a Jew is not allowed onto). I want to find the gate, the point of transition where one can go from "it's wrong to be racist" to "a Jew wouldn't be here on my property" (Cabb and Theroux 2003). And yet here lies another paradox – how do I know I have found the gate without stepping through it, without opening it a crack? If I do not touch it or interact with it, how can I be sure it is not just another immovable part of the fence? The gate *is*, of course, a part of the fence too, a literal in-between space that exists *in* and *between* as well as potentially beyond. And Louis, as possibly Jewish in Skip's eyes, is a part of the fence, occupying an in-between reality that resists scrutiny. Significantly, then, the Jew the far right imagines also exists in between. And from this in-between space, a space that defies the Skip/Louis binary, then perhaps I (the Jew) can resist going *through* the gate, as even if I crack it ajar, or flick open the latch, I am simultaneously, always, *between* the sides of the fence. Whilst the far right's proximity is inherently threatening, I cannot fall onto Skip's side, I cannot fall into the belief of "a Jew wouldn't be here on my property". Not only through my Jewishness do I resist such a binary, but as I exist in-between, I inherently undermine the claim "a Jew wouldn't be here", for wherever I am a Jew also is.

From within the in-between space, I have power. I am otherworldly. Through the impossibility of pinning me down, the far right talk around me (the Jew) – not *to* me. Just as talking around the far right in gaming arguably gives them power, there is power in the way the far right talk around me; I am always, potentially, walking around Skip's yard. I do not have to arrive at Skip's home, I am *already there*. In my own way I, the Jew, have already won. Skip is constantly alert, patrolling his fence (both literal and metaphorical) because of the threat of my proximity – even when I have no intention of going near it. In my failure to arrive, I leave Skip to perpetually anticipate me (Ahmed 2004: 123–125). I *haunt* him. Significantly, I, unlike the vocal minority, do not deny Skip's agency; he denies it from himself. The ghost of the vocal minority is indicative of a real threat, a very real phantom pain. But the Jew who might cross Skip's fence is not real, nor does she need to be. Just as the vocal minority minoritises themselves as a clever ideological mechanism, they simultaneously police borders, both literal and gaming borders, for imagined threats. Whilst such policing *does* by action propagate harmful ideas (if you are on the defensive – surely you have something to be defended from?) it is also quite funny to imagine Skip being haunted by a Jew who is not real and has no ontological status beyond the ideological, beyond the fence that entraps him within.

Concluding thoughts

Maybe as I turn away from spaces that might harm me, I do not enter a non-space but carve new space and new possibility. This chapter, this *space*, speaking (writing) frankly about Jewishness and gaming already feels meaningful. There will always be an element of contradiction, of paradox, in my work. I seek to understand a vocal minority without giving them a voice but cannot directly do so without endangering myself and my Jewish body, and without platforming dangerous ideas. But there *is* power in the paradox. Whilst the vocal minority might present a methodological contradiction, I can counter it with my own; from the in-between space that is the fence, I can fail *and* win. I simultaneously conduct research about how to eradicate the far right whilst my spectre haunts Skip's yard. In failing to arrive, I never leave.

I understand that this chapter may sound tortured, like I am tangled up in ideological, ethical, and methodological knots. I would like to assure you that even if I am tangled, I enjoy it. I enjoy researching the far right in gaming, I enjoy catching them out, pinpointing the words and ideas that indicate that they have already, and always have, arrived. Maybe I queer my failure through my derived pleasure. I cannot say if Skip enjoys his torture, but I can confidently say I do enjoy mine. Happiness allows us to carve out new space, new worlds (Ahmed 2010). And I have made one – right here.

References

Ahmed, S. 2004. 'Affective Economies', *Social Text*, 22(2), 117–139.

Ahmed, S. 2010. *The Promise of Happiness*. Durham, NC and London: Duke University Press.

Allan, J. A. 2016. 'Phallic Affect, or Why Men's Rights Activists Have Feelings', *Men and Masculinities*, 19(1), 22–41.

Anon. 2022. 'Roblox Removes Nazi Concentration Camp "Experience" with Gas Chambers', *StopAntisemitism.org*. https://www.stopantisemitism.org/antisemitic -incidents-105/roblox-removes-nazi-concentration-camp-experience-with-gas -chambers (accessed 3 March 2022).

Atton, C. 2006. 'Far-Right Media on the Internet: Culture, Discourse and Power', *New Media & Society*, 4(8), 573–587.

BBC 2021. 'Plymouth Shooting: Jake Davison Was Licensed Gun Holder', *BBC News*. https://www.bbc.co.uk/news/uk-england-devon-58197414 (accessed 15 March 2022).

Bezio, K. M. S. 2000. 'Ctrl-Far-Del: GamerGate as a Precursor to the Rise of the Far-Right', *Leadership*, 14(5), 556–566.

Campbell, C. 2019. 'The Anita Sarkeesian Story', Polygon. https://www.polygon
.com/features/2019/6/19/18679678/anita-sarkeesian-feminist-frequency
-interview-history-story accessed 3 March 2022).

Flick, U. 2007. *Designing Qualitative Research*. London: SAGE Publications.

Halberstam, J. 2011. *The Queer Art of Failure*. Durham, NC: Duke University Press.

Hall, S. 2011. 'The Neo-Liberal Revolution', *Cultural Studies*, 25(6), 705–728.

Kimmel, M. 2013. *Angry White Men*. New York: Nation Books.

Love, H. 2009. *Feeling Backward*. Cambridge, MA; London: Harvard University
Press.

Mahdawi, Arwa. 2017. 'PewDiePie Thinks "Death to All Jews" Is a Joke. Are You
Laughing Yet?', *The Guardian*. https://www.theguardian.com/commentisfree
/2017/feb/15/youtube-pewdiepie-thinks-death-to-all-jews-joke-laughing-yet
(accessed 3 March 2022).

O'Reilly, K. 2004. *Ethnographic Methods*. Abingdon: Taylor & Francis.

Tracy, S. J. 2010. 'Qualitative Quality: Eight "Big-Tent" Criteria for Excellent
Qualitative Research', *Qualitative Inquiry*, 16(10), 837–851.

Games

Bioware. (2009–2014). *Dragon Age* series.

Interviews

Participant 4. 16/07/2021.
Participant 6. 08/07/2021.
Participant 7. 19/07/2021.
Participant 8. 07/07/2021.

Film and TV

Cabb and Theroux. 2003. 'Louis and the Nazis', BBC Two England.

8

On the incompleteness of ethnography: embracing and navigating failure as a principle in research on the far right

Balša Lubarda

There are many ways in which ethnography can fail and be incomplete – in fact, probably not many in which it can be fully successful. Its "triple hermeneutic" (Yanow 2009: 279), situating the knowledge production and interpretation between the reader, the subject, and the object of research, is often too difficult to follow, especially if the agency of the non/more-than-human is brought into the picture. But failing and incompleteness should not bring a sense of despair. Building on the notions of 'dark ethnography' (Ortner 2016) and 'failure' (Kušić and Záhora 2020) in far right research, I introduce the notion of 'incomplete ethnography' to capture the outcome of complex ethical and practical dilemmas related to the research of the far right. By drawing from more than seventy interviews during four years of ethnographic research on far-right ecologism in Eastern Europe (Lubarda 2023), this chapter attempts to make sense of failures in the field by reflecting on the practical steps and decisions made in the course of fieldwork preparation. In doing so, this chapter goes against the scholarly attempts at "taming the unruliness of ethnography", assuming a normative ethnographic standard from which deviations can be identified (Eggeling 2021: 156). As such, it speaks to the previous and future ethnographic research on the far right troubled with potentially similar issues.

Much like anything else, incomplete ethnography is a relational term, depending on what "complete" stands for – and whether it exists. Its very completeness is arguably undermined by methodological triangulation, as ethnography is often conflated with qualitative interviews and "participant observation" (Poets 2020: 106). Merely standing for "writing an account of the way of life of a particular people" (Hammersley 2017: 3) is a definition of ethnography that no longer suffices in far right research. Is it really that we want to know about the 'way of life' of our interlocutors, and more importantly, does this help us explain the underlying structural circumstances that condition their existence and support? Yet, without tempering or even overlooking the antifascist ethos with which (I hope) the researcher enters the field, both the positionality and 'distance/proximity' as the fundamental principles of a good (dark) ethnography cannot be meaningfully fulfilled (on these and other principles, see Faust and Pfeifer 2021).

Fieldwork is a legitimising experience, an opportunity for researchers to rain-check their privilege by engaging with those they wish to write about. While there may be many ways to conduct fieldwork, such an experience is 'failable'. Some of the failures write off the very possibility of conducting fieldwork, e.g., failing to convince the ethical board. Others can be manageable: unanswered emails, accounting for limited subjectivity, maintaining mental health amid a towering sense of loneliness, and even the language barrier. The danger lurks also in the very attempt to "obscure ourselves in the method that is inevitably embodied" (De Guevara and Kurowska 2019: 163) and assume equivalence between different contexts in comparative case studies. The 'incomplete' character of my ethnography was conditioned by numerous failures I will unpack below but predominantly refers to its multi-sited nature and the continuous hesitancy to become fully immersed in the context and livelihoods of my respondents.

The first and the main failure of my (incomplete) ethnography is in its very existence. My original intention was to do (just) qualitative interviews with the far right. Expectedly, the first couple of interviews already turned into informal conversations and prolonged contact with my interlocutors, leading to several situations in which the 'data' was not collected solely during the interview. This also meant that my ethnography notably deviated both from the (imagined) ideal-type application encountered in textbooks (Mitchell 2007) and the existing ethnographies of the far right (Blee 2002; Thorleifsson 2018, to name only two). The multi-sited/multi-country nature of the ethnography I conducted in the countries of the Visegrad Four, paired with my continuous hesitancy to become fully immersed in the context and livelihoods of my respondents, rendered impossible the principle of immersion. For instance, keeping regular field notes or prolonged contact with the object of the study, i.e., the far right, was virtually impossible due to my frequent changing of locations and security concerns. While I spent the majority of my doctoral research in Hungary (Budapest), I took short trips to Poland (November 2018, June–July 2019, and September–October 2019), Slovakia (June 2018 and July 2019), and Czechia (December 2019) to conduct my fieldwork. Each of these trips involved moving places frequently in my futile quest for the 'perfect sample' but also meeting as many respondents and thus, naively, maximising the fieldwork experience amid limited funding. In the presentation of my research and its outcomes, I often hid behind this rationality that moving places provided me with, whereas my main motivation was to avoid mental health hardships characteristic of the 'embodied fieldwork' (Okely 2007) and interacting with the far right on a virtually daily basis.

Obviously, the downsides of such a decision are equally mounting. Being often surrounded by members of violent political organisations, establishing a shallow rapport, and misinterpreting the findings, I might have failed with the very choice of method. Ethnography of the far right in my research was conditioned by "the pull of holism" (Hammersley 2006: 6), that is, a need to construct a more or less coherent ideological picture – in my case, that of far-right ecologism. Obviously, my limited immersion entailed a range of dubious encounters, for which none of the classes in my or (I dare presume) any other university can fully prepare the researcher. Physical presence in the field brings about consequences, exacerbated by the focus on the far right. Being unable to meet the respondents because they were arrested for possessing antisemitic materials, or making ethical decisions related to intervening and/or observing in the spur of a moment are all cases in point. For instance (swiftly) deciding whether to enter pubs in which the initiation process for new members was about to commence or to accept the invitation to go to a private party for the inner circles was not always beneficial to the research or the researcher (for similar dilemmas, see Ramalingam 2020). Entering potentially dangerous situations from the perspective of physical or mental health is also a sign of a frantic chase for the 'good data' in a futile quest for competitiveness in the academic market – a market characterised by precarious, short-term stints and overwhelming solitude.

A separate set of issues entails both the physical proximity to and the ideological distance from those I researched. Handshaking, fist-bumping, hugging, drinking from the same bottle of alcohol, and even faux boxing sparrings, all the potential signs of amiability and camaraderie in the far-right worlds, were the acts that I, more often than not, accepted to do. Being aware that a refusal to do most of these would likely result in an estrangement from my interlocutors that I could not afford, knowing how hard it was to interact with these groups, still made me feel profoundly dishonest as a researcher. Have I not been upfront enough about who I am and where I stand politically, that these people are still so eager to embrace me as their interlocutor? Has my antifascism, a conviction which I had personally nurtured for as long as I can remember, waned in light of my personal encounters with the far right?

The answers to these questions may seem obvious but they contributed to a certain sense of revulsion coming from both in and outside the scholarship. Getting acquainted with the far right even with the aim of understanding and ultimately opposing it is bound to raise suspicion. Far too many times, I found myself addressing these suspicions of not only fellow researchers and other interested individuals but even my family and close friends: have I 'crossed the line' by becoming a part of the private lives of my respondents, congratulating on their first child, providing travel advice about my home country, etc.? Coming from the Balkans, that continuously othered and 'less than European' semi-periphery, I have come to experience first-hand both the consequences and the (short-term) perks of the nationalist frenzy.

Perhaps in an act of scholarly vanity towards sceptics, I also occasionally found myself engulfed by an unwarranted feeling of contempt towards fellow researchers who never dared to soil their "moral hygiene" (Gingrich and Banks 2006: 7) by interacting with or, at least, trying to understand (and not justify) the motivations behind far-right activism. Much as my positionality was malleable and dependent on an interplay of events that occurred in preparation for the field, during the very interactions and in the write-up phase, the end goal was clear – to probe the ideological tenets of the far right, that is, to "tangle the web of political meaning" (Freeden 2022: 35) by focusing on its very source: the meaning-makers. Tangling this web is reminiscent of hiking over a sharp ridge, where the researcher/hiker is continuously expected to keep in mind the non-existent 'safe' side or a backdrop of humanity against which these aberrations can be examined.

If ethnography with the far right is 'hiking over the ridge', then negotiations are that ridge. But negotiating with subjects with whom one does not share a frame of reference (Whittier 2002) requires navigating between the "ethics of fairness" towards the subjects and mitigating the consequences of these social movements (Blee 2007: 125). This is where another source of failure and incompleteness whittles down the imagined core of ethnographic rigour. Being upfront about my research and its goals, in spite of that resembling "an openness about the irreconcilability" of our worldviews (Saglam 2021), has proven to be of immense value in deepening the rapport. Of course, this was partly due to the 'nature of the topic' – being portrayed as a harmless researcher interested in an un(der)explored dimension of far-right nationalism diminished the scepticism that usually comes as a consequence of such intrusions (Damhuis and de Jonge 2022). As Benjamin Teitelbaum (2017: 12) has noted in his often-critiqued ethnography of far-right music, exactly on the grounds of its attitude towards his respondents, this was not a consequence of "the silly fetish of an unattainable neutrality" or the lack of concern towards the radical nationalism of the far right. It is an attempt at producing an authentic commentary which, amid unescapable criticisms, brings about reflection in the readers. Such commentary should also bring about a reflection in my respondents, without which such commentaries would not exist (on the range of issues arising from this proximity, see Tenold 2018). Still, the difference between 'an authentic commentary' and the ideological rendition is often confusing, probably due to the inescapably ideological nature of any interpretation.

The sense of failure and incompleteness associated with ethnographic research is also derived from informality and the inability to decide on a strategy for approaching and interacting with the interlocutors. Some of my far-right informants appreciated the more 'professional' approach, with a lengthy introduction on informed consent, ethics, and storing data; others, instead, looked for a more unstructured, relaxed discussion, relieved of procedural Q&A patterns. I insisted on integrating the former: telling my respondents about the purpose of the research, the rules for recording, and the willingness to remain available and visible to them after our meeting. Nonetheless, the richest ethnographic accounts proved to be with those respondents who preferred my informal approach.

Yet the informality of ethnographic research (see Laurier et al. 2001) may easily become a double-edged sword, possibly leading to a lack of interest from the informants (Teitelbaum 2017: 13). As a relatively young researcher in his mid-twenties, growing up in the settings somewhat similar to those of my respondents, I may have avoided this trap (for more suggestions, see Damhuis and de Jonge 2022). One of the particularly daunting situations I had to anticipate in each of my 'new' encounters was the inescapable 'Soros moment'. Even though I ensured that my respondents were familiar with my institutional affiliation before I obtained informed consent, I deliberately chose to 'postpone' revealing, until later in the interview, the fact that George Soros, the meta-enemy of the far right (particularly in Hungary), is the founder and honourable chairman of Central European University, where I was studying.[1] The strategy behind such a decision was to establish a rapport, which was, in all of the cases, unaffected by the 'finding' of my informants. Informality allowed me to establish contacts with my respondents, learn about their lives (but also share my own life stories), and continue my research journey without ever being physically endangered.[2] The threat of physical violence was significantly diminished by my positionality: a white, heterosexual sportsman, which mitigated the position of being a 'foreigner' and 'outsider' to my respondents. Using deflective techniques in discussions in order to re-centre the debate on their own and not my opinion proved to be another helpful practice in narrowing the immense gap in values. Discussions and disagreements should always be an option but they should also be planned – avoiding such moments early on in the conversation can mitigate potential consequences.

The informality of far-right ethnography has its own limits and failures. Purged of the possibility of entailing the 'co-creation' and collaboration, reinscribed in the creed of the method, or at least its anthropological appro-priations (see Kemper and Royce 2002), the ethnography of the far right is bound to end bereft of its imagined completeness. One of the moments that amplified this feeling was my intentional sidestepping of respondents in spreading the word about the drafts I produced or works I published. Growing closer with some of them, I find it increasingly difficult to navigate between the repulsive comments of my interlocutors and the (even if justi-fied) criticisms of far right scholars who have never encountered an actual nationalist. This overcasting discourse of moralisation evident in far right research, while arguably necessary to distinguish those who subscribe to far-right ideas from those genuinely interested in countering the far right, situates the researcher in an uneasy position of being associated with the worldviews of their respondents. Yet, it is also easy to fall into the trap of both-siderism, being overtly sympathetic towards hate as a sentiment. Being well aware of my values (e.g., refusing to appear in any photos that promote far-right slogans or merchandise) proved to be helpful in drawing the much-needed boundaries of an imagined epistemic and decontextualised dualism I pushed for.

Ethnography is ultimately about care (Schatz 2009: 12) – yet, one can only care as much. Caring towards the victims of far-right ideas and actions cannot be compared to the care towards the far right as the 'objects of study'. The latter obviously does not go very far, ending with the interpre-tivist 'care to understand' and paired with the care to counter. I believed I came into the field without an obligatory activist impetus but also with an obligation towards victims of far-right violence. Either way, I ended up hav-ing long (and tiresome) conversations in an admittedly futile attempt to per-suade my respondents to abandon some of their argumentative positions. Maintaining the delicate ethics of care, stuck between the poles of complic-ity and evangelism, brought forth the fundamentally extractive nature of ideological (and incomplete) ethnography. For the researcher to sufficiently grasp this range and avoid extractivism, even if aimed at those they aim to defeat, any form of 'moral relativism' (Montesinos Coleman 2015) is sim-ply not attainable. Addressing these caveats is far from a straightforward and unidirectional process, especially in an attempt to come to terms with a looming ecological disaster – the one which my respondents also tried to make sense of. Enlisting the possibility of this ecological disaster to the well-established fear of cultural decay professed by the far right creates a sense of incompleteness not only for the researcher but for the objects of study as well. Being aware of the startling contradictions between the exclusionary politics they were advocating for and the holistic and essentially inclusive environmental agenda, my respondents often espoused logical contradic-tions in an attempt to produce a sensible ideological account.

Finally, the incomplete ethnography is not necessarily used in the descrip-tion of far right research, but also of other, pragmatic flaws in the research design and the execution of the method. As Neumann and Neumann (2015: 804) indicate, the emphasis on "pragmatism", constituent of ethnography, is "fair enough as far as it goes, but that is not very far". In spite of being familiar with the languages, the majority of the interviews I conducted in the six countries where I did my research were in English. This unwillingness to speak the language I did not fully master, even if this was the language of my interlocutors, has significant limitations. Yet, this limitation made me value the need to work closely with my informants, to the extent to which that was possible, in order to ensure the correct meaning. The somewhat different, and consequently more difficult, approach to obtaining informed consent forms was a consequence of my outlook on transcription as a necessary interpretation. Instead of having my respondents sign the consent form during or immediately after the interview, I contacted them after the transcription was prepared: in some cases, this was even one or two years after our interview. However, this also entailed difficulties in obtaining consent forms, so I had to sometimes rely on the audio consent and respondent's recognition of participation in a scientific study.

Apart from obtaining verbal or recorded consent after providing the basic information about my research and the ethics of storing the data acquired through the research process, I deliberately wanted to ensure that my respondents would have another opportunity to amend the transcripts of our conversation but also to obtain help in contacting other far-right interlocutors. Fulfilling this requirement entailed prolonged contact with my respondents (often via private cell phones or Facebook profiles).

As was previously noted, the basic idea behind ethnography is to capture the mundane aspect of research objects. The 'capturing' process, apart from the audio or video materials, is also based on field notes. For this research, keeping a log of everything that happens in the field is a prerequisite to successful fieldwork (Emerson et al. 1995). In far right research, keeping track of field notes can be rather dangerous. Many times during my interviews, my respondents took the freedom to snatch and flick through my topic guide. To some, this can be read as a violation of personal space: though I did not appreciate it at first, it always proved to be a sign of amiability. Eventually, maintaining a systematic log of events in the field was yet another failure in the field – in an attempt to treat myself to a leisure trip to Belarus, I had to destroy my field notes to avoid having to explain their content to the Belarus border officers, which proved to be a very wise choice.

It may sound like an academic cliché, but acknowledging and embracing failure is an inevitable product of reflexivity, "both on the subject written and the subject writing" (Minh-Ha 1989: 76). In something as amorphic as ethnographies can be, identifying ineluctable ideas characteristic of political ideologies may seem essentialistic, foundational, and ultimately, contradictory. It was exactly the ethnography I conducted, with all its incompleteness, that helped identify the morphology of far-right ecologism. The limitations and failures of the research have arguably elongated the identification of the ideological features. Still, it also allowed me to understand that ideologies are not only doctrinaire or dogmatic, even in the far-right cases, but pliant and vibrant with respect to their contextual appropriations. This I could not have found without the moments of abruptness and incompleteness, the moments which have long bothered me as a scholar and as a human being. Yet it is thanks to such moments that this account on ideological morphology, constructed both from a theoretical inquiry, but also from the very lived accounts of the people I have encountered over the last five years, has been made possible.

Notes

1 As I always ensured my respondents know who they are talking to, the Soros-moment was sometimes met with surprise or even laughter by my respondents but never with a visible negative reaction.
2 The only situation in which I found myself expecting a violent confrontation was in Poznań. As my two informants were showing me around this city, one of them silently pulled a pepper-spray out of his pocket without saying a word. It was only a couple of (tense) seconds later that I learned that we just passed the local ANTIFA pub, where my informants had numerous altercations with the pub's guests.

References

Blee, K. 2002. *Inside Organized Racism: Women and Men in the Hate Movement.* Berkeley, CA: University of California Press.

Blee, K. 2007. 'Ethnographies of the Far Right', *Journal of Contemporary Ethnography*, 36(2), 119–128.

Damhuis, K., and de Jonge, L. 2022. 'Going Nativist: How to Interview the Radical Right?', *International Journal of Qualitative Methods*, 21, 1–11.

de Guevara, B. and X. Kurowska. 2019. 'Building on Ruins or Patching Up the Possible? Reinscribing Fieldwork Failure in IR as a Productive Rupture'. In: Kušić, K. and Záhora, J. (eds). *Fieldwork as Failure: Living and Knowing in the Field of International Relations.* Bristol: E-International Relations.

Eggeling, K. A. 2021. 'At Work with Practice Theory, "Failed" Fieldwork, or How to See International Politics in an Empty Chair', *Millennium*, 50(1), 149–173.

Emerson, R. M., Fretz, R. I., and Shaw, L. L. 1995. 'Processing Fieldnotes: Coding and Memoing', *Writing Ethnographic Fieldnotes*, 142–168.

Freeden, M. 2022. *Ideology Studies: New Advances and Interpretations.* London: Routledge.

Faust, L. and Pfeifer, S. 2021. 'Dark Ethnography? Encountering the 'Uncomfortable' Other in Anthropological Research: Introduction to this Special Section', *Zeitschrift für Ethnologie*, 146, 81–90.

Gingrich, A. and Banks, M. (eds). 2006. *Neo-Nationalism in Europe and Beyond: Perspectives from Social Anthropology*. New York and London: Berghahn Books.

Hammersley, M. 2006. Ethnography: Problems and Prospects. *Ethnography and Education*, 1(1), 3–14.

Hammersley, M. 2017. 'What Is Ethnography? Can It Survive? Should It?', *Ethnography and Education*, 13(1), 1–17.

Kemper, R. V. and Royce, A. P. (eds). 2002. *Chronicling Cultures: Long-Term Field Research in Anthropology*. Lanham, MD: Rowman Altamira.

Kušić, K. and Záhora, J. 2020. *Fieldwork as Failure: Living and Knowing in the Field of International Relations*. Bristol: E-International Relations.

Laurier, E., Whyte, A., and Buckner, K. 2001. 'An Ethnography of a Neighbourhood Café: Informality, Table Arrangements and Background Noise', *Journal of Mundane Behaviour*, 2(2), 195–232.

Lubarda, B. 2023. *Far-Right Ecologism: Environmental Politics and the Far Right in Hungary and Poland*. Abingdon: Routledge.

Minh-Ha, T. 1989. *Woman, Native, Other: Writing Postcoloniality and Feminism*. Bloomington, IN: Indiana University Press.

Mitchell, J. 2007. 'Ethnography'. In: Outhwaite, W. and Turner, S. (eds). *The Sage Handbook of Social Science Methodology*. Los Angeles, CA: Sage.

Montesinos Coleman, L. 2015. 'Struggles, over Rights: Humanism, Ethical Dispossession and Resistance', *Third World Quarterly*, 36(6), 1060–1075.

Neumann, C. B. and Neumann, I. B. 2015. 'Uses of the Self: Two Ways of Thinking about Scholarly Situatedness and Method', *Millennium*, 43(3), 798–819.

Okely, J. 2007. 'Fieldwork Embodied', *The Sociological Review*, 55(1), 65–79.

Ortner, S. 2016. 'Dark Anthropology and Its Others: Theory since the Eighties', *HAU: Journal of Ethnographic Theory*, 6(1), 47–73.

Poets, D. 2020. 'Failing in the Reflexive and Collaborative Turns: Empire, Colonialism, Gender and the Impossibilities of North-South Collaborations'. In: Kušić, K. and Záhora, J. (eds). *Fieldwork as Failure: Living and Knowing in the Field of International Relations*. Bristol: E-International Relations.

Ramalingam, V. 2020. 'Overcoming Racialisation in the Field: Practising Ethnography on the Far Right as a Researcher of Colour'. In: Ashe, S., Busher, J., Macklin, G., and Winter, A. (eds). *Researching the Far Right: Theory, Methods, and Practice*. London: Routledge, 254–270.

Saglam, E. 2021. 'Darkness Unbound: Insights from Ethnographic Research with Nationalist Groups in Contemporary Turkey', *Journal of Social & Cultural Anthropology/Zeitschrift fuer Ethnologie*, 146, 129–150.

Schatz, E. 2009. 'Introduction'. In: Schatz, E. (ed.). *Political Ethnography: What Immersion Contributes to the Study of Power*. Chicago, IL: University of Chicago Press.

Teitelbaum, B. 2017. *Lions of the North: Sounds of the New Nordic Radical Nationalism*. Oxford: Oxford University Press.

Tenold, V. 2018. *Everything You Love Will Burn: Inside the Rebirth of Far-Right Nationalism in America*. New York City: Nation Books.

Thorleifsson, C. 2018. *Nationalist Responses to the Crisis in Europe: Old and New Hatreds*. London: Routledge.

Whittier, N. 2002. 'Meaning and Structure in Social Movements'. In: Meyer, D., Whittier, N., and Robnett, B. (eds). *Social Movements: Identity, Culture, and the State*. New York: Oxford University Press, 289–308.

Yanow, D. 2009. 'Dear Author, Dear Reader: The Third Hermeneutic in Writing and Reviewing Ethnography'. In: Schatz, E. (ed.). *Political Ethnography: What Immersion Contributes to the Study of Power*. Chicago, IL and London: University of Chicago Press.

9

Ethnographic empathy and research ethics as methodological whiteness

Catherine Tebaldi and Rae Jereza

The ethnographer of the far right is portrayed in many variations of the straight white male: Indiana Jones saving cultural treasures from the Nazis, Louis Theroux's middle-class English befuddlement at the skinheads and Baked Alaska. The ethnographer is a middle-class, cis white man unthreatened by the subjects he studies, the liberal columnist who reframes racism as populism, the manarchist[1] who uses his masculinity to fit in with the white nationalists. His embrace of this heroism, while seemingly against the right, ultimately grants him the same kind of militant white masculinity the far-right desires. His counterpart is the 'uneducated', left-behind, unreconstructed right whom he encounters in ways not unlike how the early colonial anthropologists might have an 'isolated tribe'.

This version of the far right researcher is reproduced as default by bureaucratic university processes aimed ostensibly at evaluating research ethics. In the US the context from which we write, such processes are overseen by university Institutional Review Boards (IRB):[2] committees tasked to assess research studies involving human participants. Many have criticised the IRB's narrow treatment of ethics in qualitative studies, calling into question their efficacy in ensuring the protection of research participants, especially from marginalised groups (see Blee and Currier 2011). Additionally, we assert that the IRB neglect: (1) the safety and welfare of marginalised researchers who study far-right communities; and (2) how researchers belonging to socially privileged groups might inadvertently reproduce cis, white, straight, male dominance in their interactions with far-right adherents and through their analyses of such interactions. The IRB's indifference towards marginalised researchers' experiences among far-right adherents and its failure to hold accountable cis, white, straight, male researchers of the far right contribute to the whiteness and maleness of far right studies.

Ethnographers reflect this indifference in their work, effectively excluding marginalised researchers who arguably have the greatest stake in dismantling far-right politics within the academy. Their analyses often frame far-right adherents as economically dispossessed (Brownlow and Wood 2017) and recast racism as populism, which, as Brown and Mondon (2021) point out, can legitimise and mainstream far-right politics through awarding 'populist' politics with "democratic value as *the* alternative to the status quo" (2, emphasis in original). Moreover, framing far-right adherents as unequivocally 'left behind' creates room for researchers to make claims about how ethnographers ought to treat far-right interlocutors with empathy regardless of social positionality.

We are not arguing that economic processes are not central to the grammar of far-right discourses or the self-understanding of far-right adherents. Rather, we assert – and we are not the first to do so (Bhambra 2017; Mondon and Winter 2020) – that ethnographers tend to neglect how white supremacy informs far-right adherents' understandings of their experiences. We assert that ethnographic calls to empathy and narratives 'through the eyes of the other' elide this fact by constructing a sharp difference between the ethnographer and his other. By eliding this reality, ethnographers of the far right inadvertently justify far-right politics in ways that ignore the violent effects and implications of the latter's practices and discourses on cis women, LGBTQ+ communities, and Black, Brown, Indigenous, Latinx, and Asian and Pacific Islander people. Furthermore, we argue that in doing so, researchers reproduce the colonial ethnographer – white, impartial, and emotionally neutral – as default.

In this chapter, we, two anthropologists from very different backgrounds, explore the institutional reproduction of the colonial ethnographer as default and assert the importance of utilising anti-colonial, feminist approaches to counter this tendency. Cat is an unwilling insider to the right-wing women she studies, raised a white woman within the world of 'traditional gender roles' and now a proud participant in 'Cultural Marxist' conspiracies to undo them. With critical feminist methods, which emphasise reflexivity, affect, and vivid writing, moments of disconnection or complicity, Cat aims to question or subvert the genre (Briggs and Bauman 1992) of ethnographic writing to help understand gender and the mainstreaming of the right. Rae is a queer, non-binary Filipino person, who migrated from the Philippines to the US when they were 12 years old. They feel like an outsider within the anthropology of the right not only because the field is dominated by white Euro-Americans, but also because they investigate 'extreme' politics in the 'mainstream' spaces of tech.

In the first section, we illustrate how ethnographers reproduce methodological whiteness in their written work. We then look ethnographically at our own experiences and attempt to challenge this. Rae draws on personal experience to illustrate how methodological whiteness can extend to interactions between colleagues. Next, Cat uses an excerpt from her field notes to discuss methodological whiteness in ethnographic writing. We conclude by discussing suggestions for anti-colonial and feminist methodologies that are politically engaged, challenge mainstream racism, and work towards dismantling barriers in far right studies that limit the contributions of marginalised scholars.

Methodological whiteness among ethnographers of the right

Ethnographers have made important contributions to our understanding of far-right politics, revealing the role of affect (Cramer 2016; Hochschild 2018) and analysing the figured worlds of the far right (Westermeyer 2019). Yet ethnographic narratives tend to elide the role of race and racism in the development of far-right ideologies and, at times, frame far-right adherents as victims of economic dispossession with whom we must build more meaningful connections. Many ethnographers ask us to 'scale the empathy wall' (Hochschild 2018); focus on how far-right adherents are 'othered' (Pasieka 2017, 2019); and pursue friendship – and thus an 'immoral anthropology' – with white supremacists (Teitelbaum 2019). While many have pointed out the dangers of attributing far-right politics to class dispossession (Bhambra 2017; Brownlow and Wood 2017), we add that the narrative of dispossessed actors, with whom we must empathise, assumes and reinforces the white, cis, male ethnographer as default who is neither targeted by nor implicated in far-right politics (Holmes 2000; Hochschild 2018; Pasieka 2017, 2019; Teitlebaum 2019).

Peter Hervik (2021) defines empathy in the context of researching far-right communities as "a positively laden emotion and strategy to pursue because it holds recognition, mutuality, reciprocity, and attempts to bring a non-hierarchical form of genuine dialogue" (99). He differentiates empathy from 'sympathy' which he describes as "the caring and feeling of pity or sorrow for those who suffer. Sympathy does not include sharing distress and therefore easily leads to victimisation" (99). Likewise, Pasieka (2017) writes that empathy "indicates a need to grant or restore agency to far-right propagators/supporters ... taking into account that their views ... are their ways of engaging with and changing the world" (S28). Hochschild (2018) argues that doing so requires us to scale the empathy wall, which is "an obstacle to deep understanding of another person, one that can make us feel indifferent or even hostile to those who hold different beliefs or whose childhood is rooted in different circumstances". Finally, Teitlebaum (2019) calls for "scholar-informant solidarity", which foregrounds "collaboration, reciprocity", and "solidarity" with informants against what he describes as the moralising turn in anthropology reflected in the American Anthropological Association's (AAA) 2012 ethics statement (415).

Empathy can function as a form of methodological whiteness when it aims, solely, at understanding and presenting the world as it might look to far-right adherents without troubling such perspectives. In his ethnography of far-right Berlin youth, for instance, Shoshan (2016) describes, in minute detail, how racist youth regard Muslim women walking in Berlin streets as 'foreign bodies':

> Douglas Holmes has noted how the constant encounter with "foreign bodies" triggers a sense of collective humiliation for far-right residents of multiracial underclass neighbourhoods in London (Holmes 2000) ... here, too, tangible, quotidian encounters with embodied otherness redefine the urban landscape: Muslim women strolling in the park and past the benches on which my informants congregate, bus and tram stops where the shifting gazes of commuters betray a sense of discomfort at the presence of people of Middle Eastern appearance, or a range of ethnically marked and immigrant-owned businesses – restaurants, Internet cafés, kiosks, flower shops, grocery stores – that dot central avenues with a variety of ethnic indexes (Greek, Indian, Vietnamese, Turkish). (61)

Because Shoshan does not follow up this description with a criticism of white Berlin youth's objectification of Muslim people, he ends up reproducing their racist perspective.

While both Shoshan (2016) and Teitlebaum (2019) – the latter more so than the former – reflect on how ethnographic empathy has yielded them to align, in troubling ways, with their white nationalist interlocutors, they present little critical reflection. In the case of Shoshan, a Jewish person, he describes anxiety-inducing moments where his Jewish identity was nearly revealed to right-wing extremist interlocutors, which could have threatened his safety. He also grapples with the tension between representing his interlocutors "as multidimensional, beyond their repugnant racism" on the one hand and "not representing them negatively *enough*" (Shoshan 2016: XIII, emphasis in original). Yet, he concludes that this tension ultimately cannot be resolved and characterises it as one that "exceeds the negotiation of analytical detachment and personal familiarity so common to many ethnographic studies" (Shoshan 2016: XIII). While these conclusions might be true, they do not excuse the lack of engagement with anti-racist perspectives to frame his participants' perspectives.

Teitlebaum (2019), in contrast, embraces the 'immorality' that attends ethnographic empathy with far-right interlocutors despite his Jewish identity. He argues that the AAA's attempts to "eliminate" scholar-informant solidarity are "a strategy of reversing long-standing efforts to collapse physical, social, and power differentials in anthropological research, a strategy to secure distance and assert control" (422). This statement draws problematic equivalencies between power differentials that shape encounters between Western ethnographers and Global South communities on the one hand and encounters between Western ethnographers and white supremacists on the other. Here, he reproduces methodological whiteness by assuming that power dynamics between those doing the studying and those 'studied' are straightforward. This excludes the possibility – indeed the reality – that some researchers inhabit positionalities marginalised relative to white cis straight maleness.

Such assumptions affect not only the quality of academic research on the far right but also interactions between researchers. Specifically, scholars who ignore how white supremacy shapes interactions between researchers and their interlocutors can end up dismissing the experiences of researchers of colour. Consider my (Rae's) encounter with a colleague recounted below.

> In the summer of 2020, as thousands in the U.S. protested racist, anti-Black policing, I was conducting ethnographic fieldwork with Facebook moderators in the U.S. and Ireland, some of whom were encountering posts related to anti-racist uprisings. This context, coupled with my own participation in anti-racist protests, shaped my conversations with moderators. While they acknowledged anti-Black racism to some degree, they simultaneously voiced white supremacist rhetoric. For instance, over Zoom drinks one afternoon, Abigail, a white woman in her 30's, told me that while anti-racist posts made sense in light of the fact that "white people have been horrible to Black people", some posts "went too far" by posting "anti-white" content. Such rhetoric is based on an understanding of race as mere difference and of racism abstracted from the reality of enduring power relations that maintain white supremacy. It is part of the same logic that enables narratives of so-called "white genocide", which contemporary white nationalists use to justify their goal of an exclusionary, genocidal "white ethnostate". (Stern 2020)

> After speaking to interlocutors who took up Abigail's stance, I sought advice from a senior colleague: a white cis male scholar with years of experience working with far-right interlocutors. Specifically, I solicited input on how to manage my relationships with interlocutors as a Filipino ethnographer, whose people continue to be oppressed by white, Euro-American imperialism on a global scale. In response, this colleague told me to put my politics aside and transitioned, abruptly, into a criticism of white privilege as a concept. Voicing authors like Arlie Hochschild (2018) and J. D. Vance, who argue that "white working class" racism is a byproduct of economic disenfranchisement and call for empathising with such groups (see Brownlow and Wood 2017), he brushed off my concerns and launched into a rant about how we could not possibly regard white, rural working-class people as privileged.

I highlight this interaction to demonstrate how ethnographers of the right practice methodological whiteness not only in their writings but also in interactions with racially minoritised colleagues. Here, my colleague refuses to engage the concerns of ethnographers belonging to marginalised communities, for whom interactions with far-right actors are shaped less by political/moral dislike and instead by a concern for *survival* in a cissexist, heteropatriarchal, white supremacist world. Furthermore, his advice to put aside my political beliefs suggests a gap in understanding the experiences of people belonging to racially marginalised groups at best and at worst, implies an alignment with whiteness as a socio-political project. In this way, my colleague reasserted whiteness and cis maleness as the default perspective from which anthropologists ought to understand far-right adherents and their politics.

For scholars belonging to marginalised communities, interacting with far-right adherents can be fraught, because their beliefs are underpinned by the same white supremacist, imperialist logics that continue to fuel the oppression of Black, Brown, and Indigenous peoples all over the world. If there is 'hostility' towards the right, as Hochschild (2018) put it, it may stem from the realities of ongoing violence, not only by far-right terrorists but also by state actors in the West whose policies are guided by the notion of white, cis, straight, abled, Christian, male as default. Ethnographers of the far right reproduce this default script, embodied in the figure of the white male ethnographer, when they dismiss anthropologists' reluctance to practise 'scholar-informant solidarity' with far-right adherents as moralising in ways that contradict the goals of anthropology (Teitlebaum 2019).

This is not to say that existing ethnographies of the far right have no critical import, nor do I mean to suggest that the goal of understanding far-right people's realities through ethnography is not worthwhile. Rather, I urge ethnographers to move beyond neutrality, empathy, and solidarity as frameworks for studying the lives of far-right adherents by considering ethnographers' positionalities. We might do so by taking seriously the reality that proximity to far-right groups, parties, and communities, as well as their respective agendas, can not only lead to troubling complicities but also constitute terrifying closeness to politics that threaten marginalised peoples' existence.

Who does the university serve?

The question of who the appropriate subject of empathy is and how they must be constructed as such is revealed not only in ethnographic texts but in the official scripts which regulate research practices. In US universities, the Institutional Review Board (IRB) governs research with human subjects to, ostensibly, protect the welfare of research subjects. The board comprises five people, including at least one scientist and one representative from outside the university. Any researcher hoping to conduct research with human beings, from biologists to social anthropologists, must have their projects approved by the IRB before they can do research. Approval requires a brief (some might argue perfunctory) training on research ethics and history, and the submission of an application report to the IRB detailing research aims, methods, sites, participants, and, in the case of social scientific research, sample interview/survey questions as well as recruitment scripts and informed consent documents. The IRB then reviews the researcher's application according to its stated values of beneficence, justice, and respect for persons.[3] If the board decides that the researcher's application does not sufficiently address issues related to these values, the board asks the researcher to revise their application, often repeatedly.

This process was instituted in 1974 as a response to myriad violent and profoundly unethical twentieth-century biomedical studies where scientists experimented on marginalised peoples. Examples include the US Public Health Service's 1932 Tuskegee experiments, during which scientists refused to treat Black men with syphilis to learn about the disease's progression,[4] and Nazi medical experiments on Jewish and Roma peoples during World War II. Thus, the IRB exists, ostensibly, to protect vulnerable groups, such as children, the mentally ill, or pregnant women, and to protect all participants from physical, economic, psychological, or social harm during research.

However, the IRB reproduces methodological whiteness through a 'hidden curriculum' (Giroux and Pena 1979) that perpetuates 'race-blind' approaches to research ethics. IRB protocols assume a cis, white, male researcher when they neglect to consider how, in some circumstances, researchers can also be harmed by subjects, effectively limiting access to researchers at the sharp end of right-wing politics or who have a different – that is, critical – vision of ethnography or ethnographic writing. Moreover, the IRB lacks mechanisms for holding researchers of the far right accountable for potentially reproducing the racist, antisemitic, misogynistic, and anti-LGBTQ politics they seek to understand. If the IRB were truly designed to promote research ethics, its protocols would reflect how power dynamics operate in messy, sometimes contradictory, ways.

Cat endured multiple iterations of internal review for both her research methods and first publications, spending more than eight months waiting for approval to conduct interviews with far-right adherents and more than four rounds of revisions from the editorial and then the legal team at Taylor and Francis. This stood in stark contrast to her pilot research on low-income students in France, which was approved within three weeks. This process exposed her to significant social and economic harm in terms of wasted research funding and extended time to her degree, adding stress and uncertainty to an already difficult subject. Yet, at no point did the IRB provide mechanisms to mitigate such harm or inquire about potential threats to her personal safety as a researcher of the far right. Given that a project on middle-class white women was subject to much more scrutiny than one on a more marginalised population, Cat felt that not only did the university not care about her welfare, or about those targeted by the far right, but it was using the idea of protecting participants to protect the university. It seemed the university knew what many researchers refused to acknowledge – far-right women could be powerful, and they are not afraid to use their power in media and legal institutions.

During the publication of her first two research articles, Cat went through more revisions with the legal team than the editorial board. Despite receiving IRB approval, which would permit publication, legal boards censored much of the data and her argument. The journal's legal office targeted not only her use of publicly available social media data but also her affective, reflexive writing, claiming that they were less 'objective' and thus more objectionable. Her personal experiences with right-wing politics amongst family members and feelings of anger, fear, love, and confusion were seen as libel, not data. By discounting reflective writing as less objective, the journal asserted their preference for what they termed more 'objective' research with an impartial tone, one that they could read as neutral – an outsider approach to ethnography, what we call methodological whiteness in ethnographies of the right.

Methodological whiteness privileges affluent, white, liberal, outsider approaches to ethnographies of the far right, limiting our capacity to produce critical, anti-racist scholarship that foregrounds marginalised groups who are most directly impacted by far-right political activities. As Cat's experiences demonstrate, the colonial ethnographer shapes our vision of what counts as 'legitimate' epistemology: one void of critical reflection or personal connection and one that favours 'objectivity' and political 'neutrality'.

Empathy as methodological whiteness in ethnographic narratives

I (that is, Cat) am not an outsider ethnographer, probably not 'objective' and certainly not 'neutral', unless you think that the far right being bad is an objective fact. Femininity and the far right are as close to home for me as my mother – a far-right QAnon supporter who would beg me, hands clasped together in prayer, not to marry a Jew – one of the 'people of the eye'. The rest of the family, while more liberal, shared her gender politics: gender roles were natural, traditional, and desirable. This shapes my engagements with critical feminist approaches to the study of the far right and its interaction with the mainstream. Following Hemment (2007), I understand critical feminist approaches as emphasising affect, reflexivity, and a critique of power. Reed-Danahay (2009) explores how reflexivity illuminates the power relations one is enmeshed in, while Abu Lughod (2008) shows this critique can become entwined with new forms of academic writing questioning an opposition between affect and analysis. I share an early attempt below:

I'm on the way to an old sugar plantation outside New Orleans, curious how the city remembers its past – and who wants to enjoy it. The tour bus is filled with squishy couples and too much air conditioning. I'm the only one without a partner. We pass a sign for Oak Alley plantation valentine's day's brunch [and] several women snuggle up to benevolently bored men. (You know, the guys who elaborately perform soft patriarchy while waiting for their woman to buy shoes, they are very much MEN and don't like silly women things but look how good they are for waiting) are they turned on by this tour? Will they go to this Valentine's brunch and drink bottomless mimosas with the ghosts of suffering? Get me some pearls to clutch. Alone and chilly, imagining them at plantation weddings I realize all those chubby cupcake say-yes-to-the dresses are southern belle gowns. I'm warm with embarrassment. Pass me one of those racist old lady fans; my style's better but I like fairy tale romance – and brunch.

We get to the plantation and the sorority mommas and their sentient pair of chinos wander through the terrible luxury of it, the lines of live oak trees shading some and lynching others. They stand there in the dining room, pointing to a set of silver or a well-constructed cupboard admiringly as though it was HGTV. The tour guide explains the house's construction to keep both the home and the chat breezy, built by expert Senegalese carpenters no mention they were brought over in chains. Once the fancy house tour is over there is a brief mention of slavery and the individual cruelty of one of the owners, before a return to a bar where you can get a mint julep. Here affect and domesticity intertwine with terror, gendered visions of the happy home or the weekend romance making cruelty normal, desirable, for the tourists, one of our everyday engagements with white supremacy.

I finished my research during covid and the Black Lives Matter protests and wage theft protests in New Orleans, where service industry workers asked for fewer statues of slave owners and more of the city's tourism taxes be returned to the workers. As we marched past the empty Lee circle, with its toppled statue of the confederate general, two counter protesters waved the American flag at us – so close to getting it! White supremacy isn't just plantations when you're living in a city where white people profit off of black people, black culture and labour, you might not go to Valentine's brunch but who makes your hangover eggs? Suburbs named after old plantations, built on them, your house itself a little symbolic plantation with decorative columns and lawn jockeys, segregation and wealth gaps.

This piece began with my field notes, a way of writing what I saw that was critically entangled with what I felt, what I thought about it. No more smooth line separating the feeling, the judgment, from an 'objective' observation or the emotional 'objectivity' of empathy. I turned my field notes, my feelings, the next evenings, into these monologues, co-opting the genres of the right – the long-winded conspiracy monologue, the sermon, the love story, the fairy tale. This story became part of a presentation on genre and critical beauty for the sociolinguistics symposium, linked to Gershon and Prentice (2021), and Taylor Neu's work on genre parasitism (2020) – taking up the language, the concerns, the genres of the right and twisting them around to write against it.

Critical feminist ethnography, with its emphasis on reflexivity and affect, is a crucial way to understand the mainstreaming of the right (or the extremism of the mainstream). Femininity is an excellent instance of this enmeshment, as it is a way of normalising and depoliticising the right. Affect helped me engage with the mainstream, using my own reaction, feelings, and experiences not as a wall to jump over, but as a space to explore. Where does this far-right femininity shock, disgust me? Where are there moments of uncomfortable complicity or lessons to unlearn? I learned, through my own entanglements, the ways in which white supremacy was framed as a romance, or misogyny a domestic idyll. This complicity with modes of being feminine was not a kind of solidarity with the plantation tour meets home and garden television show crowd, but a moment of productive discomfort. It led me to further investigate how love and beauty were used to normalise racism, to make racism appealing by coding it in idealised gender roles (Mattheis 2021), and how this ideal romance was used to sell white nationalism historically and in the present as *Metapolitical Seduction* (under review). It appeals to our fear of being alone, our need for love, all while making racism seem as normal as a dinner plate. And, in a certain sense, it is.

Reflexivity is especially important for studying mainstreaming, the connection between ourselves and our research participants often reflecting the links between extreme and mainstream. As multiple movements from the radicalisation of the Republican party to the growing conspirituality[5] movement show, the space in between the far right and the so-called mainstream demands more study – even, perhaps, questioning the idea of the mainstream itself and engaging more with other forms of criticism of everyday white racism. We must look beyond a one-line positionality statement to our own real engagement with the right: you may not have a conspiracy-believing racist parent, but you probably know a Republican.

The imagined ethnographer is both white and knows no racist people, a strange combination given the long enmeshment between far right and centre (Mondon and Winter 2020). We need, then, more engagement with intersectional feminisms and their call to denaturalise this vision of upper-class whiteness as femininity common to both the far right and certain sections of feminism (especially the 'gender critical' kind). We need more than empathy – we need anger, love, and self-criticism, to tell new stories which move beyond methodological whiteness and white romance.

Towards anti-colonial and feminist approaches to ethnographies of the right

We reviewed ethnographies of the far right to show how empathy reproduces a colonial script, a narrative of the ethnographer and the dispossessed other. The research experiences described above, coupled with these examples, illustrate how ethnographic empathy can reproduce racist and heteropatriarchal scripts which guide research, writing, and interactions with colleagues. Moreover, by neglecting to account for the potential harms far-right research participants might inflict upon researchers, especially those belonging to marginalised communities, university ethics processes assume – and reproduce – the white cis male ethnographer as default. Such processes, we argue, ignore or excuse racism in the mainstream.

Ethnographic empathy is an argument in three steps:

1. We (researchers) are not the far right.
2. We must empathise with far-right interlocutors.
3. Empathy is the essence and contribution of ethnography.

The first point refers to the assumption that far-right adherents cannot be found in our communities, nor are our community members harmed by their politics. Relatedly, the ignorant far right constitutes the opposite of the impartial, knowledgeable, and objective academic community, even though many US universities were founded for the slave trade (Wilder 2013) and enable the work of scholars who practice racial science (Lykes and van der Merwe 2019).

Second, far-right interlocutors are worthy of our *uncritical* understanding and emotional work. We must see through the eyes of the racist teens and access the 'deep story' (Hochschild 2018) of the David Duke supporter. These stories are framed in ways that conflate ethnography with the practice of revealing participants' inner truths. This practice of empathy covers patronising distance in a fine veneer of criticality while it exceptionalises and euphemises the dangers they pose. Such empathy reinforces ideas of the far right as 'left behind' and academia, in contrast, as an enlightened vanguard. Empathy often means privileging narratives of economic or social dispossession, encouraging us to accept far-right perceptions of disenfranchisement and divorce their stories of loss and mourning from longstanding fears of white 'replacement'. In other words, we are asked to accept narratives of white victimhood. Far-right politics becomes about a loss of meaning and identity rather than the defence of power and hierarchy. Perhaps paradoxically, when we pretend to be objective, empathic observers, we participate in the mainstreaming of the far right. On the other hand, affect from disgust to complicity, increases our critical awareness of the process of mainstreaming.

Despite the importance of affect, empathy is framed as the essence and core contribution of ethnography: a type of emotional neutrality that produces its own kind of objectivity in smooth narrative form. The notion that empathy is ethnography's most valuable contribution positions it as excavating pre-existing 'deep stories' yet ignores the ways in which this creates its own fable of the heroic colonial academic redeeming the culturally and economically left behind. This vision of the dispossessed further elides how white supremacist narratives construct desirable forms of personhood: beautiful women and heroic men battling the decline of civilisation – stories which sit uncomfortably close not only to the mainstream fairy tale but to the ethnographic narrative as well. Recording these with empathy as emotional neutrality then disconnects our feelings and ourselves from our analysis, a disconnection that mirrors' the colonial ethnographic narrative's sharp division between academic and other in a division between extreme and mainstream.

We call for new ways of writing not for their own sake, but for the development of an anti-colonial and feminist anthropology of the right – and of the mainstream. Anthropologists have noted the ways in which ethnography is *rooted* in "unequal power [encounters] between the West and the Third World" (Asad 1973: 16). Baker (1998) writes that anthropology – and ethnographic methods – gained scientific and professional legitimacy through anthropologists' justification of racist ideologies. Encounters between ethnographers and far-right interlocutors are rarely situations where the researcher is 'studying' the experiences of minoritised participants. Yet, ethnographers of the far right reproduce racialised and gendered colonial inequalities when they advocate for empathy, friendship, or even solidarity with their interlocutors. We urge instead empathy for those affected by these inequalities, even when studying those who cause them. Calls for empathy discursively create difference and repeat colonial power hierarchies, not themselves that distinct from the values the far right holds. We urge ethnographers to take up an anti-colonial approach, which we understand here as practices that *actively* counter tendencies to normalise white supremacist, misogynistic, and anti-LGBTQ ideas when analysing and representing far-right experiences. This requires continuous and critical reflexivity but cannot stop at internal reflection. Rather, ethnographers must take their reflections and apply them to fieldwork encounters, interactions with colleagues, and any presentation of their work. We ask researchers to situate issues of complicity and empathy within the history of colonial oppression and ongoing racism, seeing the far right in connection with the settler colonial mainstream.

To help accomplish this, we have critiqued the narrative of the colonial ethnographer and asked for ways of writing ethnography differently. This begins with institutional scripts of the IRB to better reflect the complex power relations that attend studying, interacting with, and writing about far-right adherents. We also call for writing that goes beyond ethnography as empathy, stock narratives, and distant observers, returning instead to ethnography as thick description with its close entanglement of affect and knowledge, to the passion and political commitments that emerge from affective responses to these challenges. At the same time, we call on universities to establish funding and safety networks that permit minoritised and early-career researchers to engage in emotionally difficult research.

Finally, above all, we call for a deeply political study of the far right which takes as its foundation empathy for those who are targeted by it, not those who perpetuate it. This may include institutional support for researchers, and institutional support for engaged, activist, and critical research methods which seek not only to understand the (far) right but to stop it. We cannot aim for emotional objectivity about those things which are harming us and those we love. While ethnography is about seeing the world through people's eyes, our research, and our obligations, cannot and do not stop there.

Notes

1　Manarchist is a portmanteau of man and anarchist used to refer to those who imbue anarchist politics with male supremacist forms of personhood or practices. Many thanks to Chelsea Ebin of IRMS for the term.
2　IRB is the American term for ethics review boards, which are located within universities and offer approval for studies with human subjects, originating primarily from concerns with our long history of medical experimentation on marginalised people. However, many places outside the US have ethics review boards and therefore these concerns apply to ethics issues outside the US as well.
3　See https://hrpo.wustl.edu/participants/institutional-review-board/ (accessed 10 October 2023).
4　See https://www.cdc.gov/tuskegee/faq.htm (accessed 10 October 2023).

5 Conspirituality is a portmanteau of conspiracy and spirituality, which refers to the spread of conspiracy theory in New Age and, increasingly, wellness spaces. The term was coined by Ward and Voas (2011), who have since been revealed to have links to these movements themselves. We are never outsiders.

References

Abu-Lughod, L. 2008. *Writing Against Culture*. Abingdon: Routledge.

Asad, T. 1973. *Anthropology and the Colonial Encounter*. Ithaca, NY: Ithaca Press.

Baker, L. D. 1998. *From Savage to Negro: Anthropology and the Construction of Race, 1896–1954*. Berkeley, CA: University of California Press.

Bhambra, G. K. 2017. 'Brexit, Trump, and "Methodological Whiteness": On the Misrecognition of Race and Class', *The British Journal of Sociology*, 68(S1), S214–S232.

Blee, K. and A. Currier. 2011. 'Ethics beyond the IRB: An Introductory Essay', *Qualitative Sociology*, 34(401).

Briggs, C. L. and Bauman, R. 1992. 'Genre, Intertextuality, and Social Power', *Journal of Linguistic Anthropology*, 2(2), 131–172.

Brown, K. and Mondon, A. 2021. 'Populism, the Media, and the Mainstreaming of the Far Right: The Guardian's Coverage of Populism as a Case Study', *Politics*, 41(3), 279–295.

Brownlow, R. and Wood, M. 2017. 'Not about White Workers: The Perils of Popular Ethnographic Narrative in the Time of Trump', *Lateral*, 6(2).

Cramer, K. J. 2016. *The Politics of Resentment: Rural Consciousness in Wisconsin and the Rise of Scott Walker*. Chicago, IL: University of Chicago Press.

Gershon, I. and Prentice, M. M. 2021. 'Genres in New Economies of Language', *International Journal of the Sociology of Language*, 2021(267–268), 117–124.

Giroux, H. A. and Pena, A. N. 1979. 'Social Education in the Classroom: The Dynamics of the Hidden Curriculum', *Theory & Research in Social Education*, 7(1), 21–42.

Hemment, J. 2007. 'Public Anthropology and the Paradoxes of Participation: Participatory Action Research and Critical Ethnography in Provincial Russia', *Human Organization*, 66(3), 301–314.

Hervik, P. 2021. 'Neo-Nationalism and Far-Right Studies: Anthropological Perspectives'. In: Ashe, S. D., Busher, J., Macklin, G., and Winter, A. (eds). *Researching the Far-Right*. Abingdon: Routledge, 92–108.

Hochschild, A. R. 2018. *Strangers in Their Own Land: Anger and Mourning on the American Right*. New York: The New Press.

Holmes, D. 2000. *Integral Europe: Fast Capitalism, Multiculturalism, Neofascism*. Princeton, NJ and Oxford: Princeton University Press.

Lykes, M. B. and van der Merwe, H. 2019. 'Critical Reflexivity and Transitional Justice Praxis: Solidarity, Accompaniment and Intermediarity', *International Journal of Transitional Justice*, 13(3), 411–416.

Mattheis, A. 2021. '#TradCulture: Reproducing Whiteness and Neo-Fascism through Gendered Discourse Online'. In: Hunter, S. and van der Westhuizen, C. (eds). *Routledge Handbook of Critical Whiteness Studies*. London: Routledge.

Mondon, A. and Winter A. 2020. *Reactionary Democracy: How Racism and the Populist Far Right Became Mainstream*. London: Verso.

Pasieka, A. 2017. 'Taking Far-Right Claims Seriously and Literally: Anthropology and the Study of Right-Wing Radicalism', *Slavic Review*, 76(51).

Pasieka, A. 2019. 'Anthropology of the Far-Right: What If We Like the Unlikeable Others?', *Anthropology Today*, 25(1), 3–6.

Reed-Danahay, D. 2009. 'Anthropologists, Education, and Autoethnography', *Reviews in Anthropology*, 38(1), 28–47.

Shoshan, N. 2016. *The Management of Hate*. Princeton, NJ: Princeton University Press.

Stern, A. M. 2020. *Proud Boys and the White Ethnostate: How the Alt-Right is Warping the American Imagination*. New York: Penguin Random House.

Taylor-Neu, R. H. 2020. 'Parasites and Post-Truth Climate', *Journal of Linguistic Anthropology*, 30(1), 4–26.

Teitlebaum, B. R. 2019. 'Collaborating with the Radical Right: Scholar-Informant Solidarity and the Case for an Immoral Anthropology', *Current Anthropology*, 60(3), 414–435.

Ward, C. and Voas, D. 2011. 'The Emergence of Conspirituality', *Journal of Contemporary Religion*, 26(1), 103–121.

Westermeyer, W. H. 2019. *Back to America: Identity, Political Culture, and the Tea Party Movement*. Lincoln, NE: University of Nebraska Press.

Wilder, C. S. 2013. *Ebony and Ivy: Race, Slavery, and the Troubled History of America's Universities*. New York: Bloomsbury.

10

Emotions in methodology: resisting violent ideological structures in the knowledge-production of extremisms

Elsa Bengtsson Meuller

Often when the radical voice speaks about domination we are speaking to those who dominate ... Words are not without meaning, they are an action, a resistance. (hooks 1989: 16)

Researching extremisms can be tricky: not just because recruitment tactics, ideologies, and the way extremisms look, may change and adapt through time, but also because of how the research itself affects the researcher; how the research affects societal understandings of extremisms; and how this, in turn, affects people who are associated with, or are victims of, extremist ideologies. It is, therefore, important that we consider the ethical and political implications of our research.

In this chapter, I draw on decolonial and Black feminist thought as I reflect on the risks of enhancing the messages of antifeminist and male supremacist (extremist) ideologies through my role as an academic and producer of knowledge. I argue that the use of emotions in our research methodology can help us resist the reproduction of antifeminist and male supremacist extremist ideologies. I do this as I examine how embracing emotions and care in research can be a way of taking responsibility for the people affected by our work (hooks 2001: 54). In addition, I draw on my own experiences of researching male supremacist groups and reflect on how the feelings of numbness and vulnerability can help us (re)encounter our political and ethical commitments. These reflections contribute to the growing literature on ethics and extremism, but take it further by arguing for the incorporation of emotions in the research process.

The first section of this chapter, therefore, looks at the hegemonic stance of objectivity in knowledge production. I show how objectivity is used to assert power both in the academy and among misogynist incels by devaluing the use of emotions as knowledge. The section that follows lays out how emotions can help us resist the reinforcement of male supremacist knowledge production. It does this by explaining the ways in which emotions can make us more ethically and politically conscious about the effects of our research. The next section contains a brief story of my own experiences of both resisting and embracing emotions in my research. In the last section, I draw on my experiences and reflect on how being vigilant to feelings of numbness and vulnerability is useful for researching extremisms. I conclude this chapter by emphasising how emotions as methodology can serve as a radical counterweight to male supremacist ideologies.

Objectivity in the academy and male supremacist ideologies

In many ways, I have found the hegemonic stance of the objective in the academy to be an idea and framework I need to resist. This is, firstly, because of its relationship to domination in sites of knowledge production and secondly, because of its foundational part in keeping up ideological structures of antifeminism and male supremacism. Since objectivity is used to assert power in traditional sites of knowledge production (e.g. the university) as well as in alternative sites of knowledge production (e.g. antifeminist and male supremacist online spaces), I find it necessary to counter this assertion of power with what it often contrasts itself to – that of subjectivity and emotions. The side-lining of emotions in the search for knowledge reflects patriarchal and imperial structures of knowledge production. Hence, to do research is a site of struggle, a site wherein the ways of knowing and the interest of some (e.g. the West) have come to dominate and resist the interest of "the Other" (Tuhiwai Smith 2012: 2). The devalued position of using emotions in research thus encapsulates a historic and continuing dominance of the objective researcher due to its relationship with advancing the power of the West and the social construction of the masculine man: the institutionalised idea that one (the West/the man) ought and need to dominate and actively control the passive other (the 'non-West'/the woman and 'non-man') to enlighten and help them to fight their irrationality (Cheng 1999: 296; Connell 1987: 167; Mosse 1996: 6–7, 14). Through this dominance, the idea of objectivity has been used to further colonial and patriarchal knowledge (Antony and Witt 2001: xv).

The problem with objectivity is not its meaning in theory, such as the idea of neutrality and being free from bias. The problem is that its meaning lacks completion in practice. It cannot be done. The centrality of objectivity in research has been used to create a distance between what is researched and the researcher – such as from the practice of separating the collection of data and the analysis thereof. A distance can thus be created from an extraction-collection-analysis order within one's research practice (D'Ignazio and Klein 2020: 76). Furthermore, this way of researching also implies that objectivity cannot be realised unless enough material evidence exists so that one can confidently claim an objective result (Sandler and Apple 2010: 325–326). In the social sciences, the collection of evidence will many times be incoherent and the result complicated. As has been shown in data science, the evidence collected from objective methods tends to reflect structural power imbalances (D'Ignazio and Klein 2020: 8–9). The result can, therefore, never be free from bias.

Claiming objectivity thus reinforces hegemonic knowledge production and power, a practice that male supremacists have learnt to use to their advantage – for example, in the site of producing and reinforcing misogynist incels' male supremacist extremist ideology of the BlackPill. In brief, the BlackPill is an ideology that symbolises an extension of the metaphor of the red and blue pill in *The Matrix*. In the view of people in the Alt-Right and Manosphere spaces, taking the red pill symbolises being 'enlightened' to the real hierarchical order of society, such as that Jews, feminists, and women overall hold the utmost power and control. In comparison, people who have taken the blue pill would thus be us who reject red pillers' view of the world. In misogynist incel spaces, they have developed this idea by adding a black pill (the ideology is often named *the BlackPill*). The BlackPill encapsulates a nihilistic and deterministic continuation of the red pill: whilst red pillers believe they can do something concrete to change the 'world order', black pillers believe they are determined to live in their state of hopelessness. Consequently, the state of hopelessness leads to one of three (self-proclaimed) outcomes: cope with the situation, rope (attempt suicide), or 'go ER' (commit violence, e.g. mass murder, that ideally leads to suicide by cop). Misogynist incels who believe in the BlackPill engage in knowledge practices to 'scientifically' prove this idea by creating dictionaries and knowledge banks on their forums that reference pseudointellectual and scholarly articles – a practice you can also see some red-pill actors doing (Kelly et al. 2021). Thus, within the BlackPill ideology, misogynist incels advocate their belief by claiming an objective stance on topics concerning relationships and power. For example, on their Wiki, they describe their ideology as the "Scientific Blackpill" that delivers a "neutral tone and scientific findings" for "common dating issues" for men. However, at the same time, they argue that women enjoy and deserve physical and mental pain (Incels Wiki 2022). Although the majority of their ideology reflects their subjective hatred and dehumanisation of women, people of colour, trans, and Jewish people, they use the frame of 'objective science' to argue for their beliefs. Hence, misogynist incels devalue the stance of subjectivity and emotions through their misogyny (even though they are, in practice, using both).

The use of emotions as part of my methodology aims to resist this framework by providing and producing knowledge that considers power structures, biases, and the effects of our research. Consequently, by using a methodology that directly counters the claim of objectivity, the research carries the opportunity of being a radical counterweight to the extremist ideology. As such, this methodology is a political and ethical engagement that aims to counter antifeminism and male supremacism, along with other oppressional structures that upkeep them, such as white supremacy. If emotions are used as a way to incorporate and extend oneself from the research, for example by examining whose emotions are seen and whose are not, we can elevate our ability to make ethically and politically conscious research on extremisms. In the next section, I explore this further by considering the impressions of emotions (Ahmed 2014) and who are allowed to feel or be visible with their feelings (Tuhiwai Smith 2012) in order to show the benefits of emotionality when conducting research.

Emotions can help us make ethically and politically conscious research

By exploring the ways our bodies, souls, and minds are part of the processes of creating knowledge, our emotions can equip us with the power to challenge structures that work against our ethics and politics, such as structures that fertilise harm (Toyosaki 2018: 33). What we perceive as harmful or beneficial depends on how we are affected by it. In turn, this reflects and shapes our thinking about it (Ahmed 2014: 6). In the context of research on extremisms, what we consider harmful or beneficial determines what we deem is important and worthy of research – and what we think is an extremist ideology. For example, when it comes to misogynist incels, what does it mean when we conceptualise them as extremists rather than actors of mainstream misogyny? Why are other actors of misogyny, such as Donald Trump and Boris Johnson, not considered extremists? The misogyny by all actors just mentioned affects us individually and systematically. As Kelly (2020), Jasser et al. (2020), and DeCook and Kelly (2022) point out, by assigning more importance within research on extremism to one particular extreme misogynist ideology, we risk obscuring how similar sentiments and ideas are prevalent in other misogynist actors and societal structures (Kelly 2020; DeCook and Kelly 2022; Jasser et al. 2020) including in inter-personal abuse (Jasser et al. 2020) and academic practices. Consequently, we may let other harms pass by relatively 'unnoticed'. Emotions are, therefore, foundational to the production of knowledge, both for the individual and the community (Ahmed 2014: 10).

The use of emotions as methodology needs to be accompanied by reflexive and introspective practices of the visible and the invisible. Tuhiwai Smith (2012) argues that the intention to advance knowledge can many times reflect patronising power imbalances rooted in colonial and patriarchal power relations. This is not avoided just because we may refuse some parts of the processes of hegemonic knowledge production (e.g. the claim of objectivity). There is still a risk that I reinforce colonial and patriarchal structures with my research when I am using emotions to produce knowledge, particularly considering my positionality as a white academic in a Western institution. For instance, practices of patronisation through assuming unawareness, as commonly claimed when seeking to further knowledge, can create power imbalances (Tuhiwai Smith 2012: 2). We, therefore, need to be attentive to what we are making visible and invisible – as well as who we are making it visible or invisible to.

In the case of misogynist incels, for example, I want to make their violence visible in order to make people aware of their harm, so that we can counter it. But, in line with the above discussion of misogynist incels' status as extremists and/or mainstream misogynists, I also need to ask myself: do forms of their violence not already exist elsewhere? And, if I emphasise their harmful practices, do I reify their form of male supremacy to the detriment of the struggle against male supremacism overall? Indeed, we need to further investigate the ways in which our own theoretical practices affect the general understanding of who is seen as a harmful actor – to properly see our role in reinforcing structural violence. To properly develop answers to these particular questions is beyond the scope of this chapter. However, we may still presume that the answers to these questions are affected by what we deem harmful or beneficial.

Emotions may then be used as a tool that can both advance and regress political rights for people in society. This means that we need to be careful with the ways we are working with emotions in sites of knowledge production. Social norms are, indeed, playing a role in determining who is allowed to feel and who is not, as well as where one is allowed to show feelings. There is politics in place to make emotionality more convenient for some than others. For example, white middle- to upper-class men tend to have their expressions of emotions believed, whilst women tend to be disbelieved – as recently seen in the Depp–Heard 2022 trial when Amber Heard was mocked for crying on the stand, whilst Johnny Depp's smirking was, in comparison, given less attention (Donegan 2022).

Moreover, emotions are racialised through politics. People of colour's emotions are seen as more political than white people's expressions of emotion. For example, white people's guilt and/or defensiveness assign negative emotions to people of colour (hooks 2000: 10). To illustrate this point, Bonilla-Silva (2019) tracks racialised relationships through practices of emotionality, such as how "Whites fear Blacks in interracial encounters ... [that can lead to that] many people of color experience anxiety and discomfort when entering 'white spaces' (Denzin 1984)" (Bonilla-Silva 2019).

Emotions can thus also be forced onto you as a result of dominant political practices and be a performative, and powerful, act in politics (Eklundh 2020: 108). Hence, as researchers using emotions, we carry the responsibility to understand the potential ethical and political consequences of emotionality in research.

We, therefore, need to use emotions as a critical practice. In particular, to use emotions in our methodology would mean to critically examine the visibility and invisibility of our and others' emotions. As Ahmed states, the emotions we encounter, the experiences we gather from them, and how they affect us leave us with impressions (Ahmed 2014: 6). This extends to our research. Our research affects us and we affect it. Hence, if we incorporate ourselves and our emotions in our knowledge production, we need to be critical of our research and stretch our ability to see its effects. If we do, we may also get better at seeing the things that did *not* leave an impression. How would our research be affected if we reflect on the knowledge we decide to leave out? The use of emotions in our methodology is, therefore, an active political and ethical engagement as it challenges us to extend our understanding of our own positionality. It can make us reflect more on our roles as producers of knowledge as well as the product that comes out of it.

To embrace emotions in research can be especially important when studying antifeminist and male supremacist extremisms; not just how emotions are gendered, but also how they are racialised. For example, Nash points out how defensiveness is a recurrent feeling and position for Black feminists in academic spaces. Black feminists need to defend their theories, critiques, and their own existence in these spaces. The defensiveness can as such be seen as an obstructive agency; however, Nash sees Black feminist defensiveness as an active resistance and cathartic experience as it is produced on behalf of the intellectual production of Black women (Nash 2018: 26–28). Indeed, whilst emotions can be a source of political control to oppress, they can also serve as a force of resistance. The assignment of emotions to the feminine, personal, and racialised domain/s (Ahmed 2014: 3; Krystalli and Schulz 2022: 6) can thus be used as a radical resistance to antifeminist and male supremacist ideologies through actively resisting traditionally forced positionalities. For example, whilst misogynist incels constantly want to justify and see the legitimisation of their feelings, they reject outsiders' expressions of emotions by repeatedly irrationalising and dehumanising us who work to resist their ideological beliefs. The expression and use of emotions to advance male supremacism by misogynist incels have been observed and detailed by Kelly (2020) where misogynist incels have been given mainstream platforms to share their beliefs without any critical examination of the effects. Whilst emotions are present in incels' own arguments and behaviours, they seek to monopolise allowed emotions around themselves, within their communities and people reacting to their communities. This is a way of exerting male supremacism, by establishing a dominant narrative around who is allowed to feel and who is not allowed to feel (hooks 2001: xxiv, 6). If we then use emotions on our own terms to understand the effects of their actions and ideology, we resist their efforts to dominate us.

The ethical and political consciousness that is in circulation when researching with emotions will, as seen in this section, evoke many questions and sometimes less straightforward answers. However, in the next two sections, I show how adhering to and using emotions can help us in a more straightforward way too. In the next section, I illustrate how emotions are an unavoidable part of my research on antifeminism and male supremacy by reflecting on my story of emotionality and vulnerability during my digital ethnography of a misogynist incel forum.

A story of emotionality and vulnerability when researching

In late 2021, the third month of my yearlong observational research period for my PhD, I went on to a misogynist incel online forum and noticed a thread that was receiving a lot of attention. The thread was made to discuss a high-profile murder case in the US and had grabbed incels' attention. Perhaps this was due to the identity of the perpetrator: a young white man seemingly rejected by society – a type of man many incels decide to relate to. I scrolled through the thread's posts. The posts discussed the look of the perpetrator, his chances with women, and how they found his violence justified. There were also loathsome comments about the victims and their families. Many comments were vile, foul, and offensive – they were misogynistic, racist, and antisemitic. It was depressing to read. Exhausting. Two feelings I had come to experience a lot during my observations.

I read one awful and gruesome comment after another, comments the participants in the forum seemed to devour with comfort and ease. But then, an anomaly of content and emotions popped up. Something shocked me. A wave of new emotions and reactions swept over me: horror, nausea, sadness, and pain. A post was attached with a photo of one of the victims, dead. Pale and lifeless. In an effort to gather together all that had swept over me, my mind went into a sort of investigative mode. I hoped that I could find evidence for the photo's fabrication. I wanted it to not be real.

Whilst I tried to make sense of it all, subconsciously fighting the wave of horror, nausea, sadness, and pain, I performed the role of the emotionally disconnected and objective researcher. I did not want to be vulnerable to the people I studied so I, ironically, mimicked their sense of ease with horrific content. However, not long after, I had to embrace my vulnerability.

Another wave of emotions swept over me, more immense this time, and generated additional discomfort and distress. Tears started to form, my heart raced and my body froze. I was slung back to the memory of seeing one of my dearest, loving, persons in the world in a similar, but also so different, state. But pale and lifeless.

In this snippet of emotions felt during my observations of the misogynist incel forum, there were several aspects of emotionality that affected me and my research. The systematic exposure to the dehumanising content misogynist incels post on their forum had made me somewhat numb to parts of the content they continued to post. However, at the same time, previous experiences of mine had made me further distressed by other parts. Whilst both the numbness and the vulnerability are reactions and feelings, they both seemed at the time to be completely different aspects of my research. And for a moment, not relevant. However, this was far from it. Instead, these two emotions have come to mean a lot when I do my research now. In the following section, I want to briefly reflect on how both the feeling of numbness and vulnerability can make us better researchers through the evocation of care these put forward, such as the need to be attentive to our feelings and recognise the emotional effect our research bring to our participants, readers, and ourselves.

Checking in: feeling numb and vulnerable as a way to care

> I want to welcome Vulnerability as the way in which we make ourselves open to ourselves and to others. (Cvetkovich and Michalski 2021: 19)

To feel numb and vulnerable in our research on extremism can make us more attentive to the effects that may come out of it. Being attentive to the feelings of numbness through embracing vulnerability also allows us to care for ourselves and the product of knowledge we disseminate. For example, Blee (1998) reflects on how her feeling of fear had come to fade as she continued and got deeper into her research on racist women. She "was becoming numb to the horrors of organized racism, a situation that was not only personally dismaying but also signaled the need … to end fieldwork and regain emotional separation from the research" (Blee 1998: 396). Blee was attentive to her emotions, particularly that of numbness, to know when she needed to take a break from her research. Her reflection on her feelings in research served as a mechanism to reconnect with her ethical and political engagements. Being aligned with one's emotions can therefore serve as a way to check in on oneself to minimise the risk of producing harmful research.

Numbness can thus be beneficial if acted upon: it can help us to grasp when what we are researching is systematically foul or heavy. However, if we do not realise or act upon it, numbness might risk making our research unreflective of its effects. When my observations had made me numb, I only got reminded again of the harm when something *personally* horrific crossed my path. I knew about misogynist incels' harm before I started my observations. Hence, it was not that I could not see, or noted down, the systematic harm misogynist incels purported when I observed them. But to be able to deal with it for an extended amount of time I had, in the process, felt the need to emotionally distance myself from it. Now I understand that the exhaustion and numbness I felt were indeed reactions to the systematic harm – and a sign to stop, slow down, and reencounter my political and ethical commitments (including that of care).

If I had not gotten into this research with emotions as methodology, I would have continued with my observations despite my strong reaction to the thread with that photo. If I did, I would have potentially lost out on some effects of the study. But as a result of coming across that photo, I took some time off from my observations. However, I came back to it a bit too soon and continued to feel a sense of numbness when I scrolled through the forum. This time, though, I recognised the effect it had had on me. Consequently, I took a break from my observations for almost two months, to give myself some time to care for myself and my research. When I went on to do my first session after the break, I noticed how the posts affected me more. I even asked myself if the posts had always been this grim. Just like Blee, being close to my feelings and reflecting on the change in my emotions helped me realise some potential ways the effects of my research would lack if I continued to be emotionally disconnected.

The incorporation of emotions and care into our research process may thus be a necessity to manage our work. Before I started my observations, I had prepared myself and built methods and defences to deal with gruesome things to try to avoid vulnerability (it is scary) (Behar 1997). However, it did not work. Instead, I found that I had to embrace feelings of vulnerability as a form of care maintenance.

Conclusion

In this chapter, I presented how emotions can help us make ethically and politically conscious research on extremisms. I particularly reflected on how embracing the emotion of vulnerability in the process of knowledge production can help us resist hegemonic power structures that uphold extremisms. Indeed, by embracing vulnerability and working with it early on in the research process, we may learn how to better and continuously spot harmful content. If we emotionally protest the violent content we are routinely exposed to in our work, content that has made us go 'numb', we may reduce the risk of overlooking harm that, eventually, disguises as 'less violent'. Furthermore, I argued that using emotions in research leads to an increased ability to reflect on one's research process and findings, which in turn can make us more critical of how our research habits may reinforce harm. Black feminist scholars and activists have dealt extensively with emotions as knowledge-making by showing how the use of anger (Lorde 1997), defensiveness (Nash 2018), and love (hooks 2001) contribute to making political and ethical research. To illustrate the basis of my argument, I gave the example of how the hegemonic stance of objectivity in academic research reflects patriarchal and colonial structures of dominance which refuse to deal with emotions as valuable knowledge. This conceptualisation of valuable research praxis is being used by misogynist incels to advance their male supremacist extremist ideology of the BlackPill.

I reflected on how using emotions as methodology functions as a 'check-in' for researchers, both for our mental health and for the risk of obscuring harmful effects generated by the extremisms we study. As I briefly shared in my story of emotionality and vulnerability, even though we might learn or try to deal with the harmful content we come across, emotions will always be present. Sometimes, we may have no other choice than to embrace them. This 'check-in' also serves a larger purpose. The use of emotions in our research can help us deal with the power we as knowledge producers have in furthering the understanding of extremisms. By looking at what we make visible and invisible (Tuhiwai Smith 2012) through our work with emotions as impressions (Ahmed 2014), we can critically examine the phenomena and structures we deem beneficial and harmful, such as different kinds of extremisms.

References

Ahmed, S. 2014. *The Cultural Politics of Emotion*. Edinburgh: Edinburgh University Press.

Antony, L. M. and Witt, C. E. 2001. *Feminist Essays on Reason and Objectivity*. New York: Routledge.

Behar, R. 1997. *The Vulnerable Observer: Anthropology That Breaks Your Heart*. Boston, MA: Beacon Press.

Blee, K. M. 1998. 'White-Knuckle Research: Emotional Dynamics in Fieldwork with Racist Activists', *Qualitative Sociology*, 21(4), 381–399.

Bonilla-Silva, E. 2019. 'Feeling Race: Theorizing the Racial Economy of Emotions', *American Sociological Review*, 84 (1), 1–25. https://doi.org/10.1177/000312241 8816958

Cheng, C. 1999. 'Marginalized Masculinities and Hegemonic Masculinity: An Introduction', *The Journal of Men's Studies*, 7(3), 295–315. https://doi.org/10.3149%2Fjms.0703.295

Connell, R. 1987. *Gender and Power: Society, the Person and Sexual Politics.* Cambridge: Polity Press in association with Blackwell.

Cvetkovich, A. and Michalski, K. 2021. 'The Alphabet of Feeling Bad Now'. In: Hollenbach, J. and McDonald, R. A. (eds). *Re/Imagining Depression: Creative Approaches to 'Feeling Bad'*. Cham: Palgrave Macmillan.

D'Ignazio, C. and Klein, L. F. 2020. *Data Feminism*. Cambridge, MA: The MIT Press.

DeCook, J. R. and Kelly, M. 2022. 'Interrogating the "Incel Menace": Assessing the Threat of Male Supremacy in Terrorism Studies', *Critical Studies on Terrorism*, 15(3), 706–726.

Donegan, M. 2022. 'The Amber Heard-Johnny Depp Trial Was an Orgy of Misogyny', *The Guardian*, 1 June, https://www.theguardian.com/commentisfree/2022/jun/01/amber-heard-johnny-depp-trial-metoo-backlash (accessed 24 September 2022).

Eklundh, E. 2020. 'Excluding Emotions: The Performative Function of Populism', *PArtecipazione e COnflitto (PACO)*, 13(1), 107–131.

hooks, b. 1989. 'Choosing the Margin as a Space of Radical Openness', *Framework: The Journal of Cinema and Media*, 36, 15–23.

hooks, b. 2000. *Feminist Theory: From Margin to Center*. London: Pluto Press.

hooks, b. 2001. *All About Love*. New York: HarperCollins.

Incels.Wiki. 2022. 'Scientific Blackpill', incels.wiki. https://incels.wiki/w/Scientific_Blackpill (accessed 9 May 2022).

Jasser, G., Kelly, M., and Rothermel, A.-K. 2020. 'Male Supremacism and the Hanau Terrorist Attack: Between Online Misogyny and Far-Right Violence', *ICCT*. https://icct.nl/publication/male-supremacism-and-the-hanau-terrorist-attack-between-online-misogyny-and-far-right-violence/ (accessed 10 May 2022).

Kelly, M. 2020. 'The Mainstream Pill', *Public Eye*, Spring/Summer, 3–9, https://politicalresearch.org/2021/07/01/mainstream-pill (accessed 10 May 2022).

Kelly, M., DiBranco, A., and DeCook, J. 2021. 'Misogynist Incels and Male Supremacism', *New America*, 18 February. http://newamerica.org/political-reform/reports/misogynist-incels-and-male-supremacism/ (accessed 10 May 2022).

Krystalli, R. and Schulz, P. 2022. 'Taking Love and Care Seriously: An Emergent Research Agenda for Remaking Worlds in the Wake of Violence', *International Studies Review*, 24(1), 1–25.

Lorde, A. 1997. 'The Uses of Anger', *Women's Studies Quarterly*, 25(1/2), 278–285.

Mosse, G. L. (George Lachmann). 1996. *The Image of Man: The Creation of Modern Masculinity*. New York: Oxford University Press. http://archive.org/details/imageofmancreati0000moss (accessed 24 September 2022).

Nash, J. C. 2018. *Black Feminism Reimagined: After Intersectionality*. Durham, NC: Duke University Press. https://muse.jhu.edu/book/70558 (accessed 24 September 2022).

Sandler, J. and Apple, M. W. 2010. 'A Culture of Evidence, a Politics of Objectivity'. In: Leonardo, Z. (ed.). *Handbook of Cultural Politics and Education*. New York: Routledge.

Toyosaki, S. 2018. 'Toward De/postcolonial Autoethnography: Critical Relationality with the Academic Second Persona', *Cultural Studies ↔ Critical Methodologies*, 18(1), 32–42.

Tuhiwai Smith, L. 2012. *Decolonizing Methodologies*. London: Zed Books.

11

Reflections on researching armed Nazis as an unarmed left-wing Jew: politics, privilege, and practical concerns

Aaron Winter

The title of this chapter is not a provocation or the start of a bad joke, but my response to a serious question that I was frequently asked during my postgraduate studies in the late 1990s/early 2000s. The question was why I decided not to do ethnography or interviews with far-right figures as part of my DPhil research into the Christian Identity and Patriot movements in the US. It is something that I have also been asked many times since then about that project and my subsequent research. Sometimes this question was asked as a challenge or criticism, but mostly out of interest and curiosity. In either case, I suspect that it was related to trends and conventions in my field and discipline. I am thinking particularly about how my research and this question overlapped with the ethnographic, as well as affective and empathetic, emphasis and turns in sociology and the social sciences more broadly, but also specifically in terms of far right research at the time.

At the time of writing, we have seen a resurgence of the far right globally and a boom in research on it. This has been accompanied, if not dominated, in some contexts, by two research trends: the first is the 'populist' 'left behind' narrative that presents the far right as an expression of white working-class inequality and grievance. This narrative and approach provides both a material basis and legitimacy to the far right and, building on the ethnographic and affective turns, both relies on and encourages first-person engagement, data collection, and even empathy. The second trend is P/CVE (Preventing and Countering Violent Extremism), and wider terrorism problem-solving research that seeks to understand vulnerability to recruitment and radicalisation, including but not limited to the 'left behind'. This type of research often involves engagement with past, present, and potential (or at risk) 'extremists'.

The fact that engagement with far-right figures and racists, as well as the need to be objective about and empathetic to them, has become a convention and imperative in research is interesting as a development and for what it reveals about the assumptions underlying the field. These assumptions not only concern the object of the research but also the researcher, particularly the challenges and implications for those who belong to a racialised or otherwise targeted group. This is because they can be exposed to individuals and material that target them and their communities, and this is rarely considered. Ironically, I find myself asked about the threat of 'left-wing antisemitism' from colleagues in the field, often more than I am asked about that coming from the far right. What requires greater consideration in the field and by the research community are the implications of privileging such methods, as well as resisting or refusing them, and the pressure to be objective or apolitical and empathetic about our research topics and participants. There also needs to be greater awareness of how institutional ethical, counterextremism, and counterterrorism policies play out differently for researchers with different identities. I am thinking particularly about Muslim researchers who may not only work on a far right that targets them but also come into contact with or under the gaze of institutionally racist state agencies that treat them as a suspect community. Following on from these issues, there needs to be greater understanding and development of specific types of support needed and provided by institutions and the wider research community in light of these different challenges, experiences, and potential risks. I am not opposing such methods wholesale, but calling for serious reflection and change to address such challenges and implications, as well as the assumptions underpinning them, as they highlight and perpetuate the unequal racial politics of far right research. I have found it both deeply troubling and ironic that the racial politics of such research and its undertaking are largely ignored in a field focused on racist movements.

This chapter will reflect on my research experience and decisions about how to engage with the far right as part of a wider examination of the racial politics of research on the far right, most notably how research into the far right often: (1) underplays race and racism; (2) assumes the whiteness and white privilege of the researcher and relies on white ignorance, including when it comes to risks and harms; and (3) underplays its politics and subjectivity while constructing anti-racist and anti-fascist work as biased, political, or non-objective. I will discuss these issues and their implications, as well as how addressing them can help us understand and oppose racism more effectively and promote a more reflexive and anti-racist approach to far right studies.

While I engage with some research in the field, this chapter is more about my experiences and thus is non-exhaustive. While my experiences will not apply to all and some of my points will meet with disagreement, including from researchers who also belong to targeted groups, I do hope that what I have drawn from it resonates with others and contributes to a wider discussion. I would also note that when I use the term 'white privilege', I am excluding myself from that. Not because I do not have white privilege structurally and institutionally, but in the face of a far right that is anti-semitic (which is what I research), I am a racialised target (despite some tactical philosemitism from the far right). I am also speaking in a context of increasing and emboldened antisemitism, seen most explicitly in chants of 'Jews will not replace us' at the Unite the Right rally in Charlottesville in 2016 and the attack on worshippers at the Tree of Life Synagogue in Pittsburgh in 2018, as a migrant in the context of anti-immigrant movements, politics, and policies, and about my family history from a time when they were not considered white.

A personal introduction

I should start by introducing myself, my research, and my reasons for focusing on the far right, as well as for choosing not to do ethnographic research or interviews. The decision to study the far right was explicitly political and connected to my identity, family, and community history and experiences. These also influenced my anti-racist and anti-fascist politics, which in turn informed, and continue to inform, my work. Although conceiving of the far right as a field of study and topic of research and professional expertise did not come until I was in university in the 1990s, the seeds were planted much earlier. I can trace it back to growing up as the grandchild of Holocaust survivors, descendant of many murdered, and others who escaped antisemitism earlier from Poland and Russia and were part of the working-class, immigrant Jewish community in Montreal's garment or 'schmatta' (rag) industry, and experiencing a skinhead and wider far-right revival in Toronto as a teenager in the 1980s.

These formative experiences politicised me and motivated my research on right-wing extremism. Although predicated and focused on experiences with fascism, this did not distract me from structural, systemic racial inequality and state and institutional racism. It is a common problem, as liberal democracies like Canada and the UK use fascism and extreme or illiberal forms of racism as a distraction from and denial of their own systemic racism and legacies of colonialism. I am specifically thinking of how the antisemitism my family experienced in post-war Canada and the racism that I witnessed and others experienced were often overshadowed or displaced by discussions about European fascism and 'worse' American racism, including in school where we were taught *To Kill a Mockingbird* (Lee 1960) many times. In fact, while working on this chapter, my family also reminded me that my first piece of writing on the far right was a primary school report I did on the Ku Klux Klan after reading an article about them in the *Toronto Star*. This is of vital importance to me because of the ways in which fascism,

Nazism, the Holocaust, and antisemitism, as well as American segregation and the Klan, as exemplars of illiberal racism, have been used to displace, exceptionalise, and externalise racism and deny or minimise other forms and experiences. In addition, my family history and experiences, and thinking about this, would later be developed in my work with Aurelien Mondon on 'illiberal vs liberal racism' and mainstreaming, my wider work on racism, counterextremism, and counterterrorism, and our critique of the white working class 'left behind' narrative (Mondon and Winter 2019 and 2020a; Winter 2018).

My experiences also made me question the belief that the far right and racism are an expression of working-class inequality and disenfranchisement, which has long received wisdom and a dominant narrative in academic research, political discourse, and media representation, reaching what seemed like a peak in the context of Brexit and Trumpism. My own grandparents, who escaped antisemitism in Europe and worked in garment factories in Canada during the Depression and post-war period, were not targeted by fascists for the purposes of recruitment. They were at the sharp end of such activist antisemitism and xenophobia, as well as institutional and state versions that all supported one another. As a teenager, many of those with whom I got into confrontations with skinheads were working-class kids who were anti-racist, anti-fascist, and racialised. These friends, as well as their families and communities, were targeted by skinheads and doubly disenfranchised by the racist state and the capitalist system, challenged the widely held assumption and often repeated narrative that working-class people are white, racist, and turn to fascism in response to inequality for me. These were issues that I wanted to explore and understand more about, and these experiences definitely shaped my interest in researching the far right, but at that point, I had not thought about becoming an academic. The fact that I ended up in Britain to study may have been influenced by my musical education from that time, particularly 'Concrete Jungle' by The Specials, 'Two Swords' by The Beat, and 'Down in a Tube Station at Midnight' by The Jam, as well as reading Stanley Cohen's *Folk Devils and Moral Panics: The Creation of the Mods and Rockers* (1973). Thinking back, Britain sounded politically and sociologically interesting, but not that green and pleasant.

Research and methods

I started my DPhil on *Christian Patriotism and the Politics of the American Extreme Right in Post-Civil Rights Era America* at the University of Sussex in 1999. This was between the Oklahoma City bombing in 1995 and the millennium, which many thought would bring more attacks, as well as 9/11 and the war on terror, when racist terrorists were replaced by the racialisation of terrorism and legitimisation of Islamophobia. My research focused on the turn towards fascism, white separatism, anti-government activism, armed insurgency, and rejection of the system and mainstream by far-right activists and organisations that occurred in the post-civil rights era. It was something that I saw as a reflection of and response to the movement's perception that white supremacy was over and white people were persecuted victims, despite the fact that systemic and institutional racism carried on. In spite of the focus on something that was so 'extreme' and illiberal, I did not think that the far right was the problem in and of itself or that the mainstream and liberal democracy were benign or a bulwark against it. Instead, I wanted to examine how the changing character of the far right and its relationship to the mainstream operated as a response to and reflection of the changing status, configuration, and acceptability of racism in that mainstream and the needs of the governing white supremacist system. By this, I am referring to the ways the far right can defend the system as its foot soldiers and border guards at some points and distract from it or even serve as the unacceptable face of racism that can be scapegoated and expunged in others. If race and racism were central to the analysis, and I was implicated as a target of their antisemitism, then racism and antisemitism could not just be my topic. They also had to be central to my research design and methods.

My research involved a systematic review of Aryan Nations, Posse Comitatus, The Order, and National Alliance, as well as older Ku Klux Klan ephemera such as newsletters, manifestos, magazines, and flyers from archives in the US and UK. I also collected transcripts and reports from government hearings into the Klan, Aryan Nations, anti-government groups, domestic terrorism and Ruby Ridge, material from the trials of far-right activists, and local and national media reports throughout the period that I was working on. In addition to this, I conducted interviews with representatives of monitoring organisations such as the Southern Poverty Law Center (SPLC) and Political Research Associates (PRA). Doing this in the post-9/11 era – particularly requesting such material and travelling through the US and internationally with it – was itself instructive. It was a lesson in privilege, not belonging to a suspect community, and how little the far right was on the radar as a threat so soon after the Oklahoma City bombing and during a war on terror.

I was initially surprised to be asked about ethnography and interviews with far-right activists, as if these were the most obvious, natural, and effective methods of researching and understanding the phenomenon, but perhaps I should not have been. In addition to disciplinary conventions, this was, after all, the same period in which Kathleen Blee's *Inside Organized*

Racism: Women in the Hate Movement (2002) came out, partly based on invaluable access and first-person interview data. There was also a popular culture boom in far-right ethnography and interviews, which everyone I encountered seemed to know about. The most notable mainstream media example was Louis Theroux, who visited the Aryan Nations compound in the 1998 episode of the BBC's *Weird Weekends* 'Survivalists' and wrote about it in *The Call of the Weird: Travels in American Subcultures* (Theroux 2006). Far-right extremists and conspiracy theorists were also visited by Jon Ronson for his TV series *Secret Rulers of the World* and book *Them: Adventures with Extremists* (Ronson 2001). I even attended one of his talks in Brighton with my supervisor, but sadly did not have my question about the place of interviewer identity answered. Despite all the mainstream media attention, this was not a mainstream movement. They were fringe figures of fun, amusement, and derision that made our society, with the documentarian serving as a proxy for it, appear more liberal, tolerant, and progressive, as well as intelligent. Such is the function of illiberal racism (Mondon and Winter 2020a).

My reasons for choosing not to do ethnography and interviews were multiple, not least because I considered my methods and material to be the most appropriate for my topic and questions, but also because of political, personal, methodological, and ethical issues. I thought that documentary research and discourse analysis focused on organisational ephemera would be the most effective way to control for and map changes to movement, its discourses, narratives, ideologies, and tactics over time. I could not access organisations that were gone or had transformed over time, nor actors who had moved between movements, organisations, or ideologies. Those whom I might be able to interview would provide less breadth and possibly even clarity on the precise changes that the organisations implemented to recruit members and mobilise activists. They might not even care and put them all in an ever-expanding repertoire of racisms. Not that this is uninteresting or unimportant. It would, though, be a different issue if I was looking at individual interpretations, beliefs, motivations, and recruitment, but I was not.

My methodological rationale for this decision always seemed easier to explain and marginally more convincing to colleagues than my personal and political reasons, articulated best by the title of this piece. I am an unarmed left-wing Jew and they were armed far-right antisemites. I get the argument that such representations can perpetuate and exacerbate fear and stigma, but it is also a real concern. Such research would come with obvious risks, as well as possible challenges to access that would not affect all researchers equally. The other issue that concerned me at the time was granting further opportunities for racists and fascists to spread their hate and debate their ideas in legitimate forums. It was something demonstrated by the boom in TV documentaries and media platforming, often under the auspices of free speech to represent 'diverse' voices or expose the far right to scrutiny. This saw the appearance of Nick Griffin of the British National Party (BNP) on *Question Time* in 2009. While Griffin and the party would go into decline following this, regular appearances by far-right figures followed and this fed both a resurgence and mainstreaming, which was itself becoming the focus of my more recent research. Even Theroux returned with a new visit with right-wing extremists in 2022.

If the far right could be conceived of as fringe and funny then (not that they should have ever been), they certainly cannot now, having enjoyed a period of mainstreaming. Mondon and I argue that this mainstreaming is partly predicated on the legitimisation and platforming of far-right ideas, particularly around a white working-class 'left behind' grievance narrative (Mondon and Winter 2019, 2020a), which was honed by the BNP in the 2000s and taken up and legitimised by politicians, media, and academics. In the case of the latter, we saw a run of work in sociology, criminology, and political science giving voice to such grievances through ethnography, interviews, surveys, and analysis in the 2010s (e.g. Goodhart 2017; Goodwin and Ford 2014a, 2014b; Hochschild 2016; Inglehart and Norris 2016; Pilkington 2016; Winlow, Hall, and Treadwell 2017; see also Mondon and Winter 2019, 2020a). Trump and Brexit were widely seen, by media and academics, as giving voice to this constituency, and their victories confirmed the narrative for many, as opposed to confirming how deftly these campaigns and their media supporters weaponised and mainstreamed a far-right narrative. These political developments and far-right activity in the form of Unite the Right, 6 January, the Canadian Convoy, and various marches and attacks became part of that narrative and led to new research opportunities, studies, and problems, as well as the reproduction and escalation of established ones. The most notable problem was, and still is, the representation, amplification, and legitimisation of far-right ideas, narratives, and figures. It is a fast-moving train with most eyes on getting access, funding and publications, and addressing the problem, as opposed to critical reflection and resistance.

At the same time, we are also seeing important discussions about the politics, ethics, and challenges of far right research, notably in this collection and *Researching the Far Right: Theory, Methods and Practice* (Ashe et al. 2020). The latter includes a range of reflections and differing views on interviews, ethnography, engagement, and empathy (Ashe 2020; Busher 2020; Dobratz and Waldner 2020; Klandersman 2020; Ramalingam 2020; Mondon and Winter 2020b). There has also been a new emerging discussion on ethics, support, and safeguarding in far right and wider terrorism studies (Kingdon and Mattheis 2021; Morrison et al. 2021; Pearson et al. 2023). Crucially, there is increasing discussion about how this needs to address specific unequal relations of power and privilege in research, as well as institutionally. This pertains particularly to race and gender, early career researchers (ECR) and postgraduate researchers (PGR), precarity and mental health, and the implications these have for opportunity, access, funding, and risk or harm. With increased attention comes pressure to do the work in ways that might increase the risk or to stay silent and even get left out. It is also occurring on the back of social media trolling, inappropriate and abusive behaviour, particularly by those in power, and wider debates about systemic racism, misogyny, transphobia, and ableism in higher education and wider society.

Discussion about issues related to race and racism in far right studies is less developed and recognised – possibly due to the whiteness of the field (Mondon 2022) and the function of the far right to distract from everyday, systemic, and institutional racism (Mondon and Winter 2020a). Yet, we do see a growing body of important work and reflection on race and far right research, including about researcher identity and experience, in this collection and elsewhere (Ashe 2020; Dixit 2022; Jereza 2022; Mondon 2022; Mondon and Winter 2020b, 2020c; Pai 2016; Ramalingham 2020). These are issues that affect and are reflected by researchers in related disciplines and sub-fields, including sociology, international relations, criminology, and wider terrorism research (Abu-Bakare 2017; Fernandez and Johnson 2020; Lumsden and Winter 2014; Qureshi 2020; Sabir 2022; Younis 2020).

While there is increasing awareness and support for researchers, and it is to be applauded, I wonder if it can address the assumptions and inequalities that create such challenges and problems for researchers in the field, or represent a band-aid that may actually gloss over and distract from specific and diverse structural and institutional inequalities that exist? I would argue that what is required is a deeper critique of the field, its assumptions, and its methods, particularly around race. This is particularly important because the subject matter is racist and the field is disproportionately and analytically white, supports and legitimises a system that is institutionally racist, and exceptionalises racism as 'extremism'. It is for this reason that I pull out three assumptions, issues, and challenges which are underpinned by structural and institutional white privilege and white ignorance, and can both disproportionately impact racialised or otherwise targeted researchers and exacerbate both racism or its displacement, if not denial, within the field, and need to be challenged. Support and care are not enough for what are structural and institutional problems in our field.

I've got issues

First-person research

The first issue is the reliance on and prioritisation of first-person research in the field. There are many assumptions that underpin such an approach and these have serious implications. As noted earlier, a great deal of work on the far right is often underpinned by 'left behind' and radicalisation narratives and a deradicalisation and disengagement problem-solving logic and imperative. Because of this, and despite the fact that the focus is on movements and implicates a wider demographic (e.g. the white working class), such research privileges experiences and stories of individuals at risk of radicalisation, recruitment, and engagement or are active in right-wing extremism and terrorism.

This not only limits the range of research problems and questions asked, but also perpetuates the individualisation of white extremism and terrorism and places far-right activists, formers, and racists as a main source of data and means to understand and address the problem. This also occurs because extremism and terrorism are defined as the problem and not racism, whiteness, or inequality, except where the latter explains far-right radicalisation. This approach also assumes who the researcher is and what the access issues and risks are, with whiteness constructed as a universal, objective, and neutral position of observation. This occurs with little reflection on whether a far-right organisation, activist, and racist will grant access to and share experiences honestly and safely with someone who does not share their racial, religious, and national identity, and whether a racialised researcher can or will take up such research, get access, and be safe. In their work, both Blee and Pete Simi acknowledge and reflect on the role of their white identity and appearance in gaining trust and a rapport with their research participants (Blee 2002: 13; Simi and Futrell 2010: 129). The relationship between white supremacy and white privilege and between recruitment of activists and research participants is closer than is comfortable in this context.

We can see the ways that whiteness is reproduced in these assumptions and practices. This is also evident in all-white teams and panels on white supremacy, where you not only have white researchers but former white supremacists explaining how to fight racism. This is a growth field with many formers and representative organisations seeking opportunities. While they can be a useful resource and there are good people working in the field, it can serve to conflate or confuse their role as research subject, data source, expert, and partner and promote their voices above others. This practice is even more serious as there is little attempt to engage with the voices and experiences, as well as expertise, of those at the sharp end of racism and the far right (Braune 2022 and in this collection; Dixit 2022), including racialised working-class people and researchers. Yet, to do so would likely mean asking them to engage or work with and sit side by side with those who are or represent their victimisers. In a context where the role and value of far-right and former voices are privileged and assumed, they would have to accept and consent to participate and this re-affirms the unequal terms of inclusion and exclusion in this context. This has many serious implications. If such approaches have the greatest legitimacy and currency in the field and are reproduced through established operating logics and gatekeeping, this can lead to limited opportunities and exclusion, as well as increased risks and harms, for racialised and otherwise targeted researchers and research participants.

Risks and harms

The second issue is that of how risks and harms are constructed and discussed. It is closely connected to the first-person research issue but also extends to engaging with online and print material and disseminating our research, as well as being active on social media. In fact, it was being trolled and hearing about or witnessing friends' and colleagues' experiences with online harassment, abuse, and threats that partly motivated this piece.

To quote a 2019 *Wired* article on this, 'The Existential Crisis Plaguing Online Extremism Researchers': "Chronicling the internet's worst impulses can be depressing" and "soul sucking" (Martineau 2019). While the points are important, such analysis flattens out and universalises researcher identity, assuming they are white and not directly affected by racism. Speaking for myself, that 'existential' has an altogether different meaning and implication when my life, the lives of my family, and my people's existence are threatened or our genocide celebrated. This is in addition to the targeted antisemitism, anti-Muslim, or anti-Black racism that is more specific than the generic language of 'hate', 'othering', or 'minority' used in the field, along with euphemisms such as populism and nativism, or the way that forms of racism become merely part of an exercise in about labelling and definitions. What is often lost in this process and practice is the ways in which racism actually harms those it is directed at and to which it applies as more than a concept for academics to apply and debate.

Risk and harm also apply to those who read or are exposed to our work. We also have to be careful about reproducing and amplifying racist and wider hate speech, text, and images, particularly when it targets someone other than ourselves. This is particularly important in the case of ethnography and particularly participant observation, when a researcher may directly or indirectly aid activists or take part in a racist march that is actively targeting racialised communities in real time. While it is important to protect and represent research participants and researchers, in far right research, too often this is understood in terms of the researcher as having power and privilege and the participant being 'left behind' and vulnerable. What is lost in this schema is the specific risks and harms for not only racialised and otherwise targeted researchers, but also the wider communities most targeted and affected by the far right who should be centred.

Objectivity vs politics

The final issue concerns claims of objectivity in the field. When raising the issue of racism and issues with counterextremism and counterterrorism research or policies, many of us are told by colleagues that we are being 'political', 'activist', 'biased', or 'subjective' as opposed to objective and unbiased scholars who can provide policymakers with the data and evidence they need to understand and solve the problem. What strikes me about this argument is how it often comes from those who self-define as objective and apolitical, yet made the decision to combat extremism and terrorism, engage with political parties, governments, and state agencies, including those that mainstream far-right ideas, and are complicit with racist and repressive policies and practices. While I would not oppose anyone claiming to be political, I do not understand how anyone can be objective or apolitical, or crucially claim to be, about racism, these issues, or such work.

The question that I frequently ask (and may become the title of another researcher's reflective piece one day) is: what drew you to this work studying and combatting racist far-right extremism and terrorism? I assume that most are against it, seeing that it is constructed as a problem in the field and the work as problem-solving. This is readily acknowledged and sometimes the answer is 'hate' or 'racism' (in addition to 'violence' and 'threat to democracy'), but typically not in the way that it is seen as subjective because it is linked to someone's identity, experiences, feelings, or activism. In addition to this, because of the way that the far right is often constructed as a proxy for and distraction from systemic and institutional racism, such work often serves instead of challenging the political status quo and thus can escape charges of being political in an activist sense. This is far easier if you are positioned (or position yourself) outside the racialised system, do not experience racism or listen to anyone but other 'experts', government officials, and former far-right racists who, coincidentally, often all come from the same communities and identity groups. Sometimes, anti-racists and anti-fascists, or the 'left' are even targeted as proof of objectivity and balance, or to claim that it is 'polarisation' and not racism that is the problem.

My favourite argument received from 'insiders' and gatekeepers in response to my criticism of the field is that I am not privy to the seriousness of the threat. Saying that to a fellow researcher, and to any target of the far right who will know the threat viscerally, is quite a statement. I find it ironic that many of us have the place of our identity in the research process negated because it is political but our critical anti-racist, anti-fascist, and wider left politics included in the analysis for such purposes.

My hope is that my arguments and analysis, and those from others (including in this collection), as well as wider anti-racist, antifascist, decolonial, and abolitionist scholars and activists and communities at the sharp end of racism and the far right, will be heeded and that this is the start of much-needed reflection and change. If anything, the far right is becoming more mainstream and their ideas more powerful and influential, so the current research approaches, and particularly the problem-solving ones that exceptionalise the far right (and racism with it) and serve existing state policies, are not working.

References

Abu-Bakare, A. 2017. 'Why Race Matters: Examining "Terrorism" through Race in International Relations'. *E-International Relations*. https://www.e-ir.info/2020/10/05/interview-amal-abu-bakare/ (accessed 22 March 2023).

Ashe, S. D. 2020. 'Whiteness, Class and the "Communicative Community": A Doctoral Researcher's Journey to a Local Political Ethnography'. In: Ashe, S. et al. (eds). *Researching the Far Right: Theory, Method and Practice*. Abingdon: Routledge, 284–306.

Ashe, S. D., Busher, J., Macklin, G., and Winter, A. (eds). 2020. *Researching the Far Right: Theory, Method and Practice*. Abingdon: Routledge.

Blee, K. M. 2002. *Inside Organized Racism: Women in the Hate Movement*. Berkeley, CA: University of California Press.

Braune, J. 2022. 'Experts Who Study Far-Right Mass Violence Must Center the Communities Affected', *Range*. https://www.rangemedia.co/highland-park-ideology-mass-shooting/ (accessed 22 March 2023).

Busher, J. 2020. 'Negotiating Ethical Dilemmas During an Ethnographic Study of Anti-Minority Activism: A Personal Reflection on the Adoption of a "Non-Dehumanization" Principle'. In Ashe, S. et al. (eds). *Researching the Far Right: Theory, Method and Practice*. Abingdon: Routledge, 270–283.

Cohen, S. 1973. *Folk Devils and Moral Panics: The Creation of the Mods and Rockers* St Albans: Paladin.

Dixit, P. 2022. *Race, Popular Culture, and Far-Right Extremism in the United States*. London: Palgrave.

Dobratz, B A. and Waldner, L. K. 2020. 'Interviewing Members of the White Power Movement in the United States: Reflections on Research Strategies and Challenges of Right-Wing Extremists'. In: Ashe, S. et al. (eds). *Researching the Far Right: Theory, Method and Practice*. Abingdon: Routledge, 212–224.

Fernandez, S. and Johnson, A. 2020. 'Navigating Refusal within the Academy'. In: Qureshi, A. (ed.). *I Refuse to Condemn: Resisting Racism in Times of National Security*. Manchester: Manchester University Press, 90–100.

Ford, R. and Goodwin, M. J. 2014a. 'Understanding UKIP: Identity, Social Change and the Left Behind', *The Political Quarterly*, 85, 277–284.

Ford, R. and Goodwin, M. J. 2014b. *Revolt on the Right: Explaining Support for the Radical Right in Britain*. Abingdon: Routledge.

Goodhart, D. 2017. *The Road to Somewhere: The Populist Revolt and the Future of Politics*. London: Hurst.

Hochschild, A. R. 2016. *Strangers in Their Own Land: Anger and Mourning on the American Right*. New York: The New Press.

Inglehart, R. F. and Norris, P. 2016. 'Trump, Brexit, and the Rise of Populism: Economic Have-Nots and Cultural Backlash', *HKS Working Paper*. RWP16–026.

Jereza, R. 2022. 'Inheritance as Alternative to Ethnographic Empathy with the Far Right', *C-Rex RightNow*. https://www.sv.uio.no/c-rex/english/news-and-events /right-now/2022/inheritance-as-alternative-to-ethnographic-empathy.html (accessed 22 March 2023).

Kingdon, A. and Mattheis, A. 2021. 'Does the Institution Have a Plan for That? Researcher Safety and the Ethics of Institutional Responsibility'. In: Lavorgna, A. and Holt, T. (eds). *Researching Cybercrimes*. London: Palgrave, 457–472.

Klandermans, B. 2020. 'Life-History Interviews with Rightwing Extremists'. In: Ashe, S. et al. (eds). *Researching the Far Right: Theory, Method and Practice*. Abingdon: Routledge, 225–237.

Lee, H. 1960. *To Kill a Mockingbird*. Philadelphia, PA: J. B. Lippincott & Co.

Lumsden, K. and Winter, A. 2014. 'Reflexivity in Criminological Research'. In: Lumsden, K. and Winter, A. (eds). *Reflexivity in Criminological Research: Experiences with the Powerful and the Powerless*. Basingstoke: Palgrave, 1–19.

Martineau, P. 2019. 'The Existential Crisis Plaguing Online Extremism Researchers', *Wired*, 2 May. https://www.wired.com/story/existential-crisis-plaguing-online -extremism-researchers/ (accessed 22 March 2023).

Mondon, A. 2022. 'Epistemologies of Ignorance in Far Right Studies: The Invisibilisation of Racism and Whiteness in Times of Populist Hype', *Acta Politica*, 58, 876–894.

Mondon, A. and Winter, A. 2019. 'Whiteness, Populism and the Racialisation of the Working Class in the United Kingdom and the United States', *Identities: Global Studies in Culture and Power*, 26(5), 510–528.

Mondon, A. and Winter, A. 2020a. *Reactionary Democracy: How Racism and the Populist Far Right Became Mainstream*. London: Verso.

Mondon, A. and Winter, A. 2020b. 'From Demonization to Normalization: Reflecting on Far Right Research'. In: Ashe, S. et al. (eds). *Researching the Far Right: Theory, Method and Practice*. Abingdon: Routledge, 370–382.

Mondon, A. and Winter, A. 2020c. 'Racist Movements, the Far Right and Mainstreaming'. In: Solomos, J. (ed.). *Routledge International Handbook of Contemporary Racism*. Abingdon: Routledge, 147–159.

Morrison, J., Silke, A. and Bont, E. 2021. 'The Development of the Framework for Research Ethics in Terrorism Studies (FRETS)', *Terrorism and Political Violence*, 33(2), 271–289.

Pai, H.-H. 2016. *Angry White People: Coming Face-to-Face with the British Far Right*. London: Zed.

Pearson, E., Whittaker, J., Baaken, T., Zeiger, S., Atamuradova, F., and Conway, M. 2023. *Online Extremism and Terrorism Researchers' Security, Safety, and Resilience: Findings from the Field*. VOX-Pol. https://www.voxpol.eu/publications/ (accessed 22 March 2023).

Pilkington, H. 2016. *Loud and Proud: Passion and Politics in the English Defence League*. Manchester: Manchester University Press.

Qureshi, A. (ed.). 2020. *I Refuse to Condemn: Resisting Racism in Times of National Security*. Manchester: Manchester University Press.

Ramalingham, V. 2020. 'Overcoming Racialization in the Field: Practicing Ethnography on the Far Right as a Researcher of Color'. In: Ashe, S. et al. (eds). *Researching the Far Right: Theory, Method and Practice*. Abingdon: Routledge, 254–269.

Ronson, J. 2001. *Them: Adventures with Extremists*. London: Picador.

Sabir, R. 2022. *The Suspect: Counterterrorism, Islam, and the Security State*. London: Pluto.

Simi, P. and Futrell, R. 2010. *American Swastika: Inside the White Power Movement's Hidden Spaces of Hate*. Lanham, MD: Rowman & Littlefield.

Theroux, L. 2006. *The Call of the Weird: Travels in American Subcultures*. London: Pan.

Winlow, S., Hall, S., and Treadwell, J. 2017. *The Rise of the Right: English Nationalism and the Transformation of Working-Class Politics*. Bristol: Policy Press.

Winter, A. 2018. 'The Klan is History: A Historical Perspective on the Revival of the Far-Right in "Post-Racial" America'. In: Morrison, J. et al. (eds). *Historical Perspectives on Organised Crime and Terrorism*. Abingdon: Routledge, 109–132.

Younis, T. 2020. 'The Duty to See, the Yearning to Be Seen'. In: Qureshi, A. (ed.). *I Refuse to Condemn: Resisting Racism in Times of National Security*. Manchester: Manchester University Press, 67–77.

Part III

The haunting past: memory and far right studies

12

Heritage, archaeology, ancestry, and the far right

David Farrell-Banks and Lorna-Jane Richardson

The construction of collective belonging is often reliant on the use of the past. Creating a sense of group connectivity is facilitated by the assertion of a historical legitimacy, the sense of a collective ancestry (both literal and figurative) that is common to the articulated group. The growth of anti-intellectual populism and the sharpening social, cultural, and political divisions of post-Brexit Britain has made cultural heritage a political 'hot potato' in service to the (re)construction of national identity as much as education and enlightenment. The offerings of museum exhibitions, or the results of archaeological fieldwork, are increasingly under scrutiny, and the outcome of heritage work is 'used in ways that we neither intended, nor fully understand' (Brophy 2018). Extreme conservative sentiment in the United Kingdom has centred the past as a battleground for contemporary national identity, nationalism, and the so-called 'culture wars', from the reconstruction of ancient human remains via DNA evidence for migration, to the removal and reinterpretation of statues. The past is at the heart of group belonging and identity. This is particularly true of belonging constructed along lines of national identity (Guibernau 2013). As researchers working across museums, heritage and archaeology, we are drawn to the past, its role and meaning in our lives in the present, and how it can inform our conception of shared futures. This is a thread that runs through every aspect of our work.

In this short chapter, we offer some reflections drawn from our experience in archaeology, heritage, and museum studies. We look at uses of the past in the discourse and recruitment tactics of far-right groups. Such groups often focus on notions of ancestry and the construction of a deep historical exceptionalism for particular in-groups (i.e. white, English, Christian). Allusions to ancestry and belonging are frequently a hallmark of archaeological and heritage discourse. While there is an increasing acknowledgement that the far right appropriates the past by sections of academic archaeology (Hakenbeck 2019; Frieman and Hofmann 2019; Niklasson and Hølleland 2018), we see the continued use of potentially nationalistic discourse as an ethical priority that these fields must confront.

The past and the far right

To date, the twenty-first century has seen a political shift to the right in British politics, policy, and media commentary. Far-right sentiment and authoritarianism continue to flourish across Europe and North America. Biologically determinist notions of nationhood, heritage, and white 'cultural erasure' have relocated to mainstream cultural and political discourse. The past, as understood through archaeology, heritage sites, and museums, has a long, historical, and mutually beneficial relationship with imperialism and nationalism. The reinterpretation and manipulation of the past by the right springs from these deep roots in imperial expansion and colonial subjugation of other nations and peoples.

The study of the past, through historical enquiry, archaeological work, and the growth of museums and archives, has expanded in complexity alongside the concept of the nation-state. The study of the past has acted as a buttress to national cohesion, has been exploited to support claims to territory, and has been held up as a mirror to reflect present-day identities. The link between the past and present-day politics has been a focus of archaeological and heritage scholarship for a number of decades. This includes, but is not limited to, the use of heritage and the past in fostering national belonging (De Cesari and Kaya 2020; Guibernau 2013) or promoting nationalist politics (Bonacchi 2022; Kohl and Fawcett 1995; Sommer 2017; Yahya 2005); Brexit discourse (Farrell-Banks 2020; Bonacchi, Altaweel and Krzyzanska 2018); xenophobic constructions of racial identities (Kolvraa 2019); and promoting the far right (Farrell-Banks 2021; Niklasson and Hølleland 2018; Wodak 2015).

Far-right uses of the past have been made explicitly, publicly visible on a number of occasions in the past decade. At the 2017 Unite the Right rally in Charlottesville, a national mobilisation of far-right groups in the United States, people holding flaming torches marched through the city chanting a series of Nazi slogans including 'blood and soil' and 'you/Jews will not replace us'. The location, Charlottesville, was chosen ostensibly to voice opposition to the planned removal of a statue of Confederate General Robert E. Lee. Local movements to remove monuments to a racist past became a focal point through which far-right groups could mobilise. These statues, and the pasts they represent, become a tool to reflect the far-right desire for an exclusionary, racist society in the present.

Active since 2019, the UK-based far-right nationalist group Patriotic Alternative (PA) was founded by former members of the British National Party. On 4 July 2020, the group unfurled a 'White Lives Matter' banner at the top of Mam Tor in the Peak District, the site of a late Bronze and early Iron Age hill fort and burial mounds, and a Scheduled Ancient

Monument. PA presents itself as a voice for the 'indigenous' white British and promotes a hardline white British ethnostate based on 'native' ancestry (Davis and Lawrence 2021). PA has also held events to coincide with the annual International Indigenous People's Day, including the raising of a banner at Clifford's Tower in York, the site of an antisemitic massacre in 1190 (Hope Not Hate 2023). This activity is an attempt to subvert the aim of the day to align with the 'white indigenous British' ideology of PA. The group repeatedly appropriates archaeological and historical events, places, and discoveries from British contexts. These are filtered through a lens of white supremacy and misinterpreted by the group to support their claims to 'indigeneity' and the superiority of British/English life, history, and cultural heritage.

As these two examples demonstrate, the past is often a central component of far-right discourse and action. One of the key tactics utilised by PA is to gain publicity by attracting controversy and outrage, especially on social media. References are made to mythological gloried pasts, with these often presented as under threat (Wodak 2015). At their most potent, these versions of the past create an emotional response among the target audience, simultaneously constructing a sense of group belonging, suggesting that this group is threatened by perceived status loss and economic instability. By uniting an in-group against an excluded 'other', the past can be effectively, and affectively, used to mobilise people in support of extreme and far-right identitarian politics. Interpretations of the past are at the heart of the emotional components of far-right political discourse.

These uses of the past are visible, too, in discourse surrounding far-right acts of violence. The far-right extremists responsible for the 2011 Oslo and Utøya attacks and the 2019 Christchurch attacks each referred to the 1683 breaking of the Ottoman siege of Vienna in material surrounding their actions. The Norway attacker produced a manifesto entitled *2083: A European Declaration of Independence*. The Christchurch attacker wrote a series of names, places, and dates onto his weaponry, including '1683 Vienna'. While the Siege of 1683 represents a moment in a long and complex to-and-fro between multiple empires and interests, in far-right discourse the moment is reduced to a moment of victory for white, Christian Europe against a non-white and non-Christian other. The use of this particular moment has not emerged from the ether, but rather it forms part of the frequent use of this moment across far-right networks, encompassing extremist blog sites, the Identitarian movement, and more mainstream far-right parties such as the Freedom Party of Austria (see Farrell-Banks 2021; Wodak and Forchtner 2014). These groups find potency in their use of this moment because they see it as representing a clear, racist vision of European identity. Europe, according to this narrative, is white and Christian. This was reinforced in 1683, and these groups are those who will stand up for this form of European identity in the present. This position is enhanced by the construction of a group belonging, which suggests a direct connection between past and present. It seeks to construct a sense of ancestry.

While the uses of 1683 represent an extreme example, references to Christianity as representing a 'shared European heritage' are frequent in the discourse of European far-right, nationalist, and right-wing populist parties (De Cesari, Bosilkov, and Piacentini 2020: 29). The far-right Identitare Bewegung Österreich (IBO; Identitarian Movement Austria), for example, link their nationalist ideology to the protection of 'traditional values', with these values presented as tied to a Christian heritage. These groups seek to attach cultural symbols of Christianity to their constructed notion of a legitimate national or transnational (European and white-colonial) superiority. Those who fit into these cultural brackets are allowed to belong, while others are excluded and identified as illegitimate. PA have echoed this tactic, arguing that to be 'white-European' (noting that to be European, for these groups, is necessarily a white identity) involves experience of Christian cultural traditions. This connection to a cultural identity is reinforced through interaction with heritage, through visits to sites such as ruined churches and campaigns to preserve existing churches. Again, an exclusionary vision of identity is given legitimacy through the use of heritage and archaeology.

The ubiquity with which the past emerges in far-right discourse presents a challenge to archaeology, heritage, and museum researchers and practitioners alike. Within heritage research, the past is often viewed relationally, or as an assemblage (Macdonald 2013; Harrison et al. 2020; Chidgey 2018). We have to ask, therefore, how we view pasts utilised in far-right discourse in relation to their emergence within archaeology and heritage discourse. This line of questioning brings researchers in these sectors into contact with the far and extreme right. It also necessitates a questioning of our practice.

Archaeology and ancestry

The use of ancestry and inheritance, too, has been at the heart of the recruitment tactics of far-right groups in the United Kingdom. Patriotic Alternative has focused campaigning around natural heritage and conservation of what it calls 'our national inheritance', with an indistinct relationship between natural and cultural heritage in its sense of nationhood and perceived threats from immigration. During the UK COVID-19 lockdowns of 2020 and 2021, the organisation turned to nature hikes, outdoor physical fitness, or visits to heritage sites as group activities to encourage new recruits. The connection between landscape, the past, and constructions of collective identity by PA reflects the use of the notion of *Heimat* by the IBÖ, with *Heimat* referring not just to homeland, but a mythologised connection between physical landscape and national identity.

For PA, recent campaigning has concentrated on changing demographics in the UK, and what it perceives to be 'white replacement' by 2066. Its so-called Demographic Replacement Awareness Month of April (DRAMA) has focused attention on delivering leaflets about the effects of immigration and refugees, identifying threats from immigrants to everything from transport to white British culture. The organisation also offers what it calls an 'alternative curriculum' in order that white British children might 'appreciate their rich ancestral heritage' (Patriotic Alternative 2022). This includes resources such as 'Be Proud of Your People', 'The People of England', and 'Who Were the Anglo-Saxons?' Threaded throughout these resources and campaign literature is a resolute belief in the exclusively white ownership of human activity in the past on these islands. From language, art, and literature to engineering success and historic monuments, all are carefully woven into the narrative of ancestry, natural inheritance, and belonging.

In the UK public consciousness, ancestry and heritage appear to be fundamentally linked. Biology and nationhood are often presented as forged in the European mediaeval period – an era which saw multiple migrations across Europe. The advent of the notion of 'Germanic' cultural influence from the continent in these islands is the result of the direction of travel of historiography during the expansion of the British imperial, and German unification and imperial expansion (Harland and Freidrich 2020). Terminology such as 'Anglo-Saxon', used to describe the ethnicity of the population of what is now England in the early mediaeval period, has a long and uncritical history in the Anglosphere. The mapping of contemporary ethnic identity onto archaeological sites and monuments, material culture, and peoples from the past, such as Germanic or 'Celtic' cultures, is inherently problematic. However, this misconception can still be seen in everyday life in the National Curriculum for schools in England, popular history books, TV programmes, and even museum displays. Perceptions of an unbroken continuity between the ethnic identity of 'ancestral' populations and modern populations are commonplace, and almost always unchallenged.

Recent research in the field of mediaeval studies has demonstrated that the term 'Anglo-Saxon' is 'an identity label associated with whiteness and is often the self-identification preferred by white supremacists' (Wilton 2020: 425). Work by Allfrey (2021), Lomuto (2020), Rambaran-Olm et al. (2020), Whitaker (2015), and others to challenge the use of the term has met with resistance from many academic archaeologists in the UK (Clarke et al. 2019; Williams 2020). Despite Clark's (1966: 173) warnings of the 'obsessive and dangerous' misunderstandings of prehistory, it seems that it is only in the past few years that archaeologists have started to investigate how the public, and particular interest groups, make use of their work. In both traditional and social media, archaeology is used 'to draw parallels, support arguments and define personal and national identities' (Brophy 2018: 3). It is, then, difficult to know how to wean our national misunderstanding of the relationship between material culture and exclusionary mythologised ethnicity, when many experts in these fields are unable or unwilling to appreciate the penetrative effects of centuries of ethnonationalism and exploitation of these misconceptions by the far right.

The ubiquity of social media platforms has enabled the spread of these myths and biases to a wider and international audience, many of whom are unwilling to engage critically with tropes about ancestry and nationhood. The mythologising of ancestry and landscape, and their relationship to 'belonging', evoke strong emotions, and this is hard to challenge with science and nuance in the post-truth era (Allfrey 2021). The sense of belonging facilitated by this mythologised shared ancestry can aid in giving groups confidence to engage in political action (Guibernau 2013). Ruth Wodak (2015) outlines how this operates in far-right political discourse, where past events are used to instigate political action in the present. Research into digital discourse on archaeological sites, heritage, and national identity (Bonacchi et al. 2018; Bonacchi and Krzyzanska 2021; Bonacchi 2022; Booth and Richardson 2017; Farrell-Banks 2023; Richardson and Pickering 2021) provides an abundance of evidence for bad-faith actors using archaeological work to discuss issues such as race and ethnicity, attitudes to migration, and to promote concepts of an ethno-state and racial superiority. The complex relationship between understandings of ethnic identity in the present and 'ancient DNA is misunderstood, over-simplified' such that it finds potent use in 'nationalist narratives' that 'support ideas of white supremacy' (Richardson and Booth 2017: 2).

The concept of national identity and ancestry has special importance in these digital discussions. Ownership of the present landscape, by way of ancestral links, is used as a device to support discussions of British and English exceptionalism. Archaeological sites and heritage are used to harness discussions of British cultural and technical superiority and individualism both in the past, from ancestral 'precociousness', or in the present, because of inheritance of these traits through DNA or 'blood ties' to past cultural groups.

The imaginary pasts of neo-Nazi identitarian groups exploit numerous symbols, sites, and characters from history, be they early medieval folk heroes, old gods, runic script, or battle dates. The IBÖ carry banners to historic leaders in their march to 'commemorate' the end of the 1683 Siege of Vienna. Biographies of these figures are presented through social media to connect these events to a global audience. Even deep, prehistoric pasts such as that of Stonehenge are somehow connected to national identities and belonging in the present. Complex narratives about life, death, and migration in the past become reduced to a linear sense of ancestry, with each appropriated and adapted version of the past legitimising the exceptionalism of a particular in-group in the present. The fact that these versions of the past reflect centuries of establishment mythologising does not seem to matter.

Reflections

To return to the central focus of this book, there is a series of ethical challenges that emerge from the increased focus and attention to far-right uses of the past. Firstly, and primarily, there is an urgent need for those of us working in the public presentation of the past to recognise and acknowledge how these versions of the past are used in the present. These uses of heritage can contribute to very real damage in everyday life, from the horrific immigration policies of the present Conservative government to state-endorsed decisions about the retention of memorials to slave traders. The wealth of research outlined above is a testament to an increasing recognition of these uses of the past in some academic and professional circles. This has been reflected in recent conference proceedings, where discussions of archaeology, heritage, museums, and the far right or nationalism have been on the increase. There has, too, been increased focus on the colonial and racist history that sits at the heart of British archaeology, heritage, and museums, through recent works such as Orson Nava's documentary *Decolonising the Curatorial Process* (2021), Olivette Otele's *African European: An Untold Story* (2020), Dan Hicks' *The Brutish Museums* (2020), and Corinne Fowler's *Green Unpleasant Land* (2020). Janes and Sandell's Museum Activism collection (2019) has given greater focus to the activist work already taking place within institutions across the country, while Subhadra Das and Miranda Lowe (2018) have shown how decolonial approaches can be applied to natural history collections, as much as human pasts.

However, this work continues to emerge from academic and professional fields that are severely lacking in diversity. In the 2019–20 Profiling the Profession survey, 97 per cent of archaeologists working in the United Kingdom were white, with no statistically significant progress since similar studies in 2012–13, 2007–08, and 2002–03 (Aitchison, German, and Rocks-Macqueen 2021). The stasis within archaeology is counter to an increasing diversity in the UK workforce in its entirety. The story is similar within the museum sector. In 2017–18, just 5 per cent of staff at major museums in England identified as Black or from minoritised communities – better representation than present in archaeology, but still lower than the full breadth of Arts Council England organisations (12 per cent) and the wider British population (16 per cent). These figures will likely not be a surprise to readers who work within or are familiar with the sector. It is a whiteness clearly visible at conferences, clearly at play in the lack of willingness to engage with complex debates around the terminology outlined above and, it should be acknowledged, reflected in the authorship of this piece and a significant portion of the academic work referenced. We still have work to do.

Museum Detox, a network for people of colour working in museums, galleries, libraries, archives, and heritage, campaign to 'enable a sector where the workforce and audience is reflective of the UK's 21st century population' (Museum Detox 2022). This necessary work has drawn greater attention to the lack of diversity in the sector and, importantly, its impacts on the stories told by museums and heritage sites and the audiences who visit these sites. In the sections above we outlined how frequently archaeology, heritage, and the past are mobilised within the discourse of the far right. While it is important to avoid an exaggeration and potential mainstreaming of these uses of the past, there is an ethical duty within the sector to consider how narratives presented might be used beyond the edges of the archaeological/ heritage site or the museum. This requires an unpicking of the dominant whiteness of the sector and the narratives produced. While some of this work is taking place, it is necessary that this comes hand in hand with changes across the sector.

This links to a second ethical challenge. As the level of research which engages directly with the politics of the past increases, support structures within universities need to adapt and update to reflect these changes in practice. Personal experience has brought home to us the pressures that come from researching or engaging with some political uses of the past. The use of social media platforms has had a profound impact on how museums and academic archaeologists and historians manage and share their work through these media. However, there are hidden costs to digital public discourse. Many scholars working and undertaking public engagement in this field have experienced online harassment, trolling, and abuse from far-right actors. Online abuse by non-archaeologists during academic public engagement, online or in person, remains commonplace (Perry et al. 2015; Richardson 2018; Richardson and Hobbs, personal communication). Archaeologists, historians, and other academic scholars working at the intersection of heritage and society who critique the mythologising of the past risk misinterpretation, attempts at professional damage, and even the threat of physical harm when engaging with the public through social media, and there is a vulnerability to any public-facing research. In the Netherlands, politically engaged historians have seen their homes targeted with posters that warn them: "you are being watched" (Matthews 2021). Professor

Corinne Fowler has spoken of threats received from the far right following the publishing of an interim National Trust report on links between their properties and histories of colonialism and slavery (Doward 2020). These threats are exacerbated by the actions of the national right-wing press and government officials. Nadine Dorries, Culture Secretary under Boris Johnson's prime ministership, had previously complained about "left wing snowflakes [...] tearing down historic statues, removing books from universities [...] and suppressing free speech" (Demianyk 2017). Her predecessor, Oliver Dowden, had called on museums to notify the government of any activities relating to the interpretation of historical statues, with a thinly veiled threat to funding if museums did not comply (Museums Association 2020). Since leaving his post, Dowden has complained of "woke psychodrama" (Mason 2022) in the United Kingdom. These cynical comments reflect a government discourse that adds significant risks and pressures to researchers across the United Kingdom.

If we accept that: (a) the past is political, (b) far-right uses of the past are worthy of attention, and (c) this is a necessary area of research, then we must make sure that the conditions are in place to allow this research to take place. The risks outlined here, and the associated vulnerabilities, will be felt even more starkly by people of colour or other marginalised groups who raise their voices. There is a challenge in making minority researchers feel protected and safe within the heritage, archaeology, and museums research environment, particularly when these environments are so white-dominant. Claims of mythical ancestral pasts are far from harmless and have real-world effects. We desperately need a better understanding of the practical and emotional effects of targeted abuse on academic researchers engaged in this type of work, especially scholars of colour. We need to advocate for the implementation of institutional anti-abuse policies and well-being provisions to support those targeted. This work will also highlight the need for platforms to do more to act against abusive behaviour in online spaces. Most of all, we need to find better ways to actively challenge the claims of superior ancient ancestors. We have to bring public attention and nuance to discussions of victorious past migrations by warlike Germanic tribes and openly condemn claims of so-called 'indigenous rights' to inhabit these islands.

References

Aitchison, K., German, P. and Rocks-Macqueen, D. 2021. *Profiling the Profession*. London: Landward Research Ltd.s

Allfrey, F. 2021. 'Ethnonationalism and Medievalism: Reading Affective "Anglo-Saxonism" Today with the Discovery of Sutton Hoo', *Postmedieval*, 12, 75–99.

Bonacchi, C. 2022. *Heritage and Nationalism: Understanding Populism through Big Data*. London: UCL Press.

Bonacchi, C., Altaweel, M., and Krzyzanska, M. 2018. 'The Heritage of Brexit: Roles of the Past in the Construction of Political Identities through Social Media', *Journal of Social Archaeology*, 18(2), 174–192.

Bonacchi, C. and Krzyzanska, M. 2021. 'Heritage-Based Tribalism in Big Data Ecologies: Deploying Origin Myths for Antagonistic Othering', *Big Data & Society*, 8(1).

Brophy, K. 2018. 'The Brexit Hypothesis and Prehistory', *Antiquity*, 92(366), 1650–1658.

Chidgey, R. 2018. *Feminist Afterlives: Assemblage Memory in Activist Times*. Basingstoke: Palgrave Macmillan.

Clark, G. 1966. 'The Invasion Hypothesis in British Prehistory', *Antiquity*, 40, 172–89.

Clarke, C., Dockray-Miller, M., Hines, J., Jayatilaka, R., Rambaran-Olm, M., Rauer, C., ... and Williams, H. 2019. 'Should British Archaeology Stop Using "Anglo-Saxon"?', *British Archaeology*, 170, 24–29.

Das, S. and Lowe, M. 2018. 'Nature Read in Black and White: Decolonial Approaches to Interpreting Natural History Collections', *Journal of Natural Science Collections*, 6, 4–14.

Davis, G. and Lawrence, D. 2021. *Patriotic Alternative: Britain's Fascist Threat*. London: Hope Not Hate.

De Cesari, C. and Kaya, A. 2020. *European Memory in Populism: Representations of Self and Other*. Abingdon: Routledge.

De Cesari, C., Bosilkov, I., and Piacentini, A. 2020. '(Why) Do Eurosceptics Believe in a Common European Heritage?' In: De Cesari, C. and Kaya, A. (eds). *European Memory in Populism*. Abingdon: Routledge, 26–46.

Demianyk, G. 2017. 'Nadine Dorries Thinks "Left-Wing Snowflakes" Are "Dumbing Down Panto" and People Are Done', *Huffington Post*, 27 December. https://www.huffingtonpost.co.uk/entry/nadine-dorries-panto_uk_5a43bc80e4b0b0e5a7a417a7 (accessed 20 February 2023).

Doward, J. 2020. 'I've Been Unfairly Targeted, Says Academic at Heart of National Trust "Woke" Row', *The Guardian*, 20 December. https://www.theguardian.com/uk-news/2020/dec/20/ive-been-unfairly-targeted-says-academic-at-heart-of-national-trust-woke-row (accessed 20 February 2023).

Farrell-Banks, D. 2020. '1215 in 280 Characters: Talking about *Magna Carta* on Twitter'. In: Galani, A., Mason, R., and Arrigoni, G. (eds). *European Heritage, Dialogue and Digital Practices*. Abingdon: Routledge, 86–103.

Farrell-Banks, D. 2021. 'Crossing Borders and Building Walls in Right-Wing Uses of the Past', *Anthropological Journal of European Cultures*, 30(1), 104–113.

Farrell-Banks, D. 2023. *Affect and Belonging in Political Uses of the Past*. Abingdon: Routledge.

Fowler, C. 2020. *Green Unpleasant Land: Creative Responses to Rural England's Colonial Connections*. London: Peepal Tree Press.

Frieman, C. J. and Hofmann, D. 2019. 'Present Pasts in the Archaeology of Genetics, Identity, and Migration in Europe: A Critical Essay', *World Archaeology*, 51(4), 528–545.

Guibernau, M. 2013. *Belonging: Solidarity and Division in Modern Societies.* Cambridge: Polity.

Hakenbeck, S. E. 2019. 'Genetics, Archaeology and the Far Right: An Unholy Trinity', *World Archaeology*, 51(4), 517–527.

Harland, J. M. and Friedrich, M. 2020. 'Introduction: The "Germanic" and Its Discontents'. In: Friedrich, M. and Harland, J. M. (eds). *Interrogating the 'Germanic': A Category and Its Use in Late Antiquity and the Early Middle Ages.* Berlin: Walter de Gruyter GmbH, 1–18.

Harrison, R., DeSilvey, C., Holtorf, C., Macdonald, S., Bartolini, N., Breithoff, E., Fredheim, H., Lyons, A., May, S., Morgan, J., and Penrose, S. 2020. *Heritage Futures: Comparative Approaches to Natural and Cultural Heritage Practices.* London: UCL Press.

Hicks, D. 2020. *The Brutish Museums: The Benin Bronzes, Colonial Violence and Cultural Restitution.* London: Pluto Press.

Hope Not Hate. 2023. *State of Hate 2023: Rhetoric, Racism and Resentment.* London: Hope Not Hate. https://hopenothate.org.uk/2023/02/26/state-of-hate -2023-rhetoric-racism-and-resentment/ (accessed 20 February 2023).

Janes, R. R. and Sandell, R. (eds). 2019. *Museum Activism.* Abingdon: Routledge.

Kohl, P. L., and Fawcett, C. P. (eds). 1995. *Nationalism, Politics, and the Practice of Archaeology.* Cambridge: Cambridge University Press.

Kølvraa, C. 2019. 'Embodying "the Nordic Race": Imaginaries of Viking Heritage in the Online Communications of the Nordic Resistance Movement', *Patterns of Prejudice*, 53(3), 270–284.

Lomuto, S. 2020. 'Becoming Postmedieval: The Stakes of the Global Middle Ages', *Postmedieval*, 11, 503–512.

Macdonald, S. 2013. *Memorylands: Heritage and Identity in Europe Today.* Abingdon: Routledge.

Mason, R. 2022. 'Tory Chairman Says "Painful Woke Psychodrama" Weakening the West', *The Guardian*, 14 February. https://www.theguardian.com/politics /2022/feb/14/oliver-dowden-says-painful-woke-psychodrama-weakening-the -west (accessed 20 February 2023).

Matthews, D. 2021. '"Anti-Left" Group Targets Dutch Academics with Home Visits', *Times Higher Education*, 7 April. https://www.timeshighereducation.com/news/ anti-left-group-targets-dutch-academics-home-visits (accessed 12 October 2023).

Museum Detox. 2022. *About Us.* https://www.museumdetox.org/museumdetox -about-us (accessed 20 February 2023).

Museums Association. 2020. *Our Response to Oliver Dowden's Letter on Contested Heritage.* https://www.museumsassociation.org/campaigns/ethics/our-response -to-oliver-dowdens-letter/ (accessed 20 February 2023).

Nava, O. 2021. *Decolonising the Curatorial Process.* https://vimeo.com/464558806 (accessed 20 February 2023).

Niklasson, E. and Hølleland, H. 2018. 'The Scandinavian Far-Right and the New Politicisation of Heritage', *Journal of Social Archaeology*, 18(2), 121–148.

Otele, O. 2020. *African Europeans: An Untold History.* London: Hurst & Company.

Patriotic Alternative. 2022. 'Alternative Curriculum'. https://www.patrioticalter native.org.uk/alternative_curriculum (accessed 30 October 2023).

Perry, S., Shipley, L. and Osborne, J. 2015. 'Digital Media, Power and (In)equality in Archaeology and Heritage', *Internet Archaeology*, 38.

Rambaran-Olm, M., Breann Leake, M., and Goodrich, M. J. 2020. 'Medieval Studies: The Stakes of the Field', *Postmedieval*, 11, 356–370.

Richardson, L.-J. 2018. 'Ethical Challenges in Digital Public Archaeology', *Journal of Computer Applications in Archaeology*, 1(1), 64–73.

Richardson, L. and Booth, T. 2017. 'Response to "Brexit, Archaeology and Heritage: Reflections and Agendas"', *Papers from the Institute of Archaeology*, 27(1), Art. 25.

Richardson, L. and Pickering, T. 2021. 'What's the Meaning of Stonehenge', *Epoiesen: A Journal for Creative Engagement with Archaeology and History*. https://doi.org/10.22215/epoiesen/2021.7 (accessed 16 October 2023).

Sommer, U. 2017. 'Archaeology and Nationalism'. In: Moshenska, G. (ed.), *Key Concepts in Public Archaeology*. London: UCL Press, 166–186.

Whitaker, C. 2015. 'Making Race Matter in the Middle Ages', *Postmedieval*, 6.

Williams, H. 2020. 'The Fight for "Anglo Saxon"', *Aeon*, 29 May. https://aeon.co/essays/why-we-should-keep-the-term-anglo-saxon-in-archaeology (accessed 20 February 2023).

Wilton, D. 2020. 'What Do We Mean by Anglo-Saxon? Pre-Conquest to the Present', *The Journal of English and Germanic Philology*, 119(4), 425–454.

Wodak, R. 2015. *The Politics of Fear: What Right-Wing Populist Discourses Mean*. London: Sage.

Wodak, R. and Forchtner, B. 2014. 'Embattled Vienna 1683/2010: Right-Wing Populism, Collective Memory and the Fictionalisation of Politics', *Communication*, 13(2), 231–255.

Yahya, A. 2005. 'Archaeology and Nationalism in the Holy Land'. In: Pollock, S. and Bernbeck, R. (eds). *Archaeologies of the Middle East: Critical Perspectives*. London: Wiley Blackwell, 66–77.

13

Another way to do ethics: uses of the landscape in the far-right cultural milieu and the ethics of researching them

Andrew Fergus Wilson

Introduction

This chapter asks researchers to consider a broader ethical framework than is typically addressed when approaching their work. 'Ethics' is typically a procedural engagement that reflects on the risks of the research to participant(s) and researcher(s). Whilst there is always a political dimension to all research in the field of extremism studies – and related areas across the human sciences – the broader ethical setting is the inadmissibility of the extreme ideologies under study. Having produced work concerned with delineating aspects of far-right ideology that draw on conspiracy theories, millennial beliefs, folklore, and minority religions, I found myself reflecting on the purpose of the work aside from adding to the growing mini-industry in academic work doing similar things. And I arrived at this ethical question: what is the work *for*?

Is it enough to expose, explore, and explain, or should the work be conducted in order to discover possible countermeasures? In other words, it is not enough to write history in the hope that others may learn from it but to show *how* they can learn from it. It is argued here that by delineating the repertoire of beliefs and cultural practices associated with, but not exclusive to, extremist ideologies, strategies for intervening in their attempts to mainstream their ideas can be devised. It is in the promotion of forms of resistance to the spread of extremist ideology in the communities in which they are active that a wider ethical framing of extremism research can be understood.

This chapter explores these questions through the relatively narrow focus of the language and discourses that are used to describe and engage with 'the countryside' and 'landscape'. It does so through an analysis of the use of the countryside by Patriotic Alternative (PA) in both their public statements and public actions. Patriotic Alternative have been chosen due to their increasing presence in the far-right scene, the presence among their membership of former members of the banned terrorist organisation National Action, and their attempts to gain wider public acceptance for their ideology of hate. Hope Not Hate have described them as having "reinvigorated British fascism" (Davis, Lawrence, and Mulhall 2021: 9). It is their use of the countryside as a cultural signifier of their ethnonationalism that will form the focus of the subsequent discussion.

Culture, folklore, landscape

It has been well known since the interventions of Alain de Benoist that the far right has waged a cultural war. Benoist's ideas have been seen as influencing an ideological shift among the far right that emphasises discrete regional European identities within a homogeneous pan-European community; this shift places identity (and thus culture) at the heart of anti-immigrant politics rather than race (and thus blood). Benoist's influence is explored in detail by Tamir Bar-On (2007, 2008, 2013) and Alberto Spektorowski (2003, 2007, 2012). Academic work that comments on, critiques, unpacks, and negates far-right ideology is therefore involved in an ongoing struggle over the extent to which culture and identity are maintained as open and inclusive. To imagine academic work to be dispassionate and unconnected from the cultural sphere is to cede ground without contestation. Thus, the question that I confronted in my work was: how can this understanding of, say, the millennialist impulses of David Lane's Wotanism be of use in stemming – or at least contesting – the spread of the politics of hate (Wilson 2013)? And, let's be clear, this needs to be part of our ethical concerns. We should not only ask ourselves as researchers if we have followed correctly the institutional or disciplinary ethical processes associated with our chosen methodologies, but also: have we made clear the use to which our work may be put?

This chapter will address this question through a reflection on a wider ethical commitment to using research as a means to counter far-right extremism. It develops themes raised by earlier research exploring far-right usage of 'the folkloresque' in the appropriation and vernacular restaging of extant and reimagined religious iconography and concepts (Wilson 2021). Acting as a precursor to further work, this chapter develops the key theme of the incursion of far-right groups and individuals into folkloric practices with a particular focus on landscape and 'the countryside'. Here, then, the intention of the far right is to limit access to the countryside as a resource that contributes to stories about origin and belonging: to produce folklore and myth that connects the land to a single cultural identity. This, of course, coincides with Nazi and neo-Nazi articulations of racial nationalism around 'blood and soil'. Thus, this chapter will argue that a broader ethical agenda needs to address the role of intellectual work in amplifying alternate and disruptive 'lore' that dynamically remakes the countryside as an open and free space, in a folklore that is continually being told and retold in inclusive and diverse voices.

This use of the land in the racial nationalist milieu is commonplace. For instance, Dan Stone (2004) outlined, and Roger Cutting (2016) expanded upon, 'indigenous organic fascism' in the 1930s. Emily Turner-Graham (2020) has written about the place of nature and the environment in British National Party materials; and Amy Hale (2011) has analysed the resonance between John Michell's Earth Mysteries, the 'New Age', and right-wing Paganism. This chapter situates current far-right 'land-making' activity within this milieu. In doing so, the chapter will demonstrate the importance of recognising the ongoing and open-ended work of engaging with an enchanted landscape that makes available the sacred landscape as a heterodox and multi-faith resource that offers multiple places of meaning within its open spaces. As such, it will explore ethnonationalist use of the rhetoric of indigeneity as context-driven situated knowledge that requires an active, targeted response.

Research ethics and the ethics of writing

In making this suggestion, it draws attention to a broader point about the ethics at work here. To research the far right and to do so ethically raises broader questions than those typically inferred by discussions of 'research ethics' *per se*. There is a tendency to frame questions of ethics within the instrumental tendencies that result from the ethical frameworks required by the institutional setting of most research. Universities, professional organisations, think tanks, and funding bodies typically frame ethical concerns in discourses of risk: to researchers, research subjects, institutional reputation, and so on. Berger (2019) also points out that when funding for research is won from governments or commercial sources, such as social media platforms, their agendas may skew the character and balance of the research. Clearly, although there is scope for discussion of the ways in which these frameworks might better enable or protect researchers of extremism and their subjects, the importance of this aspect of ethical reflection is necessary and apposite. In the case of the work from which this chapter is derived, research has meant drawing predominantly on the Patriotic Alternative (PA) webspaces. The group are a straightforwardly ethnonationalist organisation that seeks to promote a racist agenda. By posting as representatives of the group, all contributors do so understanding the politics and position of the space to which they are contributing. Despite the best efforts of racists and their sympathisers, there is still sufficient stigma associated with ethnonationalism for most of the contributors to hide behind assumed names. Whilst the leaders of PA operate under their real names as the organisation's 'public figures', the most frequently recurrent voices are those of members hiding behind assumed names.

So in terms of the institutional ethics of the university or the funding council, there is a necessary discussion to be had here. But I would like to suggest that in focusing on these typifying ethical questions there are other, more searching ethical considerations that are sometimes overlooked. What we tend to focus on are the instrumental concerns of ethics. But what of the ethical role of the intellectual? Here, I mean the wider, Gramscian understanding of the idea of the organic intellectual – the active thinker and organiser who is concerned with the role of ideas in a field of contestation. This is the idea of contestation I referred to in the introductory paragraphs. As a researcher contributing to the field of research on the far right, I know that they seek to win over converts to their ideology by promoting a distorted version of British folklore. Is it enough to point out the distortions? Or can we do more by demonstrating how these distortions can be countered and how the extremist ideological reading can be undone? I am arguing here that it is important that we, as researchers, continually reflect on this wider ethical role. It is in this understanding of ethics, of the wider 'good' as opposed to what is institutionally 'right', critical instead of instrumental reason, that many of us orient ourselves to the study of extremism. To reveal its mechanisms, networks and tactics is work that is ethically satisfying and necessary in this sense.

The work, in and of itself, is an ethical endeavour. Although there is an ongoing discussion about the exact nature of 'the good', there is, at least, the possibility of a shared assumption that 'we' (as heterogeneous as we may be) have common goals: to work against the propagation of extremism, especially that which seeks to systemise division, to make barriers to citizenship, and to diminish or eliminate outgroups and whole communities. In so doing, such work contributes to the undoing of what Paul Gilroy describes as "modernity's insistence that the true, the good, and the beautiful had distinct origins and belong to different domains of knowledge" (Gilroy 1993: 39). That he situates the sundering of these domains of knowledge in the dis-ease in Enlightenment thought brought about by the centrality of slavery in the development of European thought, social, cultural, and economic life should make evident its relevance here.

One of the things Gilroy shows us in *The Black Atlantic* is the importance of recognising that folk cultures are a constituent part of the working through of experiences that have no other outlet. The remaking of the world through Black folk cultures' retelling of it offers at once a mechanism for communal resilience but also a means of building an "alternative body of cultural and political expression" (1993: 39). For Gilroy, Black music cultures have integrated politics and ethics in a mode of expression that incorporates the Black diaspora into a rearticulation of humanity's story of itself. To extend these ends to the current context entails being engaged with the ethical dimension, asking how to better frame our questions, reflecting on the ends to which we are working, and in whose interests, as a simultaneously political endeavour – in short, to consciously reintegrate the work into the whole of social life. In spite of the symbolic ruptures that would separate intellectual work from social contexts ('anti-intellectualism' or, in contrast, the closed worlds of the ivory towers' own echo chambers), the production of knowledge is an engaged public endeavour. Ethical awareness of this is evident in the concerns over researcher safety (n.b. Massanari 2018) or over the exposure of research subjects. But is there more that can be done with the topographies of ideology, practice, and belief that are delineated through our findings? Here, there is an ethics, too.

How fascists pollute the land

Here, then, is a justification (and perhaps it will take another reflective piece to consider why I feel I need one) for spending the next few years talking to people from a variety of faith communities about what the countryside means to them. There is an established and growing literature concerned with geographies of belief (e.g. Park 1994; Stump 2008; Wynn 2009; Hopkins, Kong and Olson 2013; Matsui 2014) so there is no need to justify the project as such. Instead, I mean the ethical justification, a statement of ethical aims that address the 'good' whilst I'll leave the 'right' to the institutional frameworks within which it unfolds. There is not the space here to rehearse the full argument I will go on to make for the importance of the accretion of meaning taken on by 'the land' in human meaning systems. What will be familiar to those engaged with thinking about the land, place, and meaning in the study of extremism will be the heightened role 'the land' (scare quotes to signify the coupling of fantasies and geological physicality) plays in narratives of belonging and exclusivity among ethnonationalists: the enchanted land beneath the sacred canopy.

On the PA website, this theme is repeatedly underscored. The centrality of the connection between 'land', 'nature', and 'people' is made repeatedly. So, for instance, in an article published in May 2022, Fenek Solère writes a brief but rambling paean to anthropomorphised animals in English literature; inspired by an encounter with badgers under the moonlight, he cites Kenneth Grahame, C.S. Lewis, Aeron Clement, Richard Adams, A.A. Milne,

J.M. Barrie, and the Nazi sympathiser Arthur Bryant. Barrie's 'Neverland' is invoked as a warning against ceasing to believe, "Because it is only through activism that we will achieve our goals [...] For we will be robbed forever of the magical dreamscape conjured by Barrie of Peter Pan's Neverland if we do not fight for it" (Solère 2022a). Following this call to arms, Solère draws on Bryant's English exceptionalism as inspiration for such a fight.

Although bordering on whimsy, Solère's piece is usefully pertinent here. It makes clear the interwoven nature of the strands that I suggest can inform at least part of the underlying ethics of a consciously antifascist approach to research. For Solère, what is being contested is an imaginal realm in which the meaning of England (or, from Bryant, Albion, or Barrie's Neverland) is determined. This resolves and clarifies the actions in which Patriotic Alternative seek to have their symbols and banners stretched across the landscape, layering it with a strata of hate-filled exclusivity. But how to respond to this? It is not enough simply to call it out and identify the mechanisms of meaning-making and symbolic appropriation that are at work in these gestures but also to counter it, to leave no significatory space for racist or fascist interventions.

Intervening in open spaces

It is thus imperative that the countryside and the rural landscape are not abandoned as being overly marked by 'tradition' or allowed to be used as the basis for narratives of a romanticised past idyll. Clearly, these would make the symbolic appropriation sought by fascists like Solère all too easy. In this enfolding of discourses charged with fascism's palingenetic ultranationalism (Griffin 1991) into the signifying space of 'the rural', Ana Carolina Balthazar's reflections on meaning in nationalist constructions of time and space provide extensive opportunity for reflection (Balthazar 2021a, 2021b). Her study shows that in an enjoyment of 'the outside', in seaside towns, there is a pleasure in temporarily escaping from the instrumentalist rationalities of capitalism's incessant commodification of subjective time and space. Balthazar's following point is crucial here. She identifies the pleasure of unstructured meaning-making from spaces of (cultural) memory and the collective national imaginary:

> For example, certain appropriations of the national at the British seaside engender a temporal experience that challenges capitalist normative conceptions of time and productivity. In this sense, retired right-wing voters in Southeast England are in their own way performing some sort of cultural criticism and resisting the oppressive norms of capitalism. (Balthazar 2021b: 338)

So, in Balthazar (2021a), this is described in terms of hours spent wandering around charity shops, using objects in them as occasional and contingent mechanisms for reconstructing memory, and reminiscing about old music, fashions, and objects. It is 'wasted' time that is meaningful for the people who she accompanies as they recompose continuities between pasts and presents. But in what way is this ethical and how is it of relevance to the concerns of the present volume?

What Balthazar does is make her interlocutors complex. As older, white, working-class, Brexit-supporting people who bemoan the erosion of the 'character' of the seaside town of Margate, it is easy to imagine them dismissed as racist. Balthazar recognises that they are susceptible to nationalist rhetoric about culture and identity. She describes this in terms of an attempt to manage the space of national belonging that they feel to be theirs, "people who perceive themselves as authentically British feel some sort of privileged right over space and act as a sort of 'spatial manager', a person who feels entitled to push away 'intruders'" (2021a: 121). Clearly, in this, we can see a shared impulse with Solère to maintain a racial structuring of the nation's space through management of the character and composition of place. But this would be to overlook Balthazar's main insight. Her interlocutors fall into ethnonationalism as a retreat from local authority-backed gentrification and as a means of maintaining a hold on spatial and temporal meaning in a world remade by capital and its logic.

What Balthazar draws our attention to is the extent to which contestation over spatial and temporal meaning has combined with a sense of exclusion from processes of change that proceed without them. Following Evans (2017), she highlights in the 'left behind' narrative "how right-wing parties have attempted to 'inculcate' […] a sense of 'indigenous' entitlement among the white working class" (Balthazar 2021a: 124). We can see, here, a perception of white Britons as an 'indigenous' people acting as 'spatial managers' seeking to recompose 'empty time' with a (to them) recognisably 'English; character. The racist Patriotic Alternative repeatedly return to these themes: in their policy document, 'Immigration, Asylum, and Border Control', they explicitly link immigration to "large-scale destruction of the British countryside" (Patriotic Alternative nd: 2); in a typically rambling Fenek Solère article, an appeal to indigeneity is made, claiming Britain as "the land that is ours by right of inheritance" (Solère 2022b); a regular column on folklore plays on the idea of the sleeping hero in the land (Taliesin 2022). The examples continue throughout their materials and are most clearly evident in the 'White Lives Matter' banners displayed at multiple rural sites annually on 9 August, UNESCO's International Day of the World's Indigenous Peoples.

These strategic uses of the landscape by PA have multiple ends that tend to converge on the semiotic embedding of specific forms of whiteness onto and into the landscape. In so doing, there is an apparent confirmation of the reclamatory desire delineated by Balthazar in her engagement with Brexit voters in Margate. But should those individuals be aligned with PA? Balthazar (2021a; 2021b) describes her work as 'ethical' in the sense that she has treated her subjects as anthropological subjects and not as 'racists' or 'gammons'. And it is here that the ethical response proposed in the current chapter is hopefully clarified. The Kent seaside and the Derbyshire hills are both filled with memories of happiness and a 'time outside' the daily grind. The pleasure they offer is fleeting but it contributes to collective and individual culture, identity, and meaning. These are the faultlines which are weakened when history and memory are arranged around narrow and exclusive versions of 'the nation'.

Concluding comments

In a piece titled 'Subversion' that is concerned with LGBTQ+ and ethnic diversity in fantasy novels, Fenek Solère warns his readership of "A relentless and insidious campaign in the ongoing culture war that needs to be resisted at all costs" (Solère 2022c). Clearly, this is an effort worth making and the value of work like Balthazar's is in charting those domains of contestation where resistance to neoliberal empty time can be made. A further ethical demand, then, is that for the potential of the good to be fulfilled then those domains of contestation, such as – here – the landscape, need to be engaged with as living systems of vernacular meaning through which it can be shown how they might offer a meaningful alternative to the dead time of proto-fascist formations.

During the spring of 2021, not long after the end of COVID-19 restrictions in England and Wales, I took my kids for a walk in the White Peak region of the Peak District. On a hillside, overlooking Cromford, a short, nameless tributary of the Derwent emerges from a spring and trickles down into the main river after a few hundred yards. As we walked past, I could see a man teaching his children how to perform *wudu* (an Islamic ritual to mark physical and spiritual cleansing) in the stream. Months later, I was at Nine Ladies stone circle on Birchover Moor for the small, inclusive Winter Solstice celebration held there. In between these moments, Muslim Hikers had been formed with the aim of 'Championing diversity outdoors', joining other groups with similar aims such as Black Girls Hike UK CIC. Thinking about each of these, I was haunted by PA's 'White Lives Matter' banner on Mam Tor. And it struck me that as an academic, intellectual even, my work – which, I hope, contributes to the exposure and analysis of moments like the latter – also needs to address and incorporate the man enchanting the

Derbyshire countryside with his children; the pagan groups seeking to excise exclusivist appropriations of their rituals, practices, and locations of belief; faith and community groups undoing and remaking assumptions about who the countryside 'belongs to'. It is here that the 'subversion' Solère frets about takes place, and this is the ethical demand made here – to make difficult the claims to any cultural 'ownership' that the far right might seek to make. As is so frequently the case, their claims are spurious or false but this seldom seems to matter to their converts and followers. It is their appeal to the 'spatial managers' of a national imaginary that needs to be thwarted.

Although the story is contested (Rothman 2012; Hey 2011), it is fitting that the Peak District should repeatedly feature in this destabilisation of old prejudices about 'the land'. It was here that the first national park was formed in the aftermath of the 1932 Kinder Scout mass trespass. The trespass was organised by communist youth groups and led by Benny Rothman, the son of Jewish migrants from Eastern Europe. The groups travelled into the countryside by bus, rail, or bicycle. That this iconic story joins together the urban and the rural, working-class youth, immigrants, and left radicalism in a watershed moment for access to 'the land' still matters because who gets to claim that land as theirs continues to be contested. And, I'm suggesting here, it is there that our key ethical concerns remain.

References

Balthazar, A. C. 2021a. *Ethics and Nationalist Populism at the British Seaside Negotiating Character*. London: Routledge.

Balthazar, A. C. 2021b. 'Ethnography of the Right as Ethical Practice', *Social Anthropology Journal*, 29(2), 337–338.

Bar-On, T. 2007. *Where Have All The Fascists Gone?* Aldershot: Ashgate.

Bar-On, T. 2008. 'Fascism to the Nouvelle Droite: The Dream of Pan-European Empire', *Journal of Contemporary European Studies*, 16(3), 329–345.

Bar-On, T. 2013. *Rethinking the French New Right: Alternatives to Modernity*. London: Routledge.

Berger, J. M. 2019. *Researching Violent Extremism: The State of Play*. Washington, DC: RESOLVE Network.

Cutting, R. 2016. 'Reflections on Outdoor Education and English "Indigenous Organic Fascism" in the 1930s', *Journal of Adventure Education and Outdoor Learning*, 16(2), 105–116.

Davis, G., Lawrence, D., and Mulhall, J. 2021. *Patriotic Alternative: Britain's Fascist Threat*. London: Hope Not Hate.

Evans, G. 2017. 'Social Class and the Cultural Turn: Anthropology, Sociology and the Post-Industrial Politics of 21st Century Britain', *The Sociological Review Monographs*, 65, 88–104.

Gilroy, P. 1993. *The Black Atlantic: Modernity and Double Consciousness*. London: Verso.

Griffin, R. 1991. *The Nature of Fascism*. London: Routledge.

Hale, A. 2012. 'John Michell, Radical Traditionalism and the Emerging Politics of the Pagan New Right', *Pomegranate: The International Journal of Pagan Studies*, 13(1).

Hey, D. 2011. 'Kinder Scout and the Legend of the Mass Trespass', *The Agricultural History Review*, 59(2), 199–216.

Hopkins, P., Kong, L., and Olson, E. (eds). 2013. *Religion and Place: Landscape, Politics, and Piety*. London: Springer.

Massanari, A. L. 2018. 'Rethinking Research Ethics, Power, and the Risk of Visibility in the Era of the "Alt-Right" Gaze', *Social Media + Society*, 4(2). https://doi.org/10.1177/2056305118768302

Matsui, K. 2014. *Geography of Religion in Japan: Religious Space, Landscape, and Behaviour*. London: Springer.

Park, C. C. 1994. *Sacred Worlds: An Introduction to Geography and Religion*. London: Routledge.

Patriotic Alternative. n.d. 'Immigration, Asylum and Border Control'. https://assets.nationbuilder.com/patrioticalternative/pages/1432/attachments/original/1652267066/Point_Two_Immigration_Asylum_and_Border_Control.pdf?1652267066 (accessed 23 May 2022).

Rothman, B. (with Smith, R. and Waghorn, T.). 2012. *The Battle for Kinder Scout: Including the 1932 Mass Trespass*. Timperley: Willow.

Solère, F. 2022a. 'Neverland'. https://www.patrioticalternative.org.uk/neverland (accessed 20 May 2022).

Solère, F. 2022b. 'Raise the Shield Wall'. https://www.patrioticalternative.org.uk/_raise_the_shield_wall (accessed 24 May 2022).

Solère, F. 2022c. 'Subversion'. https://www.patrioticalternative.org.uk/subversion (accessed 22 May 2022).

Spektorowski, A. 2003. 'Ethnoregionalism: The Intellectual New Right and the Lega Nord', *Global Review of Ethnopolitics*, 2(3), 55–70.

Spektorowski, A. 2007. 'Ethnoregionalism, Multicultural Nationalism and the Idea of the European Third Way', *Studies in Ethnicity and Nationalism*, 7(3), 45–63.

Spektorowski, A. 2012. 'The French New Right: Multiculturalism of the Right and the Recognition-Exclusionism Syndrome', *Journal of Global Ethics*, 8(1), 41–61.

Stone, D. 2004. 'The Far Right and the Back to the Land Movement'. In: Gottlieb, J. V. and Linehan, T. P. (eds). *The Culture of British Fascism: Visions of the Far Right in Britain*. London: I. B. Tauris, 182–198.

Stump, R.W. 2008. *The Geography of Religion: Faith, Place, and Space*. Plymouth: Rowman & Littlefield.

Taliesin. 2022. 'Folklore on Friday: The Wizard of Alderley Edge'. https://www.patrioticalternative.org.uk/folklore_on_friday_the_wizard_of_alderley_edge (accessed 24 May 2022).

Turner-Graham, E. 2020. '"Protecting Our Green and Pleasant Land": UKIP, the BNP and a History of Green Ecology on Britain's Far Right'. In: Forchtner, B.

(ed.). *The Far Right and the Environment Politics, Discourse and Communication*. London: Routledge, 57–71.

Wilson, A. F. 2013. 'From Apocalyptic Paranoia to the Mythic Nation: Political Extremity and Myths of Origin in the Neo-Fascist Milieu'. In: Gibson, M., Trower, S., and Tregidga, G. (eds). *Mysticism, Myth and Celtic Identity*. London: Routledge, 199–215.

Wilson, A. F. 2021. '"Our Community Could Start Our Own Traditions": The Commingling of Religion, Politics and the Folkloresque in a Far-Right Groupuscule'. In Cheeseman, M. and Hart, C. (eds). *Folklore and Nation in Britain and Ireland*. London: Routledge, 246–261.

Wynn, M. R. 2009. *Faith & Place: An Essay in Embodied Religious Epistemology*. Oxford: Oxford University Press.

14

Researching memory and heritage during a culture war

Meghan Tinsley, Ruth Ramsden-Karelse,
Chloe Peacock, and Sadia Habib

In September 2020, the National Trust published a 115-page report on the historical connections to colonialism and slavery of its five hundred-plus properties. The foreword, by former trustee Gus Casely-Hayford, situated the project as part of the Trust's founding mission to "speak to, and for, everyone … to see the ongoing diversification, the broadening of those we serve, as being a core, consistent and unending goal" (Huxtable et al. 2020). The report, in other words, sought to make sense of history in a way that would be relevant to the public at large, across the lines of ethnicity, class, age, and political persuasion. By extension, both history and national heritage should belong to the public at large. Spotlighting histories of slavery and colonialism, the authors of the report said, would demonstrate the profoundly international character of national history and identify some ways in which Black and Asian visitors might have links to properties associated with elite, white owners.

Given the Trust's stated goal of appealing to a broader public, what happened next is particularly jarring. Immediately following the report's publication, MPs and Government ministers condemned the National Trust for straying from its mission. A group of twenty-six Conservative MPs accused the Trust of pandering to a leftist ideology, writing in *The Telegraph* that "a clique of powerful, privileged liberals must not be allowed to rewrite our history in their image" (Hope 2020a). The Heritage Minister, Nigel Huddleston, reported with thinly veiled delight that the Trust was "being bombarded with complaints from its members wanting it to focus on managing the beautiful houses and gardens and not the historic links to slavery and empire" (Hope 2020b). Indeed, at the Trust's annual general meeting on 19 September 2020, one member noted that they "just want to see beautiful houses and gardens, not have others' opinions pushed down their throats" (Hope 2020a). Another asked, "Why doesn't the Trust concentrate on their upkeep and stop being political? History is history – you will lose members and waste money" (Hope 2020a). Even more explicitly, one member claimed that they "wish to enjoy the properties gifted in good faith without having to endure the unfortunate woke agenda of the modern Trust management".

The report's authors were subjected to direct and personal attacks questioning their credentials, their political views, and their ability to write a 'neutral' report. The right-wing press joined the furore, with Simon Heffer (2020) writing in *The Telegraph* that "many more [members] could end up resigning, if members visit properties and are confronted with a tsunami of wokeness that impresses the sort of people who now run the Trust, but nauseates much of their clientele. The latter visit Trust properties for a recreational experience culminating in a cream tea, not to be lectured by a cultural thought police." The far-right backlash culminated in an official inquiry by the Charities Commission, which cleared the National Trust of any wrongdoing but cautioned that it should

> remain mindful of the opposing views and diverse opinions within its membership and wider society. Charities need to be constantly alert to the impact their actions may have on the people on whose support they rely – their beneficiaries, supporters, volunteers, members, donors – and be aware of the wide range of views and sensibilities that exist within the public on whose support all charities ultimately rely. (Stephenson 2021)

The embattled National Trust report illustrates the pitfalls of public-facing research on memory and heritage – which are compounded for Black and minority ethnic researchers. In Britain (though not only in Britain), imperial nostalgia, amnesia, and melancholia have produced a deeply fraught public memory of empire and slavery. Britain's ambivalent relationship with its own history is not new; however, amidst the mainstreaming of the far right, recent calls to decolonise the curriculum and to remove statues of colonisers and slavers from public space have met with a particularly violent response from certain sectors of the government and media. Increasingly, attempts to engage critically with the imperial past are framed as attacks on the nation and its history. In the context of this 'culture war', in early 2021 we embarked upon a five-country comparative study of contested statues that commemorate (and often celebrate) slavery and empire. In our interviews with activists and local stakeholders, workshops with young people, public engagement activities, and writing, we found that detached neutrality was neither desirable nor possible: memory, always contested, had become a prominent battlefield in the far right's 'culture war'. Consequently, researching memory is an inherently political project that is bound up with the contestation of past and present.

The changing shape of cultural activism

Between January and May 2021, in the wake of a global wave of anti-racist protests and punitive backlash, we conducted a comparative study of fifteen contested statues in five countries. Among them were a statue whose removal had propelled a global student movement (Cecil Rhodes in Cape Town), a statue that had garnered global attention despite its defenders' intransigence (Cecil Rhodes in Oxford), a statue that had become a locus for protests and a canvas for public art (Robert E. Lee in Richmond), a decapitated and bloodied statue that was toppled decades later (Josephine de Beauharnais in Fort-de-France), and a statue removed by the state after being set alight (Leopold II in Antwerp). Our goal was to trace the transnational trajectories and local particularities of anti-racist cultural activism (as well as patterns in the racist backlash), in the hope of identifying lessons for activists about which strategies were most likely to be effective.

From the outset, we aligned ourselves with the project of anti-racist cultural activism and hoped that our research would validate the dynamic contestation of statues. We sought to do this in two ways: first, by building a 'toolkit' of effective strategies where possible, and second, in the absence of such a toolkit, by demonstrating that there is no 'right way' to remove a statue in the eyes of far-right 'statue defenders'. We also sought to use our platform as academics to refute criticism of cultural activism and to equip activists with data about its effectiveness. Finally, we sought to provide spaces for young people to collectively explore the prevailing narratives about statues of empire and colonialism.

Across forty interviews, the participants in this study revealed that each case carries a distinctive history and politics. Similarly, the workshops with young people (aged eighteen to twenty-five, predominantly members of the Manchester Museum Our Shared Cultural Heritage Collective) highlighted the significance of context. We did, however, identify several themes that hold implications for cultural activism at large. First, memory is always contested, even when far-right narratives do not appear to focus on the past. In virtually all cases, activists had sought for years to remove a statue, and in many cases, various groups (and, even more frequently, generations) of activists had proposed different courses of action. In Richmond, for example, African-American lawmakers and journalists had publicly opposed the statue of Lee since its erection in 1890. Yet in 2020, the statue's supporters claimed that it was a fundamental and immovable piece of the city's heritage.

Second, statues reveal what matters to people in power. Alongside their material form, they are symbols of ideologies and policies. Consequently, when those in power resist calls to remove a statue of a slaver or coloniser, they will also resist challenges to white supremacy in governance, curricula, and the allocation of resources. Such was the case in Oxford, where the Rhodes Must Fall movement targeted the statue as a 'test case' of a larger set of demands, and met with entrenched opposition to even this simple gesture.

Third, and finally, the act of removing a statue is not an erasure of history. Rather, it *is* history. Removing a statue brings to light long-suppressed memories, and it makes activists agents who shape the present and future. In Fort-de-France, Martinique, for example, members of the elder generation of activists who had decapitated the statue of Josephine, and who had continually dabbed the neckline with red paint, celebrated its toppling in 2020. As one longstanding activist remarked, "They finished the job".

Researching cultural activism during a far-right 'culture war'

As a research team, we met biweekly to refine our approach, to report back from interviews, and to troubleshoot difficult situations as they arose. At the beginning of the research process, this entailed drafting an ethics application, including an interview protocol and distress protocol, and consulting with criminologist colleagues to determine how to protect our participants and ourselves in the event of any disclosure of illegal activities. Once we began conducting interviews, we shared difficult conversations – in particular, concerning our own positionalities and how we were perceived by participants. In the final few months of the project, we wrote summaries of each case study and began to collate emerging themes. The diversity of our case studies and participants, and the subjectivity of our own standpoints, made it challenging to draw any clear conclusions about the contestation of statues at large. Our conversations, however, pointed us to several critiques of research on memory and heritage that proved particularly salient during the political moment of a far-right 'culture war'.

As researchers affiliated with academic institutions and working on a government-funded project, we were compelled to demonstrate that our work was 'objective' (a term, and a concept, we grappled with during the research process) and methodologically sound. At stake were our perceived legitimacy as academic researchers, our access to potentially critical or defensive participants, and our ability to disseminate our findings and access future funding. For those of us who were racially minoritised, and who participated publicly in scholar-activism, the stakes were particularly high. The subject of our research, however, was deeply political, and the stakes were high for the people we interviewed. Further, we had undertaken this project in order to garner support for cultural activists and create spaces for important conversations, and our own politics were aligned with those who sought to challenge statues of slavers and colonisers. All of this meant that we had to think carefully about how we represented ourselves to participants and how we positioned our work in our academic and public-facing outputs. This took on an additional salience as we saw a growing number of academics targeted by far-right policymakers and members of the public for engaging with histories of empire and slavery.

Our interactions with activists and academics made us increasingly critical of any approach that emphasised the validity of 'both sides' of the issue. Whilst opponents and defenders of statues alike expressed strong views and claimed that the issue was important to them, the impact of the issue was felt unevenly. The reality of white supremacy meant that for racially minoritised people, their very humanity was at stake in the debate. Statues that celebrated slavery and colonialism also denigrated the people who had been oppressed by these systems and their legacies. Additionally, it became increasingly clear during the research process that power was aligned with those who sought to keep the statues in place. The statues had been erected by councils, states, and wealthy benefactors, and their successors maintained the sites decades or centuries later. In some instances, cultural activists had sought modest alterations to statues for years (e.g. in the case of Bristol's Colston statue, changing the wording of a plaque), only to be rebuffed by the statue's powerful defenders.

In rapid succession, a series of policy changes in Britain heightened the already acute disparities in political power and highlighted the mainstreaming of far-right narratives of the past. Robert Jenrick, the Communities Secretary, restricted the ability of councils to remove contested statues. Henceforth, whether or not a site is listed, a council must secure the agreement of Historic England before removing any statue. When the council and Historic England disagree, the Communities Secretary will have the final say. Since the implementation of this policy change, councils (Stroud, Gloucestershire) and other decision makers (Oriel College, Oxford) have cited their expectation of bureaucracy as an obstacle to action. In March 2021, an additional development further restricted the ability of cultural activists to act outside of legal channels: the government tabled the punitive Police, Crime, Sentencing, and Courts Bill, which would raise the maximum custodial sentence for damaging a statue from three months to ten years.

These policy changes meant that many of our participants would be risking custodial sentences for any future direct action, and they led us (and the media) to closely watch the prosecution of four activists involved in toppling the statue of Colston in Bristol. As we continued to interview stakeholders and analyse contested statues, we increasingly found the opportunity – and the obligation – to respond.

Listening to, and learning from, young people through a series of four workshops is a particular focus of our work, since young people were at the forefront of cultural activism during the amplification of Black Lives Matter in 2020. Emphasising young people also counters their marginalisation in public discussions of contested heritage; the young people valued the workshop series because of a lack of formal spaces to critically explore empire and colonialism. Young people recognise that dominant narratives of heritage elevate 'British values' at the expense of lived experiences of class and race (Habib 2018). Since the younger generation will gradually take on a larger role in memory politics, now is the time to grapple collectively with the intersections of memory and heritage with identity and belonging.

How should researchers respond?

As we continue to make sense of data, write up results, and disseminate outputs, we also reflect on the ethics of researching memory and heritage during a far-right 'culture war'. We have arrived at a (non-exhaustive) list of best practices, which we continue to revise in dialogue with our participants and each other.

Critique 'neutrality'

Post-imperial Britain is not 'neutral' on issues of race and racism; political, economic, and cultural institutions are bound up with histories of slavery and empire, and continue to perpetuate white supremacy today. As researchers, we interact with and belong to these same institutions, and our standpoints are shaped by our own ascribed identities and lived experiences. Within this environment, claiming detachment from the social systems that shape our case studies would be both inaccurate and undesirable. Instead, as our interviews progressed, we were increasingly explicit about our own backgrounds, our own political sympathies, and the purpose of our research.

With activists, this clarity about our own positionalities and perspectives helped to facilitate dialogue. On one occasion, an activist asked to see samples of our writing before agreeing to an interview. When we provided them with some of our public-facing outputs (which critiqued the criminalisation of cultural activism), they agreed to speak with us. In other instances, we remained in contact with participants following the interviews, shared a platform on public panels, and facilitated cross-national networking.

Foregrounding our own views was more challenging when working with research participants who were critical of activism. We decided at the outset of the project not to interview self-proclaimed 'statue defenders' or people who had expressed racist or threatening views. In so doing, we aligned ourselves with researchers who seek to produce and disseminate knowledge about the far right without amplifying these already dominant voices. Equally, we sought to protect the researchers' safety amidst the far right's targeting of academics. We felt it important, however, to access the perspectives of some of those who had been central to local decision-making processes and who may have sought to retain statues, to better understand the often complicated histories of contestation and some of the political, cultural and ideological factors at play. These encounters highlighted the difficulty of being transparent about our own positionalities and perspectives in this context.

Some potential research participants we contacted, who had been critical of the activism around their local statue, asked for reassurance that our research was 'totally impartial', concerned that we might only include the views of those supportive of removing statues. We explained that while we all have our own views that we bring to research on any topic, we were keen to include a variety of perspectives on the issue. This allowed us to proceed with interviews whilst being honest about our own positions.

Other issues arose in an interview with a local politician in Louisiana, who had headed a decision-making body that voted to retain a Confederate monument, in the face of a long-standing campaign by local residents for it to be removed. The conversation had felt somewhat tense, with the interviewee rather defensively stating his reasons for voting to keep the statue (which included the frequently heard claim that the Civil War was about states' rights, rather than slavery). As we were closing the interview, he asked the researcher's opinion of the statue. The researcher explained that in the UK context much contestation had centred on statues of figures who had played major roles in the slave trade or who made their fortunes from slave labour and that we were sympathetic to activists' assertions that these were not appropriate monuments for twenty-first-century public space. When the participant responded by minimising the historical significance of transatlantic slavery and its inherent connection to racism (stating that "slavery was an issue for thousands and thousands of years", that it had "happened everywhere", that white people had been enslaved, and that it was now irrelevant: "we've grown and we've got away from it, so just move on") it was clear that there was a deep gulf in understanding and political conviction. The interview ended shortly thereafter, without resolution. In such situations, political arguments may well be futile, but there is arguably an ethical imperative to be clear about our own commitments when it is safe to do so. Taking a neutral stance risks reinforcing, or being perceived to be complicit in, deeply troubling viewpoints.

Tell neglected and obscured stories

Statues are not factual records of history; rather, they set in stone the highly partial perspectives of their elite funders. By extension, statues erase memories and histories that contradict the narratives they enshrine. These may entail critical perspectives on the individuals that statues depict, associating oppression and violence with events that are publicly celebrated, or recalling histories that are neglected and forgotten by the dominant narrative. The pattern continues when statues are openly contested: in the context of a mainstreamed far right, people and institutions with power affirm the dominant narrative whilst denying space for other stories.

During interviews, participants regularly shared stories that had been omitted from either the official narrative of a statue or media coverage of its contestation. As researchers with an academic platform, we have sought to provide a platform for these stories. For example, charges of historical erasure that had been levelled against Rhodes Must Fall activists at the Universities of Cape Town (UCT) and Oxford were contested during interviews. Participants pointed out that the statues of Cecil Rhodes erected at these universities were intended to obscure bloody histories of extraction and exploitation and to craft as opposed to reflect popular opinion.

During his lifetime, Rhodes's reputation was by no means uniformly favourable. Participants stressed that statue defenders' claims that Rhodes was 'a man of his time' discount Rhodes's many African contemporaries whose colonisation, displacement, mass murder, and exploitation he dreamt of and oversaw. Yet Rhodes had "carefully planned and choreographed his own immortalisation" (Maylam 2002: 39). When erected nine years (Oxford) and thirty-two years (Cape Town) after his death, the statues did not only frame Rhodes's theft and redistribution of resources as a form of benevolence worthy of celebration. They cast Rhodes in a new light, reimagining his ambivalent historical reputation. Thus, participants stressed, the statues cannot be understood as representative of history in any neutral sense. Rather, their prominent placement and heroic style obscured histories that the student movements sought to highlight and protest.

Share research publicly

The emphasis on publishing in academic journals with high impact factors, on citations, and on 'REFability' in British universities means that social scientific research is often inaccessible to the people it depicts (and on whom it relies). Feminist and decolonial scholars have long argued that these practices are extractive, and have advocated giving research participants control over their own narratives by data sharing and accountability. Given the political salience of cultural activism, it was particularly important for us to share our research publicly. We did this in two ways: first, we prioritised public-facing outputs such as policy briefs and articles, publishing these before we turned to academic outputs. Second, we hosted and participated in public events, where cultural activists and the Manchester Museum OSCH Young Collective were among our co-presenters and audience members.

We jointly authored a policy brief laying out our opposition to the policing bill (Habib et al. 2021) and made the case for actively contesting statues in *The Guardian* (Younge 2021), *The Conversation* (Peacock 2021), *Red Pepper* (Tinsley 2021a), and *The Fabian Review* (Tinsley 2021b). We hosted and participated in panels alongside cultural activists in order to lay out the academic case for contesting statues, with events in Manchester (Habib, Tinsley, and Younge) and Cambridge (Ramsden-Karelse and Younge). Under Habib's leadership, young people from the OSCH Young Collective contributed to a roundtable discussion in Manchester attended by policymakers, academics, and heritage sector managers ('From Bristol to Manchester' 2021). In early 2022, the young people were active in sharing their perspectives at the London Commission for Diversity in the Public Realm's Contested Heritage Roundtable consultation event (co-chaired by Habib). We also created a video in support of contesting statues for social media, and are authoring a zine in collaboration with young people as a learning resource for schools and the cultural sector.

Create critical, creative spaces for young people

A series of workshops with twenty-five young people, led by Habib, was a pivotal component of our research. Over the course of four sessions, each participant in the 'Whose Statues, Whose Stories?' workshop series selected a local statue, researched its subject and history, and spoke back to it by composing poetry (Habib 2021). Subsequently, several of the young people shared their poems and reflections in the research team's social media campaign and participated in panels and roundtables with the researchers and policymakers. The young people's critical reflections explored how removing statues should be a starting point rather than an eventual goal, revealed their wariness of claims that statues were fixed and permanent, and highlighted their understanding that material culture is only one of many expressions of racism in contemporary Britain.

One Young Collective member noted,

> In a country that has 'wilful amnesia' over the negative and violent histories of its past, thinking critically about the meanings that statues hold, the histories

they make visible and invisible, and the impact of their existence on communities and individuals is extremely necessary. The workshops created a space in which timely and important discussions could be held around memorialisation, identity & belonging, and offered an opportunity for creative reflection wherein participants could express their thoughts and opinions through powerful pieces of poetry.

Another Young Collective member explained,

Attending the statues workshops was a fantastic opportunity to voice my opinions, in an empowering space alongside other young people. Each workshop allowed for us to think critically about the political, moral and historical implications of such tainted commemorations. It was a pleasure to attend these workshops alongside other young people who shared such inspirational views and creative capacity when we began to put our thoughts into writing … I'd love to do more workshops like this!

Recognise the risks these practices create

Deliberately positioning ourselves as supporters of anti-racist cultural activism, providing a platform for neglected stories and for young people, and sharing our work publicly does create risks for both researchers and participants. This issue has become particularly salient in recent years, as far-right policymakers and media outlets have subsumed Critical Race Theory, decolonial thought, and critical perspectives on empire under the label of 'wokeness' and demonised them on that basis. The risk of far-right attacks on our safety and our careers is felt disproportionately by academics who are at the sharp end of racism and misogyny, as well as early career and precariously employed researchers.

At times, we experienced these attacks directly: when prominent cultural institutions retweeted or shared details about the 'Whose Statues? Whose Stories?' sessions, Habib and Manchester Museum OSCH Young Collective members who run the OSCH social media accounts were targeted by online trolls and statue defenders. "Aren't museums for preserving the past?" asked one. Another replied, "As a Mancunian whose family has been here hundreds of years and built this city I object to this woke signalling rubbish, stop with the politics and wasting money during a pandemic".

Conclusion

The re-ignition of the far-right 'culture war' has thrust research on cultural heritage into the political and media spotlight. Given the proliferation of cultural activism and draconian laws restricting it, research on this topic will continue to be highly visible and politicised for the foreseeable future. As researchers, we should acknowledge the ethical risks of our work. We should also recognise the impossibility (and undesirability) of adopting a 'neutral', apolitical standpoint. Instead, we should pursue research that is critically engaged, anti-oppression, public-facing, and protective of our own standpoints.

References

Habib, S. 2018. *Learning and Teaching British Values: Policies and Perspectives on British Identities*. London: Palgrave Macmillan.

Habib, S. 2021. 'Histories of Empire and Colonialism: Whose Statues? Whose Stories?', Our Shared Cultural Heritage blog, 23 June. https://sharedculturalh eritage.wordpress.com/2021/06/23/histories-of-empire-and-colonialism-whose -statues-whose-stories/ Accessed 12 October 2023.

Habib, S., Peacock, C., Ramsden-Karelse, R., and Tinsley, M. 2021. 'The Changing Shape of Cultural Activism: Legislating Statues in the Context of the Black Lives Matter Movement'. Runnymede and CoDE COVID briefings. https://pure .manchester.ac.uk/ws/portalfiles/portal/204662114/Runnymede_CoDE_Cultural _Activism_and_statues_briefing_FINAL.pdf (accessed 12 October 2023).

Heffer, S. 2020. 'I've Read the National Trust Report and It's a One-Sided Take on History, Full of Woke Prejudices', *The Telegraph*, 13 November. https:// www.telegraph.co.uk/art/architecture/read-national-trust-report-one-sided-take -history-full-woke/?utmsource=email (accessed 12 October 2023).

Hope, C. 2020a. 'National Trust Members Accuse Board of "Woke Agenda" in Stormy Virtual AGM', *The Telegraph*, 8 November. https://www.telegraph.co.uk /politics/2020/11/08/national-trust-members-accuse-board-woke-agenda-stormy -virtual/ (accessed 12 October 2023).

Hope, C. 2020b. 'National Trust Colonialism Report Was Flimsy and Offensive, Say MPs', *The Telegraph*, 12 November. https://www.pressreader.com/uk/the-daily -telegraph/20201112/281560883321972 (accessed 12 October 2023).

Huxtable, S.A., Fowler, C., Kefalas, C., and Slocombe, E. 2020. *Interim Report on the Connections between Colonialism and Properties Now in the Care of the National Trust, Including Links with Historic Slavery*. Swindon: National Trust.

Maylam, P. 2002. 'Monuments, Memorials and the Mystique of Empire: The Immortalisation of Cecil Rhodes in the Twentieth Century', *African Sociological Review*, 6(1), 138–147.

Peacock, C. 2021. 'A Meaningful Debate about Statues Is Happening – The Government Just Doesn't Seem to Be Taking Part', *The Conversation*, 27 January. http://theconversation.com/a-meaningful-debate-about-statues-is-happening-the -government-just-doesnt-seem-to-be-taking-part-162806 (accessed 12 October 2023).

School of Arts, Languages and Cultures. 'From Bristol to Manchester: History and Memory in our Cities', University of Manchester, 20 October 2021. https://www .youtube.com/watch?v=-64tG4vt2g0 (accessed 12 October 2023).

Stephenson, H. 2021. 'Engaging with Controversial and Divisive Issues – Reflections for Charities', Charity Commission blog, 11 March. https://charitycommission .blog.gov.uk/2021/03/11/engaging-with-controversial-or-divisive-issues -reflections-for-charities/ (accessed 13 October 2023).

Tinsley, M. 2021a. 'Statues, Street Names, and Contested Memory', *Red Pepper*, 21 February. https://www.redpepper.org.uk/statues-street-names-and-contested -memory/ (accessed 13 October 2023).

Tinsley, M. 2021b. 'Policing History', *The Fabian Review*, 14 September. https:// fabians.org.uk/policing-history/ (accessed 13 October 2023).

Younge, G. 2021. 'Why Every Single Statue Should Come Down', *The Guardian*, 1 June. https://www.theguardian.com/artanddesign/2021/jun/01/gary-younge-why -every-single-statue-should-come-down-rhodes-colston (accessed 13 October 2023).

15

Archiving the extreme: ethical challenges in sharing, researching, and teaching[1]

Daniel Jones

The question of ethics around the use of far-right or extreme material has particular interest when we consider the question of Higher Education Institution–based archives. Not only do these archives support researchers of different types on a regular basis, but they also play an important role in introducing this material into the wider consciousness through public engagement. To explore these questions, this chapter will explore the experiences gathered from the operation of the Searchlight Archive at the University of Northampton during its almost ten years of existence. The Searchlight Archive is an important university-held resource on British and international far-right and antifascist movements, based around the collection on long-term loan from the leading antifascist magazine *Searchlight*. Much of the material it holds from the far right contains racism, homophobia, antisemitism, and other forms of hate and was designed to radicalise others into this thinking.

In such archives, the responsibility to ensure that material is cared for appropriately exists in balance with a further ethical duty to ensure any harm from the extreme material is mitigated. The simplest solution, to simply seal the material away, cannot exist alongside the fundamental purpose of an archive to preserve material for study. Institutional archives must also bear in mind, as Baron (2014: 2) observed, that the rigid lines around archives are blurring and there will be ever-increasing pressure to engage with community work, in order to have an impact. However, this chapter will contend that the use of the material with appropriate care is not just ethically acceptable, but in fact desirable because of the positive learning impacts and the revelation of marginalised histories. The material held not only shows the hate directed at minority groups within society but also their resistance to that – and in that, it reflects a part of their history. It is also an important part of our social history, covering a debate and struggle that has helped forge modern Britain, even if it was often played out at the margins. There is also the much wider duty of any academic institution to promote research and study. This last duty falls as heavily on an archive as it does more traditional academics; as Ellis (2005) observes,

Higher Education Institution–based archives have an important role beyond their work as repositories in establishing and embedding research cultures within the institution.

Making the extreme accessible

The most fundamental ethical concern of an archive handling extremist or radical material is to ensure that its material is preserved for future researchers in an accessible manner, and also that the material is used in a responsible way that does not cause harm. The preservation is handled through standard archival practice and professional standards, but in the case of radical material, preservation also must include the mitigation of risks posed by activist access.

In the case of the Searchlight Archive, the two activist groups are the far right and antifascists. The former very obviously carries greater risk, as they might seek to damage the material to block study, seek to abscond with parts of the archive that might be valuable for them for internal movement reasons (such as letters from famous figures), or even pose a risk to the archive staff themselves. Equally though, as archivists, we do need to consider that antifascist activists may also give rise to questions of suitability of access due to the intent behind access – with differing ethical values and intent, some antifascist activists, for example, will take photos from archives and share them freely on websites. While this is done through a positive endeavour, to share the history of their movements and counter the extreme right, nonetheless it is important for the archivist to consider the unintended risks of such activity. At the Searchlight Archive, these risks are mitigated at the most basic level through the application of access controls, requiring those who access the archive to demonstrate need and suitability, and through specific measures such as the use of lone working applications for staff to ensure security can be quickly summoned, alongside standard archival practice such as constant monitoring of users in the reading room.

The access control serves two purposes: ensuring that those who access the material are aware of its harmful nature and are suitably prepared for the immersion in that material that archival research brings and that they are responsible researchers who can be trusted with the material. It must be considered, however, that such systems will inevitably show bias in favour of researchers attached to institutions – where the provision of references from supervisors can be used to show the person is complying with an existing ethics structure, or where assumptions can be made of ethical oversight through university ethics boards. Accordingly, it is necessary that such access controls be balanced so as to be rigorous enough to serve their primary purpose, but not so strict or reliant upon institutional academic structures that the process excludes independent or community researchers.

At the same time, this should not be presented as a binary – where access is granted fully or refused. This would create too high a bar which would risk unnecessary exclusion and dissuade interest. Therefore, there must be an obligation on the archive to be adaptable in their standards and consider sensible and proportionate restrictions where there are concerns, or where supporting credentials cannot be obtained. In the case of the Searchlight Archive, these have consisted of restrictions on digital image taking or a restriction to purely pencil notes to ensure that the researcher can gain access for their own use but that facsimiles of the material do not leave the archive. In this way, broad access can be maintained that both adheres to professional standards within the sector and also respects the additional duties of radical collections to engage with community and public histories.

In saying this, however, what is not argued for is a relaxed approach that would enable access in all situations, such as that of simple casual interest. While it opens the archive up to accusations of paternalistic attitudes, it cannot be forgotten that the material in the archive – both from the extreme right or other radical groups – can often be upsetting. While, of course, the onus is on researchers to be responsible for what they access, the potential greater gap between the knowledge and experience of archive staff and someone with a casual interest places a greater ethical burden on the archive staff. In those cases, it must be the case that, for the well-being of the interested party, access is denied unless sufficient reason can be presented.

It must also be borne in mind by archive and special collection staff that not all contacts will be positive or well intentioned. Specifically, for our Archive, contact may come from the far right or associated movements. Not all of this will, in and of itself, pose a risk to the Archive or its staff – as has been alluded to previously (Jones 2015), the extremist website *Stormfront* commented on the wealth of information held in the Searchlight Archive. It is easy to dismiss such contacts, but sensible precautions should still be taken for the safeguarding of staff, researchers, and the archive. Whenever contact is made by the far right with the Searchlight Archive, the content is copied and stored as a physical medium – such as a printed screenshot. This is then stored within the archive, so should anything happen, there is a ready list of recent contacts. No request for access from the far right has yet been considered, with such prospective users ceasing contact after being presented with the access request form. However, it is unlikely that such access would be granted on the grounds of staff safety as well as the risk to the material – the majority of which is held on loan rather than by donation to the University.

For wellbeing purposes, after a received email is identified as being from the far right, the sender is blocked at the server by IT, and when we are engaged on social media we have a policy of not responding to far-right trolling or comments. It is worth considering who is monitoring social media during archive-hosted events, as these have attracted greater interest from the far right. If someone is from a group traditionally targeted by the far right, the archive must consider whether the engagement of the posting outweighs the potential upset. This is a choice for individuals to make based on what they are comfortable with, and for institutions to consider as well on an ethical basis.

In general, the experience within the Searchlight Archive has been that contact from the far right is quite irregular and takes place almost exclusively online. One thing the Archive has always emphasised is that it recognises the serious nature of the far right as a movement and the real threat it presents to those it targets. The Archive does not ridicule far-right beliefs but treats them as serious and worthy of study – indeed, this is the Archive's entire justification for existence. While it is believed that this approach also minimises the animus the far right may feel to contact the archive, it must be emphasised that there is no firm basis for this assumption. Accordingly, as an institution, the Archive must develop policies and procedures assuming such contact will occur.

Moving beyond the question of access to the accessibility of material within the archive, this, again, often places competing obligations on the archivist. As part of the academy, there is an ethical obligation towards ensuring free access to information where possible, yet this must be balanced against an ethical duty to ensure that material under the care of the archive is not used to harm or allowed to create unnecessary harm. As Chambers (2020) discusses in their exploration of film archives, these tensions between researcher, archivist, and public consumption have always existed, and, though these tensions are exacerbated by the modern digital world, archivists have a history of balancing the competing needs. Material that is fragile is withdrawn from handling, material that contravenes the data protection regulations is redacted, and copying of items is restricted by copyright legislation. When dealing with extreme-right material, archives must keep ethical considerations as much in their mind as standard archival practice.

This does not mean changing the principles of an archive or special collection: one of the founding principles of the Searchlight Archive was to maximise access to the material, which had not been accessible to academics previously in a meaningful way. What it means, however, is that to maximise what it is possible to share, the archive must constantly remain in dialogue with its users about the intended use of archival materials to find a balance between their needs and ethical practice. It is also worthwhile to consider the work of Stevens et al. (2010), who emphasise how community-based archives should prioritise the sharing of knowledge and be flexible around existing professional practice to achieve this.

Radical archives, the classroom, and decolonisation

After its opening in the summer of 2013, one of the first questions that the Searchlight Archive sought to address was how to make the material more accessible to students. Working with undergraduate students on two small-scale funded projects led by Dr Paul Jackson, material was provided to focus groups of students from criminology, sociology, law, psychology, and history. These projects showed the material was wanted, but raised the question of how it was to be done, and why such material should be used.

As noted by Beilin (2017: 80), history and its associated subjects also remain overwhelmingly white at the university level. Alexander and Weekes-Bernard (2017) highlighted that BAME students represented around 25 per cent of the students in school, but only 8.7 per cent of those studying historical or philosophical subjects at the undergraduate level. Though Alexander and Weekes-Bernard focused on the impact this had in terms of diversity within student teachers in these subjects, the impact must be considered much broader than this, on the wide range of history-related professions that feed into our heritage and its public engagement, such as museums, or indeed feeding back into archives themselves. This is commented upon by Eastwood (2017), that those who make use of archives within their education are those most likely to enter that profession. Archives have to engage a diverse background of people from a range of disciplines if they are to contribute to a healthy, varied, and more representative heritage sector.

This supports the approach highlighted by Landes (2018: 6–8) and others who see radical styles of collections held by libraries and archives as having an important role to play in breaking down many of the traditional barriers that exist in terms of access to these collections and the histories they hold. This engagement, often seen through the lens of a wider part of decolonising the curriculum, also provides an opportunity for addressing the awarding gap that exists between white British and Black, Asian, and Minority Ethnic (BAME) students at universities. As Schucan Bird and Pitman (2020: 904–905) observe, diverse reading lists and sources are one method of approaching the awarding gap.

With these principles in mind, internally funded pedagogical research projects were run from 2016 to 2017 that looked to make material from the Searchlight Archive available to lecturers across the University of Northampton. The Active Blended Learning model in place at the University of Northampton, which uses interlinked and mutually supportive online and face-to-face learner activities (Lomer and Palmer 2023), meant that this involved both electronic and physical resources. As well as helping broaden the source material available for lecturers, the presentation of online material in easy-to-integrate formats also helped reduce the barrier to ABL take-up due to prevailing academic attitudes that valued face-to-face over online resources (MacKeogh and Fox 2009: 150–151).

To overcome concerns over the specialist knowledge surrounding the complex nature of the extreme right, briefing videos were created by specialist academics. The briefing videos and online material were then used in conjunction with physical material in class, drawn from the Archive's duplicate stocks. This use of third and further duplicates within an archive for educational purposes is long established in the heritage sector as collection handling boxes, but with extreme material, this also represents an ethical use for these items that, by their duplicate nature, hold no archival value. Collections often dispose of excess copies through distribution (such as selling items or donating to other collections), but for extremist material, this option was never considered ethically justifiable. Distribution of some items in the archive was legally questionable due to its extreme messaging, and, even where this was not the case, a decision was made that disposed of material could get into the hands of those who might misuse it. This use of duplicates then justifies the shelf space given over to continued storage of duplicates by transforming them into active teaching items.

The project engaged with modules in criminology, history, and sociology, with approximately 200 student participants in total across the courses. The material chosen for modules under these pilot schemes was done in discussion with the academics who would be teaching, ensuring that between their own knowledge and the briefing packs, the academics would be comfortable in framing the material for students. Extreme material was often shown alongside radical material opposing those groups, an advantage that the archive had as a collection of antifascist as well as far-right resources. This is an important point in the representation of this material – that excessive focus on campaigning material of the far right can lead to a portrayal of marginalised communities as passive victims. The inclusion of material opposing these groups not only provides a fuller context but helps restore voice to groups ordinarily ignored and rendered voiceless by traditional histories.

The results from this project were successful, with 93.9 per cent of students responding that the material enhanced their knowledge and 90.9 per cent reporting that it made the subject more engaging. When asked, however, whether they would want this style of engagement rolled out to other modules, 90.9 per cent answered positively, while 9.1 per cent of students gave a neutral or negative response to this proposition. While this may seem like an overwhelmingly positive response, it carries with it a concern – for the 9.1 per cent of students who did not want this in further modules, was this due to concern or trauma from its use, and were there ways in which the engagement could be improved?

This was one of the questions explored in a project by Dr Paul Jackson, Dr Rachel Moss, Dr Daniel Jones, and Siobhan Hyland during 2019 and 2020. More broadly, the project examined how material could be used to particularly engage with BAME communities and to assemble best practices for the use of radical collections in teaching and engagement. However, it also sought to understand how students reacted to this material, what barriers might exist, and how these might be mitigated.

This was achieved through exploring the findings of the previous projects in focus groups, facilitated by the project team. While these were curtailed due to the COVID-19 pandemic, they nonetheless provided interesting findings. What the discussions revealed was that these materials were indeed engaging, and they did reflect histories that were generally hidden and which spoke to a number of groups and their lived experiences of society that are often unknown by mainstream populations. It also highlighted that the material was upsetting and that students emphasised a need to be aware that it was coming and also that it should be used where appropriate. Most interestingly, though, was an observation from students that they did feel it was appropriate to highlight the nature of the racist, homophobic, or otherwise contentious language in the extreme material, even though they also felt it should still be used. More than this, they indicated that once the warning is given, there should not be an overemphasis on that upsetting nature.

The reason given for this was that though students recognised the words were upsetting, they also may not be upsetting in a context – either denatured due to the academic work, due to familiarity, or because the content was not felt to affect them personally. In those cases, it was felt overemphasis of the harmful or upsetting nature could lead to an unintended novel source of upset, where students felt they were expected to react and their failure to do so meant they were somehow bigoted or lacking emotion.

The focus groups also highlighted that an understanding of the vocabulary around the issues raised in the material was important – the direct but also coded terms used within the far right to target ethnic groups and other communities. Understanding the terms and having a safe space to explore them was seen to be valuable – both in helping discussions be free and fruitful and also in taking away some of the raw upsetting nature. It was felt this kind of linguistic framework helped denature terms and helped students themselves read them with academic interest and not feel upset or shock, even while recognising the terms possess those qualities.

What is clear from these projects is that the material has a use in exploring a diverse set of histories, which helps the experience of marginalised communities to be recognised within teaching. Beyond the ethical need for academics to help enable access to these histories, the material also was seen to engage and embed learning, helping uplift student attainment across different groups, but this must be done in a conscientious and ethically conscious manner. It is important in trying to use extreme material in this way that we do not create new sources of trauma for students from diverse backgrounds, and thus further amplify – rather than reduce – the awarding gap within higher education. If done right, however, the teaching of extreme-right behaviour and the community responses can play an important role in helping students from marginalised communities feel they belong in higher education.

Engaging beyond the academy

As has been mentioned, engagement with this material is vital for promoting a better understanding of community histories in Britain and for diversifying the ways in which history is studied, written about, and taught. This means an obvious step is engaging with those outside of the academy, and even outside of the confines of Higher Education Institutions. This, however, provides new ethical risks and considerations which must be considered and the different contexts respected.

Within the institution, there are – in effect – ethical safety buffers in place at all times. Students are beholden to codes of conduct and to staff supervision, and staff members are beholden to professional ethics, institutional ethics frameworks, and institutional policies. When engaging within the community there are far fewer checks in place – yes, staff are still beholden to professional ethics, ethics boards, and policies, but often the monitoring is far less robust than activity within the institution. Equally, those with whom you are engaging cannot be assumed to have such constraints.

Over its decade of operation, the main area which has caused additional considerations and concern is those items made available as digital items, which can easily transform once outside of the archive environment due to the ease of use, transfer, and transformation that exists with digital material compared to traditional physical items. This means that though an image of radicalising material might be shared for educational purposes, alongside contextualising information, it could be taken and have that contextualising information stripped away and then be used for its original intent – to radicalise and promote hatred.

Any material chosen for presentations, advertisement, or other use must be considered carefully by an archive and its researchers. In his examination of the extreme material of Islamic State, Johnston (2022) observes how repeated exposure to material from radical extremism alters the audience's perception of violence, desensitising them to what is beyond normality – this desensitisation can, in many cases, be the very purpose of the material. Archive staff and researchers should not presume that, though not the target audience for the radicalising material they examine, they are immune to this desensitising effect. An image chosen for a presentation may feel appropriate at 4 pm after a day of examining 1960s American Nazi Party material that will, when the presentation occurs, be obviously excessive. A policy introduced by the Searchlight Archive to mitigate this is that any presentation images are chosen at least one day before so that they can be examined first thing the following day. These items will never be without their unpleasant nature, and their extreme nature is often an important part of the lesson they teach; however, it is incumbent on the researcher never to cause needless upset by choosing images more extreme than is necessary.

Collections such as the Searchlight Archive are held on loan from parts of the activist community, rather than being held as outright donations. Even beyond this, the histories it contains are considered important and seen in a protective light by antifascist and antiracist groups, and this is similar to the way other communities see affiliated community-originated or radical collections. As well as the perceived duty to contribute back to these communities by sharing the work of your research, it is also practically useful for collections. As trust is built, so may future collections be garnered and the histories can become better preserved, stored, and more accessible.

This is especially important when it comes to oral history projects. The Searchlight Archive undertook such a project with Dr Gavin Bailey and Dr Benjamin Lee, and later Siobhan Hyland, in 2015 and again in 2018. This was to interview antifascist and antiracist campaigners and activists and record especially the stories of those who were ageing and passing. These oral histories are important to undertake, as they record histories that have traditionally been under-valued and which preserve the voices of activists and others. For key moments in antifascist history, in particular, events like Cable Street have already lost their last participants.

Oral recordings, however, come with other ethical points and concerns. Practically, participants must be made aware of intended use, as is standard within such projects, but when dealing with radical activist stories, they may contain problematic content. In this, rather than being worried about racist language, the concern must be about the potential admission of crimes. With antifascist histories as an example, this might be of violence or other crimes against the far right, or crimes undertaken while in the far right by those who defected to antifascism.

In 2011, an oral history collection held at Boston College related to the Northern Irish Troubles was accessed by authorities to try to pursue charges against IRA members (Inckle 2015). Archivists did object to this, and it ran counter to assurances and agreements they had in place. Nevertheless, disclosure did occur. As archivists, the law will always be superior to a deposit agreement, and so it is important to be honest not just about how you will use the items but also about what you cannot do and cannot accept. This approach, of negotiating a balance between the ethical principle of avoiding harm while also accepting the unpredictability of events, was among the lessons drawn by Kay Inckle (2015) in their examination of this and similar cases. This need for care when engaging marginalised groups who experience cultural or legal vulnerability is further underlined by Yiu Tung Suen (2015), who explored the question of LGBT+ interviews in Hong Kong. From these, it can be taken that if the interview will cause direct harm, then it must be reconsidered seriously in that context – no matter its historical value.

One area over which there remains a great deal of active debate is the ways and extent to which archives should engage with activist and community groups depositing material. Within the context of the Searchlight Archive, questions have been raised as to whether staff feel they are antifascist or what relation they have to *Searchlight*. The answer to this is still unfolding, and there is a range of practice and comfort within the Archive and its related staff. Institutionally, the focus remains on shared goals – not just the preservation of the materials as a research collection, but on using them and knowledge created from them to help combat intolerance and hatred.

Conclusion

In the decade since the opening of the Searchlight Archive, a lot has changed around the subject of archiving material from the far right and antifascist groups. The question of ethics was not one that was widely raised, and there was very little advice available on how to set up such an archive. It is still the case that there is not much written about the subject now but, as Espley and Landes (2018) show, there is a growing discussion occurring within academia and connected professions about how we can best share the lessons learnt. That debate, by its nature, has to be free and frank – open about our failures as well as our successes, as well as about those things that are as of yet still unknown. It is inevitable that in establishing and building such an archive there will be moments where you had to use your best judgement or had to balance competing ethical directives. Equally, the unknowns attached to such archives can often cause concern about risk for staff unfamiliar with the material, and it will fall on the archivist to reassure the institution.

The answer for the archivist is to be proactive, to create systems of control and protection – as the Searchlight Archive has done with the access controls and considerations around online materials. Though the experience has been that such systems are rarely needed, the confidence they provide to the archivist is one that allows the archive to engage actively with the research community, to maximise how much it can make available to researchers, while at the same time minimising the harm that might occur. Having those systems in place also allows staff to handle any adverse contacts or experiences with a degree of distance.

This work, though, as this chapter has detailed, is not all about predicting harm and acting to mitigate risks. While that is an important ethical consideration, archives must also consider the duty that falls on them to share the material they hold. This material is engaging to students, researchers, and communities and allows the archive to play a genuine role in transforming how the histories of minority communities are taught and understood by showing some of the ways in which hate was directed against them and the ways in which the communities responded to the far right – histories that are often not captured by more traditional archive sources.

What the Searchlight Archive's work with students has shown, repeatedly, is that these extreme sources are ones that bring history alive for the students. It engages them more deeply with the study of politics, law, and society, and in doing so embeds the learning and improves outcomes. As an archive, the experience built up in this work enabled the support of community-led projects, such as Race Act 40, which sought to capture the oral histories of people who experienced racism in Northamptonshire. That, ultimately, is the only way in which the ethical handling of collections such as the Searchlight Archive will improve – through the heuristic process of trying and, whether a failure or success, sharing those experiences.

Note

1 Parts of this chapter draw upon the experiences and outcomes of ILT Teaching and Learning projects run at the University of Northampton. The author would like to acknowledge and thank the University, particularly the Institute for Learning and Teaching, as well as the academics and research assistants who worked on these projects, in particular Prof Paul Jackson, Dr Rachel Moss, Dr Siobhan Hyland, and Billy Mann.

References

Alexander, C. and Weekes-Bernard, D. 2017. 'History Lessons: Inequality, Diversity and the National Curriculum', *Race, Ethnicity and Education*, 20(4), 478–494.

Baron, J. 2014. *The Archive Effect: Found Footage and the Audiovisual Experience of History*. Abingdon: Routledge.

Beilin, I. 2017. 'The Academic Research Library's White Past and Present'. In: Schelssman-Tarango, G. (ed.). *Topographies of Whiteness: Mapping Whiteness in Library and Information Science*. Sacramento, CA: Library Juice Press, 77–96.

Chambers, C. 2020. 'Ethics and the Archive: Access, Appropriation, Exhibition'. In: Dodd, S. (ed.). *Ethics and Integrity in Visual Research Methods*. Bingley: Emerald, 133–151.

Eastwood, T. 2017. 'A Personal Reflection on the Development of Archival Education', *Education for Information*, 33(2), 75–78.

Ellis, M. 2005. 'Establish a Research Centre for Archive Administration in the UK', *Education for Information*, 23(1–2), 99–101.

Inckle, K. 2015. 'Promises, Promises: Lessons in Research Ethics from the Belfast Project and "The Rape Tape" Case', *Sociological Research Online*, 20(1), 59–71.

Johnson, N. 2022. 'Selling Terror: A Multidimensional Analysis of the Islamic State's Recruitment Propaganda', *Australian Journal of International Affairs*, 76(2), 194–218.

Jones, D. 2015. 'The Searchlight Archive Collection at the University of Northampton: A Research Note', *Journal for Deradicalisation*, 3, 210–215.

Landes, J. 2018. 'Introduction: Radical Collections and Radical Voices'. In: Landes, J. and Espley, R. (eds). *Radical Collections: Re-Examining the Roots of Collections, Practices and Information Professions*. London: University of London, 1–9.

Lomer, S. and Palmer, E. 2023. '"I Didn't Know This Was Actually Stuff That Could Help Us, with Actually Learning": Student Perceptions of Active Blended Learning', *Teaching in Higher Education*, 28(4), 679–698. https://doi.org/10.1080/13562517.2020.1852202

MacKeogh, K. and Fox, S. 2009. 'Strategies for Embedding E-Learning in Traditional Universities: Driver and Barriers', *Electronic Journal of e-Learning*, 7(2), 147–154.

Schucan Bird, K. and Pitman, L. 2020. 'How Diverse Is Your Reading List? Exploring Issues of Representation and Decolonisation in the UK', *Higher Education*, 79, 903–920.

Stevens, M., Flinn, A., and Shepherd, E. 2010. 'New Frameworks for Community Engagement in the Archive Sector: From Handing Over to Handing On', *International Journal of Heritage Studies*, 16(1–2), 59–76.

Suen, Y. T. 2015. 'Methodological Reflections on Researching Lesbian, Gay, Bisexual and Transgender University Students in Hong Kong: To What Extent Are They Vulnerable Interview Subjects?', *Higher Education Research and Development*, 34(4), 722–734.

16

Researching racism in racist times

Jean Beaman

> For scholarship that strives to overcome racism cannot be content with making black persons visible, but rather needs to recognise the very particular toll that the theoretical and political invisibility of others, through the process of racism, has taken on the world. (Smith 2006: 436)

I begin this chapter with two anecdotes. First, I have been conducting research on race and racism in France, particularly in the Parisian metropolitan region, for about fifteen years now. I typically fly in and out of France through Paris's Charles De Gaulle Airport. Often when I go through customs leaving France to fly back to the US, the French customs or border patrol officer will examine my US passport, comment on the spelling of my name ('Jean' as I spell it is read as a male name in France, not a female one), and then ask what I was doing in France (especially since I usually stay for a couple of months during these trips). I respond that I'm a sociologist, a professor (or graduate student when that was the case) and that I was here in France to conduct research. 'Research on what?' is usually the reply. I briefly respond, saying that I research racism in France. And the response is usually something like, 'Oh does that exist here in France?' or 'Racism is a problem in France?' To which I respond, yes. Racism exists in France and is a big problem worthy of study. Then I typically get a weird look from the customs or border official and a stamp on my passport, and then I'm on my way.

Second, when I was a graduate student and was first conceptualising what was to be my dissertation on marginalisation, racism, and second-generation Maghrébin immigrants in France, I was warned to be careful to not impose a US-based conception of race, ethnicity, and racism to the French context. I remember a prominent French social scientist meeting with me during an extended stay at my doctoral institution. He told me definitively that race does not mean anything in France, particularly compared to the United States, and that terms such as 'white' or 'black' do not mean anything to French people or in French society. Yet, as I'll discuss shortly, when I moved to France and began my research, I found the reality was quite the opposite.

To me, both of these anecdotes speak to the complexities and challenges of conducting research on race and racism in France, including from the vantage point of a Black woman and US citizen. Race, although not officially measured or acknowledged by the French state, still marks individuals as distinct and creates and reinforces a racial order or hierarchy, as the work of many scholars including me has shown (Keaton 2010; Mazouz 2020; Ndiaye 2008). Throughout my many years of conducting research, my interlocutors have been quick to invoke race, racism, and ethnicity, both directly and indirectly, without my prompting.

In what follows, I will use insights from my qualitative research in France on these questions to discuss the nuances and complications of examining race, racism, and ethnicity in a different societal context. I chose the title, 'Researching racism in racist times', as a way to think through how France is simultaneously race-avoidant and race-conscious and how that impacts research conducting research on these questions. While I do not explicitly research the far right, I research issues directly impacted by the far right or issues that challenge far-right discourses – namely acknowledging the humanity of racialised populations and documenting the extent of racism in France (and Western Europe more broadly).

As France is always in a period of 'racist times', research on racism is unfortunately always timely and always crucial. As my epigraph suggests, such research on racism must interrogate the myriad tolls it takes on those populations subjected to it.

As a sociologist, my intervention in this forum primarily focuses on how racism becomes manifest in 'postcolonial' France through ethnographic research with France's 'visible minorities', i.e. descendants of France's colonial empire throughout parts of Africa, the Caribbean, and Asia. I also acknowledge my identity as a non-European, a US citizen, and Black scholar, all of which inform my research and how it is received by others.

How race is interpellated and read in France

One of the difficulties of researching race and racism in France is even naming it as such, given overarching colourblind ideologies. In much of Europe – the UK being a notable exception – so-called 'ethnic statistics', or collecting demographic information on race and ethnicity in the census, are prohibited. Especially in France, race is therefore not seen as a legitimate category – not something to be measured or understood as significant or consequential. This is reflected, for example, in one of the anecdotes I shared earlier, in which a French social scientist told me racial categories do not mean anything to French people. The fact that I quickly discovered the opposite – as I'll discuss later – evidences how France simultaneously avoids, denies, and yet is conscious of race and the differences it creates.

If race is difficult to name, racism is particularly impossible to name without facing significant hostility. France's universalist and colourblind Republican ideology enables what philosopher Charles Mills (1997) terms an 'epistemology of ignorance'. Such ignorance allows for racial reproduction and perpetuation of white supremacy. Mueller (2017) extends this to consider how colourblind ideologies are grounded in such an epistemology for white individuals, revealing a "process of knowing designed to produce not knowing surrounding white privilege, culpability, and structural white supremacy" (2017: 220).

So, if race and racism cannot be named, it is therefore also because they do not exist. Moreover, as David Theo Goldberg (2006) has argued, race is framed as exceptional in Europe, i.e. the far right or the Holocaust, and relegated elsewhere (and such a framing is particularly illustrative of how France's ongoing 'racist times', as I alluded to earlier, is related to the mainstreaming of far-right discourse in France and Europe more broadly (Mondon and Winter 2020)). Particularly in France, race and racism are deemed imported concepts from the United States, and those in the French public sphere decry how 'wokeisme' is threatening the French academy and French society more generally (Beaman and Fredette 2022). In the moments where racism is named, it is significantly minimised, downplayed as phenomena of the past, or rendered the acts and behaviours of individual racists, never as a macro-level or structural phenomenon. There can be individual racists, but they are an exception and do not at all reflect wider French society.

Discussing certain populations as racialised or as racial or ethnoracial groups is, moreover, complicated. In contrast to the term 'ethnic and racial minorities', the term 'visible minorities' is used in French academic parlance. According to French scholar Pap Ndiaye,[1] 'visible minorities' is defined based on "the presence of phenotypical characteristics that racially or ethnically characterise those persons concerned ... that is, people whose supposed ethno-racial membership can be deduced from their appearance" (Ndiaye 2008: 57–58). Research that has sought to examine ethnoracial disparities in France has had to rely on proxies for race and ethnic origin such as individual name, socioeconomic status, immigrant status (or parental immigrant status), or residential location (Acolin et al. 2016; Bonnet et al. 2016; Oppenheimer 2008; Quillian et al. 2019). As race and ethnic origin can be correlated with these other markers of difference, this empirical evidence is useful, yet still limited in explaining what is not captured, or the effects of race or ethnic origin alone. One example is the 2009 joint INED and INSEE study, *Trajectoires et Origines* (TeO), which by identifying individual respondents' immigrant status and that of their parents was able to approximate percentages of different second-generation populations. It was also able to identify the disparate treatment of these various populations, including their experiences with discrimination (Simon 2012). This study also identified a dissonance between these individuals feeling French and perceiving that others actually see them as French, "as Frenchness is based rather on a restricted vision of who 'looks French'" (Simon 2012: 13). This finding suggests the ethnoracial parameters around who is actually accepted as French.

Citizen outsider: children of North African immigrants in France

My first book is an ethnographic examination including semi-structured interviews with forty-five middle-class adult children of Maghrébin, or North African, immigrants in France. The central question of my research is understanding how citizens remain on the margins of mainstream society and what this reveals about how race and ethnicity operate in practice. In my book, I argue that the continued marginalisation of children of Maghrébin immigrants – and visible minorities in France – reveals the continuing significance of race for shaping life chances in French society.

This book serves as an ethnographic complement to much of the TeO study. I demonstrate how the source of the dissonance Simon (2012) identifies lies in how the North African second generation is denied cultural citizenship because they are non-white. The majority of individuals I studied do see themselves as French as any other French person, yet find that their claims to 'Frenchness' are denied by others. I use the framework of cultural citizenship to explain this dynamic. I further argue that my respondents – and visible minorities in France more generally – are denied cultural citizenship,[2] which inhibits them from being seen as French as anyone else, despite how they themselves see Frenchness as constitutive of their identity. I frame the North African second generation as 'citizen outsiders', a term which Cathy Cohen (2010) uses to characterise the precarious social locations of African-American youth. Cohen considers the degrees to which Black American youth feel like full members of the citizenry as a way of complicating the relationship between race, citizenship, and belonging.

The middle-class North African second generation is both inside and outside of the citizenry – they have made it, so to speak, but only to a point, as they are continually reminded of how their citizenship is 'suspect' and often questioned by others. They are denied cultural citizenship from a young age, which continues into adulthood in a variety of domains, including the workplace, higher education, Islam, residential location, and the public sphere or in everyday public life. They are suspect at both micro and macro levels, from having their identity checked by the police – *les contrôles d'identité* – in public spaces to growing up with few representations of Maghrébin-origin individuals in government or popular culture.

As I alluded to earlier, despite being warned that race (and racial categories) were meaningless to many French people, I found quite the opposite once I arrived in Paris as a graduate student and began conducting fieldwork and interviews. I approached people telling of my interest in identity formation and experiences of second-generation North African immigrants, and often race and racism implicitly or explicitly came up. Respondents were quick to bring up these issues without my prompting. That is undoubtedly partly related to my own identity as Black, but does not fully explain this. (And I would argue that this is not a limitation of my ethnographic research, but rather reflects a more complex understanding of how difference and race are both similar and different in two societies.)

Rather, in conducting my research, I saw first-hand how second-generation Maghrébin immigrants connected with minoritised populations worldwide, including in the US, as they made sense of their own social locations. They were deeply aware of how they are treated differently because they are not white, or because of their Maghrébin origins. They understood themselves as minorities and minoritised by other French people, even though they understood themselves to be as French as any other French person. My respondents have had to grapple with French Republicanism professing *liberté*, *égalité*, *fraternité* while simultaneously denying them full societal membership.

As an ethnographer, I am simultaneously constructed as an insider and an outsider, which undoubtedly shapes how individuals perceive and respond to me. I was an insider as another racial and ethnic minority, or a 'visible minority', in French social science parlance. Yet I was also an outsider as a native-born American citizen and non-French person. Being an American carried a particular 'weight' during my field research that I had to reckon with. Black feminist scholar and sociologist Patricia Hill Collins (1986) has theorised about the 'outsider-within' or the multiple positionalities individuals can possess from having multiple social group memberships. In other words, individuals can simultaneously remain both inside and outside of mainstream society – or be citizen outsiders. Just as my respondents or interlocutors were 'citizen outsiders' or 'outsiders-within', so too was I, both in terms of my individual identity and in terms of my relationship to the field and to conducting ethnographic research.

Studying anti-racism and anti-racist movements

My current research builds upon remaining questions from research for my first book to consider how people fight against racism in a seemingly colourblind society. Specifically, I am conducting ethnographic research with anti-racist activists on mobilisation against police violence in France. Here, I detail how the spectre of police violence constructs a suspect citizenship, denying full societal inclusion for minoritised populations. By considering the multifaceted dimensions of citizenship and belonging in France, I demonstrate the limitations of full societal inclusion for France's non-white denizens and how French Republicanism continues to mark, rather than erase, racial and ethnic distinctions.

Both in doing anti-racist work and studying anti-racism, it is a challenge to name race and racism. In other words, this is a (somewhat related) struggle for activists and scholars working with them – and scholar-activists more broadly. In line with Goldberg's framework of racial Europeanisation, racism – and therefore phenomena ascribed to racism – is a problem elsewhere, so police violence targeted at ethnoracial minorities cannot exist in France. It cannot be interpellated as a systemic societal problem. French media can report on incidents of police violence in the US and point to that as a problem, but cannot do the same work with France's own incidents of police brutality.

To give one example: Ramata Dieng is one Black French activist who has been mobilising against police violence ever since her brother, Lamine Dieng, was killed by the police in 2007 in Paris's twentieth *arrondissement*. She created a collective, *Vies Voleés* (loosely translated as Stolen Lives), as a way to mobilise others against state violence. She and the other members of her collective regularly hold commemorative demonstrations marking the death of Lamine and other victims, push for changes to policing tactics and techniques, and advocate for better police accountability for incidents of brutality and death. One of the challenges she faces is naming police violence as a systemic problem, as well as countering the negative framing of her brother as a delinquent or criminal. Once when I spoke with her following a commemorative demonstration in 2017 for the tenth anniversary of her brother's death, Ramata told me that police violence is far worse in the US as there are many more victims than in France. "Yet, this happens in all Western countries because it comes from the state. The state is racist." That a French person, a France-born person, says this belies the supposedly colourblind ethos upon which France rests. It also makes her easily dismissed by a French public sphere that too readily frames systemic racism as a solely US phenomenon. Other Black French activists, including Assa Traoré (who has received much attention in recent months as the movement for justice for the police killing of her brother Adama in 2016 has gained steam) and journalist, documentarian, and author Rokhaya Diallo, have been accused of relying on US conceptions of racism when they provide their *own* analyses of racism in France, based on their own experiences of being born and raised in France.

Challenges and questions in doing this work

As an African-American and US citizen conducting this research, I myself have faced related questions and accusations of importing US frameworks of race, ethnicity, and difference to the French context and forcing them to 'fit' when they otherwise do not. I have been disregarded or not taken seriously, by both scholars and others, because I lay to rest the notion of French exceptionalism with regards to differentiation and illustrate how French Republicanism as an ideology excludes rather than includes all members of French society. To give one recent example, on a conference panel discussing my work on activism against police violence, a member of the virtual audience immediately dismissed my reference to the relationship between police violence and racism culled from my interviews and ethnographic observations because race is not part of the official state discourse, considered inappropriate and illegitimate. What I was really describing was related instead to the importance of nationalism and national identity. Again, before we can even analyse racialisation, and the impacts thereof, one must fight to even name race or racism.

Relatedly, I have often been warned about issues of 'objectivity' in conducting research related to race and identity as a racial minority myself (both in the context of France and more broadly), and have often received questions as to whether I naturally saw race and racism in every interaction, versus understanding these issues through the lens of the people in the field. My experiences are similar to what other minority researchers encounter studying race within the United States and how the research findings are filtered through the race and ethnicity of the researcher and not the research itself (Truesdell 2013; Young 2008).

This is particularly ironic when we consider the historical origins of conceptions of race and differentiation in the US, which were heavily influenced by European notions of inherent differences and inferiority of Black individuals, including by French thinkers such as Arthur de Gobineau (Beaman 2017). Yet it is easier and strategic for France to imagine race and racism as US conceptions with no relevance in France. This is perhaps most recently evident in President Macron's declaration that French academia, and French society more broadly, is being wrongly influenced by US ideas of race, racism, intersectionality, and post-colonialism (Beaman and Fredette 2022).

For this and many other reasons, it is important to centre individuals' lived experiences in our scholarship on societal conditions such as racism. In order to fully make sense of the areas we study, we should take seriously our identities as scholars, how those circulate globally, and how participants engage with their perceptions of our identities. This is crucial for understanding the totality of individuals' lives. I end this essay circling back to the epigraph quote by encouraging us as scholars, especially ethnographers, to focus less on 'proving' that racism exists and more on exposing the real and significant tolls it takes, even in 'colourblind' societies.

Notes

1 Ndiaye was appointed in 2022 as Minister of National Education, Youth, and Sports in President Macron's administration. Ndaiye is the first Black person to serve in this role. He says he sees himself as a "symbol of diversity" (Hird 2022).
2 By cultural citizenship, I am referring to the markers that would allow an individual to traverse the cultural-symbolic boundaries around a particular national identity and be fully accepted by one's compatriots (Beaman 2017).

References

Acolin, A., Bostic, R. and Painter, G. 2016. 'A Field Study of Rental Market Discrimination across Origins in France', *Journal of Urban Economics*, 95, 49–63.

Beaman, J. 2017. *Citizen Outsider: Children of North African Immigrants in France*. Oakland, CA: University of California Press.

Beaman, J. and Fredette, J. 2022. 'The US/France Contrast Frame and Black Lives Matter in France', *Perspectives on Politics*, 20(4), 1346–1361.

Bonnet, F., Lalé, E., Safi, M. and Wasmer, E. 2016. 'Better Residential Than Ethnic Discrimination! Reconciling Audit and Interview Findings in the Parisian Housing Market', *Urban Studies*, 53(13), 2815–2833.

Cohen, C. J. 2010. *Democracy Remixed: Black Youth and the Future of American Politics*. Oxford: Oxford University Press.

Collins, P. H. 1986. 'Learning from the Outsider Within: The Sociological Significance of Black Feminist Thought', *Social Problems*, 33(6), S14–32.

Goldberg, D. T. 2006. 'Racial Europeanization', *Ethnic and Racial Studies*, 29(2), 331–364.

Hird, A. 2022. 'Right-Wing Outcry as Historian Pap Ndiaye Heads Up French Educational Ministry', *RTI*, 24 May.

Keaton, T. D. 2010. 'The Politics of Race-Blindness: (Anti) Blackness and Category-Blindness in Contemporary France', *Du Bois Review: Social Science Research on Race*, 7(1), 103–131.

Mazouz, S. 2020. *Race*. Paris: Appaloosa LHS Editions.

Mills, C. W. 1997. *The Racial Contract*. Ithaca, NY: Cornell University Press.

Mondon, A. and Winter, A. 2020. *Reactionary Democracy: How Racism and the Populist Far Right Became Mainstream*. London: Verso.

Mueller, J. C. 2017. 'Producing Colorblindness: Everyday Mechanisms of White Ignorance', *Social Problems*, 64(2), 219–238.

Ndiaye, P. 2008. *La Condition noire: Essai sur une minorité française*. Paris: Editions Calmann-Lévy.

Oppenheimer, D. B. 2008. 'Why France Needs to Collect Data on Racial Identity … in a French Way', *Hastings International & Comparative Law Review*, 31, 735.

Quillian, L., Heath, A., Pager, D., Midtbøen, A. H., Fleischmann, F., and Hexel, O. 2019. 'Do Some Countries Discriminate More Than Others? Evidence from 97 Field Experiments of Racial Discrimination in Hiring', *Sociological Science*, 6, 467–496.

Simon, P. 2012. *French National Identity and Integration: Who Belongs to the National Community?* Washington, DC: Migration Policy Institute.

Smith, M. 2006. 'Blackening Europe/Europeanising Blackness: Theorising the Black Presence in Europe', *Contemporary European History*, 15(3), 423–439.

Truesdell, N. 2013. 'Researching Race While Being Raced: Reflections on Race Politics in Anthropology', *Anthropologies*, 18, 24 May.

Young, A. A., Jr. 2008. 'White Ethnographers on the Experiences of African-American Men: Then and Now'. In: Zuberi, T. and Bonilla-Silva, E. (eds). *White Logic, White Methods: Racism and Methodology*. Lanham, MD: Rowman & Littlefield, 179–202.

Part IV

Care and safety

17

How do you respond when you feel under threat? A reflective exploration into my experience with the far right online

Alice Sibley

Researching the far right can be daunting especially when engaging in close-up research (Dobratz and Waldner 2020). The far right often poses a threat to academics and researchers due to their hostile positioning of academia as left-wing. Consequently, the left is frequently identified as an enemy of the far right (Pilkington 2019). Although this type of research holds challenges for both established academics and early-career researchers alike, early-career researchers are at a disadvantage due to their academic inexperience (Conway 2021; Moujaes, Yankova, and Marques 2021). Despite this inexperience, little research discusses the emotional and mental well-being challenges of researching the far right online (Conway 2021). As a result, this chapter discusses how I, an early-career PhD candidate, responded to a difficult experience online with a British far-right group during my fieldwork.[1] I am a third-year PhD candidate at Nottingham Trent University (NTU). My thesis consists of three studies: (1) a Facebook demographic analysis focusing on who supports three far-right groups, (2) a YouTube qualitative thematic analysis, and (3) a series of face-to-face online interviews with supporters and leaders of three far-right groups. During my final interview-based study one of the three far-right groups focused on posted my Facebook profile picture with a message advising people not to talk to me. Subsequently, I received online abuse which will be the focus of this chapter.

In my third study, I used qualitative semi-structured interviews, a common method in some academic disciplines. However, within far right research specifically, interviews are uncommon. Further, researchers who conduct interviews normally do not reflect on the interview process and simply report the data collected (Ellinas 2021). This reporting of findings alone does not help future researchers understand the process of interviewing including sampling, recruiting, ethics, and most importantly potential dangers associated with researching the far right. Despite emergent literature emphasising researchers' emotional and mental well-being (e.g., Baele et al. 2018), there is little academic research detailing how to practically respond to ethical challenges researchers may face during far right research (Ellinas 2021). Therefore, this chapter will first outline and follow Gibbs's reflective six-step cycle to evaluate and explore the complexity of my experience and reactions. It will finish with recommendations for responding to online abuse while conducting far right research.

Gibbs's reflective six-step cycle

As highlighted above, this chapter will reflect on my hostile online experience with a British far-right group. To do this, I use Gibbs's (1988) reflective six-step cycle. Although there are other more complex reflective models, Gibbs's has been selected as it is accessible and clearly defined (Adeani, Febriani, and Syafyadin 2020; Moon 2007). I, therefore, adhere to the following process: (1) describing what happened, (2) discussing how it made the researcher feel, (3) evaluating what was positive and negative about the experience, (4) analysing how to make sense of the situation, (5) concluding what else the researcher could have done, and finally, (6) outlining what the researcher would do next time in an action plan. This cycle focuses on the past with the intention of learning to inform future experiences (Gibbs 1988).

Description: what happened?

First, as argued above, researching the far right can be anxiety-provoking (Dobratz and Waldner 2020). This is especially true when you receive unwanted attention. Between September 2021 and March 2022, I attempted to recruit participants for my final interview-based study. Out of the three far-right groups I contacted, only one refused to talk to me. It is the subsequent online abuse I experienced from this group that I will discuss in detail. I was using Facebook to recruit people by going onto the far-right group's official Facebook page and observing who had liked or reacted to recent posts. As Schaffar and Thabchumpon (2019) recommend, I then contacted those individuals directly via Facebook Messenger with a comment about who I was, what I was doing, and why I was contacting them. For individuals who expressed interest, I then sent the participation sheet which had further details. In total, I sent over 100 messages to individuals that expressed support for this group. I only received one response and we were discussing a date for the interview. However, after a week, the individual withdrew from the study, stating that they were no longer interested in taking part. I was surprised by this and as a result, I returned to the group's Facebook page to view their recent activity. The group's admin had written a detailed post about me and my research and had attached my Facebook profile picture which contained my name and academic position. Although the post was respectful, they had advised people not to talk to me as they claimed I was a journalist who may attempt to manipulate their words. There was nothing aggressive about the post itself, but the post received 250 likes, twenty-eight comments, and sixteen shares. Of the twenty-eight comments, five were insulting or threatening with offensive language and reference to rape jokes. I also received a private message that said "kys" which is internet speak for "kill yourself".

Unsurprisingly, previous research suggests that online abuse, especially related to rape and death threats, can be traumatic. Despite the impact of such abuse, sadly it has become somewhat normalised in online discourse (Lewis, Rowe, and Wiper 2017). In response to my exposure, the first point of contact was to get emotional support from my partner, friends, and family. I then took screenshots of the perpetrators' Facebook profile pages and the post, comments, and private messages I had received. At the same time, I contacted my supervisors who emailed the pro-vice chancellor of research and the chair of the ethics committee. My supervisors put me in touch with the mental health support team at NTU and offered me the chance to discuss my concerns with them personally. During the meeting with the mental health professional, I was referred to a free University-linked cognitive behavioural therapy programme, a self-help online course which teaches positive coping mechanisms when dealing with stress and anxiety. However, the process to contact the relevant people and to enrol on the course was long and by the time I was enrolled, I no longer felt I would benefit from such a course. Therefore, I decided not to continue with the programme. During this period, I also met with student support services and Nottingham Trent Student Union who advised me to contact the police to ensure I had additional non-university protection. Subsequently, I contacted the police and attached the screenshots of the abuse I had received as evidence. After the police responded to my first email detailing what had happened, they did not reply to my second email despite my attempts to contact them. As there was no indication that there was any threat, I assumed this meant that the police were not concerned about my physical safety. However, even though there may have been little physical threat, I experienced emotional and psychological threat. This perceived threat was exacerbated by the lack of external protection from the police.

Feelings and thoughts: how did it make me feel?

While the initial message from the group's admin was matter-of-fact, non-aggressive, and inoffensive, some of the subsequent comments and direct messages were threatening. Because of this, I felt anxious for a period of time which impacted both my work and my personal life. It made me wary of my physical movements as my work address was publicly available. I was also concerned about personal information online which could identify my location, as well as personal details relating to my family and friends. I therefore deleted all my old accounts, contacting admins to ask for my profile to be removed after proving my identity. In total, I deleted nine online profiles that could have been used to target me. Most of these profiles were old and related to previous home addresses and phone numbers that were no longer relevant. Nevertheless, I deleted all personal information as even old information could be used to find more personal information, such as family members' names. Fortunately, nothing physically unpleasant happened, but in the far right, the tactic of doxing is a reality; this involves releasing personal information about a person, such as their address or phone number (Conway 2021) which can lead to physical abuse. Pertinent to me as an early-career researcher was the possibility of false information being spread to negatively affect my professional job prospects. In contrast to established academics, PhD students are in a more precarious professional environment, making targeted false information potentially more damaging (Massanari 2018).

Undoubtedly, my lack of experience in the field and my precarious professional position increased my anxiety response. This was my first attempt at recruiting participants from the far right to interview. Consequently, my supervisor team and the NTU ethics committee encouraged me to keep a diary of any untoward attention I received. They also advised me to open a line of communication with the IT department and relevant academics and university personnel to ensure I could discuss any threatening behaviour with the relevant people. Based on the complexity of online research, we decided to deal with each situation on a case-by-case basis. Despite implementing these protective steps, I was still inexperienced in how to deal with this online situation and how to feel about it. In total, it took about four months for my anxiety to dissipate. During this time, I had a persistent feeling of being under threat. However, this reaction may also have been related to my general emotional makeup and the stress of COVID-19. The pandemic had increased my stress generally and just as COVID-19 restrictions were easing, this happened. It is likely then that a combination of factors increased my anxiety, but the online abuse was a significant trigger.

Evaluation: what were the positive and negative effects of this experience?

Like most experiences, there were both negative and positive effects. The negative effects were obvious. I became anxious, I felt out of control and unprotected (even though I did have people protecting me as outlined above). As a result of this event, I discussed what had happened with certain people, informed my supervisors, and got the help I needed. I also had to take some time to reflect and regain my confidence. I took a couple of days out of my research and prioritised my mental health. Arguably the most serious negative effect was that I could no longer interview people for my third group in my thesis. This reduced my interview pool substantially and forced me to re-evaluate my final study, resulting in further anxiety about my ability to finish the PhD.

However, it also allowed me to take care of my well-being and prioritise my mental health (Conway 2021). PhD candidates are under time pressure and, therefore, we often do not take time to reflect on our experience and pause to assess our positioning, mental well-being, and progress. We do not think we have enough time. This experience forced me to pause, reflect, and temporarily prioritise my mental health and well-being *over* my research which, I think, made me a more mature researcher. Finally, it allowed me the opportunity to feel protected by my university and understand the ethical and supportive channels available to me. As a result of the experience, my supervisors were informed and informative; they knew my interview schedule and met with me after interviews to ensure I felt fully supported. This brought me closer to my supervisors but also connected me with other notable people within NTU who supported me through the process. Consequently, this experience made me feel like a more valued member of the NTU research community.

Analysis: how else could I have interpreted the situation?

In this research, I assumed that my ethnicity would give me a certain level of protection. As previous research has highlighted (Simi and Futrell 2015), being a white far right researcher positioned me as part of the accepted in-group rather than the identified out-group. This was clear in the interviews that I conducted with other far-right groups where supporters spoke with candour about race, ethnicity, and immigration (Sibley 2023), a finding that supports previous research (Hall 2020). As far-right groups are often characterised by their anti-immigration, anti-Muslim position, they are more likely to respond to a Black woman or Muslim woman with suspicion and hostility, resulting in less open communication (Conway 2021). My ethnicity, then, provided me with a significant layer of protection which meant that I was unlikely to be identified as a substantial threat and facilitated a more open discussion.

Although my ethnicity likely positioned me as part of their in-group, being female increased my chances of online harassment. Women are much more likely to receive online harassment compared to men (Veletsianos et al. 2018). Further, I found that my assumed socio-economic status (being part of the educational elite (Rydgren 2018)), my assumed values (being left-wing), and my assumed profession (being a journalist) counteracted the lack of perceived threat provided by my ethnicity. There was certainly a lack of trust as to what my intentions were during this research. As a researcher of the far right, some individuals may be suspicious of you and not feel comfortable talking. Some may even position you as the enemy and, therefore, researching the far right comes with certain potential dangers (Ellinas 2021; Klandermans 2020). It is difficult to access certain groups that are suspicious of academic or left-leaning institutions (Ellinas 2021). Some researchers prefer to gain access to a group via the gatekeeper as this ensures a level of trust and reputation, but this can create difficulties as the gatekeeper may withhold access (Pilkington 2016; Minichiello et al. 1990). Therefore, some, for example, Dobratz and Waldner (2020), choose to contact individuals directly, which is what I also chose to do (Sibley 2023). It is likely, then, that the group's admin was suspicious of me because I had not gone through what they saw as the appropriate channels to gain permission to access the group. Further, I did not immediately send each individual the participant information sheet as I wanted to gain their permission to send this document first. This meant that they did not have proof that I was not a journalist, nor did they have a detailed understanding of who I was and why I was conducting the research. Many far-right groups have been infiltrated by journalists and are presented negatively in the media. Therefore, there are understandable reasons as to why such groups are suspicious of researchers (Klandermans 2020).

Being the target of suspicion made me revaluate my own position. I had to ask myself: *did I trust individuals that expressed support for these groups?* Far-right supporters are frequently represented as dangerous in the media. Further, the British far right themselves often position academic researchers and universities as part of the United Against Fascism (UAF) movement, one of the far right's enemy groups (Pilkington 2019). The groups themselves, therefore, do pose a threat to left-leaning researchers and institutions. It is understandable then that I was nervous about being singled out by a group that could potentially harm me. This perceived threat was further heightened as I revealed certain personal information about myself to a supporter of this group when I shared the participant information sheet and my researcher profile page. However, in order to build rapport with individuals to ensure trust, it is necessary to disclose some information about yourself and the research you are conducting so that individuals can make an informed decision about whether they want to take part in the research (Ellinas 2021). This potentially may make you vulnerable as a researcher because you have to reach out to unknown people who are likely to be suspicious of you, and you may have to disclose some personal information about yourself (Dobratz and Waldner 2020). My implicit suspicion of far-right supporters then, in turn, may have increased their suspicion of me.

When online abuse happens, it is natural to respond in an anxious, threatened way. Online abuse can be distressing (Veletsianos et al. 2018). However, now, I would not respond in the same way as I previously did. Research suggests that one of the best approaches to online abuse is normal-isation, the acceptance that online abuse is part of the far right research jour-ney, especially for researchers who reach out to far-right groups personally (Lewis, Rowe, and Wiper 2017). However, this process of normalisation is easier once you are an established researcher with more experience (Lewis, Rowe, and Wiper 2017). Therefore, for an early-career researcher, one of the most useful ways to interpret the situation would be mindfully with curiosity rather than as a threat. Being mindful is to be receptively atten-tive and interested in what is happening in the present moment (Kummar, Correia, and Fujiyama 2019; Kashdan et al. 2011). Previous research sug-gests that being curious *and* mindful can decrease your defensive response, thereby reducing the perceived threat. However, being mindful *without* curiosity may heighten defensiveness and anxiety, suggesting that curiosity is the key to reducing threat perception (Kummar, Correia, and Fujiyama 2019; Kashdan et al. 2011). Through being mindful *and* curious, I could, therefore, have interpreted the event as what it was; a few hurtful comments and threats which caused me emotional distress. However, because I only responded with anxiety and mindfulness, not curiosity, I ruminated about the potential physical danger as well as the emotional danger, which caused me further emotional distress. Although the online abuse affected me emo-tionally, it provided an opportunity, albeit an unwelcome one, to reflect on my practice by engaging in self-protection, resistance, and acceptance tactics (Veletsianos et al. 2018). I did this by gaining academic support and sharing my experience. It was mainly the potential physical threat that concerned me which led me to feel powerless. This was primarily due to the possibility of what *could* happen rather than what actually *did* happen. For example, as previous research highlights, while online abuse may cause emotional distress, it is also more common than physical abuse, indicating that online abuse rarely leads to physical abuse (Baele et al. 2018). Mindfulness and curiosity, therefore, would allow me to interpret the threat more accurately in the future.

However, it should be noted that the far right generally does pose a significant threat to researchers and doxing is a tactic that is used to target identified enemies. This mindfulness and curiosity response then is only beneficial in less extreme types of online abuse where the researcher is not in a significantly dangerous position. If used in more dangerous situations, researchers may misinterpret the severity of the threat, thereby, putting themselves in more danger. The appropriateness of this response, therefore, depends on how extreme the group being researched is, the profile of the researcher including their ethnicity, and the severity of the online threat. In a seriously dangerous situation, anxiety and a perceived increased threat may encourage a more proactive response, possibly saving your life. Further, some academics claim that fear and anxiety may be an advantage in extremism research. As Blee (2002) argues in her organised racism research, losing a heightened sense of fear can decrease your analytical edge as a researcher. Therefore, a reduction in the level of fear felt may be preferable to losing a sense of fear altogether.

Conclusion: what else could I have done?

This experience encouraged me to develop as a researcher. However, there are further steps I could have taken to minimise negative impacts. My anxiety was partly driven by my lack of network with people who had experienced similar threats in relation to far right research. I could have built an emotional support network with other early-career researchers and academics who work in similar fields. This would have given me further psychological and emotional protection. However, because of COVID-19, I had not attended physical conferences and, therefore, had not been able to network with many people in my field. Further, as the abuse took place online, I could have reported the activity to Facebook as they follow a strict online abuse policy. This would ensure that the abusive material was removed and could also result in the perpetrators' accounts being disabled (Mendonca-Richards 2021). Finally, had the threat been more significant I could also have continued my line of enquiry to the police to increase my level of protection.

Action plan: what would I do next time?

Based on my experience, there are many things I will do next time I encounter online abuse during my research, as I am sure there *will* be a next time. First, preparation before conducting research is key (Conway 2021). Before beginning my research, therefore, I will delete all personal information from the internet (both past and present) to ensure my location and other identifying details are protected. As I did in this research, I will prepare a plan of action with my supervisors and relevant staff members to provide a supportive network (including counselling services offered by the university). I will also network with other relevant early-career researchers and academics to reinforce this support network. I will take screenshots of all relevant comments, posts, direct messages, and perpetrators' Facebook profile pages. These screenshots can be given as evidence of online abuse. In addition to contacting the police to report the abuse, I will also report the perpetrators to the relevant social media platform (Mendonca-Richards 2021). Further, when I receive future threats, I will immediately take time to reflect and do something that I love, physically and mentally detaching myself. Finally, depending on the severity of the abuse, I will also try to change my mentality by responding mindfully with curiosity rather than defensively with anxiety. I will remind myself that there is a low chance of something physically serious happening and that the majority of people who are commenting, responding, or messaging are not likely to be a physical threat, even if they appear threatening online.

Concluding thoughts

Researching the far right can be daunting (Dobratz and Waldner 2020). This situation was threatening not because of what *did* happen, but because of the potential of what *could* have happened. The PhD experience is already precarious and filled with insecurity, so something like this can exacerbate those feelings making you react in detrimental ways. This, I think, is what happened to me. One important lesson learnt during this process was that perceived threat is not the same as actual threat. In my case and likely due to my ethnicity, most of the online responders were respectful and reasonable and only a few were threatening. However, researchers in this field also have to ask the question: *does this potential danger come with the job?* Perhaps working closely with supporters of the far right *is* dangerous, and perhaps we need to be aware that negative events may happen, so we are ready for them. As Blee (2002) argues, this could give us, as researchers, an analytical edge. When I received the threats in this research I responded with high levels of anxiety, which led me to feel the need to prioritise my mental health *over* my research. I now understand that a better research approach is to give due attention to both my mental health and research so that the two can be held in balance without the need to prioritise one over the other. When threats do arise, responding in a mindful way with curiosity whilst at the same time perhaps retaining a degree of fear, will ensure our ongoing well-being as researchers in less dangerous situations. I certainly feel that this experience, after reflection, made me a more critical, mature researcher, and I feel more engaged in my research as a result.

Note

1 I am not going to name the group personally as this may put both me and the group in question at risk.

References

Adeani, I. S., Febriani, R. B. and Syafryadin, S. 2020. 'Using Gibbs' Reflective Cycle in Making Reflections of Literary Analysis', *Indonesian EFL Journal*, 6(2), 139–148.

Baele, S. J., Lewis, D., Hoeffler, A., Sterck, O. C. and Slingeneyer, T. 2018. 'The Ethics of Security Research: An Ethics Framework for Contemporary Security Studies', *International Studies Perspectives*, 19(2), 105–127.

Blee, K. M. 2002. *Inside Organized Racism: Women in the Hate Movement*. Berkeley, CA: University of California Press.

Conway, M. 2021. 'Online Extremism and Terrorism Research Ethics: Researcher Safety, Informed Consent, and the Need for Tailored Guidelines', *Terrorism and Political Violence*, 33(2), 367–380.

Dobratz, B. A. and Waldner, L. K. 2020. 'Interviewing Members of the White Power Movement in the United States: Reflections on Research Strategies and Challenges of Right-Wing Extremists'. In: Ashe, S. D., Busher, J., Macklin, G., and Winter, A. (eds). *Researching the Far Right: Theory, Method, and Practice*. London: Routledge, 212–224.

Ellinas, A. A. 2021. 'The Interview Method in Comparative Politics: The Process of Interviewing Far-Right Actors', *Government and Opposition*, 1–21.

Gibbs, G. 1988. *Learning by Doing: A Guide to Teaching and Learning Methods*. Oxford: Further Education Unit.

Hall, N. A. 2020. *Taking Back Control: The Online Political Engagement of Pro-Leave Non-Digital-Native Facebook Users*. Doctoral dissertation, University of Manchester.

Kashdan, T. B., Afram, A., Brown, K. W., Birnbeck, M., and Drvoshanov, M. 2011. 'Curiosity Enhances the Role of Mindfulness in Reducing Defensive Responses to Existential Threat', *Personality and Individual Differences*, 50(8), 1227–1232.

Klandermans, B. 2020. 'Life-History Interviews with Rightwing Extremists'. In Ashe, S. D., Busher, J., Macklin, G., and Winter, A. (eds). *Researching the Far Right: Theory, Method, and Practice*. London: Routledge, 225–238.

Kummar, A. S., Correia, H., and Fujiyama, H. 2019. 'A Brief Review of the EEG Literature on Mindfulness and Fear Extinction and Its Potential Implications for Posttraumatic Stress Symptoms (PTSS)', *Brain Sciences*, 9(10), 258.

Lewis, R., Rowe, M. and Wiper, C. 2017. 'Online Abuse of Feminists as an Emerging Form of Violence against Women and Girls', *British Journal of Criminology*, 57(6), 1462–1481.

Massanari, A. L. 2018. 'Rethinking Research Ethics, Power, and the Risk of Visibility in the Era of the "Alt-Right" Gaze', *Social Media+Society*, 4(2): 1–9.

Mendonca-Richards, A. 2021. 'Part 1 – The Rise of Online Abuse in Lockdown: How to Deal with Online Harassment'. 21 January. Farrer & Co. [Online]. https://www.farrer.co.uk/news-and-insights/the-rise-of-online-abuse-in-lockdown-how-to-deal-with-online-harassment-stalking-and-revenge-porn/#3.%20What%20can%20I%20do%20if%20I%20am%20being%20harassed%20online? (accessed 12 October 2023).

Minichiello, V., Aroni, R., Timewell, E. and Alexander, L. 1990. *In-Depth Interviewing: Researching People*. Melbourne: Longman Cheshire.

Moon, J. 2007. 'Getting the Measure of Reflection: Considering Matters of Definition and Depth', *Journal of Radiotherapy in Practice*, 6(4), 191–200.

Moujaes, G., Yankova, D. and Marques, P. 2021. 'Opening Up about PhD Uncertainty', *POLISS*, 1 July. [Online]. https://poliss.eu/opening-up-about-phd-uncertainty/ (accessed 12 October 2023).

Pilkington, H. 2016. *Loud and Proud: Passion and Politics in the English Defence League*. Manchester: Manchester University Press.

Pilkington, H. 2019. '"Field Observer: Simples": Finding a Place from Which to Do Close-Up Research on the "Far Right"'. In: Toscano, E. (ed.). *Researching Far-Right Movements*. London: Routledge, 23–40.

Rydgren, J. (ed.). 2018. *The Oxford Handbook of the Radical Right*. Oxford University Press.

Schaffar, W. and Thabchumpon, N. 2019. 'Militant Far-Right Royalist Groups on Facebook in Thailand: Methodological and Ethical Challenges of Internet-Based Research'. In: Toscano, E. (ed.). *Researching Far-Right Movements*. London: Routledge, 121–139.

Sibley, A. 2023. 'Behind the British New Far-Right's Veil: Do Individuals Adopt Strategic Liberalism to Appear More Moderate or Are They Semi-Liberal?', *The British Journal of Politics and International Relations*, online first.

Simi, P. and Futrell, R. 2015. *American Swastika: Inside the White Power Movement's Hidden Spaces of Hate*. Lanham, MD: Rowman & Littlefield.

Veletsianos, G., Houlden, S., Hodson, J., and Gosse, C. 2018. 'Women Scholars' Experiences with Online Harassment and Abuse: Self-Protection, Resistance, Acceptance, and Self-Blame', *New Media & Society*, 20(12), 4689–4708.

18

Community building as a response to care in studying the far right

Kayla Preston

A neglected topic in research ethics and qualitative and quantitative research in social sciences is the idea of self-care and emotional and often physical trauma when doing research. This is particularly salient when engaging in research that can be emotionally draining, traumatising, or taxing. Researchers of the far right have highlighted the potential to experience such problems (Blee and Cresap 2010; Massanari 2018). For example, far-right groups have created multiple platforms to 'expose' researchers and professors who they believe threaten their ideology, one of which is the Professor Watchlist which highlights professors who are espousing 'leftist propaganda' (Massanari 2018). This chapter will consider the following questions: what impact do the possibilities of these actions have? How do researchers separate themselves when looking at explicit or troubling content? Is this possible? This chapter will highlight these questions and examine literature that discusses the problems scholars face when they navigate the emotional labour of research. I argue that coping strategies are often insufficient for researchers who study the far right. This is because they rely on individualising research emotional labour without addressing the underlying isolation of the research enterprise. Ultimately, community building and membership provide better solutions to research stress as they mediate the above problems. I begin by addressing the importance of community building and support in research on the far right. What follows is a discussion on how the pitfalls of other forms of research care, such as emotional labour, research ambivalence, and self-care, can be elevated by community building. I will also discuss how privilege influences access to care.

Community and research

A primary sector of support for researchers is the research community itself (Petrova and Coughlin 2012; Vaughn, Jacquez, and Zhen-Duan 2018). While some studies have found that community-centred research yields promising results (Vaughn, Jacquez, and Zhen-Duan 2018), other research has also found that writing retreats and peer mentorship are key to creating nurturing and supportive spaces for researchers to share ideas and challenges in both the writing and research processes (Paltridge 2016; Petrova and Coughlin 2012). This is especially important for early career researchers (Petrova and Coughlin 2012). Understanding ourselves as researchers as part of a collective can also be highly beneficial, especially in isolating work such as academia (Jones and Whittle 2021). Alongside the peer research community, studies have also shown the importance of mentorship to researchers and clinicians, especially those who may experience additional boundaries due to racism, sexism, etc. (Remaker et al. 2021). Individuals who have supportive mentors are more likely to combat research career loneliness and are more likely to be able to access resources to improve their work environments (Remaker et al. 2021).

The separation between researcher and their field

While I argue that community is vital to addressing trauma, other tools include the separation of the researcher from the field. However, for many, this is impossible due to positionality and the nature of the topic, especially when considering research on the far right, a community that spews racism and xenophobia. Due to these reasons, some scholars have complicated the idea of the separation of the researcher from the field by placing the individual into the research process as an inalienable feature of data collection and analysis (Behar 2020; Kleinman, Copp and Henderson 1997; Piper et al. 2019; Tuhiwai-Smith 1999). These scholars inquire about neutrality and objectivity in scientific inquiry. They ask how researchers separate themselves from the field during studies. What happens to the research process if this cannot be done? The research itself would benefit from more scholars being critical about fitting into the research process. Researchers should consider how a lack of critical analysis of the research process as inherently objective fails to understand research implications as a colonial tool and how racialised researchers have been encouraged to separate identity from the research processes (Hordge-Freeman 2018). Literature on researcher and field relationships also highlights the emotional impact that the field can have on scholars (Hahonou 2019). This is especially important to consider when studying the far right, as the far right often targets marginalised groups, making studying the far right an emotional and taxing experience for those in these communities.

As a result of the possibility of complicated relationships to the data, participants, and the field, some literature has considered embracing the imperfections of research (Luttrell 2000), a topic discussed in further detail below.

Being a 'good enough' researcher means creating a feeling of mutual trust between the people who are being researched and the researcher (Luttrell 2000). In this method, the participants can negotiate the definitions placed on them by the researcher. Disagreement between researcher and participant may also in itself yield important insights into the far right. For example, if a researcher labels a group as a far-right group and participants disagree, this tension could yield insight into how far-right individuals, even former far-right individuals, understand far-right groups and white supremacy. In synopsis, the relationships researchers have with the field, how they navigate their interactions with participants, and the emotions that occur when doing research are all central to the research.

However, in far right studies, the act of coming to participants is complicated. This may be because at times scholars disagree on the correct definition of the far right. Such definitions are contentious in this field, especially to people who may be labelled as a member of the far right. There may also be an inability to develop a rapport between participant and researcher with research participants in far right studies. Mutual trust also might not be able to be achieved. This is because when researching the far right, scholars often come in contact with intense, traumatic, or offensive content. For example, in far right studies, the contention between researcher and participant may be too difficult or even dangerous to subvert. Researchers in this field daily risk being exposed, threatened, and attacked because of their identity as a researcher or because of the intersections of their scholarship and their gender, race, ethnicity, and sexuality (Blee and Cresap 2010). Therefore, the idea of the separation of the researcher from the field may be impossible for researchers of the far right, meaning alternative modes of care are needed.

Discomfort and ambivalence in research

Literature has spoken about the discomfort of feeling changed by the field (Buford May 2014; Connell 2018; González-López 2010; Pugh 2013). In this research, the authors speak to the benefits and pitfalls of discomfort, exploring how ambivalence in research can be an analytical tool and an opportunity for personal growth. This may occur through outsider status with participants (Buford May 2014) or reflection on the ambivalence and the comfort in discomfort when faced with participant interactions during the research (Connell 2018; González-López 2010).

While some scholarship on emotions and discomfort examines outsider relationships that participants might have with researchers (Buford May 2014), a growing set of literature has taken up this conversation by speaking about being uncomfortable or questioning the relationships that are built as an insider during the research process (Connell 2018; González-López 2010). For example, in their article about participant and research discomfort, González-López (2010) speaks about research discomfort when talking to participants about emotionally charged topics. Being able to join participants during the interview in that moment of vulnerability may be uncomfortable. In some research projects, scholars are asked to be emotional support for their participants as they speak about their experiences (González-López 2010: 576). This would require being comfortable in very emotional moments that many would find uncomfortable. Still, it also would require a deep relationship with participants that comes from trust and understanding. However, being able to go to participants in moments of vulnerability and being vulnerable is not always possible (Connell 2018). Connell (2018) further adds to this conversation by arguing that, as researchers, we should be okay with the discomfort of having mixed feelings about our research and its outcomes. Much like González-López (2010), Connell finds a way to move past this discomfort in research toward analytical clarity, or at least meaningful analytical ambivalence that can propel research.

Literature has spoken about how researchers should not shy away from uneasy and mixed feelings about their data and time in the field (Connell 2018; Buford May 2014; González-López 2010; Pugh 2013). In her article, Hordge-Freeman (2018) argues that we construct our research, field, and analysis through our emotional responses. For example, Hordge-Freeman's (2018) experience with discrimination in the field drove her research process and impacted how and what she studied and questioned. In their article, Kovach et al. (2013) take up a similar claim. By highlighting their own stories about their work as researchers, they emphasise the importance of 'going home' and reconnecting with yourself during the research process. Grounding and reconnecting with oneself are integral parts of the reflexivity process and should be included in academic research.

Analytical insights are created in this discomfort and tension (Buford May 2014; Pugh 2013), and we grow as researchers in these convergences (Connell 2018; González-López 2010). However, researchers can be ambivalent about these experiences, instead of seeing them as analytical moments to advance the field (Connell 2018). It is in these spaces where care can become important. Discomfort and ambivalence are emotionally taxing and when researchers must sit in that space during data collection, analysis, and writing, the prolonged exposure can have severe consequences. This is even more pronounced when dealing with participants or data collected from the far right. Due to the nature of far-right discourse that is often homophobic, transphobic, sexist, Islamophobic, and racist, researchers in marginalised groups are even more at risk of experiencing trauma in the research process. Therefore, much like the separation of the researcher and the field, being comfortable in ambivalence and discomfort at times is impossible for researchers of the far right whose communities may be under attack by their own participants.

Benefits and pitfalls of self-care in research

While being uncomfortable and ambivalent about research may be a site of further data analysis, it is also impossible or particularly distressing for some researchers. When this occurs, some may propose self-care during the research process. However, engaging in this type of process may be impossible for some for a variety of reasons which I will discuss. There has been an extensive amount of research done on self-care in research in general (Jones and Whittle 2021; McGourty et al. 2010; Rager 2005). Many of these studies highlight the need to engage in self-care practices when conducting research that looks at trauma or topics that can be significantly troubling to researchers and readers (Kumar and Cavallaro 2018; Rager 2005). Some of this research has been done in the health sciences, addressing novice researchers and doctoral students' self-care practices when studying anxiety-inducing and emotionally distressing topics. Kumar and Cavallaro (2018) highlight in their article how important it is to engage in self-care when researching an issue that you have a personal connection to. This emotional drain and need to engage in self-care are even more prominent in qualitative research, where often researchers are engaging with participants and are themselves tools in the research and methodology process, gaining rapport with participants, and constantly hearing or reading first-hand accounts of traumatic or violent content (Kumar and Cavallaro 2018). For example, many people who researched the far right may have family members who are part of these groups or are engaged in far-right electoral politics. Researchers are also regularly subjected to violence emotionally, and at times physically, by far-right participants. Self-care and the idea of engaging in restorative practices such as meditation, exercise, etc. may seem ineffective to individuals who are at the sharp end of far-right violence. Far right researchers may be harassed by their research participants and may read and engage with racist, transphobic, homophobic, sexist, and xenophobic content about their own communities when researching the far right.

However, being able to engage in self-care is a privilege denied to many researchers who may be under financial strain to continue to work, or who may be deeply impacted by the discourse of the participants they are studying. Self-care often requires monetary funding. For example, taking time off work, a common practice meant to help with self-care, is not an option for many. In some research fields and professions, such as the field of counselling (Nelson et al. 2018), there are concrete strategies given to researchers and professionals when they start their careers to combat this strain. This includes keeping tabs on emotional responses to the project, checking in on fellow researchers, and creating communities of those who may also be engaging in this type of work (Rager 2005; Jones and Whittle 2021). It may also be time for far right researchers to engage in some of these practices and acknowledge our projects' often emotionally taxing work. This is of particular importance because some people in the field do receive backlash on their publications, even in the form of hate mail and derogatory messages on commonly used social media from members of the far right.

Separation, privilege, and research

While self-care, comfort in discomfort in research, and separation from the field are ways to limit research emotional strain, only certain researchers can participate in these strategies. Being so detached from your research participants and their experiences and being so separate from your field that you are not influenced by traumatic things that happen are reserved for people who hold such significant power in society. In research on the far right, this is even more prevalent. When scholars examine content that can be racist, sexist, transphobic, and homophobic and may be in a marginalised community, the ability to separate oneself from the research might not be possible. It is a privilege not to be significantly changed by any discrimination or trauma you experience in the field. It is a privilege not to share these phenomena in general.

Self-care is particularly one area in which researchers who study the far right may be unable to participate. Self-care requires time, financial stability, and an ability to separate yourself from your research, all of which might not be possible for racialised and queer researchers who study the far right. In research, in general, racialised scholars have experienced large-scale discrimination in the academy (Henry and Tator 2012). The research enterprise also has a history of being used for colonial purposes, further isolating racialised researchers (Piper et al. 2019; Tuhiwai-Smith 1999). Queer people have also faced discrimination based on their identities when conducting research (Bacio and Rinaldi 2019). Therefore, for these communities, self-care may feel like a band-aid solution, especially when researching groups who may themselves be discriminatory.

Bringing it back to community

Because self-care and research separation are not possible, an alternative to counter research fatigue and trauma when studying the far right is through community. Community may also counter isolation and loneliness in the field. Academia and research enterprise in general have not been immune to the neoliberalisation of the university (Jones and Whittle 2021). Through this process, scholars have been conditioned to the idea that research should be done alone, meaning it is often an isolating endeavour (Jones and Whittle 2021: 381). Scholars are typically left alone to cope with the trauma and stress of the research process. However, the ability to separate the self from the field and heal through research is difficult and isolating as discussed above. This is even more prominent when researching topics such as the far right, which inherently results in the researchers being exposed to violent content.

Forming research communities as spaces of healing and support is just one way to mediate the isolation and trauma of the research process. Scholars have investigated the meaning of community space and support during research and writing; Jones and Whittle's (2021) discussion of communiversity draws particular attention to community in research. Kinpaisby (2008) originally utilised the term 'communiversity' to examine the role of community and researcher identity in scholarship. This term also signifies the idea that within the university itself, communities are pervasive and should be highlighted as an important research tool (Kinpaisby 2008: 296). Other studies have also highlighted the benefits of community and support for graduate students (Ginn 2014). Feminist researchers have highlighted the need for supportive mentorship and emotional reflectivity in the research relationship to counter the neoliberalisation of the university and research process (Fem-Mentee Collective 2017).

Subverting the neoliberal idea of the academy as a space of competition where one student or professor must beat out another for promotions, grants, or jobs means also highlighting what care looks like in the academy. Research has shown that for marginalised communities, having a supportive network of peers and mentors to discuss problems that may arise in funding and research is crucial to researcher well-being (Deanna 2022). Care in these spaces can be open communication, support, and mentorship. This is important in far right studies as researchers from all levels of the academy may face emotional difficulty. Moving forward, it will be vital for far right researchers to undertake such a compassionate turn towards community and away from research in isolation. By doing so, individuals who research the far right can foster strong community support systems which can assist in emotional trauma that may be inflicted during the research process. Alternatively, people who research the far right would benefit from community-led healing and support to share intellectual insights in a safe environment, often an element of the research process that those studying the far right miss out on as safety in their research and discussion with participants is not guaranteed. While self-care and reflectivity can be steps to healing and connecting to ourselves and participants during research, those who study the far right should have access to a community of those who have gone through similar research experiences to negate feelings of isolation and trauma during the research process.

Conclusions

What can these discussions bring to the study of the far right? It's essential to build a supportive community to assist researchers in pursuing often tricky subjects. Peer communities and supportive mentorship that can provide spaces of connection for junior and senior researchers are also vital in the care processes. As the literature has shown, it is hard to separate the researcher from the field, engage in the emotional labour of research, and unpack the feelings and emotions that research findings and participants may bring forth. This is particularly more pronounced in studies surrounding violence, trauma, or research subjects that may wish to do harm. These problems are even more pronounced for researchers who may face oppression both in and outside academia. Moving forward, if far right research wishes to contribute to decolonial and anti-racist work, then building a community of supportive, encouraging, and engaging researchers and activists is needed to navigate the discomfort and at times violent circumstances that come with researching the far right. Care in communities may look different depending on the individual. However, providing supportive peer and supervisor mentorship, and a space to speak about problems that arise in research including feelings of ambivalence, fear, and even anger may be a step forward in assisting far right researchers in their pursuits.

References

Bacio, M. and Rinaldi, C. 2019. 'The Queer Researcher: Challenging Homonormativity in Research and Educational Settings'. In: Magaraggia, S., Mauerer, G., and Schmidbaur, M. (eds). *Feminist Perspectives on Teaching Masculinities*. London: Routledge, 29–43.

Behar, R. 2020. 'Read More, Write Less'. In: McGranahan, C. (ed.). *Writing Anthropology: Essays on Craft & Commitment*. Durham, NC: Duke University Press, 47–53.

Blee, K. M. and Creasap, K. A. (2010). 'Conservative and Right-Wing Movements', *Annual Review of Sociology*, 36, 269–286.

Buford May, R. A. 2014. 'When the Methodological Shoe Is on the Other Foot: African American Interviewer and White Interviewees', *Qualitative Sociology*, 37(1), 117–136.

Calabro, S. 2018. 'From the Message Board to the Front Door: Addressing the Offline Consequences of Race- and Gender-Based Doxxing and Swatting', *Suffolk University Law Review*, 51(1), 55–75.

Connell, C. 2018. 'Thank You for Coming Out Today: The Queer Discomforts of In-Depth Interviewing'. In: D'Lane, R., Compton, T. M., and Schilt, K. (eds). *Queer Methods in Sociology*. Berkeley, CA: University of California Press, 126–139.

Deanna, R., Merkle, B. G., Chun, K. P., Navarro-Rosenblatt, D., Baxter, I., Oleas, N., ... and Auge, G. 2022. 'Community Voices: The Importance of Diverse Networks in Academic Mentoring', *Nature Communications*, 13(1681), 1–7.

Fem-Mentee Collective (Bain, A. L., Baker, R., Laliberté, N., Milan, A., Payne, W. J. ... and Saad, D.) 2017. 'Emotional Masking and Spill-Outs in the Neoliberalized University: A Feminist Geographic Perspective on Mentorship', *Journal of Geography in Higher Education*, 41(4), 590–607.

Ginn, F. 2014. '"Being Like a Researcher": Supervising Master's Dissertations in a Neoliberalizing University', *Journal of Geography in Higher Education*, 38(1), 106–118.

González-López, G. 2010. 'Ethnographic Lessons: Researching Incest in Mexican Families', *Journal of Contemporary Ethnography*, 39(5), 569–581.

Hahonou, E. K. 2019. 'Emotions as Method: Obtrusiveness and Participant Observation in Public Bureaucracies', *Critique of Anthropology*, 39(2), 188–204.

Henry, F. and Tator, C. 2012. 'Interviews with Racialized Faculty Members in Canadian Universities', *Canadian Ethnic Studies*, 44(1), 75–99.

Hordge-Freeman, E. 2018. 'Bringing Your Whole Self to Research: The Power of the Researcher's Body, Emotions, and Identities in Ethnography', *International Journal of Qualitative Methods*, 17(1), 1–9.

Jones, C. H. and Whittle, R. 2021. 'Researcher Self-Care and Caring in the Research Community', *Area*, 53(2), 381–388.

Kinpaisby, M. 2008. 'Taking Stock of Participatory Geographies: Envisioning the Communiversity', *Transactions of the Institute of British Geographers*, 33(3), 292–299.

Kleinman, S., Copp, M., and Henderson, K. 1997. 'Qualitatively Different: Teaching Fieldwork to Graduate Students', *Journal of Contemporary Ethnography*, 25(4), 469–499.

Kovach, M., Carriere, J., Barrett, M. J., Montgomery, H., and Gillies, C. 2013. 'Stories of Diverse Identity Locations in Indigenous Research', *International Review of Qualitative Research*, 6(4), 487–509.

Kumar, S. and Cavallaro, L. 2018. 'Researcher Self-Care in Emotionally Demanding Research: A Proposed Conceptual Framework', *Qualitative Health Research*, 28(4), 648–658.

Luttrell, W. (2000). '"Good Enough" Methods for Ethnographic Research', *Harvard Educational Review*, 70(4), 499–523.

Massanari, A. L. 2018. 'Rethinking Research Ethics, Power, and the Risk of Visibility in the Era of the "Alt-Right" Gaze', *Social Media+Society*, 4(2), 1–9.

McGourty, A., Farrants, J., Pratt, R., and Cankovic, M. 2010. 'Taking Your Participants Home: Self Care within the Research Process', *Counselling Psychology Review*, 25(4), 65–73.

Nelson, J. R., Hall, B. S., Anderson, J. L., Birtles, C., and Hemming, L. 2018. 'Self-Compassion as Self-Care: A Simple and Effective Tool for Counselor Educators and Counseling Students', *Journal of Creativity in Mental Health*, 13(1), 121–133.

Paltridge, B. 2016. 'Writing Retreats as Writing Pedagogy', *Writing & Pedagogy*, 8(1), 199–213.

Petrova, P. and Coughlin, A. (2012). 'Using Structured Writing Retreats to Support Novice Researchers', *International Journal for Researcher Development*, 3(1), 79–88.

Piper, D., Jacobe, J., Yazzie, R., and Calderon, D. 2019. 'Indigenous Methodologies in Graduate School'. In: Windchief, S. and San Pedro, T. (eds). *Applying Indigenous Research Methodologies: Storying with Peoples and Communities*. Milton: Taylor & Francis, 86–100.

Pugh, A. 2013. 'What Good Are Interviews for Thinking About Culture?', *American Journal of Cultural Sociology*, 1(1), 42–68.

Rager, K. B. 2005. 'Self-Care and the Qualitative Researcher: When Collecting Data Can Break Your Heart', *Educational Researcher*, 34(4), 23–27.

Remaker, D. N., Gonzalez, M. M., Houston-Armstrong, T., and Sprague-Connors, G. 2021. 'Women of Color and Mentorship in Graduate Training', *Training and Education in Professional Psychology*, 15(1), 70–75.

Taylor, J. and Patterson, M. 2010. 'Autonomy and Compliance: How Qualitative Sociologists Respond to Institutional Ethical Oversight', *Qualitative Sociology*, 33(2), 161–183.

Tuhiwai-Smith, L. 1999. 'Introduction'. In: *Decolonizing Methodologies: Research and Indigenous Peoples*. London: Zed Books, 1–18.

Vaughn, L. M., Jacquez, F., and Zhen-Duan, J. 2018. 'Perspectives of Community Co-Researchers about Group Dynamics and Equitable Partnership within a Community-Academic Research Team', *Health Education & Behavior*, 45(5), 682–689.

19

Negotiating contradiction in success and safety: a consideration of environmental constraints on risk management

Antonia Vaughan

Discussions around the safety of researchers of extremism have acquired a more substantial presence on Twitter, at conferences, and in literature, including for those researching the far right. As part of this, the scholarly community has incorporated a broader understanding of the range of harms including networked harassment, threats to livelihood, and vicarious trauma (Conway 2021). The impact of these harms can be substantial, leading to trauma, "logistical and financial burdens", and social isolation (Doerfler et al. 2021: 12). Pivotal moments for academia for discussing such harms came with #OperationDiggingDiGRA (part of Gamergate) when the far right turned its focus and energy towards harassing feminist gaming academics (Massanari 2018), whilst Maura Conway (2021) points to research on content moderators to explain how we have acquired the language to discuss vicarious trauma. With ethical approaches to research seeking to minimise "undue harm" (Morrison et al. 2021), incorporating researcher safety is critical. However, Conway argues that such consideration is undermined by an almost complete "dearth" of advice on the topic (2021).

In response to the increased breadth of threats, attention has turned to how to minimise the impact of the harms associated with working in the field. Some guidance for individuals has been produced by a range of think tanks, in opinion pieces and blogs, and in academic chapters (Marwick et al. 2016). However, the individual focus of advice has been critiqued by Conway (2021), Mattheis and Kingdon (2021), and Doerfler et al. (2021) who argue that individuals only have so much power and capability due to the lack of comprehensive advice, the economic and temporal barriers to implementation, and the embedded nature of harms faced. Mattheis and Kingdon particularly critique institutions for failing to support their own researchers (2021).

Similarly, scholars have challenged the centrality of ethics requirements such as informed consent, arguing that this unnecessarily jeopardises the safety of researchers by requiring identification towards likely hostile groups. Research that attracts the 'gaze' of the far right – including research on the far right – can see the traditional power balance favouring the researcher shift towards the participants, rendering the former vulnerable (Massanari 2018). When considering harm to researchers, positionality is critical as it can substantially mediate the risk, magnitude and impact of harm (Conway 2021). Researchers at the sharp end of the far right are significantly more vulnerable researching the far right, especially if they present or publicly discuss their identity as they are "likely to prove a more attractive and persistent target" (Conway 2021: 370). Outside of threats specific to the subject area, Veletsianos et al. (2018) and Kawahara and Bejarano (2009) have identified pervasive structural discrimination and harm within academia and in online spaces impacting on experiences and progression for scholars at the sharp end of the far right.

However, within the conversations on harm, the structural and environmental obstacles to safety and care have been largely overlooked. Like every researcher in academia, researchers of the far right work within an environment with shifting demands like 'publish or perish', the measurement of value through impact, the precarity of employment, and university reputation management. In considering an area where harm is said to 'come with the territory', this chapter aims to show how individualising responsibility for safety harms researchers by creating an antagonistic relationship between success and safety, with implications for who we enable to stay in academia. In framing behaviours as choices, the current system invisibilises its own role in mandating or discouraging behaviour. With the trends affecting researchers across academia, this chapter argues that the response should not be to individualise responsibility for a structural problem. First, I will discuss the neoliberal environment and the measurement of success, then I will detail how two harms highlight the contradictions, before finally discussing the implications.

The neoliberal academic environment

The neoliberal turn in academia has greatly impacted how knowledge has been "conceptualised, produced, and disseminated" (Ward 2012). It is visible in the management of institutions and research (Deem 2001), academic capitalism (Croucher and Lacy 2022), precarity as the norm (Loher and Strasser 2019), individualisation rather than collegiality (Rosa 2022), the imposition of metrics quantifying success, the focus on productivity, output, and assessing the value of research (impact) (deRond and Miller 2005). The quantification of success produces metrics which determine what is rewarded and who progresses as they become highly relevant at review boards, for promotions, during job applications, and in the production of hierarchies such as university rankings (deRond and Miller 2005). Collectively, the metrics imagine the 'ideal worker' with implications for gendered, racialised, and disabled academics (Rosa 2022).

Underlining the importance of productivity to succeed in academia, the phrase 'publish or perish' has become common currency. 'Publish or perish' is the idea that success or progression is dependent on the number of publications and citations an individual has and where these are published (deRond and Miller 2005). This phrase is used to critique the emphasis on quantity over quality and the resulting impact on work-life balance. Recently, there has been a turn to using the phrase 'publish *and* perish' (emphasis my own) due to the intense competition and pervasive precarity. This perception has been somewhat supported by research which has shown that new assistant professors "in recent years" have, on average, "published roughly twice as much as new assistant professors did in the 1990s" (Warren 2019; see also van Dijk et al. 2014).

Amplifying the emphasis on output is the h-index, which attempts to measure the impact of a scholar's work. This index takes an average of the number of citations and quantity of publications, with both being necessary for a high score. The inclusion of citations is a way of measuring impact and the quantity of publications is a way of measuring productivity. The emphasis on impact in academia has come about through the need to demonstrate and measure the value of research, particularly to funders. Impact is measured in varying ways including the number of publications, the number of citations, the presence of papers in high-impact journals, and influencing policy. 'Attention' on articles (shares on social media, etc.) is measured through the 'altmetrics' tool. Impact is tied to publication pressure because it is one way to demonstrate contribution to knowledge. The development of 'name as currency' has occurred alongside the individualisation of academia and emphasis on impact as expertise is demonstrated through publications, public scholarship, ResearchGate, and Academia.Edu profiles. Institutions have enabled (and sometimes mandated) this through the creation of online profiles which collate experience and output in the form of a public CV, a calling card, attached to the institution.

One of the most accessible avenues for impact – which has seen a corresponding spike in use – has been social media, and in particular Academic Twitter. Academic Twitter is a loose term used to refer to loosely networked accounts of scholars who use the platform for primarily academic purposes (Gregory and singh 2018). Engagement with Academic Twitter enables academics to contribute to public conversations and debates, comment on current events, and find relevant journals, articles and opportunities. The affordances of the platform mean that such engagement is a low effort with almost no barrier to entry. The use of social media to promote one's own work can contribute to success metrics, as the use of social media is positively correlated with a higher citation count (Stewart 2016; Mewburn and Thompson 2013; Terras 2012) and a higher number of media appearances (Miller and Mills 2009), as it puts expertise in front of a wider and larger audience. As noted by Barbour and Marshall (2012), the more personally engaging the Twitter profile of a researcher, the more engagement they received making it in a researcher's interest to share more, to offer the human side. This sphere taps into the attention and engagement economies, with the ability to enhance one's currency and circumvent traditional hierarchies and geographic isolation (Carrozza 2018; Barbour and Marshall 2012). The networked nature allows for connections to be built outside of the traditional spaces such as workshops and conferences – particularly critical for those unable to access such spaces.

Outside of Academic Twitter, impact is achievable in a number of ways including public scholarship, media appearances, and contributing to policy. However, these alternative venues come with their own challenges (e.g. for policy, see Chapter 27). The inclusion of public scholarship in success metrics differs between institutions. Participants reported that they were encouraged – or expected – to engage with the public sphere, but that this expectation was not reflected in the structures to report impact. This reflects the hierarchy of knowledge that devalues community or activist activities, certain topics, and research from faculty of colour (Settles et al. 2021).

Collectively, the metrics of success require productivity and output and a substantial engagement with the public sphere in order to demonstrate impact. To meet the metrics required for success, visibility in some form is necessary.

Harms

As mentioned, there is an increasing awareness of the harms associated with researching the far right, including vicarious trauma and networked harassment. The dialogue has been enabled, in part, by researchers expanding how harm is considered in ethics to incorporate researchers as a potentially vulnerable party. Massanari (2018) has identified how this is particularly important when dealing with the alt/far right because the power balance can tilt towards the participant. Exacerbating the harm has been the number of new entrants to the field seen in the growth in the volume of research (Castelli Gattinara 2020), underserved by a "dearth" of advice on ethics (Conway 2021). In this section, I outline two of the most discussed harms: vicarious trauma and networked harassment; I detail the available advice and highlight how it directly contradicts the behaviours necessary for success.

Networked harassment

Networked harassment is defined as "collaborative attacks against individuals amplified through social media" (Marwick and Caplan 2018 in Lewis et al. 2020) involving behaviours such as doxing, death threats, cyberstalking, et cetera. Its prevalence towards academics is relatively understudied, with anecdotal evidence providing the bulk of knowledge (for an exception see Doerfler et al.'s excellent piece (2021) utilising interviews with academics who have experienced harassment). Networked harassment is made possible by the digital sphere as perpetrators patch together available information and utilise communication channels to carry out and amplify the abuse. This information could be the institution the researcher works at, family members, locations, appearance, and so on. As such, the greater the engagement with the internet, the greater the vulnerability and possible harm.

One insidious aspect of networked harassment is the unpredictable nature of the attacks which can create a background level of anxiety spiking around moments of engagement and output as these bring the researcher to the public's attention. Stewart (2016) noted how context collapse means that researchers speak to a diverse and sometimes unexpected audience online, exacerbated by the far right's hostility towards academia. Doerfler et al. (2021) detail how harassment against some of their participants was directly sparked by journal publications, public scholarship and engagement with social media. These two aspects complicate core activities as publishing is both necessary and can spark harassment; similarly, engaging with Academic Twitter can prompt and enable harassment.

The majority of advice for dealing with this harm is aimed at the individual and is framed in terms of controlling engagement with the digital sphere. Researchers are advised to closely monitor and manage the amount of information available online, to make social media profiles private (personal and professional), and carefully consider what their engagement is. Proffered advice includes disengaging from social spaces, not publicising output, anonymising contributions, and refraining from contributing to the media. When harassment occurs, researchers are suggested to withdraw from the digital public sphere and refrain from public engagement in any form. In short, safety requires obscurity.

Obscurity is made necessary in part because of a broad lack of proactive and reactive support from institutions and platforms (Mattheis and Kingdon 2021; Lewis et al. 2020). Similarly, whilst Twitter has been praised for making some changes to hide abuse, helpful tools such as blocklists are privately made and require users to be aware of and implement them. This is further challenged by platforms increasingly constraining access to APIs. On the platform, the victim must individually report and block harassers – requiring a significant time and labour investment as it may involve thousands of accounts and instances. The structure of the harm means that it often does not meet the bar for criminal activity, making it nearly impossible to prosecute (Lewis et al. 2020).

Underlining the attitude of institutions and platforms is the responsibilisation of the individual. By framing networked harassment as resulting from engagement with the internet, it becomes the consequence of the researcher's activity and choice to participate, thus the researcher's fault that it happened. Conceiving online harassment like this follows through to a lack of strategy and support from institutions and ignores how success requires the behaviour. This framing has been problematised by Veletsianos et al. (2018) because it overlooks how endemic discrimination produces barriers of entry that privilege identities less subject to harassment. Moreover, with the response to harassment individualised, victims see substantial economic and temporal consequences when implementing proactive and reactive strategies, thus some seek to avoid the risk by withdrawing from public spaces (Veletsianos et al. 2018; Doerfler et al. 2021).

An insidious aspect of requiring disengagement from social media for scholars at the sharp end is that it cuts them off from community, often built through public channels on social media. Lone scholars can feel isolated at institutions and rely on these venues to connect with others in similar positions and ask for help. This is deeply unhelpful as such community and peer-led support is often critical to minimise vicarious trauma and for solidarity in a hostile industry (Allam 2022). By requiring withdrawal from the public sphere or the experience of harm, researchers are either cut off from community, solidarity, and support or repeatedly harmed. This in turn can reinforce the isolation of the individual.

Even if a researcher does engage with the public sphere in pursuit of impact, even if they tightly control all information available online, there are certain harm mitigations outside of their control. Harassment can be sparked by publications, institutional profiles, and conference presentations, enabled through traditional communication methods. Removing information verges on impossible for some researchers in country contexts where it is legally mandated to have home and/or office addresses publicly available. Institutional profiles can offer sufficient information to spark harassment by associating a researcher with their subject expertise and providing contact information. Whilst there is little evidence on the prevalence, the possibility and impact of harassment affects the researcher's wellbeing and requires risk mitigation strategies 'just in case'.

Furthermore, experiences of harassment are not uniform but rather mediated by identity, with the far right proving only too willing to use such behaviour to make the digital environment hostile for some more than others. Used to "police" victims, online harassment is seen as a "normal part of online experience" for scholars at the sharp end of far-right politics (Marwick and Caplan 2018; Veletsianos et al. 2018; Cottom 2015). This produces a "chilling effect" on engagement by victims as the toll of preventing and dealing with harassment requires both money and time (Veletsianos et al. 2018). Despite the increased endemic threat associated with engagement with the digital sphere, for those at the sharp end of the far right there is a greater pressure to be present. Discussing work-life balance and gender in academia, Lester and Sallee (2017) state that "faculty members can either choose to work increasingly longer hours, complete with more work tasks, or risk losing their jobs to someone more willing to perform that work". A similar dichotomy is present here.

Requiring obscurity for safety and visibility for success produces an obvious contradiction and requirement to perish, either from failure or harm. For example, publication is simultaneously an opportunity to make an impact and demonstrate productivity and a point of risk which could prompt harassment. Since the advice for harm minimisation is to disengage, it is supposedly the researcher's choice to disregard that. However, many researchers engage with this topic out of a moral obligation and/or self-defence; research, public engagement, and having an impact are a necessity. Thus, those on the sharp end are both researching to be safe *and* having their safety jeopardised. Furthermore, if the alternative to meeting these metrics is 'perishing', we must question whether researchers can choose to be safe *and* stay in academia or participate in the public sphere. If the environment rewards certain behaviour, to deviate from that behaviour is to go unrewarded or absent.

Vicarious trauma

Vicarious trauma – also known as secondary trauma, moral injury, or secondary stress – is defined as "the profound and lasting emotional and psychological consequences of repeated indirect exposure to the traumatic experiences of others" (McCann and Pearlman in Padmanabhanunni and Gqomfa 2022). The majority of literature on the impact on academics comes from adjacent disciplines (e.g., domestic violence) and anecdotal evidence. Impact builds with exposure and can produce effects such as hypervigilance

(Williamson et al. 2020; Padmanabhanunni and Gqomfa 2022; Pearson et al. 2023). Here as well, it can be particularly damaging to members of communities at the sharp end of the far right as they are researching an ideology that seeks harm to them; as stated by Rae Jereza, the research "can hit differently when you're reading something that spells out your extermination" (in Allam 2022). Beyond witnessing the traumatic experiences of others, those at the sharp end experience direct trauma to themselves and their communities. This harm can be particularly intense around attacks with the deluge of information alongside the need to analyse.

To minimise vicarious trauma, pre-emptive measures are more effective than reactive, as by the time reactive measures are implemented, damage has generally already occurred. There are a number of mediating factors affecting vulnerability and thus the level of preparations required varies (Conway 2021). Unfortunately, as stated by Williamson et al. (2020), researchers often cannot know what will affect them the most until they have experienced it. Among the suggestions for dealing with vicarious trauma are a good work-life balance, the need for disengagement, fresh air, exercise, mental health support, and a strong support network (Williamson et al. 2020). Community engagement with peers and antifascists can be particularly important for minimising harm as it allows for the discussion of shared struggles and the possibility of overcoming isolation.

However, protecting oneself against the harms of vicarious trauma is challenged when situated within an environment that rewards productivity. The publication churn and pressure on output disincentivise moderated and controlled exposure to harmful content, breaks, or disengagement from research. As such, researchers are faced with a 'choice' between implementing proactive practices and potentially not succeeding in academia, or attempting to match the 'ideal worker' and risking harm. The researcher is measured regardless.

Moran and Asquith suggest that "The costs of engagement with trauma may be compensated by the productive outputs and impact on policy and practice that this type of research may elicit" (2020). However, when considered alongside the advice to protect oneself from networked harassment this harm minimisation produces a different dichotomy: protection from harassment or "compensat[ion]" from vicarious trauma. With mental health provision often underfunded at institutions, proactive practices disincentivised and options for catharsis potentially leading to a different type of harm, vicarious trauma is increasingly embedded in the conduct of this research.

Faced with this contradiction, success requiring productivity, safety requiring healthy practices, researchers must decide on the balance. This is problematic not least because healthy working practices should be something to strive towards rather than being disincentivised or framed as an impediment to success. With meeting metrics a requirement to continue in academia, self-preservation becomes less of a choice.

Discussion and concluding thoughts

Comparing harm minimisation behaviours for networked harassment and vicarious trauma with success metrics and the 'ideal worker' highlights the challenges of being both successful and safe. Framing said behaviours as a choice – an individual's responsibility – is inherent to the neoliberal institution; however, those who do not meet said metrics are 'washed out' of academia, thus necessitating such behaviours as a condition of existing within the system. Rather than negotiating a balance between the two, moving towards either pole requires sacrificing some degree of safety or some degree of success.

Drew and Canavan (2021) have described how the concept of a "gender-sensitive university" is a "contradiction in terms" where diversity initiatives clash with the neoliberal environment. They highlight how initiatives like unconscious bias training are undermined by the neoliberal "market-driven climate" that prioritises "performativity, competitiveness and commodification" meaning that "isolated interventions" are not enough to undo structural inequality (Bencivenga and Drew in Drew and Canavan 2021). This is similarly true here as safety advice directed to the individual does little in the face of endemic harm. Those already privileged in the academic system are not faced with the same choice: success is less likely to lead to harm, so compromising on safety behaviours becomes less of a fraught 'choice'. Exacerbating this is that success metrics are harsher for those on the sharp end, meaning that the gulf between success and safety is deeper and further. Scholars of colour have their work evaluated and valued inequitably, their expertise questioned, and experience an "inhospitable" environment that places barriers in the way of success (Settles et al. 2021),

In individualising responsibility for safety and success, we overlook how the environment undermines the ability of individuals to protect themselves and how achieving both is easier for some than others. The need for harm in order to meet success metrics reinforces the whiteness of the field in prioritising voices that are inherently less harmed. Ward (in Allam 2022) described this as "a self-replicating system of whiteness" and called for institutions to "get more creative in finding safe ways for people of color to contribute". For example, by legitimising work in communities rather than dismissing it as activism-not-scholarship. Individualised safety advice can only go so far if it is antithetical to success. Unless Equality, Diversity, and Inclusion initiatives reconsider the structural elements integral to the experiences of academia, we risk abandoning colleagues to dangerous work without support or encouraging scholars into a hostile field with harm embedded.

Many of these challenges are not unique to this subject of study or industry but rather are representative of a broader "epistemic exclusion" that "unwarrantedly hinders one's ability … to participate in knowledge production" (Dotson 2014; Settles et al. 2021). Rather than offering advice, this chapter seeks to highlight and problematise how we understand and measure safety and success, in particular challenging the neoliberal elements that individualise responsibility for both. By framing the issue as structural not individual, we shift the burden of tackling the problem from the excluded to the community and problematise progression within the academia as purely meritocratic.

References

Allam, H. 2022. 'In the Mostly White World of Extremism Research, New Voices Emerge', *Washington Post*. https://www.washingtonpost.com/national-security /2022/06/25/extremism-researchers-diversity/ (accessed 20 July 2022).

Barbour, K. and Marshall, D. 2012. 'The Academic Online: Constructing Persona through the World Wide Web', *First Monday*, 17(9).

Carrozza, C. 2018. 'Re-Conceptualizing Social Research in the "Digital Era": Issues of Scholarships, Methods, and Epistemologies', *Análise Social*, 228, liii (3.0), 652–671.

Castelli Gattinara, P. 2020. 'The Study of the Far Right and Its Three E's: Why Scholarship Must Go beyond Eurocentrism, Electoralism and Externalism', *French Politics*, 18, 314–333.

Conway, M. 2021. 'Online Extremism and Terrorism Research Ethics: Researcher Safety, Informed Consent, and the Need for Tailored Guidelines', *Terrorism and Political Violence*, 33(2), 367–380.

Cottom, T. M. 2015. '"Who Do You Think You Are?" When Marginality Meets Academic Microcelebrity', *Ada: A Journal of Gender, New Media, and Technology*, 7. https://adanew-media.org/2015/04/issue7-mcmillancottom/ (accessed 20 June 2022).

Croucher, G. and Lacy, W. B. 2022. 'The Emergence of Academic Capitalism and University Neoliberalism: Perspectives of Australian Higher Education Leadership', *Higher Education*, 83(2), 279–295.

Deem, R. 2001. 'Globalisation, New Managerialism, Academic Capitalism and Entrepreneurialism in Universities: Is the Local Dimension Still Important?', *Comparative Education*, 37(1), 7–20.

De Rond, M. and Miller, A. N. 2005. 'Publish or Perish', *Journal of Management Inquiry*, 14(4), 321–329.

Doerfler, P., Forte, A., De Cristofaro, E., Stringhini, G., Blackburn, J., and McCoy, D. 2021. '"I'm a Professor, Which Isn't Usually a Dangerous Job":

Internet-Facilitated Harassment and Its Impact on Researchers', *Proceedings of the ACM on Human-Computer Interaction*, 5(CSCW2), 1–32.

Dotson, K. 2014. 'Conceptualizing Epistemic Oppression', *Social Epistemology*, 28(2), 115–138.

Drew, E. and Canavan, S. (eds). 2021. *Gender-Sensitive University: A Contradiction in Terms?* 1st ed. London: Routledge.

Gregory, K. and singh, s. s. 2018. 'Anger in Academic Twitter: Sharing, Caring, and Getting Mad Online', *tripleC: Communication, Capitalism & Critique*, 16(1), 176–193.

Kawahara, D. and Bejarano, A. 2009. 'Women of Color and the Glass Ceiling in Higher Education'. In: Lau Chin, J. (ed.). *Diversity in Mind and in Action*. Westport, CT: Praeger Press, 61–72.

Lester, J. and Sallee, M. W. 2017. 'Troubling Gender Norms and the Ideal Worker in Academic Life', *Critical Approaches to Women and Gender in Higher Education*, 115–138.

Lewis, R., Marwick, A., and Partin, W. C. 2020. '"We Dissect Stupidity and Respond to It": Response Videos and Networked Harassment on YouTube', *American Behavioral Scientist*, 65(5), 735–756.

Loher, D. and Strasser, S. 2019. 'Politics of Precarity: Neoliberal Academia under Austerity Measures and Authoritarian Threat', *Social Anthropology*, 27(S2), 5–14.

Marwick, A. and Caplan, R. 2018. 'Drinking Male Tears: Language, the Manosphere, and Networked Harassment', *Feminist Media Studies*, 18(4), 543–559.

Marwick, A. E., Blackwell, L. and Lo, K. 2016. *Best Practices for Conducting Risky Research and Protecting Yourself from Online Harassment*. New York: Data & Society Research Institute. https://datasociety.net/pubs/res/Best_Practices_for_Conducting_Risky_Research-Oct-2016.pdf (accessed 21 March 2022).

Massanari, A. 2018. 'Rethinking Research Ethics, Power, and the Risk of Visibility in the Era of the "Alt-Right" Gaze', *Social Media + Society*, 4(2), 1–9.

Mattheis, A. and Kingdon, A. 2021. 'Does the Institution Have a Plan for that? Researcher Safety and the Ethics of Institutional Responsibility'. In: Lavorgna, A. and Holt, T. (eds). *Researching Cybercrimes: Methodologies, Ethics, and Critical Approaches*, 1st ed. London: Palgrave Macmillan, 457–472.

Mewburn, I. and Thompson, P. 2013. 'Academic Blogging is Part of a Complex Online Academic Attention Economy, Leading to Unprecedented Readership', *LSE Impact Blog*. http://blogs.lse.ac.uk/impactofsocialsciences/2013/12/12/academic-attention-economy/ (accessed 11 June 2022).

Miller, D. and Mills, T. 2009. 'The Terror Experts and the Mainstream Media: The Expert Nexus and Its Dominance in the News Media', *Critical Studies on Terrorism*, 2(3), 414–437.

Moran, R. J. and Asquith, N. L. 2020. 'Understanding the Vicarious Trauma and Emotional Labour of Criminological Research', *Methodological Innovations*, 13(2).

Morrison, J., Silke, A., and Bont, E. 2021. 'The Development of the Framework for Research Ethics in Terrorism Studies (FRETS)', *Terrorism and Political Violence*, 33(2), 271–289.

Padmanabhanunni, A. and Gqomfa, N. 2022. '"The Ugliness of It Seeps into Me": Experiences of Vicarious Trauma among Female Psychologists Treating Survivors of Sexual Assault', *International Journal of Environmental Research and Public Health*, 19(7), 3925.

Pearson, E., Whittaker, J., Bakken, T., Zeiger, S., Atamuradova, F., and Conway, M. 2023. 'Online Extremism and Terrorism Researchers' Security, Safety, and Resilience: Findings from the Field', VOX-Pol Network of Excellence, 1–136. https://www.voxpol.eu/download/report/Online-Extremism-and-Terrorism -Researchers-Security-Safety-Resilience.pdf (accessed 4 January 2022).

Rosa, R. 2022. 'The Trouble with "Work–Life Balance" in Neoliberal Academia: A Systematic and Critical Review', *Journal of Gender Studies*, 31(1), 55–73.

Settles, I. H., Jones, M. K., Buchanan, N. T., and Dotson, K. 2021. 'Epistemic Exclusion: Scholar(ly) Devaluation That Marginalizes Faculty of Color', *Journal of Diversity in Higher Education*, 14(4), 493–507.

Stewart, B. 2016. 'Collapsed Publics: Orality, Literacy, and Vulnerability in Academic Twitter', *Journal of Applied Social Theory*, 1(1), 61–86.

Terras, M. 2012. 'The Verdict: Is Blogging or Tweeting about Research Papers Worth It?', *LSE Impact Blog*. http://blogs.lse.ac.uk/impactofsocialsciences/2012/04/19/ blog-tweeting-papers- worth-it/ (accessed 11 June 2023).

van Dijk, D., Manor, O., and Carey, L. B. 2014. 'Publication Metrics and Success on the Academic Job Market', *Current Biology*, 24(11), 516–517.

Veletsianos, G., Houlden, S., Hodson, J., and Gosse, C. 2018. 'Women Scholars' Experiences with Online Harassment and Abuse: Self-Protection, Resistance, Acceptance, and Self-Blame', *New Media & Society*, 20(12), 4689–4708.

Ward, S. C. 2012. *Neoliberalism and the Global Restructuring of Knowledge and Education*. New York: Routledge.

Warren, J. 2019. 'How Much Do You Have to Publish to Get a Job in a Top Sociology Department? Or to Get Tenure? Trends over a Generation', *Sociological Science*, 6, 172–196.

Williamson, E., Gregory, A., Abrahams, H., Aghtaie, N., Walker, S., and Hester, M. 2020. 'Secondary Trauma: Emotional Safety in Sensitive Research', *Journal of Academic Ethics*, 18(1), 55–70.

20

Spectre: covert research in digital far-right 'red zones'

Jackson Wood

Cyberspace never sleeps, and neither do I. While most rest, we netizens surf the darknet. Watchful guardians motivated only to prevent the next livestreamed terror attack …

I activate my iron-clad digital security system, also known as a VPN, before tapping into the usual far-right haunts. Parler? Zilch. GAB? Nada. Discord? Bingo. I'm going in.

In this chapter, I argue that a securitised, media-driven framing of the digital far right underpinned the approach of my university's Human Research Ethics Committee (HREC) when they labelled my doctoral research methods "the modus operandi of fictional political thrillers". Linked to actuarial logics of risk management, HRECs treat ethics as a one-off procedure, presuming that all risks can be identified and minimised in advance of the research project. This conflicts with iterative research approaches, which treat ethics as a complex social practice. Tension is magnified when HRECs lack the relevant expertise in the projects they oversee. Here, when ethical challenges arise, rather than turning to the knowledge of researchers, committees favour narrow interpretations of ethical guidelines. These logics have the ultimate effect of configuring research in particularly limited ways, stifling the use of innovative methods that are considered 'risky'. It is not ethical codes that are problematic, per se. However, when they are narrowly applied, ethics is undermined in favour of minimising institutional risks and liabilities.

My methods involved 'lurking' covertly in far-right digital spaces, which I argue posed an undue risk for the HREC for two reasons. First, my methods were considered in breach of a baseline standard of informed consent, which is typically codified in ethical guidelines as a necessary protection for participant autonomy. However, as I argue below, the distinction between overt research (with informed consent) and covert research (which lacks it) can be an arbitrary one. Second, the committee's lack of expertise meant that their understanding of extremism was sourced from popular, media-driven stereotypes. In turn, my field site posed untenable risk, construed as a met-aphorical digital 'red zone'. 'Red zones' describe physical spaces that are considered too hazardous to conduct fieldwork in – often linked to sites of conflict (Sluka 2020). These two reasons discursively positioned the com-mittee to consider my methods as *prima facie* risky, without substantively engaging with my arguments. Whilst the committee did not outright label my field site as a 'red zone', elements of their feedback can be interpreted as such. For example, the committee rearticulated covert participant obser-vation as legally dubious "undercover spying". In order to mitigate risk – rather than respond to ethical quandaries – the committee mandated that I receive advice from the university's legal office before they would consider the viability of the research.

Reflecting on this process, I argue that ethics committees would benefit from the rationalities of situated ethics and cultures of care, rather than formulaically applying ethical guidelines. These approaches acknowledge that research practices are complex, emergent, and contingent. In the context of researching the heterogeneous far right, this reframing not only provides a basis for implementing otherwise 'risky' covert methods, but also assists to dispel securitised, media-driven conceptions of extremism.

For Your Eyes Only: background to my research

This chapter reflects on my research as a PhD candidate in criminology at the University of Melbourne. My research concerned digital far-right extremism, with a particular focus on the social media platform Discord. In brief, I spent months covertly observing (and sometimes participating in) right-wing groups on the platform, adopting an 'internalist' perspective to analysing the far right (Blee 2007).

The covert nature of my research was a tension point between me and the HREC. The next section will develop some critiques of stricter notions of informed consent, but it is first important to lay out how consent is codi-fied within Australia's *National Statement on Ethical Conduct in Human Research* (NHMRC 2007) (henceforth the *National Statement*), which guides Australian HRECs in determining the ethical viability of research pro-jects. Within, informed consent is central to protecting human autonomy, which, in turn, is associated with the fundamental principle of respect for participants. However, the *National Statement* does provide specific carve-outs for the use of deception, or even waiving consent. The point being that, even within the codes adhered to by Australian HRECs, deception, or 'lim-ited disclosure' as it is termed, can be considered 'ethical'. Section 2.3.10 of the *National Statement* provides the basis for waiving consent, which

I relied upon in my ethics application. In brief, to satisfy the conditions of the carve-out, one must show that there are practical reasons to waive consent; that the benefits of the research outweigh any harm associated with not seeking consent; and there are other strategies in place to protect participant autonomy. I argued that a level of deception was necessary to even gain and maintain access to right-wing and far-right groups. It was unrealistic to expect that participants who may adopt paranoid ideologies and are especially concerned with perceived threats from 'the left' would consent to being observed by a critical university researcher. In turn, covert research was a means of reducing risks to me by, for example, mitigating potential vitriol and forms of retribution like doxing. Further, I observed hundreds if not thousands of individual users across the platform, some of whom may not have been active participants at the time of observation, but nevertheless remained in the group, 'lurking' like myself. Gaining consent from all users was unfeasible, especially when many of them had left the group, but their digital footprint remained, making the receipt of consent impossible. In my initial application to the HREC, I supported these arguments with relevant literature which sought to deconstruct strict notions of informed consent (Calvey 2008; Musante 2015), fleshing out 'lurking' as a valid method of internet research (Kavanaugh and Maratea 2020: 6).

Yet, in response, the committee cautiously aligned with stricter notions of informed consent, stifling my research until I received legal advice. There is a certain incoherency here because the committee narrowly applied the *National Statement* in such a way that overlooked the existence of the carve-out noted above. Certainly, the committee might have determined that my project did not satisfy the conditions of the waiver. But I find this unlikely because in their feedback, the committee didn't substantially engage with my response to section 2.3.10. Instead, the committee framed my approach as "undercover spying", which conjured particular legal risks that went beyond the scope of the *National Statement*.

The World Is Not Enough: universalism in institutional ethics

HRECs and ethical guidelines construct research participants as needing protection from unethical research practices (Doyle and Buckley 2017). In turn, the use of deception in research is a common vector for tension between researchers and HRECs. Under a framework that prioritises participant autonomy, informed consent is championed as a baseline requirement for ethical research. This is likely because, as Calvey (2013: 542) argues, covert research is often linked to exemplars of 'poor ethics', like Milgram's (1974) work on obedience and Humphreys' (1976) work on public homosexual encounters. In light of these examples, ethical codes like the *National Statement* provide important protections. To clarify, it is not the existence of ethical codes that I critique in this chapter, rather, it is when they are narrowly applied by university HRECs. When this occurs, entire genres of qualitative methods are suppressed under the assumption that they are ethical voids. Covert research is an example of this, whereby HRECs are positioned to guard participant autonomy from the unethical deceptive wiles of researchers.

On the other hand, the *National Statement* itself affords flexibility in applying ethical codes, stating in its preamble that ethics is more than a prescriptive list of 'dos' and 'don'ts'. For instance, the carve-out mentioned above implies that deception can be ethical even under the standards adhered to by university HRECs. However, framing deceptive practices as exceptional reifies an overt/covert binary which discursively positions university HRECs to prioritise informed consent, even if the conditions of the carve-out are satisfied. This goes some way to explaining why the HREC disregarded my methods without engaging in the substance of my response to section 2.3.10 of the *National Statement*.

There are important epistemological implications here. Ethical codes are rooted in particular historical contexts, and when committees formulaically subscribe to them, they undermine research that sits outside those contexts. As Halse and Honey (2007: 338) note, the roots of these codes lie in the Enlightenment era turn to scientific empiricism "and the veneration of the rational, autonomous subject". So-called objective research presumes that risk can be determined in advance of any research project (Halse and Honey 2007: 342). However, the positivist notion that ethics is a one-off exercise highly conflicts with iterative approaches to doing research (King 2023: 3). In turn, Whelan (2018) argues that rituals of ethics, like filling out forms, reduce ethics to a box-ticking exercise that focuses on minimising risk, even though the *National Statement* might aspire to do otherwise. This shift towards risk produces epistemological harm. As Mortimer, Fileborn and Henry (2021: 152) argue, the focus on risk management actually "curtail[s] the parameters of 'ethical' practice". To that extent, aspiring for a universal approach to ethics is incompatible with the embodied practices of research and can, in turn, undermine and restrict researchers rather than empower them to be more ethical. Hence, HRECs are positioned to suppress covert research for breaching participant autonomy, even though, as Roulet et al. (2017) argue, the routine use of 'concealment practices' in so-called 'overt' research is considered ethically viable. The overt/covert binary can therefore be an arbitrary distinction, not an ethical one.

Importantly, however, in my experience, standards of informed consent were additionally undergirded by concerns around security and legality. I argue that it was institutional rigidity *in conjunction* with the perceived dangers of researching extremist (virtual) spaces that inevitably led the committee to view my methods as legally dubious.

Licence to Kill: covert research in 'red zones'

I suggest that my research posed untenable risk for the committee, not just because it was covert but because my field site was considered inherently risky – a digital 'red zone'. 'Red zones' describe physical spaces that are assigned high levels of danger by government bodies, which, in turn, places additional restrictions on any research within those areas (Sluka 2020). Robben (2010) argues that this is connected with a broader shift in the post-9/11 security landscape which increasingly relies on a divide between safe and dangerous spaces. For Andersson (2016), the discursive effect of this is to suppress integral forms of knowledge seeking that rely on access to local areas that might be perceived as 'dangerous'. I deploy 'red zones' as a metaphor to describe far-right virtual spaces. The committee did not specifically categorise my field site as such, but elements of their feedback are linked to underlying security and legal risk.

Consider the following quote from the committee: "Faking one's identity to collect data is also questionable … isn't the researcher working at the threshold of legality himself by observing the group discussion under a fake name, and collecting data?" Here, the committee conflates digital ethnography with what they later term as "undercover spying", conjuring legal risks that required advice from the university's legal team. The securitisation of my methods in this manner indicates that the HREC considered deceptive practices to be potentially illegal themselves. I argue this is linked to the committee's lack of expertise in the field. First, they demonstrated an unfamiliarity with researching digital spaces. For example, when I indicated an intention to create a de-identified avatar, the HREC were concerned about subscribing to groups using my personal email address. That is to say, the committee did not realise you could create new email addresses at will. This is important because, as Hibben et al. (2018) found, HREC members with experience studying digital spaces were more likely to flex otherwise strict standards of informed consent. Hence, in my case, the committee's view that covert research is unethical is likely connected with their lack of expertise. Second, and more importantly, the committee also constructed 'extremist' spaces as inherently violent, dangerous, and risky. This was demonstrated by the committee's suggestion that I should inform the police about my research in advance of data collection. It is also embodied in the HREC's concern about the potential that I would become 'converted' or radicalised.

Most notably, to reiterate, the HREC labelled my methods as the "modus operandi of fictional political thrillers". Here, the way I articulated the field site was disregarded because it conflicted with popular cultural tropes used by the committee to conceptualise extremist far-right spaces. Extremism is a nebulous concept because it is contingent on a set of mainstream beliefs, meaning it is prone to change across space and time (Brown, Mondon, and Winter 2023). In turn, the remit of far-right extremist ideology is broad, particularly in virtual spaces. Lewis (2018), for example, excavates a network of right-wing content creators on YouTube, identifying slippage in their ideologies between traditional conservatism and white nationalism. My own research findings parallel this observation, with user ideology ranging from Christian conservatism to fascism and neo-Nazism. Indeed, a significant motivation of my research is paying attention to aspects of *mainstream* ideologies that legitimise harm and violence at the extremist margins. Popular conceptions of extremists as organised, hierarchical, and explicitly planning physical acts of terror elide such root causes. Yet, drawing on these popular conceptions, the committee framed my methods as a non-academic venture by associating them with the stuff of fiction. Sluka (2020: 249) has similarly argued that the perceived danger of a field site is underpinned by popular, media-driven stereotypes and that ethics committees "are generally no better informed about the actual realities of danger … than the general public are". This sits in tension with the presumption that HRECs have the ability to protect the interests of research participants – in reality, their lack of expertise undermines such.

In turn, even though my project was well-supported by academic tradition and the *National Statement*, the committee harboured serious doubts about its viability due to the construction of my field site as a digital 'red zone'. The committee's securitised approach to far-right digital space, as well as the taboo status of deceptive practices (such that covert research was itself considered to be a legal mire), led to my research being constructed as legally dubious spy-work. This, in turn, explains why the committee, in their response to my application, disregarded any substantive arguments I made to justify my research (like my response to section 2.3.10). Since my field site was constructed as such a risk as to be beyond the remit of the *National Statement* and the HREC, I was given the choice of attaining legal advice or reconceiving my project and removing 'lurking' as a research method.

Given that my research methods are not particularly novel, nor is research of extremist digital spaces uncommon, it was unsurprising that the legal advice determined there was a very low risk that I would be breaching any legal obligations. The memorandum satisfied the committee that 'lurking' does not in itself entail legal risk. Ironically, one of my risk management strategies actually went *beyond* my legal obligations. The advice of the lawyer was that I did not have a legal obligation to report any signs that individuals were planning an attack. On the other hand, I had established a strategy to do so if plans seemed specific and targeted, as opposed to 'trolling'. This shows the value of attending to ethics as an ongoing social practice – to simply adhere to the legal advice would actually entail shirking an ethical responsibility to report signs of an extremist attack. Thus, I argue for the need to expand the remit of institutional ethics by adopting reflexive approaches to ethics.

The Spy Who Loved Me: cultures of care and situated ethics

HRECs would benefit from the sensibilities of a situated ethics approach, which is compatible with iterative research by treating ethics as an ongoing social practice shaped by the context of research rather than universal codes (Roulet et al. 2017: 502). As Halse and Honey (2007: 345) posit, participant/researcher identities are often "fluid, mutable, and difficult to pin down", which is antithetical to ethics-as-risk-management that seeks to articulate all problems before the project begins. Instead, situated ethics takes into account that the research process is dynamic, and that ethical concerns are contingent on space and time (Calvey 2008: 912). King (2023) similarly offers a compelling case for adapting cultures of care to an institutional ethics environment. By focusing on empowerment and collective responsibility, cultures of care approaches flatten power imbalances by reframing ethics as an ongoing process co-shaped by all stakeholders, including participants, researchers, and the institution. Rather than universal codes, this approach attends to fundamentals like space, temporality, and relationality in forming an ethical ethos (King 2023: 9). This is compatible with Halse and Honey's (2007: 349) call to centre "respect for persons" as a critical, reflexive, and ongoing process. Indeed, although ethical codes like the *National Statement* seek to uphold an ethos of respect, I have argued throughout this chapter that the practice of institutional ethics can often be at tension with such a goal. Instead, we should attend to emergent and complex ethical conundrums on a case-by-case and critical basis; there is no one size-fits-all approach to ethics (Mortimer, Fileborn, and Henry 2021: 151).

In the context of internet research, situated ethics and cultures of care are compatible with analysing the fast-paced and evolving dynamics of digital space. Importantly, paying attention to space and time works to dispel securitised, media-driven understandings of extremism that are incongruent with the realities of multi-faceted far-right spaces. In terms of the temporal, as noted earlier, definitions of extremism rely on an articulated set of main-stream values that, in themselves, are not static, but evolve across socio-political contexts. Applying this, from my observations, users accessed far-right groups for a variety of reasons, many of them seemingly apolitical. For example, many groups I joined were framed less as far-right ideologi-cal echo chambers, but more as right-wing 'hang-out' spaces, focusing on shared hobbies like working out, movies, and video games. Users spoke about attending church and consuming content from mainstream conserva-tive pundits. However, these discussions were often underlaid by harmful normative discourses around, say, race and gender – the key word here being normative. A securitised approach obscures that most of the harmful rhetoric and behaviour emanating from such groups is justified by, or aligns with, 'mainstream' discourses.

As such, HRECs engage in epistemological harm by adopting popular, media-driven constructions of extremism. They actively reproduce harmful, securitised discourses because research (like my own) that seeks to interrogate and disentangle underlying assumptions about extremism is stifled by virtue of being a security risk. Instead of "undercover spying" – which implies a policing lens – my research process has often involved *understanding* the diversity of rationales, ideologies, and logics present in far-right 'extremist' groups. Hage (2000: 21) invites us to examine white supremacy from a de-securitised lens, offering the guiding question: "how do humans struggle to make their lives viable?" This reveals much more complexity about the underlying basis of far-right ideology within mainstream discourses than a securitised binary approach offers. The need for situated ethics is highlighted here, because it avoids essentialising participants into reductive categories such as violent, dangerous, or risky. These categories close off opportunities for research because perceived risk places boundaries on access to field sites. This is problematic because, as Blee (2007) highlights, internalist perspectives are necessary to understand how far-right digital spaces are constructed.

Moving towards other spatial elements of digital space, virtuality chal-lenges the ability to gain informed consent due to factors like increased anonymity of participants and the relative permanency of digital footprints. In my own research, users were highly transient, making the pursuit of consent impossible when their contributions to the group remained visible despite their absence. Rapidly evolving virtual landscapes make risks hard to predict in advance of the research project, which again shows the value of attending to time. For example, some groups I observed were sometimes banned within a day of being created. Others changed moderation teams multiple times in a month, which had a ripple effect on group member-ship and ideology. Additionally, users in these spaces can be paranoid and unlikely to engage with researchers in a straightforward manner. This speaks to relationality, where the known presence of the researcher changes the nature of the research task. In researching extremism, this could prevent access to groups at the outset, or it could entail danger for researchers, who open themselves up to retribution like 'trolling' or doxing. Situated ethics and cultures of care navigate these idiosyncrasies, generating an ethos that is both ethical and practical.

Further, a culture of care approach stretches to the wellbeing needs of the researcher. For example, it would acknowledge the toll of constant exposure to extremist material. More than this, relying on cultures of care salves the potentially adversarial relationship between researcher and HREC to one of collaboration and empowerment. What are the wellbeing implications of having a year of project development dismissed as 'not academic'? My own experience is far from novel, given the swathes of literature critiquing institutional ethics, some of which has been referred to throughout this chapter. Fortunately, the only significant effect of my experience was time delay. But these delays are worthy of critique when they stem from the institution clashing with the idiosyncrasies of research that it purportedly supports, particularly when doctoral researchers face additional pressures like timely completion. In other words, a culture of care or a situated ethics approach provides the basis for institutions which are more ethical *even to their own researchers*.

Diamonds Are Forever: ethical considerations for ethics committees

> Dear Mr. Neo-Nazi, can you please give me your informed consent so that I can quote your fascist tweet? (Fuchs 2018)

HRECs which narrowly adhere to ethical codes conflict with the embodied practices of qualitative research. In my experience, this tension manifested as absurdity. Informed consent as a condition for 'ethical' research was incompatible with the practicalities of my project. As if the paranoid sensibilities of my participants would allow a researcher from a left-leaning university to observe them! As Fuchs (2018) points out, more than just rejection, seeking consent could magnify danger to researchers by opening them up to retributive activity.

To reiterate, it is not necessarily ethical codes that I critique in this chapter, rather, that HRECs are discursively positioned to narrowly apply those codes despite the complexities of social research. Indeed, the *National Statement* itself offers some flexibility, navigating tensions around informed consent by providing carve-outs like limited disclosure and waiving consent.

This didn't stop the university HREC narrowly applying it, however, by labelling my research as legally dubious "undercover spying". Lacking expertise in the field, the HREC drew on popular understandings of extremism in construing my field-site as a digital 'red zone'. HRECs are positioned to stifle seemingly dangerous research because they are undergirded by actuarial logics of risk management. This might be understood as 'ethics creep' (Haggerty 2004), where, in my experience, reductive media-driven stereotypes have been codified into university processes, having the effect of suppressing rather than empowering research into the far right. The point being that HRECs do not just draw on social understandings of phenomena, but actively reproduce them, which functions to impede the remit of research that disentangles and deconstructs discourse. Certainly, my experience connects with wider critiques about the neoliberalisation of ethics, a shift which concerns itself less with the embodied practices of research ethics as an ongoing, reflexive process and is more interested with treating ethics as a one-off process of liability management.

The overarching critique in this chapter is that the committee's dogged subscription to inflexible and unfeasible standards of informed consent led them to outright dismiss my methods as risky and non-academic, instead of substantively engaging with ethical predicaments. I argue, in turn, that ethics processes should embody the logics of reflexive ethical philosophies like situated ethics or cultures of care. Rather than curbing research seen as risky, committees which are sensitive to space, temporality, and relationality can empower research to be ethical. This, in turn, shifts institutional ethics away from neoliberal logics of risk management, towards an ethics that attends to the idiosyncrasies of any given research project – even research that is, supposedly, the pretence for espionage.

References

Andersson, R. 2016. 'Here Be Dragons: Mapping an Ethnography of Global Danger', *Current Anthropology*, 57(6), 707–731.

Blee, K. M. 2007. 'Ethnographies of the Far Right', *Journal of Contemporary Ethnography*, 36(2), 119–128.

Brown, K., Mondon, A., and Winter, A. 2023. 'The Far Right, the Mainstream and Mainstreaming: Towards a Heuristic Framework', *Journal of Political Ideologies*, 28(2), 162–179.

Calvey, D. 2008. 'The Art and Politics of Covert Research: Doing "Situated Ethics" in the Field', *Sociology*, 42(5), 905–918.

Calvey, D. 2013. 'Covert Ethnography in Criminology: A Submerged Yet Creative Tradition', *Contemporary Issues in Criminal Justice*, 25(1), 541–550.

Doyle, E. and Buckley, P. 2017. 'Embracing Qualitative Research: A Visual Model for Nuanced Research Ethics Oversight', *Qualitative Research*, 17(1), 95–117.

Fuchs, C. 2018. '"Dear Mr. Neo-Nazi, Can You Please Give Me Your Informed Consent So That I Can Quote Your Fascist Tweet?" Questions of Social Media Research Ethics in Online Ideology Critique'. In: Meikle, G. (ed.). *The Routledge Companion to Media And Activism*. London: Routledge, 385–394.

Hage, G. 2000. *White Nation: Fantasies of White Supremacy in a Multicultural Society*. New York: Routledge.

Haggerty, K. D. 2004. 'Ethics Creep: Governing Social Science Research in the Name of Ethics', *Qualitative Sociology*, 27(4), 391–414.

Halse, C. and Honey, A. 2007. 'Rethinking Ethics Review as Institutional Discourse', *Qualitative Inquiry*, 13(3), 336–352.

Hibbin, R. A., Samuel, G., and Derrick, G. E. 2018. 'From "a Fair Game" to "a Form of Covert Research": Research Ethics Committee Members' Differing Notions of Consent and Potential Risk to Participants within Social Media Research', *Journal of Empirical Research on Human Research Ethics*, 13(2), 149–159.

Humphreys, L. 1976. *Tearoom Trade: Impersonal Sex in Public Places*. Routledge: New York.

Kavanaugh, P. R. and Maratea, R. J. 2020. 'Digital Ethnography in an Age of Information Warfare: Notes from the Field', *Journal of Contemporary Ethnography*, 49(1), 3–26.

King, G. 2023. 'Towards a Culture of Care for Ethical Review: Connections and Frictions in Institutional and Individual Practices of Social Research Ethics', *Social and Cultural Geography*, 24(1), 104–120.

Lewis, R. 2018. 'Alternative Influence: Broadcasting the Reactionary Right on YouTube', *Data & Society*. https://datasociety.net/library/alternative-influence/ (accessed 27 March 2022).

Milgram, M. 1974. *Obedience to Authority: An Experimental View*. London: Tavistock Publications.

Mortimer, S., Fileborn, B., and Henry, N. 2021. 'Beyond Formal Ethics Reviews: Reframing the Potential Harms of Sexual Violence Research', *Australian Feminist Studies*, 36(108), 142–155.

Musante, K. 2015. 'Participant Observation'. In: Bernard, H. R. and Gravlee, C. C. (eds). *Handbook of Methods in Cultural Anthropology*. Lanham, MD: Rowman & Littlefield, 236–276.

NHMRC. 2007. *National Statement on Ethical Conduct in Human Research*. https://www.nhmrc.gov.au/about-us/publications/national-statement-ethical -conduct-human-research-2007-updated-2018 (accessed 17 March 2022).

Robben, A. C. G. M. 2010. 'An Introduction to the Anthropological Study of the Iraq War'. In: Robben, A. C. G. M. (ed.). *Iraq at a Distance: What Anthropologists Can Teach Us About the War*. Philadelphia, PA: University of Philadelphia Press, 1–56.

Roulet, T. J., Gill, M. J., Stenger, S., and Gill, D. J. 2017. 'Reconsidering the Value of Covert Research: The Role of Ambiguous Consent in Participant Observation', *Organizational Research Methods*, 20(3), 487–517.

Sluka, J. A. 2020. 'Too Dangerous for Fieldwork? The Challenge of Institutional Risk-Management in Primary Research on Conflict, Violence and "Terrorism"', *Contemporary Social Science*, 15(2), 241–257.

Whelan, A. 2018. 'Ethics Are Admin: Australian Human Research Ethics Review Forms as (Un)ethical Actors', *Social Media and Society*, 4(2).

21

Navigating a feminist ethics of care, ethnographic methods, and academic activism in researching men's rights and the far right: a researcher's struggles

Luc S. Cousineau

Researchers who use feminist theory in immersive qualitative research like ethnography must negotiate a feminist ethics of care where the researcher is compelled to contend with their own humanity and that of their participants, engaging with and protecting them from potential harm (Hesse-Biber 2012). But what happens when the act of protecting the individual conflicts with the feminist imperative to "repair our world" (Stanley and Wise 2013: 23)? Beyond dated critiques of feminist ethnography (Stacey 1988), there are emotional and epistemological challenges when trying to work with ethnography and feminist theory on what Fielding (1990) calls "unloved groups", in this case, groups that land on the far and extreme right of the ideological spectrum. The conflict that gives rise to these difficulties is between the emancipatory and equity work essential to feminism and the imperative to expose anti-equity rhetoric and ideology.

Using a long-term study of two men's communities on the website Reddit, this chapter will explore the ethical dilemmas and decision-making required when determining what content, whose names, and what details to publish in academic work on groups that have the potential to cause social (and physical) harm. It will examine the misalignments between theory and practice when the researcher's interest in exposing dangerous ideologies conflicts with the call to protect the people who express those views. What meta-ethical hurdles might we jump to justify our own practice? In addressing some of these challenging issues, this chapter will expand the conversation between feminist ethics, qualitative/ethnographic work, and academic activism, and how these can (and cannot) come together in research on the far right.

The research setting: context

To give context to what follows, I will give a brief explanation of my research on men's rights communities on Reddit. The men's rights movement is a non-uniform collection of groups that share a belief "that society, both con-temporarily and historically, revolves around women, and that arguments claiming female oppression are a farce" (Hodapp 2017: viii). The groups that make up the men's rights movement are themselves part of a larger "loose confederation" of groups called the manosphere, where philosophies of male oppression, supremacy, and separatism orbit around a common core of anti-feminism (Ging 2019: 1; Cousineau 2021). Within this complex system of groups, I study two: the sub-community groups of /r/MensRights and /r/TheRedPill on Reddit.[1] /r/MensRights is a space where discussion, supporting studies, and links are welcomed in building "a place for those who wish to discuss men's rights and the ways said rights are infringed upon" (/r/MensRights 2019). Posts generally highlight ways in which the community members see men as disadvantaged. /r/TheRedPill presents itself as a place for "discussion of sexual strategy in a culture increasingly lack-ing a positive identity for men" (/r/TheRedPill 2019), and discussions are more focused on heterosexual conquest, coupled with the desire to return to 'traditional' gender roles and norms. I study discourses of masculinities in these spaces, as well as how community rhetorics and the platform that hosts them push men toward far-right and supremacist ideologies.

Reddit.com, for its part, is a content aggregator website and platform for user interaction that has become a hub in the North American cultural zeitgeist and an influencer in global economic markets.[2] Adrienne Massanari (2015) describes Reddit by saying "It's kind of like a community, message board, carnival, and play space rolled into one. … It's kind of like the best and worst parts of the internet and humanity rolled up into one space" (19). In March 2021, Amazon ranked Reddit nineteenth in global internet traffic and engagement over the past ninety days (seventh in the United States), with over 163,000 total sites linking in, and over 50 per cent of users coming from the US, the United Kingdom, and India (Alexa Internet Inc. 2021).[3]

Interrogating feminist ethics in researching men's rights online

The feminist and masculinities theories I have used in my research (Cousineau 2021; Johnson and Cousineau 2018) are rooted (at least in part for mas-culinities studies) within a feminist research ethos that includes acceptance of various onto-epistemological perspectives on research and knowledge, criticality of oppression and oppressive social and cultural frameworks, and an ethics of care. Each of these areas is discussed at length in feminist texts (Lorber 2012; Mandell and Johnson 2016) and significant works of theory (e.g., Butler 1990; Halberstam 2019; The Combahee River Collective 1979) and are not the focus here. However, negotiating a feminist ethics of care relative to anti-equity behaviour is necessary to help frame and understand my research decisions around community access, participant anonymity, and member checking. The centre of this discussion is whether a feminist ethics of care can, cannot, and/or should be applied when those being studied hold views and ideologies that are anti-equity in nature and antithetical to a feminist ethos.

Analysis of the ethical imperatives of researchers (both online and offline), especially feminist researchers, tends to focus on the good and bad of the relational and situational connections between the researcher and those 'being researched'. By this I mean what could happen to the participants, informants, interlocutors, etc. who are the 'subjects' of the research inquiry. How do we treat these people? Do we treat those who have provided us with research data as people, or merely as objects for production and analysis? A reflexive, qualitative approach to research must ask additional questions, including: what is the researcher's relationship to the area and people being researched? What are the implications of these relationships? How might we ensure that the data we collect are fair and representative of the individuals who contributed to the research project?

A traditional feminist qualitative inquiry calls on researchers to ask for informed consent, request access to communities we choose to study, preserve anonymity for our participants as best we can, and conduct extensive member checking to ensure that both the characterisations of research data and our conclusions about the thoughts, feelings, and expressions of our participants are properly represented in our work (Code 1995). It also works with emancipatory or social justice goals that extend beyond the individuals who might provide research data (Johnson and Parry 2016).

Feminist ethics of care

The tenets of feminist qualitative practice extend from feminist ethics of care. The feminist 'ethics of care' as an articulated approach to research has roots in Carol Gilligan's (1977, 1987) work in, and critique of, developmental psychology and her argument for an expanded conceptualisation of adulthood that included the 'feminine voice'. Gilligan's argument, which aimed to strike down the theoretical and hierarchical distinction between justice and care (also understood as the rationality of logic versus the irrationality of emotion), was that personal, ethical, and individual normative standards were centred exclusively on a male model, perpetuating norms that erased women and women's ways of being. "My critics say", explains Gilligan (1986), "that this story seems 'intuitively' right to many women but is at odds with the findings of psychological research. This is precisely the point I am making and exactly the difference I was exploring: the dissonance between psychological theory and women's experience" (325).

The acceptance of a singular human standard based on the fiftieth percentile male continues (for a series of interesting and distressing examples of this see Caroline Criado-Perez's (2019) work), but Gilligan's research and that of subsequent theorists (Fisher and Tronto 1990; Held 1993) developed the idea of care and caring into an indispensable element of feminist ethos. For Gilligan, "the distinction between justice and care cuts across the familiar divisions between thinking and feeling, egoism and altruism, theoretical and practical reasoning ... these perspectives denote different ways of organizing the basic elements of moral judgment: self, others, and the relationship between them" (Gilligan 1987: 467, 469).

This definition of care creates a flexible standard, that is carried out in action and practice and can occur in a variety of settings and institutions (Tronto 1998). Relative to research, the feminist ethics of care calls us to create a research practice that can help to "repair our world" by carrying feminist epistemological principles through, among other areas, the management of different realities and understandings between researcher and researched and complex questions of power in research and writing (Stanley and Wise 2013: 23). We are called to do so by treating our research subjects as agentic actors, real people, and to understand that our research has consequences for those researched, as well as for ourselves and society (Hesse-Biber 2012).

My purpose in exploring the nature of the feminist ethics of care in this way is to provide context for a discussion about positioning my research using feminist theory, and how the approach that I choose might be seen as a purposeful ignorance of these feminist values. In my research, I present unfiltered and obfuscated quotes from members of the communities I study. For the work that informs this discussion, I did not request access to the content of these groups from the moderators or other members.[4] I did not submit my work to the communities for member checking. A keen observer might then question whether the work can live up to a feminist research ethos having done none of these things.

What this means for my research

Negotiating a feminist ethics of care, ethnographic practices, and problematic groups like /r/MensRights and /r/TheRedPill is complicated. Rather than a single correct approach to this negotiation, there are several pathways to good quality research that take different perspectives on user identification in research data, and the associated potential for amplification of problematic messaging.

I believe when using public forum data (as I have with this Reddit research), the choice to anonymise contributors must be all or nothing – either we must anonymise usernames and obfuscate all quotes, or nothing at all. If we choose to anonymise usernames only, for example, and present research data verbatim, the data remains searchable and is easily associated with the user – rendering the obfuscation of the username pointless.[5] For the act of anonymising usernames to be effective, we must also engage with a version of Markham's (2012) fabrication to obfuscate the content as well. This discussion of all-or-nothing anonymisation relative to a feminist ethics of care is complicated since the expository work of communicating research on problematic groups might call us to present community discourses in the most effective (and affective) ways – through their own words. In taking this approach, however, we must contend with notions of dehumanisation and objectification from singling users out as representative.

Other authors who have worked with Reddit data have approached this challenge in different ways. Some authors have chosen to include usernames, including Richterich (2014), Bergstrom (2011), Springer (2015), and some of Massanari's (2017) work. None of these authors provide a justification for the inclusion of usernames in their research products. Authors like Robards (2018), Shelton and colleagues (2015), and Van der Nagel and Firth (2015) all choose to leave out usernames in their research with potentially vulnerable users, and each relies on the presumption of vulnerability of participants in leaving usernames out. Given my own consideration of unloved groups on Reddit, the decisions by authors like Gaudette and colleagues (2021) and Borton (2017) to remove or obfuscate usernames from their writing are particularly interesting. These authors are also researching misogynist communities on Reddit and acknowledge that the data they were using is public but choose to conceal author attribution anyway. Their research, while clearly critical of the extreme right (Gaudette et al.) and misogyny (Borton) on Reddit, does not do the kind of expository and academic activism that I believe is required to create change, and so begs the question of why do this type of research in the first place.

My approach to this challenge brings me back to considerations about my primary concerns in doing this research, and that (to paraphrase Fisher and Tronto (1990)) relates to a world that the most people can live in as well as possible. So, while I believe that members of /r/MensRights and /r/TheRedPill are people, and some of these people have been deeply affected in negative ways by the social policies and ways of being they complain about, their central messaging is not about the emancipation of oppressed people, but rather the perceived diminishing power of male dominance.[6] Some of the concerns and issues that these men bring up may be worthy of consideration – one example is anti-circumcision activism where the circumcision of infant boys is seen as a gender-specific violation of human rights – but the personal and collective desire for a propagandised Western gender tradition-alism, rhetorics of male domination, and intra-male hierarchy mean their rhetoric is decidedly focused on benefiting men, frequently to the expressed detriment of women, and some men. Given these considerations, I take a kind of meta-level approach to the ethics of care. I consider the exposure of both verbatim texts and usernames as having the potential to expose read-ers, in a controlled way, to harmful ideology – a move that can (hopefully) benefit the most people through a type of inoculation.[7] I feel justified in that decision given the persistent public identities and social capital/credit orien-tations of Reddit and Reddit users (Richterich 2014).

Even if we feel justified in maintaining usernames and verbatim quotes as conscious praxis, the ethical question of the amplification of problematic, anti-equity rhetoric through our research and writing remains a difficult one. While fears of amplification may prove justified for popular media arti-cles with a broad reach (e.g., Tiffany 2020), or even texts by academics writ-ten for a wider audience (e.g., Daniels 2009), the idea that dissertations or academic articles (with their limited reach, paywalls, and other challenges) would amplify counterpublic messages or convert the reader presupposes that the readers of academic texts completely miss the point.[8] Given the feminist nature of my work (for example), readers are already likely to have a critical stance on men's rights rhetorics. If they do not, I find it difficult to believe that in reading my work (or other work of this type), anyone is likely to fall into men's rights or red pill ideology.

If my work did 'go viral', the question would perhaps be how I might have obfuscated the data while maintaining its integrity. As discussed above, Markham (2012) suggests that with creative re-scripting of user data, authors can craft narratives that appropriately represent the content they wish to convey without exposing the poster. Markham calls this process fabrication, representing "the activity of combining, molding, and/or arranging elements into a whole for a particular purpose" that is "not value-laden in itself" (2012: 338) but rather accomplishes sharing the message of the content while obfuscating and shielding the creator. However, in the work of exposing problematic content to protect against it, I think obfuscating it in the ways Markham suggests does two things: (1) it ignores the agency of the person who originally posted the text in a public forum, and (2) it protects them from critique. This may feel like a defensive incongruence, but if we accept that Reddit is a kind of privately owned public space, which it is, then we should also accept that users understand that the information posted there (in public subreddits) is also public.[9] If that is the case, then do users really have the expectation of content privacy beyond the individual quasi-anonymity that is provided by Reddit accounts? How could they?

My work is expository of the discourses of masculinity and male supremacy in /r/MensRights and /r/TheRedPill. The users I quote are not confidential informants, and I include verbatim texts to best represent what users are sharing, so it also feels like the academically appropriate approach is to credit those authors in the same ways that I would credit any other author for their published work. What is the difference between Reddit posts and blogs, online articles, or other websites?

There is also the question of intentionality/expectation and whether users have the expectation that their texts would be taken up by academics and critiqued so heavily. Certainly, most users likely do not have this expectation, but I argue that this intentionality should not permit them an escape from the critical gaze. As authors in publicly accessible space, they remain open to critique of work attributed to them. Reddit runs on critique, and in both /r/MensRights and /r/TheRedPill, critical comments are significant portions of the discussions between users. Academic critique, although (mostly) more considered and extending from a more robust theoretical standpoint, is not all that different.

The act of protecting users in spaces like /r/MensRights and /r/TheRedPill in the same way that we would protect users in communities that are targets for threats and oppression also runs the risk of being protectionist and supremacist. Users from the communities I studied are not regularly under threat of physical and sexual violence in the real ways that, for example, high-profile users were/are from #Gamergate (Chess and Shaw 2015; Salter 2018), women executives have been at Reddit (Pao 2017), and women users with sexually explicit content (shared willingly or not) (Massanari 2017; Van der Nagel and Frith 2015) are or have been under threat as Reddit users. To give even the impression of protecting those who occupy dominant groups (themselves sometimes aggressors) has the potential to align us with them in dangerous ways. To cloak this protection under the veil of scientific objectivity or fairness are also arguments in bad faith, as they must be made under the presupposition that objectivity exists in science, or that we owe fairness to those in power within inequitable systems. For all these reasons, I choose to include usernames in my research.

So, having shared my own approach and decisions in the face of these ethical dilemmas, I must circle back to the discussion on the ethics of care – specifically, the question of whether I owe the same ethics of care I would afford to participants that I consider vulnerable to the individual users of /r/MensRights and /r/TheRedPill. My answer, as evinced by the previous pages, is complicated. It deals with not only what I consider explicit ethical expectations from feminist research, but also the larger and deeper praxis of feminism as a means of building a better world for the most people to live in. It considers the complex interplay between the quasi-anonymous natures of online spaces like Reddit (Cousineau 2021; Van der Nagel and Frith 2015), alongside the citational politics of using and quoting data accessed online. It plays with the humanisation of online content – content that can do multiple types of violence – through naming content authors, and by association giving them a kind of avatar of human form, but also in considering the effects of their violence on victims. It simultaneously dehumanises by allowing (or making) singular voices representative of loosely organised and complex collectives.

In my research on the far right, and particularly men's rights and red pill spaces, I believe that the meta-ethical stance of working towards a socially just world is paramount to individualised ethics of care. Simply knowing that terrible things happen (as might be the case through anonymised and obfuscated research) is not enough; we need to identify the speakers so that we can call them out when needed. I do not worry for the safety of these users, because their rights, bodily autonomy, and lives are not at risk – and will not become imperilled through my work.[10] They do, however, contribute to the growing threats to the rights, autonomies, and lives of the women they seek to subjugate and the integrity of the systems they seek to dismantle and/or redesign.[11] It is my hope that this chapter will provide others with a helpful way to think through and consider their own approach to the ethics of researching public online content, especially when that content serves agendas of subjugation and dehumanisation. As researchers, we should always be engaged in acts of consideration about the effects of our research on those who have provided our data (however we might access that data), but also on the broader implications of what that data means, what it does, and its effects on the world that the most people can live in as well as possible.

Notes

1 The website Reddit.com uses the designation /r/ before a community name to differentiate separate content-specific user forums (for example www.reddit.com/r/MensRights is the men's rights community page).

2 The influence of Reddit has sprung up on multiple occasions since the website was founded, including a very significant part in the #Gamergate controversy (Massanari 2017), and a role in upsetting Wall Street capitalism and the financial sector (Duffy 2021).

3 Reddit uses Amazon Web Services, so it is likely this data is fairly accurate.

4 It is important to note here that at the time of the research, neither of these groups had community research rules or guidelines in place requiring researchers to contact the group or ask permission to collect community content. In addition, there is some debate about whether community content from open

communities like /r/MensRights requires special permission or Institutional Review Board ethics clearance since that content is available to anyone who chooses to browse the subreddit. My work did receive IRB clearance.

5 I will acknowledge, of course, that not all public data is searchable, and this is the case for some content on Reddit.

6 With deference to the presence of bots in both communities, of course.

7 Here I am using inoculation in the way that Compton et al. (2021) discuss it in the context of the post-truth era – "immunity to counter-attitudinal messages is conferred by pre-emptively exposing people to weakened doses of challenging information" (1).

8 This statement also presupposes that those academic texts are written clearly and using an approach that acknowledges far-right rhetorics and ideologies as potential (or real) threats. There are (dangerous) instances where academic work, most often written through 'neutral' or 'objective' lensing, can seem to lend support or legitimacy to these ideologies, and these are often picked up as vanguards supporting far-right rhetoric (see, for example, the use of evolutionary psychology in this way (Diogo 2019; Siapera 2019)).

9 Here I am playing off the concept as it is used in municipal and infrastructure as an enticement to or obligation of developers (Kayden 2000; Zhang and He 2020; Lee 2020). There are also discussions on the public/private divide that are important to this argument, including Casey Fiesler's work (Fiesler et al. 2017, 2020) among others.

10 It is important to acknowledge that users have dealt with repercussions from bad behaviour online, and rarely do those consequences follow users offline in the case of misogynistic or male supremacist speech.

11 Acknowledging, of course, salient critiques of those systems that challenge whether they have any integrity to begin with (Werner and Lammert 2021).

References

Alexa Internet Inc. 2021. 'Reddit.com Competitive Analysis, Marketing Mix and Traffic – Alexa', *Alexa: An Amazon.Com Company*. https://www.alexa.com/siteinfo/reddit.com#section_traffic (accessed 19 March 2021).

Bergstrom, K. 2011. '"Don't Feed the Troll": Shutting Down Debate about Community Expectations on Reddit.com', *First Monday*, 16(8).

Borton, D. 2017, 'Masculinity and Misogyny in the Online Locker Room: Subcultural Identity Work in the Men's Rights Movement'. M.A. Thesis, Indiana University of Pennsylvania. http://search.proquest.com/docview/1944007399/abstract/CA6DF543874A4821PQ/1 (accessed 2 January 2021).

Butler, J. 1990. *Gender Trouble: Feminism and the Subversion of Identity*. New York: Routledge.

Chess, S. and Shaw, A. 2015. 'A Conspiracy of Fishes, or, How We Learned to Stop Worrying about #GamerGate and Embrace Hegemonic Masculinity', *Journal of Broadcasting & Electronic Media*, 59(1), 208–220.

Code, L. 1995. 'How Do We Know? Questions of Method in Feminist Practice'. In: Burt, S. D. and Code, L. (eds). *Changing Methods: Feminists Transforming Practice*. Toronto: University of Toronto Press, 13–44.

The Combahee River Collective. 1979. 'The Combahee River Collective: A Black Feminist Statement'. In: Eisenstein, Z. R. (ed.). *Capitalist Patriarchy and the Case for Socialist Feminism*. New York: NYU Press, 362–372.

Compton, J., van der Linden, S., Cook, J., and Basol, M. 2021. 'Inoculation Theory in the Post-Truth Era: Extant Findings and New Frontiers for Contested Science, Misinformation, and Conspiracy Theories', *Social and Personality Psychology Compass*, 15(6), e12602. https://doi.org/10.1111/spc3.12602

Cousineau, L. S. 2021. 'Sex, Power, and Body Control: Men's Rights Leisure Participation and Neoliberal Discourses of Power and Control'. In: Parry, D. C. and Johnson, C. W. (eds). *Promiscuous Perspectives: Explorations of Sex and Leisure*. New York: Routledge 73–90.

Criado-Perez, C. 2019. *Invisible Women: Data Bias in a World Designed for Men*. New York: Abrams Press.

Daniels, J. 2009. *Cyber Racism: White Supremacy Online and the New Attack on Civil Rights*. Lanham, MD: Rowman & Littlefield.

Diogo, R. 2019. 'Sex at Dusk, Sex at Dawn, Selfish Genes: How Old-Dated Evolutionary Ideas Are Used to Defend Fallacious Misogynistic Views on Sex Evolution', *Journal of Social Sciences and Humanities*, 5(4), 350–367.

Duffy, C. 2021. 'First GameStop, Now Gorillas. Redditors Are Pouring Money into Saving Apes', CNN. https://www.cnn.com/2021/03/16/investing/wallstreetbets -gorillas-reddit/index.html (accessed 18 March 2021).

Fielding, N. G. 1990. 'Mediating the Message: Affinity and Hostility in Research on Sensitive Topics', *American Behavioral Scientist*, 33(5), 608–620.

Fiesler, C., Beard, N., and Keegan, B. C. 2020. 'No Robots, Spiders, or Scrapers: Legal and Ethical Regulation of Data Collection Methods in Social Media Terms of Service', *Proceedings of the International AAAI Conference on Web and Social Media*, 14, 187–196.

Fiesler, C., Dye, M., Feuston, J. L., Hiruncharoenvate, C., Hutto, C. J., Morrison, S., Khanipour Roshan, P., Pavalanathan, U., Bruckman, A. S., De Choudhury, M., and Gilbert, E. 2017. 'What (or Who) Is Public?: Privacy Settings and Social Media Content Sharing', *Proceedings of the 2017 ACM Conference on Computer Supported Cooperative Work and Social Computing*, 567–580. https://doi.org/10 .1145/2998181.2998223

Fisher, B. and Tronto, J. C. 1990. 'Towards a Feminist Theory of Care'. In: Abel, E. K. and Nelson, M. K. (eds). *Circles of Care: Work and Identity in Women's Lives*. Albany, NY: SUNY Press, 35–62.

Gaudette, T., Scrivens, R., Davies, G., and Frank, R. 2021. 'Upvoting Extremism: Collective Identity Formation and the Extreme Right on Reddit', *New Media & Society*, 23(12), 3491–3508.

Gilligan, C. 1977. 'In a Different Voice: Women's Conceptions of Self and of Morality', *Harvard Educational Review*, 47(4), 481–517. https://doi.org/10 .17763/haer.47.4.g6167429416hg5l0

Gilligan, C. 1986. 'Reply by Carol Gilligan', *Signs: Journal of Women in Culture and Society*, 11(2), 324–333. https://doi.org/10.1086/494226

Gilligan, C. 1987. 'Moral Orientation and Moral Development'. In: Bailey, A. and Cuomo, C. J. (eds). *The Feminist Philosophy Reader*. Boston, MA: McGraw-Hill, 467–478.

Ging, D. 2019. 'Alphas, Betas, and Incels: Theorizing the Masculinities of the Manosphere', *Men and Masculinities*, 22(4), 638–657. https://doi.org/10.1177/1097184X17706401

Halberstam, J. 2019. *Female Masculinity*. Durham, NC: Duke University Press.

Held, V. 1993. *Feminist Morality: Transforming Culture, Society, and Politics*. Chicago, IL: University of Chicago Press.

Hesse-Biber, S. N. 2012. 'Feminist Research: Exploring, Interrogating, and Transforming the Interconnections of Epistemology, Methodology, and Method'. In: Hesse-Biber, S. N. (ed.). *Handbook of Feminist Research: Theory and Praxis*. Thousand Oaks, CA: Sage, 1–26.

Hodapp, C. 2017. *Men's Rights, Gender, and Social Media*. Lanham, MD: Rowman & Littlefield.

Johnson, C. W. and Cousineau, L. S. 2018. 'Manning Up and Manning On: Masculinities, Hegemonic Masculinity, and Leisure Studies'. In: Parry, D. C. (ed.). *Feminisms in Leisure Studies: Advancing a Fourth Wave*. London: Routledge, 126–148.

Johnson, C. W. and Parry, D. C. 2016. 'Contextualizing Qualitative Research for Social Justice'. In: Johnson, C. W. and Parry, D. C. (eds). *Fostering Social Justice through Qualitative Inquiry: A Methodological Guide*, 1st ed. New York: Routledge, 8–17.

Kayden, J. S. 2000. *Privately Owned Public Space: The New York City Experience*. New York: John Wiley & Sons.

Lee, D. 2020. 'Whose Space is Privately Owned Public Space? Exclusion, Underuse and the Lack of Knowledge and Awareness', *Urban Research & Practice*, 1–15. https://doi.org/10.1080/17535069.2020.1815828

Lorber, J. 2012. *Gender Inequality: Feminist Theories and Politics*. New York: Oxford University Press.

Mandell, N. and Johnson, J. (eds). 2016. *Feminist Issues: Race, Class and Sexuality*. Sydney: Pearson Education Australia.

Markham, A. 2012. 'Fabrication as Ethical Practice: Qualitative Inquiry in Ambiguous Internet Contexts', *Information, Communication & Society*, 15(3), 334–353. https://doi.org/10.1080/1369118X.2011.641993

Massanari, A. L. 2015. *Participatory Culture, Community, and Play: Learning from Reddit*. New York: Peter Lang.

Massanari, A. L. 2017. '#Gamergate and the Fappening: How Reddit's Algorithm, Governance, and Culture Support Toxic Technocultures', *New Media & Society*, 19(3), 329–346. https://doi.org/10.1177/1461444815608807

Pao, E. 2017. *Reset: My Fight for Inclusion and Lasting Change*. New York: Random House Publishing Group.

Richterich, A. 2014. '"Karma, Precious Karma!" Karmawhoring on Reddit and the Front Page's Econometrisation', *Journal of Peer Production*, 4, 1–12.

'R/MensRights'. 2019. Reddit. https://www.reddit.com/r/MensRights/ (accessed 4 January 2019).

Robards, B. 2018. '"Totally Straight": Contested Sexual Identities on Social Media Site Reddit', *Sexualities*, 21(1–2), 49–67. https://doi.org/10.1177/1363460716678563

'/R/TheRedPill'. 2019. Reddit. https://www.reddit.com/r/TheRedPill/ (accessed 4 January 2019).

Salter, M. 2018. 'From Geek Masculinity to Gamergate: The Technological Rationality of Online Abuse', *Crime, Media, Culture: An International Journal*, 14(2), 247–264. https://doi.org/10.1177/1741659017690893

Siapera, E. 2019. 'Online Misogyny as Witch Hunt: Primitive Accumulation in the Age of Techno-Capitalism', In: Ging, D. and Siapera, E. (eds). *Gender Hate Online: Understanding the New Anti-Feminism*. New York: Springer International Publishing, 21–43. https://doi.org/10.1007/978-3-319-96226-9_2

Shelton, M. L., Lo, K. M., and Nardi, B. A. 2015. 'Online Media Forums as Separate Social Lives: A Qualitative Study of Disclosure within and beyond Reddit', *iConference*, 12.

Springer, N. J. 2015. 'Publics and Counterpublics on the Front Page of the Internet: The Cultural Practices, Technological Affordances, Hybrid Economics and Politics of Reddit's Public Sphere', University of Colorado. http://noahspringer.com/wp-content/uploads/2015/12/Springer_Reddit_Dissertation.pdf (accessed 20 September 2018).

Stacey, J. 1988. 'Can There Be a Feminist Ethnography?', *Women's Studies International Forum*, 11(1), 21–27. https://doi.org/10.1016/0277-5395(88)90004-0

Stanley, L. and Wise, S. 2013. 'Method, Methodology and Epistemology in Feminist Research Processes'. In: Stanley, L. (ed.). *Feminist Praxis: Research, Theory, and Epistemology in Feminist Sociology*. London: Routledge, 20–62.

Tiffany, K. 2020. 'The Secret Internet of TERFs', *The Atlantic*. https://www.theatlantic.com/technology/archive/2020/12/reddit-ovarit-the-donald/617320/ (accessed 8 December 2018).

Tronto, J. C. 1998. 'An Ethic of Care', *Generations*, 22(3), 15–20.

Van der Nagel, E. and Frith, J. 2015. 'Anonymity, Pseudonymity, and the Agency of Online Identity: Examining the Social Practices of r/Gonewild', *First Monday*, 20(3). https://doi.org/10.5210/fm.v20i3.5615

Werner, W. and Lammert, C. 2021. 'Broken Social Contract: The Domestic Roots of US Hegemonic Decline in the World'. In: Böller, F. and Werner, W. (eds). *Hegemonic Transition*. Springer International Publishing, 43–65. https://doi.org/10.1007/978-3-030-74505-9_3

Zhang, X. and He, Y. 2020. 'What Makes Public Space Public? The Chaos of Public Space Definitions and a New Epistemological Approach', *Administration & Society*, 52(5), 749–770. https://doi.org/10.1177/0095399719852897

Part V

Complications of engaging far-right
participants and formers

22

Ethics of listening: between criticism and empathy in oral history interviews and politically charged research contexts

Vanessa Tautter

Researching the meanings of reactionary discourses and politics in society through intersubjective work with research participants, such as oral history interviews, poses several difficult ethical challenges due to the personal relationships, power dynamics, and politics involved. One central challenge revolves around the ethics of listening[1] in such work that brings together complex personal and broader public political meanings in the interview setting. Drawing on my current research on the politics of memory in Austria, this chapter reflects on the relationship – and conflict – between criticism and empathy in such intersubjective work in politically charged research settings. On the one hand, I aim to listen to my interviewees, who are willing to share their personal stories, experiences, thoughts, and feelings, on their 'own' terms, in their 'own' language to genuinely engage with their perspectives, critically, but also empathically and respectfully beyond reductionist practices, cliches, and condescension. However, as some of them also draw upon discourses linked to relativising and violent representations of the past in their narratives, such listening is not devoid of political and ethical implications. This chapter reflects critically on the meaning – and ethical problems – of listening in the context of such epistemic and discursive violence that has been firmly grounded in the structures of society over decades and which perpetuates historical violence. It also problematises my own positionality as an Austrian researcher, originally coming from a similar background as my interviewees and, as such, not directly targeted by these forms of violence. While this reflective chapter specifically focuses on my research experience in Austria, I hope that it will also offer insights, raise questions, and facilitate further discussion on similar ethical difficulties more broadly.

Background and context

Unlike much contemporary work on the right, I do not conduct research directly with or on members of far-right groups or the supporters of their politics. Rather, I critically interrogate the continuities of reactionary discourses into 'mainstream' culture. My research is situated at the intersection between public and private memory processes in relation to the memory of World War II, Nazism, and Nazi crimes in Austria. It seeks to understand the impact of and negotiations between, on the one hand, public memory politics and political mobilisations of the past and, on the other, private processes of memory making, personal life stories, and family histories. By doing so, it aims to make visible political dynamics in these highly personal and emotional processes to dissect the meaning of these embedded politics for society to critically engage with, deconstruct, and challenge them. In our conversations, many of my interviewees voiced their opposition to reactionary and revisionist mobilisations of the Nazi past by the far right and other political agents. Yet, they nonetheless occasionally deployed elements of reactionary discourses, normalised in large parts of Austrian society over decades, when composing their own family memories.

I interviewed individuals who had grown up or lived in 'traditional', previously more dominant memory cultures, mainly in the Austrian countryside, to learn about their experiences of memory change since the 1980s and 1990s. Until then, dominant cultural narratives about the Nazi past in Austria portrayed Austrians, in general, as victims of Nazism, regardless of their actual actions, complicity, and implication in the National Socialist system. Such dominant 'victim narratives', hence, not only overshadowed but violently silenced and erased the stories, experiences, and memories of the victims of Nazi persecution in public representations and cultural memory, whilst, at the same time, omitting the involvement of Austrians in these crimes (Uhl 2006, 2011; Lehnguth 2013). Even though these narratives have lost dominance over the last decades, due to their previously hegemonic position, they have nonetheless been firmly grounded, normalised, and even naturalised in some parts of society. In a Gramscian sense, they continue to underpin 'common sense' thinking about the past (Hall and O'Shea 2013), and 'residual' elements of these narratives (Williams 1977: 121–7) continue to inform processes of memory making in the present. My interviewees also drew upon aspects of these discourses when 'composing' (Dawson 1994) their own family histories.

On the one hand, interviewees – whether unconsciously or consciously – drew upon narratives with very specific and violent political meanings. At the same time, on the other hand, as 'ordinary people' rather than distinct political agents, they are 'non-elite' research participants and researchers also need to be aware of the intersubjective power dynamics between interviewer and interviewee that may impact the interview dynamics as well as the broader research process. But how to let 'non-elite' interviewees speak in their 'own' voice, with their 'own' language, when this comprises the inclusion of elements of violent discourses? And is it possible to do so in an empathetic way, respectful to their own experiences, life stories, and affective family relationships, whilst still criticising the wider power dynamics and violence of the discourses they draw upon? The following sections reflect on these ethical concerns: the first section critically explores the meaning of empathy, intersubjectivity, and power dynamics in the interview setting and the research process. The second section further complicates these approaches by interrogating them in relation to the wider politics they involve.

Empathy, intersubjectivity, and power dynamics in oral history interviews

These complex ethical and political challenges raise the question of whether empathy is needed in research in such highly political contexts that involve different forms of violence, and I fear that I am unable to fully answer that question. Rightly so, reflections on these issues are – and should be – uncomfortable for researchers, as they concern the wellbeing of others. However, in order to gain a greater understanding of the role that violent discourses, such as previously dominant 'victim narratives', continue to play in society and culture today – and to deconstruct and challenge their politics, it is necessary to genuinely engage with them and the ways in which they are used (Blee 2016; Abrams 2016: 189). Additionally, without such critical analysis, it is difficult to explore possible complexity and variation in their use, which may also lead to divergence or the development of more critical stances. In other words, going into the research environment without actively reflecting on our own preconceived notions, imaginaries, and feelings about the politics of the interview may forestall a critical and open engagement with these issues from our side, as we project our thoughts into the field, leaving little space for the unexpected. However, the value of fieldwork lies precisely in listening and learning from research participants to expand our knowledge and understanding of the world, not merely to confirm what we think we already know. In my own work, for instance, despite drawing on elements of reactionary discourses, interviewees also shared reflections about their own critical engagement with these memory politics and intimate stories of how they negotiated these political memories within their families, also in relation to their relatives' personal experiences of the war. In other words, they included personal reflections on the transgenerational memory work taking place within the private sphere of the family that I had not anticipated. But these reflective processes can only take place in an interview setting that allows for them and in which the interviewer listens to what interviewees say.

Feelings of discomfort, in this context, can be useful indicators in our work as they frequently shine a light on underlying complexities in our research, which are difficult to neatly dissect, categorise, and reconcile with our senses of self. Conducting research on these violent discourses from an empathetic, yet – importantly – critical position produces discomfort, as it transcends these binaries to some degree. This, however, is an ethically sensitive process that runs the danger of slipping into apologetic, legitimising, or justifying representations of the uses of these narratives. Hence, in this context, listening is difficult and uncomfortable. We sense these power dynamics not only between the interviewer and interviewee but especially in relation to the wider political meanings of these conversations, whether we consciously engage with them or not. In a reflective piece on feelings of discomfort in the research process from the perspective of feminist anthropology, Andrea García-González highlights that "[e]xploring discomfort makes us rethink what we study, how we study it, and what representations we create" (García-González et al. 2021: 6). In other words, awareness of these feelings enables us to reflect on the ethics and politics of our work and the violent power dynamics it is entangled with. It helps to further sharpen our critical analysis of the political meanings of the narratives we research in the context of their wider violent histories and in relation to their personal uses in society today.

Additionally, the interview setting as such is not an equal place between interviewer and interviewee either, in relation to the hierarchies, authority, and privileges afforded in the research process (Portelli 1997). Despite the increasing precarity of academia, researchers hold a privileged position that allows them to extensively engage with difficult subject matters and issues in society from a more detached and distant perspective, which is not necessarily the case for 'ordinary people' who may not have the resources for such critical analysis. It is generally the researchers who design research projects and interview questions and who conduct the analysis and interpretation. Hence, in projects that are not collaborative, ultimately, researchers make the final decisions on what is represented and how. Additionally, they oftentimes enter the research environment – the 'field' – as somewhat of an outsider but observe the highly personal lived realities and everyday lives of those they are researching. Moreover, in interviews, these research participants share their inherently personal and frequently emotional stories, meaningful to their own lives, and, by doing so, entrust us with their vulnerability. In the case of my project, these included personal stories of violence experienced during the war and thereafter, for some with emotional implications until today.

Empathy allows us to listen and hear these stories and to try to understand the perspectives of our respondents, where possible in a respectful way, even when we disagree and remain critical. In a thought-provoking reflection on the meaning of 'critical empathy', which he clearly distinguishes from sympathy and, specifically in relation to perpetrator histories, also from compassion, the South African oral historian Sean Field describes empathy as "involv[ing] researchers in ethical acts of imaginative seeing and listening to the pain and emotions in *and* between others". Yet, he highlights, "there is a tension during oral history dialogues between empathy as an imaginative tool that can expand understandings of suffering of others, and, the critical thinking required to analyse historical patterns and affective legacies of violence" (Field 2017: 661). Empathy, in this sense, is essential to learn about and from the experiences and perspectives of those we interview, but it requires critical analysis and reflection in relation to the wider history, culture, and politics.

In this context, at least for me, the conversations and dialogues that take place during the interview process are about listening and learning, and, following Alessandro Portelli, not about "preaching to" those we engage with (Portelli 1997: 63). Especially in cases that involve violent histories, politics, and discourses, this does not mean that the interview ceases to be a place for reflecting on the perspectives, positions, views, and experiences of those involved in the conversation. However, such reflection crucially builds on genuine listening and an interest in learning. A condescending and patronising approach to interviewing that entails such "preaching to" hardly allows for that. Of course, it is impossible to have open and reflective conversations in certain settings, as there are concrete limits to such empathetic approaches in political research contexts (e.g., Jessee 2011), most likely also in relation to some of the work discussed in this book. Similarly, I also experienced limits to such approaches in my own project, for instance, on the rare occasion that interviewees were not interested in any critical engagement or reflection concerning their family memories and these violent histories and politics. However, overall, most of my interviewees were, at least to some degree, open to engaging with and reflecting on critical issues discussed during the interview. These were conversations from which I was able to learn a lot. And even when these reflections do not necessarily reach our expectations as academics in terms of their rigour, it is still important to remember – to draw on Portelli once more – that our interviewees "have the information and kindly share it with us. To keep this in mind is to remember that we are speaking to, and being helped by, not 'sources', but persons" (Portelli 1997: 64). This should not lead to a departure from criticism or critical analysis, but it should be reflected in our research practice in that, whilst we approach these stories from an ethically, politically, and analytically critical perspective, we still try to meet those we engage with in conversation with empathy and respect, whenever and wherever possible.

Discursive violence, power dynamics, and the interview

Yet, due to the wider meaning of the discourses drawn upon in the interviews and the violent history that underlies them, such uses of oral history deviate from the discipline's original link to emancipatory politics. The history of oral history is strongly connected to progressive politics such as feminism. It was envisioned as a research method that challenges established power relations and oppression in society by working with "people who, historically speaking, would otherwise remain inarticulate" (Fraser in Blee 2016: 424). Ideally, it aimed to create more inclusive, collaborative, and egalitarian approaches to research (Blee 2016). These approaches, however, cannot simply be transplanted to research with 'ordinary people' who, even when not explicitly supporting far-right groups, nonetheless draw upon reactionary discourses to make sense of the lived realities around them, their families' memories of the violent past and to communicate their life stories in the interview setting. These narratives do not only have a violent historical origin but also a violent discursive history beyond the Nazi period as they continue(d) to silence and erase the experiences and memories of those persecuted by the Nazis. At the same time, they evade a critical engagement with the complicity and implication of Austrians in Nazi crimes and the National Socialist system. Any critical analysis needs to situate and interrogate oral history interviews conducted in such a context in relation to these wider power dynamics and address the violence these narratives perpetuate, not only on an individual but, especially, on a structural level.[2] Whilst I work on a specific historical context, similar reflective and critical work is also required when researching other narratives and discourses entangled with oppressive ideologies.

In this context, analysing personal life stories and engaging in intersubjective personal relationships with research participants through the interview involves the danger of becoming complicit in the perpetuation of such discursive violence. Hence, critical awareness and active reflection of this danger is necessary throughout the research process. These relationships built on the engagement with personal stories pose the additional risk of unconsciously being 'drawn into' these narrations, which may interfere with our ability to critically analyse and situate them (Abrams 2016: 189). Antonius Robben has coined the term "ethnographic seduction" for this process during which "respondents compose their narratives in a way that is intended to legitimise their versions of events" (Abrams 2016: 189), and their audience, including the researcher, are unconsciously 'seduced' by the story (Robben 1996). Thus, awareness, reflection, and open and critical analysis of these issues, including their unconscious impact on the research process, are helpful to avoid succumbing to such 'seduction' or other forms of complicity and implication (Rothberg 2019), even where we may not expect it initially.

Awareness of these issues related to becoming complicit in violent politics becomes particularly relevant and significant when researchers share some aspects of their personal background and history with research participants. On the one hand, due to feeling familiar with the stories shared, they may become more susceptible to such possible unconscious 'seduction'. On the other, and at the same time, the political meanings of these discourses become even more relevant as they raise ethical responsibilities not only in relation to the ways in which we represent this kind of work but also concerning privileges of access and the mere ability to conduct this form of research without being directly targeted by the violence of the narrations. I come from a similar rural background in Austria as many of my interviewees and grew up in a culture that perpetuates certain elements of these discourses. This makes the stories shared feel more familiar to me as well, which, however, also allowed me to notice some of the more subtle meanings in the narratives that frequently remain unaddressed, and it probably affected my relationship with my interviewees. Yet, due to this implication, such work requires awareness of and reflection on the politics of these research processes to prevent the thoughtless, uncritical, even unconscious reproduction and perpetuation of the violence of these discourses, as to deconstruct and challenge their politics.

The oral historian Valerie Yow has highlighted the importance of becoming aware of the issues that may impact our relationship with interviewees and our positioning in relation to them so that we are able to actively reflect on and negotiate these influences in our work. These include the impact of ideologies as well as our projections of personal experience on our respondents (Yow 1997). In my case, awareness of the field, the prevalent discourses, and my own relationship with them helped me to prepare for my interviews, also concerning my expectations. It allowed me to engage more deeply in conversations and reflections from the perspectives of my interviewees, without immediately reducing them solely to the discourses they were drawing on, whilst also aiming not to reproduce them uncritically. However, sharing aspects of a common background also made it more difficult when I felt respondents were not 'critical enough' of these discourses and politics, and sometimes I had to remind myself in this context of my own privileged and somewhat detached position in academia today that my interviewees did not share. In this sense, awareness of potentially shared experiences – as well as alterity (such as being in academia and having 'moved away', also in the literal sense, from the community researched) – is central to the reflection of the politics and power dynamics of the interviewing process and, furthermore, for the critical analyses in our wider research project. Researchers more generally – not only oral historians – always bring experiences, ideas, and thoughts into the field that affect their work. Thus, awareness about these influences and active self-reflection is not only helpful but an essential tool for critical research.

Concluding remarks

This chapter is not intended as a comprehensive overview of the multifarious facets of the ethics of listening in oral history interviews conducted in politically sensitive contexts. Rather it is a personal reflection on concrete challenges concerning such listening between criticism and empathy that I encountered whilst working with interviews. I hope that it will initiate and contribute to further conversation on these ethically and politically challenging issues. Interviewing, on the one hand, allows us to engage with and learn about divergent political, cultural, and social realities. On the other, however, this work is fraught with tension as it requires us to address violent discourses, power structures, and legacies of historical violence in relation to the intersubjective personal relationship in the interview. There is no easy or uniform way to approach these issues of interpersonal entanglements with political cultures of violence, and the varying practices, rationales, aims, and contexts of individual projects necessitate different approaches. Yet, awareness and reflection of political meanings that affect our work, and processes of listening in it, substantiate critical analyses that offer intricate insights for understanding cultural and political practices in society. This is especially important when it comes to the study of discursive and epistemic violence connected to these political meanings – and the implication of individual subjectivities in them. In this context, emotional responses and feelings that emerge whilst and after listening may be indicative of unconscious dynamics, easily missed yet informative about and formative for what is happening. Hence, making visible such processes by actively addressing, discussing, and reflecting on them adds depth to research. My own work centrally revolves around memory making processes that are entangled with wider cultural and political power structures in society. This research focus, I hope, offers space to render visible these sometimes 'invisible' or 'unconscious' politics by directly addressing them as a focal part of the project, also in relation to the ethical challenges they produce. While the reflections of this chapter have emerged directly out of my work on Austria, I hope that it will nonetheless also be of interest to others struggling with similar ethical difficulties in their research more broadly, contribute to ongoing debates around these issues, raise new questions, and, most importantly, facilitate further discussion.

Acknowledgements

I would like to thank Eugene Michail, Graham Dawson, Lucy Newby, Áine McKenny, Martha Beard, Timofey Agarin, Lars Cornelissen, Claudia Treacher, Aleksandra Szczodrowski, Tina Lorenz, Lennart Oschgan, Laetitia Ratiney, Petra Kostevc, as well as Anton and Roswitha Tautter for their incredible support and the inspiring, thought-provoking, and critical conversations. Every one of you has had an influence on how I think about the issues discussed in this chapter.

Notes

1 Much of my thinking on listening and hearing in oral history has been influenced by the inspiring work of Lucy Newby, and I can only wholeheartedly recommend anyone interested in these issues to engage with her current (e.g., Newby 2021) and forthcoming publications.
2 I draw on the work that emerged from and in relation to the Popular Memory Group to explore such power dynamics in processes of memory making within a 'cultural circuit' (e.g., Popular Memory Group 1982/2007; Ashplant et al. 2000; Johnson 1986; Dawson 1994; Thomson 2013; Newby 2021).

References

Abrams, L. 2016. *Oral History Theory*. Second Edition. London and New York: Routledge.

Ashplant, T. G., Dawson, G., and Roper, M. 2000. 'The Politics of War Memory and Commemoration: Contexts, Structures and Dynamics'. In: Ashplant, T. G., Dawson, G., and Roper, M. (eds). *The Politics of War Memory and Commemoration*. London and New York: Routledge, 3–85.

Blee, K. 2016. 'Evidence, Empathy and Ethics: Lessons from Oral Histories of the Klan'. In: Perks, R. and Thomson, A. (eds). *The Oral History Reader*. Third Edition. London and New York: Routledge, 424–433.

Dawson, G. 1994. *Soldier Heroes: British Adventure, Empire and the Imagining of Masculinities*. London and New York: Routledge.

Field, S. 2017. 'Critical Empathy through Oral Histories after Apartheid', *Continuum*, 31(5), 660–670.

García-González, A., Hoover, E. M., Francis, A. N., Rush, K., and Forero Angel, A. M. 2021. 'When Discomfort Enters Our Skin: Five Feminists in Conversation', *Feminist Anthropology*, 1–19.

Hall, S. and O'Shea, A. 2013. 'Common-Sense Neoliberalism', *Soundings*, 55, 8–24.

Jessee, E. 2011. 'The Limits of Oral History: Ethics and Methodology amid Highly Politicized Research Settings', *Oral History Review*, 38(2), 287–307.

Johnson, R. 1986. 'What Is Cultural Studies Anyway?', *Social Text*, 16, 38–80.

Lehnguth, C. 2013. *Waldheim und die Folgen: Der parteipolitische Umgang mit dem Nationalsozialismus in Österreich*. Frankfurt and New York: Campus Verlag.

Newby, L. 2021. 'Troubled Generations? (De)constructing Narratives of Youth Experience in the Northern Ireland Conflict', *Journal of War & Culture Studies*, 14(1), 6–24.

Popular Memory Group. 1982/2007. 'Popular Memory: Theory, Politics, Method'. In: Johnson, R., McLennan, G., Schwarz, B., and Sutton, D. (eds). *Making Histories: Studies in History-Writing and Politics*. London and New York: Routledge, 205–252.

Portelli, A. 1997. *The Battle of Valle Giulia: Oral History and the Art of Dialogue*. Madison, WI: The University of Wisconsin Press.

Robben, A. C. G. M. 1996. 'Ethnographic Seduction, Transference, and Resistance in Dialogues about Terror and Violence in Argentina', *Ethos*, 24(1), 71–106.

Rothberg, M. 2019. *The Implicated Subject: Beyond Victims and Perpetrators*. Stanford, CA: Stanford University Press.

Thomson, A. 2013. *Anzac Memories: Living with the Legend*. Second Edition. Clayton: Monash University Publishing.

Uhl, H. 2006. 'From Victim Myth to Co-Responsibility Thesis: Nazi Rule, World War II, and the Holocaust in Austrian Memory'. In: Lebow, R. N., Kansteiner, W., and Fugo, C. (eds). *The Politics of Memory in Postwar Europe*. Durham, NC and London: Duke University Press, 40–72.

Uhl, H. 2011. 'Of Heroes and Victims: World War II in Austrian Memory', *Austrian History Yearbook*, 42, 185–200.

Williams, R. 1977. *Marxism and Literature*. Oxford and New York: Oxford University Press.

Yow, V. 1997. '"Do I Like Them Too Much?": Effects of the Oral History Interview on the Interviewer and Vice-Versa', *The Oral History Review*, 24(1), 55–79.

23

Harms of the compassion narrative: ethical considerations regarding stories of disengagement from white supremacist movements

Joan Braune

Many stories are circulating in print, online media, and public lectures about how former neo-Nazis and white supremacists decided to leave their movements. These stories sometimes appear in documentary films (Kahn 2017; Ornstein 2016; Strauss 2018), in popular books (Saslow 2018), or in academic writing (Kimmel 2018), but usually, they are recounted directly by former members of hate groups. As 'exit' programmes devoted to helping people leave hate groups proliferated in Europe, so did the publication of memoirs by former neo-Nazi skinheads, confessing their acts of violence and sharing their stories of personal redemption (Fekete 2014). This trend spread to North America with the publication of books by T. J. Leyden (Leyden and Cook 2008), Kerry Noble (2010), Arno Michaelis (2012), Elisa Hategan (2014), Frank Meeink (Meeink and Roy 2017), Christian Picciolini (2017), Tony McAleer (2019), and others. Now the American and English-speaking public has also heard narratives through dozens of media interviews or speeches by former neo-Nazis or former far-right activists (Michaelis 2019; Picciolini 2017; Bates 2017; Kimmel 2018, etc.), many of whom have had public roles in 'deradicalisation' or 'countering extremism' groups and have told their stories many times.

Often such stories allege that unexpected acts of compassion from members of marginalised groups precipitated the disengagement of neo-Nazis and white supremacists from their movements. For example:

(1) Derek Black, a rising young white supremacist activist and son of prominent white supremacist leader Don Black, formed friendships with Jewish students in college (Saslow 2018).
(2) Former neo-Nazi Ken Parker had transformative encounters with Muslim filmmaker Deeyah Khan and shortly after with a Black pastor who reached out to him (Kahn 2017).

(3) Former neo-Nazi Arno Michaelis was gently challenged about his swas-
     tika tattoo by a kind African American woman working in a McDonald's
     restaurant (Michaelis 2019).

Derek Black, Ken Parker, and Arno Michaelis all credit these encounters, at
least partly, with leading them to exit white supremacist movements.

Such stories follow a familiar pattern and belong to a shared genre
that I term the 'compassion narrative'. The compassion narrative
stresses the transformative power of receiving compassion from a person who belongs to a group one has dehumanised when this is unpre-
dicted and feels undeserved. When depicted as an event in a former
hater's life, the kindness of the other is met with surprise, shame, and
cognitive dissonance on the part of the hater, who later reflects on the
meaning of receiving kindness from a member of a group they believed
to be inferior and against whom they had mobilised fear, hatred, and
violence. While these stories are inspiring to some listeners and potentially healing for some such 'formers' (former members of hate groups
or 'extremist' movements) to tell, their effects have not been adequately
considered.

In this chapter, I argue that compassion narratives may have unexpected negative impacts. They centre white perpetrators, reinforce the
status quo assumptions of mainstream racist society, and operate within
structures of Preventing and Countering Violent Extremism (P/CVE) that
can harm members of minority groups conceived as belonging to 'suspect communities' (Nguyen 2019; Kundnani and Hayes 2018; Manzoor-
Kahn 2022). In addition, the unjustified assumption that these stories are
accurate serves to further empower former perpetrators and disempower
their victims. In what follows, I address the ways in which these stories
may contribute to a racist status quo through a logic of 'colourblind-
ness', the potential for inaccuracy in compassion narratives, and potential harms to victims/survivors of hate and others. I close the chapter with
recommendations for research and ethical practice regarding compassion
narratives.

Compassion narratives and colourblindness

Compassion narratives rarely include any educational content about the
nature and history of racism or other oppressions beyond an essentially
colourblind message of shared humanity. They also often present compassionate encounters as *educative* for haters about the humanity of those they
harmed. This enables these stories to function in complex ways to maintain

both hard and soft power in the capitalist, white supremacist, and militarised societies of the global North.

The erasure of difference and uneven power relationships can contribute to policies that can worsen racism, including in the area of P/CVE – Preventing or Countering Violent Extremism. For example, in the UK, the Prevent programme (which tasks teachers, doctors, therapists, and others with reporting warning signs of 'radicalisation' to the state) often uses a 'colourblind' paradigm. That is, as Tarek Younis points out, it often tries to avoid discussing race and religious identity in its 'training' for mandated reporters, but this does not solve the problem, since Prevent's training does not occur in a vacuum. Rather, it is presented to a public already riddled with Islamophobic and racist assumptions (Younis 2019). Similarly, the US Department of Homeland Security's framework now includes a category of 'racially motivated' terrorism, which appears to merge the prior categories of 'white supremacist' terrorism and the nebulously defined 'Black Identity Extremist' (Patel 2021) terrorism. This new religion-blind and race-blind rhetoric does not erase current and historically rooted biases and inequities, including the ways in which terrorist designations in the US have targeted Black radical activism (Meier 2022; Husain 2021).

Compassion narratives function in P/CVE (Kelly and DeCook 2022) as 'counter-narratives' (Silverman et al. 2016; Braddock 2020), a term that has become a grant-winning buzzword in the world of counter-extremism initiatives. Counter-narratives, in CVE, are stories that are addressed to 'the many' (the public) to reach 'the few' (those upstream or downstream of 'extremist' movements) (Braddock 2020). Yet the effectiveness of compassion narratives as counter-narratives has not been proven. In fact, stories by formers may be unlikely to sway ideologically entrenched far-right actors, who usually dismiss formers as traitors or police (Koehler 2017).

That the world of counter-terrorism and 'countering violent extremism' sees compassion narratives as counter-narratives says much about CVE's political affiliations and loyalties. In a time when the far right is engaged in a war in state legislatures and school boards in the United States against Critical Race Theory, it is telling to see the term 'counter-narrative' used by CVE to refer to the stories of perpetrators from dominant groups. Counter-narratives in Critical Race Theory bring forward neglected experiences and histories from the standpoint of the marginalised, using stories "to cast doubt on the validity of accepted premises or myths, especially ones held by the majority" (Delgado and Stefancic 2017). By contrast, the compassion narrative, while critical of virulent and recalcitrant hatreds, does not challenge the status quo – it is hard to think of a more dominant white narrative than the idea that hate can be cured by the oppressed engaging in kind outreach and dialogue with the hater. There are deeply rooted societal assumptions about the obligations of marginalised groups that these narratives recapitulate, such as the widespread expectations that Black people must explain racism to white people in a 'gentle' and 'non-threatening' manner; that Muslims must prove their patriotism and nonviolence; that LGBTQ+ individuals must demonstrate their 'normalcy' and moral virtue; and that women must 'save' men with the power of their love.

Compassion narratives and potential for inaccuracy

Although formers' stories are often repeated uncritically (and treated in the media as heart-warming 'human interest' stories, rather than something to set an investigative journalist on), they should always be checked for accuracy. A small number of people held up as formers may be con artists, but even sincerely remorseful formers may fail to recount their exits from hate movements accurately for a number of reasons. Unfortunately, some researchers assume that these stories are trustworthy bases for explaining the factors that help people leave white supremacist groups, or even treat formers as *de facto* experts whose opinions on what 'deradicalisation' entails should determine the rhetoric and methods of CVE groups. Unsettling the assumption of the truth of formers' stories is necessary for challenging the ways in which CVE disempowers survivors of hate and bolsters the oppressive status quo.

In the worst cases, people still consciously holding fascist or white supremacist beliefs have posed as 'formers' for personal gain (such as avoiding criminal charges) or to continue to recruit for fascist or far-right politics, using a false identity as a 'former' to manipulate public opinion or gain access to new spaces. Deliberate political manipulation may have been the case with Matt Heimbach. Heimbach, the founder of the fascist Traditionalist Workers Party, reached out to the deradicalisation organisation Light Upon Light. In his initial letter, he told them that "I am not apologising and have nothing to apologise for", but in an apparent rush for publicity to demonstrate their organisation's work, Light Upon Light's Jesse Morton immediately contacted *The New York Times* to ask them to publish an article about Heimbach leaving fascism (Burley 2022). Shortly after starting a series of podcast episodes with Morton and appearing on a Light Upon Light webinar panel, Heimbach continued to promote fascist ideology, including posting online that he considered Romanian fascist leader Corneliu Codreanu "a Saint in my book" and praising fascist "degeneracy" laws used to imprison LGBTQ+ people (Burley 2022).

Although it is important to identify 'bad actors', it may not be sufficient to sort formers into categories of 'real' and 'fake' or 'sincere' and 'insincere'. Sincerely remorseful formers can still do harm. Furthermore, as others have argued, fascism is deeply insincere in the way it plays with truth and in some sense views truth as a product of violence, believing that 'might makes right' (Finchelstein 2020; Sartre 1976; Kahn-Harris 2018; Leeb 2019). Part of the process of 'exit' from fascism is about moving away from the idea that truth is a product of power and violence and returning to a notion of truth as uncovered through inquiry (Braune 2021). Asking whether someone who has recently left fascist movements is sincere, honest, and genuine may erase subtleties in the long-term process of change.

In addition, compassion narratives can contain elements of 'neutralisation', the criminological term for the tendency of those who have done harm to offer justifications or excuses. For example, victim-blaming, a tool of neutralisation (Sykes and Matza 1957), may be evident in claims that an individual was 'radicalised' by political opponents on the left (see e.g. Buckby 2020) such as antifascist or antiracist activists. Compassion narratives can suggest a dichotomy between (1) the 'good' forgiver, who is nonviolent, politically moderate, and a 'listener' who seeks to understand the underlying motivations of the extremist 'other', and (2) the 'bad' outraged opponent who may be blamed for radicalisation due to the 'extremism' of 'both sides'. The antifascist activist who is confrontational rather than forgiving may thus be accused of contributing to 'reciprocal radicalisation' or 'cumulative extremism' and thus be unfairly blamed for the fact that fascists and far-right actors are targeting their community.

Furthermore, even when taking full responsibility and avoiding neutralising, people have genuine difficulty in assessing their own motivations. Some formers may not know what led them to leave hate groups but simply assume that compassionate outreach must have played a role because of the ubiquity of this script.

Lastly, some formers probably exaggerate their descriptions of their past leadership roles in the movement or of their past violent exploits, for credentials as experts (having 'insider knowledge'), for shock value, or for 'street cred'. This possibility seems to be evidenced by cases of figures in the 'ex-Islamist' circuit who seem to have faked aspects of their past. Shehroze Chaudhry, claiming to be 'Abu Huzaifa', was the subject of a *New York Times* podcast series called *Caliphate*, in which he claimed to have fought with ISIS in Syria. Chaudhry was later brought to court in Canada for making up parts of his story, and he confessed that he had never gone to Syria (Austen 2021). Similarly, Islamophobic speaker Walid Shoebat, whose talks were funded by the US Department of Homeland Security, claimed to be a former 'terrorist' who bombed an Israeli bank, a claim Israeli officials dispute (Griffin and Johnston 2011).

Harms of the compassion narrative

The possible harms of the compassion narrative remain largely unstudied. In particular, there is no published scientific study on their impact on victims/survivors of hate attacks. It seems likely that victims could be retraumatised by seeing those who may have harmed them in the past being praised and applauded as redeemed and by hearing them retell stories of harming them.

However, some articles address other impacts. For example, Gansewig and Walsh discuss a former who is promoted by the German government as a resource for preventing the recruitment of youth into hate groups. When he speaks at schools, the former asks the kids to follow his YouTube channel, and about 50 per cent of them do (Gansewig and Walsh 2021/2). Gansewig and Walsh write that "the former's distancing from right-wing extremism and crime is not addressed" in the videos, and they worry that content in the videos about topics like drugs and guns might actually increase youth interest in the far right by glamorising it as risky and rebellious and promoting "sensation-seeking" (Gansewig and Walsh 2021/2). This example raises the possibility that, as perhaps with some anti-drug programming in schools, the stories of some formers might increase fascination with what they ostensibly are warning about, making youth more vulnerable to coming into contact with the far right.

Furthermore, there may be harms to formers themselves in the telling of these stories (Burley 2022; Hategan 2019). Daniel Koehler, Director of the German Institute of Radicalization and Deradicalization Studies (GIRDS), points out that although formers are only automatic "experts on their own biography" (Burley 2022), they can end up in long-term careers as 'professional formers' and can become so reliant on this new identity that they may experience trauma if they need to find a job in a different profession later (Koehler 2017). They may, in other words, become unhealthily dependent on telling their story.

Finally, the likely false assumption that haters need to be educated about the humanity of their victims through compassionate encounters may do harm in the way that it tasks those already endangered with outreach (which can be dangerous) and potentially blames them for their own victimisation, assuming they have not been doing kind outreach to haters. As noted above, this expectation recapitulates mainstream societal expectations that task the oppressed with 'saving' or educating oppressors. Not only is this burdensome, but it may even be false that victims need to be 'humanised' to haters. Perhaps rehabilitation of formers needs to involve meeting with people they harmed and listening to the impact their actions have had. But that does not mean that formers did not know all along that they were harming human beings. In fact, many philosophers, psychologists, and others believe that this is not how we learn that the other is human. For example, in his study of American slavery, Frederick Douglass clearly articulated the ways in which the dehumanisation of enslaved Black Americans could only have been possible through a prior knowledge of the humanity of the enslaved, leading to the slaveholders' attempts at every turn to stifle the yearning for freedom, such as by preventing and punishing literacy (Douglass 1995, 2003). More recently, in her study of misogyny in *Down Girl*, Kate Manne argues that 'humanising' women will not help stop violence against them and that perpetrators of violence against women are already aware of the humanity of their victims (Manne 2019). In short, compassion narratives continue to recapitulate the likely inaccurate assumption that a central task of social change work is 'humanising' the oppressed to their oppressors. That assumption leads to victim-blaming and also misunderstands how oppressive violence operates.

Ethical recommendations

Although new issues will likely emerge as more research is done, the following are some provisional recommendations for researchers seeking to engage the topic of compassion narratives in an ethical manner.

To engage current research ethically, researchers should:

- Fact-check formers' stories rather than assume accuracy (even when formers are affiliated with 'anti-hate' organisations or think tanks).
- Avoid amplifying and popularising compassion narratives through research.
- Learn from the work of critics of CVE and 'deradicalization', especially Muslim civil rights advocates and other critics of colour (Nguyen 2019; Kundnani and Hayes 2018; Manzoor-Kahn 2022; Younis 2019; Gowrinathan 2021; 2022).
- Challenge the widespread misconception that fixing CVE is only a matter of distinguishing sincere from insincere actors. While it is important to expose 'fake formers' who are lying for personal gain, researchers should avoid false dichotomies, and they should challenge the view that CVE can be reformed by weeding out a 'few bad apples'.
- Reject victim-blaming by affirming the right of communities to set boundaries and defend themselves. This includes challenging facile comparisons of antifascists with fascists and rejecting descriptions of fascists and antifascists as locked in cycles of 'reciprocal radicalisation' or as contributing to a new threat in the form of a soupy extremism conglomeration of right and left (e.g., "coalitional accelerationism" (Parker 2020), "salad bar extremism" (Tiflati 2022)).

To engage ethically with organisations and communities with regard to compassion narratives, researchers should:

- Build solidarity with communities negatively impacted by CVE.
- Reconsider hosting formers as guest speakers. At the very least, before agreeing to host a former, engage in conversation with impacted communities at the grassroots (dialoguing, not simply pursuing organisational 'endorsements' as evidence of buy-in).
- Amplify the voices of those most impacted by hate. This includes changing the make-up of panels, boards, and think tanks, and sometimes not simply bringing new people 'into the room' but rather deconstructing and constructing 'new rooms' (Táíwò 2022). For example, some deradicalisation organisations are little more than "right-wing grant mills", as Christian Picciolini has critically pointed out (Picciolini 2022). Organisations should not simply be reformed through the addition of more 'diverse' members on boards, but the work of prevention and disengagement from hate should be reimagined in a direction that centres and empowers those most impacted.

To fix ethical harms, researchers should undertake new areas of study, including:

- How compassion narratives are received by victims/survivors and impacted communities.
- Under-emphasised factors in hate group disengagement besides compassionate encounters, such as: doxxing; ostracism; job loss; incarceration or legal trouble; in-group or inter-group conflict; experiencing physical and/or sexual abuse in the movement; wanting to raise a family in safer circumstances; and emotional and physical exhaustion from a life lived on the edge.
- The role of whiteness in which stories are classified as 'heart-warming' and in how 'forgiveness' is popularly conceived.
- And, long-term and perhaps especially, *amends-making and abolitionist responses to hate*. Abolitionist work is emerging especially from disabled, queer and communities of colour (Dixon and Piepzna-Samarasinha 2020). 'Deradicalization' projects, such as those founded on the European 'Exit' model, are offender-centred as opposed to victim-centred models. They focus on the rehabilitation of perpetrators. While a victim-centred model could certainly acknowledge that not everyone who has left a hate group is ready to make reparations in a way that will not do further harm, the goal would be working towards repair of harm, on the terms of those harmed. This could include thinking about going beyond mere restorative justice to transformative justice

(Kaba and Hassan 2019). The transformative justice movement, led primarily by women of colour, often queer and/or disabled women of colour, has challenged society to rethink repairing harm and holding space for accountability without relying on policing and prisons. There does not seem to be any serious engagement in the 'deradicalisation' field with the work of such scholars of transformative justice and abolition. (I have encountered critics of the deradicalisation field who are influenced by abolitionist thinkers, however, and would like to assist in disengaging people from hate groups from a standpoint of greater solidarity with impacted communities.) Researchers could begin the radical work of rethinking what it would mean to give formers a path towards amends-making that shifts the balance of power, restoring power to those harmed. This would also include a need for researchers to ask victims/survivors of hate attacks what they want from formers and what they would consider to be amends-making or accountability.

These suggestions are intended to be provisional and a creative starting point for those seeking to explore the potential harm of compassion narratives and forge new, more solidaristic, antiracist, and emancipatory directions in work against hate. Those who have left hate groups and seek to do their part in undoing and reducing harm where possible may in the end benefit from and appreciate the changes that can be made in how these stories are encountered and disseminated. However, my primary purpose here is to raise the question of these stories' wider impacts, especially on those most impacted by hate. It is hoped that the questions and concerns raised here will spark further exploration and ethical research and practice.

References

Austen, I. 2021. 'Canadian Admits Fabricating Terrorism Tale in Detailed *New York Times* Podcast', *The New York Times*. https://www.nytimes.com/2021/10/09/world/middleeast/shehroze-chaudhry-caliphate.html (accessed 5 November 2022).

Bates, C. 2017. 'I Was a Neo-Nazi: Then I Fell in Love with a Black Woman', BBC, 29 August 2017. https://www.bbc.com/news/magazine-40779377 (accessed 20 August 2019).

Braddock, K. 2020. *Weaponized Words: The Strategic Role of Persuasion in Violent Radicalization and Counter-Radicalization*. Cambridge: Cambridge University Press.

Braune, J. 2021. 'Fascism and Eluded Truth', *Free Associations: Psychoanalysis and Culture, Media, Groups, Politics*, 84, December.

Buckby, J. 2020. *Monster of Their Own Making: How the Far Left, the Media, and Politicians Are Creating Far-Right Extremists*. New York: Bombardier Books.

Burley, S. 2022. 'Can You Ever Trust a Former White Nationalist?', Political Research Associates. https://politicalresearch.org/2022/05/11/can-you-ever-trust -former-white-nationalist (accessed 1 May 2023).

Delgado, R. and Stefancic, J. 2017. *Critical Race Theory: An Introduction.* New York: New York University Press.

Dixon, E. and Piepzna-Samarasinha, L. L. 2020. *Beyond Survival: Strategies and Stories from the Transformative Justice Movement.* Chico, CA: AK Press.

Douglass, F. 2003. 'Is the Slave a Man?' In: *On Slavery and the Civil War: Selections from His Writings.* Mineola, TX: Dover Thrift Editions.

Douglass, F. 1995. *Narrative of the Life of Frederick Douglass: An American Slave.* Mineola, TX: Dover Thrift Editions.

Fekete, L. 2014. 'Exit from White Supremacism: The Accountability Gap within Europe's Deradicalisation Programmes', *Institute of Race Relations European Research Programme: Briefing Number 8.*

Finchelstein, F. 2020. *A Brief History of Fascist Lies.* Oakland, CA: University of California Press.

Gansewig, A. and Walsh, W. 2021/2 Winter. 'Broadcast Your Past: Analysis of a German Former Extremist's YouTube Channel for Preventing and Countering Violent Extremism and Crime', *Journal for Deradicalization*, 2(29), 129–176.

Gowrinathan, N. 2021. 'Evident Truths: American Women at War', *Los Angeles Review of Books.* https://lareviewofbooks.org/article/evident-truths-american -women-at-war/ (accessed 1 November 2022).

Gowrinathan, N. 2022. *Radicalizing Her: Why Women Choose Violence.* Boston, MA: Beacon Press.

Griffin, D. and Johnston, K. 2011. '"Ex-Terrorist" Rakes in Homeland Security Bucks', CNN. http://www.cnn.com/2011/US/07/11/terrorism.expert/index.html (accessed 1 November 2022).

Hategan, E. 2014. *Race Traitor: The True Story of Canadian Intelligence's Greatest Cover-Up.* CreateSpace.

Hategan, E. 2019. 'Profiting from Hate: "Motivational Speakers" Compete over Who Has the Best Sob Story', *Now Toronto*, 12 December 2019. https:// nowtoronto.com/news/hate-neo-nazi-racism-profiteers (accessed 1 April 2021).

Husain, A. 2021. 'Deracialization, Dissent, and Terrorism in the FBI's Most Wanted Program', *Sociology of Race and Ethnicity*, 7(2), 208–225.

Kaba, M. and Hassan, S. 2019. *Fumbling Towards Repair: A Workbook for Community Accountability Facilitators.* Canada: Project NIA and Just Practice.

Kahn-Harris, K. 2018. *Denial: The Unspeakable Truth.* Mirefoot: Notting Hill Editions.

Kahn, D. (dir.) 2017. *White Right: Meeting the Enemy.* Fuuse.

Kelly, M. and DeCook, J. 2022. 'Not So Reformed? How Countering Violent Extremism Groups Elevate "Former" White Nationalists', Political Research Associates. https://politicalresearch.org/2022/04/01/not-so-reformed (accessed 5 September 2022).

Kimmel, M. 2018. *Healing from Hate: How Young Men Get Into and Out of Violent Extremism.* Oakland, CA: University of California Press.

Koehler, D. 2017. *Understanding Deradicalization: Methods, Tools, and Programs for Countering Violent Extremism.* London: Routledge.

Kundnani, A. and Hayes, B. 2018. 'The Globalisation of Countering Violent Extremism Policies: Undermining Human Rights, Instrumentalising Civil Society', *Transnational Institute.*

Leeb, C. 2019. *The Politics of Repressed Guilt: The Tragedy of Austrian Silence.* Edinburgh: Edinburgh University Press.

Leyden, T. J. and Cook, M. B. 2008. *Skinhead Confessions: From Hate to Hope.* Springville, UT: Sweetwater Books.

Manne, K. 2019. *Down Girl: The Logic of Misogyny.* New York: Oxford University Press.

Manzoor-Kahn, S. 2022. *Tangled in Terror: Uprooting Islamophobia.* London: Pluto Press.

McAleer, T. 2019. *The Cure for Hate: A Former White Supremacist's Journey from Violent Extremism to Radical Compassion.* Vancouver, BC: Arsenal Pulp Press.

Meeink, F. and Roy, J. 2017. *Autobiography of a Recovering Skinhead: The Frank Meeink Story as Told to Jody M. Roy, et al.* Portland, OR: Hawthorne Books.

Meier, A. A. 2022. 'Terror as Justice, Justice as Terror: Counterterrorism and Anti-Black Racism in the United States', *Critical Studies on Terrorism*, 15(1), 83–101.

Michaelis, A. 2012. *My Life After Hate.* Milwaukee, WI: Authentic Presence.

Michaelis, A. 2019. 'Essay: Dear Nice Old Black Lady at the McDonald's', *WUWM*, 3 January 2018. https://www.wuwm.com/post/essay-dear-nice-old-black-lady -mcdonalds#stream/0 (accessed 19 August 2019).

Nguyen, N. 2019. *Suspect Communities: Anti-Muslim Racism and the Domestic War on Terror.* Minneapolis, MN: University of Minnesota Press.

Nguyen, N. and Zahzah, Y. *Why Treating White Supremacy as Domestic Terrorism Won't Work and How Not to Fall for It: A Toolkit for Social Justice Advocates.* Stop CVE. http://www.stopcve.com/uploads/1/1/2/4/112447985/white_suprema cy_toolkit.pdf (accessed 1 November 2022).

Noble, K. 2010. *Tabernacle of Hate: Seduction into Right-Wing Extremism.* Syracuse, NY: Syracuse University Press.

Ornstein, M. (dir.) 2016. *Accidental Courtesy: Daryl Davis, Race & America.*

Parker, J. 2020. 'Acceleration in America: Threat Perceptions', *GNET*, 4 February 2020. https://gnet-research.org/2020/02/04/accelerationism-in-america-threat-per ceptions/ (accessed 1 November 2022).

Patel, F. 2021. 'Ending the National Security Excuse for Racial and Religious Profiling', Brennan Center for Justice.

Picciolini, C. 2017. *White American Youth: My Descent into America's Most Violent Hate Movement – And How I Got Out.* New York: Hachette Books.

Picciolini, C. [@cpicciolini]. 2022. 'I Have Found That Most "Deradicalization" Orgs Are Simply Right-Wing Grant Mills. I Trust None of Them', Twitter, 17 May. https://twitter.com/cpicciolini/status/1526596787754176514 (accessed 17 May 2022).

Sartre, J.-P. 1976. *Anti-Semite and Jew: An Exploration of the Etiology of Hate.* Trans. George J. Becker. New York: Schocken Books.

Saslow, E. 2018. *Rising Out of Hatred: The Awakening of a Former White Nationalist*. New York: Doubleday.

Silverman, T., Stewart, C. J. et al. 2016. 'The Impact of Counter-Narratives: Insights from a Year-Long Cross-Platform Pilot Study of Counter-Narrative Curation, Targeting, Evaluation and Impact', Institute for Strategic Dialogue.

Strauss, E. (dir.) 2018. *Breaking Hate*. MSNBC.

Sykes, G. M. and Matza, D. 1957. 'Techniques of Neutralization: A Theory of Delinquency', *American Sociological Review*, 22(6), 664–670.

Táíwò, O. O. 2022. *Elite Capture: How the Powerful Took Over Identity Politics (and Everything Else)*. Boston, MA: Haymarket Books.

Tiflati, H. 2022. 'The Extremism Market and Salad Bar Ideology', *European Eye on Radicalization*. https://eeradicalization.com/the-extremism-market-and-salad-bar-ideology/ (accessed 1 November 2022).

Younis, T. 2019. 'Counter-Radicalization: A Critical Look into a Racist New Industry', *Yaqeen Institute*. https://yaqeeninstitute.org/read/paper/counter-radicalization-a-critical-look-into-a-racist-new-industry (accessed 1 November 2022).

24

Voices from the past: a psychosocial reflection on interacting with a far-right activist

Yutaka Yoshida

How to build a rapport with far-right subjects has been a troublesome issue for researchers. According to some researchers' experiences, one of the key factors that can provide common ground despite political differences is when the parties share some experiences. Examples include being arrested together during fieldwork (Pilkington 2016); experiences based on gender (Suzuki 2019); and shared memories of youth (Ramalingam 2021). While I strongly agree that it is useful for researchers to have some experiences in common with research participants, I also note that it is necessary to delve into the tempting expectation that having experiences in common will produce quasi-friendship, which in turn will produce disclosure of important pieces of information. As Smyth and Mitchell's (2008) reflection on their research on abolitionists shows, while some subjects try to fill in the distance between themselves and the researcher by providing more information about their views, others refrain from giving detailed accounts precisely because of the commonality between the two parties, thinking: 'You know what I mean'. These reflections warn us that commonality might sometimes make it difficult to hear the voices of the subjects.

In reflecting on my interviews with a far-right activist, to whom I gave the pseudonym of Sato, I will demonstrate how shared experiences between us caused tension, which still resulted in producing rich data. I will apply two key notions: that of researchers and interviewees as defended subjects (Gadd 2004; Hollway and Jefferson 2000), and that of the receptive unconscious (Bondi 2014). This chapter will add to discussions about the need to humanise far-right activists (Busher 2021; Dobratz and Waldner 2021) by showing the usefulness of accepting and reflecting on the conflicts and tension between far-right activists and researchers.

Interviews as a place where two defended subjects meet

Psychoanalysis has played a pivotal role in understanding far-right subjects. Theodor Adorno and his colleagues (1950/1969) used repression and a defence mechanism against it as disposing factors for antisemitic attitudes in *The Authoritarian Personality*. Erich Fromm's (1942/2001) *The Escape from Freedom* (also known as *The Fear of Freedom*) draws key ideas from Freud's discussions in its explanation of human reactions to freedom, which gave rise to fascism in the first half of the twentieth century. Even today, psychoanalytic ideas are frequently used to explain politics of hate in many contexts, such as support for Trumpism (McAfee 2019); the cycle of mutual hate between Israel and Palestine and the possibility of the amendment of the relationship (Benjamin 2017); denialism regarding the atrocities of Austrian Nazis in the post-war era (Leeb 2018); and the emergence of hate movements against Korean minorities in Japan (Kawamura and Iwabuchi 2022).

In recent years, criminologists have used psychoanalytic ideas to understand the relationship between the perpetration of hate crime and/or participation in far-right movements and their experiences of life events (Gadd and Dixon 2011; Treadwell and Garland 2011; Yoshida 2020). Psychosocial criminologists assume that defence mechanisms play a significant role in people's investment in discourses and that this often expresses itself in their behaviours (Hollway and Jefferson 2000). They have also considered how defence mechanisms affect the production of data. As such, the Free Association Narrative Interview Method was coined to circumvent interviewees' unconscious avoidance of talking about certain topics (Hollway and Jefferson 2000). Emotional reactions and narrative inconsistencies during interviews are regarded as important sources of information to detect subjects' sources of anxiety, which might provide some pointers for how to explore the narratives that they unconsciously embrace (Gadd 2012).

Psychosocial researchers also pay attention to their own defence mechanisms. Reflecting on their interaction with the research subjects, they note how their negative feelings affect their behaviours. These feelings may include the fear that the researcher is inexperienced (Gadd 2004); the research subject's apparent reluctance to participate in the interview as it seems worthless (Gammon 2021); a sense of guilt about their laziness during fieldwork (Proudfoot 2015); and concerns about the precariousness of their academic position (Todd 2021). Some examples of behaviours and emotional reactions resulting from these feelings are attempts to present the self as an intellectual authority (Gadd 2004); identification with the research subject (Proudfoot 2015); and anger and irritation with the subject (Gadd 2004; Proudfoot 2015; Gammon 2021).

Psychosocial analysts' mode of inquiry is not limited to what happens in the minds of the interviewee and the interviewer. They also explore the intersubjective dynamics between them. Relevant to this study is the psychoanalytic idea of transference and countertransference. Transferences are "new additions or facsimiles of the impulses and fantasies [which] replace some earlier person by the person of the physician" (Freud 1905/1953: 116). Countertransference is the response of the analyst that results from receiving the patient's transference, and psychoanalysts have come to see it as a tool to inquire into the minds of patients (Akhtar 2009). Bondi (2014) coined the term 'receptive unconscious' to explain her experience of countertransference following an interview. After the interview, she found that she had a strange confusion: she remembered that there was a moment where she said words to encourage the interviewee to tell her life story from the beginning, but she could not find this in the part of the transcript where she thought it should have been. Later she discovered that there was only a long silence. (She found the remarks elsewhere in the script.) She interpreted this false memory as a product of her receptive unconscious, reflecting her interviewee's anxiety about talking about her life and the fear of being hurt in the interview. As Bondi admits, it is impossible for researchers to fully know their unconscious reactions. Nevertheless, psychosocial perspectives provide useful tools for looking back at interactions with research subjects.

Background to the case study: far-right movements in Japan

Far-right groups which are characterised by street rallies rose to prominence in Japan in the mid-2000s (Yamaguchi 2013). The movements' representative group, Zaitoku-kai (Zanichi Tokken o Yurusanai Shimin no Kai – The League of Citizens Intolerant of Zainichi's Privileges), led by Sakurai Makoto, was formed at the end of 2006. The movements became notorious after a series of harassments directed against what they regarded as their (and the Japanese people's) enemies, such as Korean schools or Korean towns. They encountered several setbacks, including the arrest of their members, compensations worth twelve million yen (approx. £73,000) paid to the Korean school targeted by the group, and the introduction of the Hate Speech Elimination Act in 2016. Sakurai and his followers started to invest more effort in sending their members to local assemblies and the national parliament. Their de facto successor, the Japan First Party (JFP) was formed in 2016 after the failed attempt of Sakurai to be elected as Tokyo Governor in the same year.

Sato (pseudonym) was one of the JFP members that I interviewed in fieldwork between 2018 and 2019. Sato's life story and my analysis were detailed elsewhere (Yoshida 2020), so I will reiterate them only to the extent that they are relevant to the discussion.

Sato's life

Sato was a sixty-one-year-old former white-collar worker in Japan. He joined the JFP in 2017 after working for a public sector organisation for more than thirty years. With his tie and a set of suits and a polite business manner, such as that of exchanging business cards, he struck me as a seasoned 'salaryman'. Indeed, 'salaryman masculinity' was the key to understanding his life. This is a type of masculinity that enjoyed hegemonic status (Connell 1995) in postwar Japan. A widely held image of the 'salaryman' is that he is heterosexual, is employed by a major company as a white-collar worker, is married to a housewife, and is the breadwinner for the household (Dasgupta 2013; Hidaka 2010).

Sato's life story revealed that he had ambivalent feelings toward masculinity. Describing his childhood self as 'timid', being bullied by girls and repressed by his authoritative father, he seemed to have developed contradictory desires to possess a masculine self and to deny the norms of masculinity. The conflict grew as he started working for the public sector organisation where he internalised salaryman masculinity. Although he was eventually promoted to the highest position that a third-class official could reach, he had always struggled when working in this environment. When he was a junior worker, he was treated like a 'slave' by arrogant bosses who would ask him to play *mahjong* (a board game) after work and make him work during the weekend. When he became a boss himself, he found himself lacking leadership qualities and was afraid of being seen as a useless boss by subordinates. Eventually, he started to abuse his wife and children and become addicted to gambling. "I was unable to say anything during my work ... looking back, such dissatisfaction surfaced [as his abusive attitude] toward family, maybe."

He rebuilt his life after quitting gambling and mended his relationship with the family. When he noticed that his children and other young people were living according to their own values, he became even more unsure about the salaryman way of life he had followed. It was around this time that he noticed Sakurai's activities. He was attracted to Sakurai's attitude, as he "persevered with his own agenda".

> I worked as a salaryman for 36 years. I could not say what I wanted to say. I shut up and obeyed [the bosses] and sometimes I projected my dissatisfaction onto my family. You know my personality; I have always listened [to what others say], putting a smile on my face. When I saw the actions of Mr. Sakurai, who will never compromise, I just envied him.

The final straw that pushed him to leave the organisation was his last boss's attitude. The boss, who was an engineer and a 'first-class' official, always described non-engineer officials like Sato as 'infesting' the engineers.

He said that every time, and I could not stand it. ... Yeah, I was very fed up, and I took a week off before retirement. ... [T]hey were surprised, saying "You are abandoning your duty!" but I just said "Let me do what I want after 34 years".

At the time of the interview, he looked satisfied with his life. After quitting the job, he joined the JFP immediately. He enjoyed recognition by other members. He was working as a part-time employee, inspecting electrical devices, and he enjoyed the 'feminine' culture of this company, where the majority of colleagues were women.

My story

Before analysing the interaction between Sato and myself, it will be necessary to introduce my side of the story. Before starting the PhD project, I worked for the National Police Agency (NPA). Although it is a police organisation, it is part of the central government, and its primary tasks are administrative, such as drafting legislation and negotiating with other Ministries. In this regard, it was more like a white-collar private company. Life-long employment was still the norm and the majority of workers were male, although the demography in terms of gender has gradually changed.

As in other governmental departments and public institutions, including Sato's, the employees at the Agency were classified into first (*isshu/'kyaria'*), second (*nishu*), and third (*sanshu*) classes, with different speeds of promotion.[1] Apart from them, there are many regular police officers who are seconded from prefectural police forces to the NPA. I was hired as a first-class official. Reflecting on my emotional reactions toward the experience of leaving the Agency, I realise that the 'class system' played an important role. The relationship between employees at such organisations is not as simple and plain as the classification suggests. It is often the case that those from the lower classes and the regular police officers have more experience in terms of both work and life in general and as such I asked for advice from them on many occasions. (Thus I remember that one of my first-class senior colleagues advised me to think of myself as a pop star, in that popularity was essential for survival.) Indeed many of them gave useful pieces of advice, from how to deal with tasks to how to maintain a good relationship with other colleagues. One of the most frequently expressed motivations behind such kindness was 'to make the force a better place', as the first-class officials were likely to be in a position to change the culture of the force in the future. Even though I do not regret the decision to leave the Agency, when I reflect on my previous career, the memories of such words and kindness leave me with a bitter-sweet taste.

Reflections on the interviews

At first, it seemed that the interview with Sato was going well. Partly due to the nature of salaryman manners, he seemed to be trying to create a friendly atmosphere between us, telling me how proud he was to be interviewed by a 'super elite' from Manchester. We had fun talking about our shared experience as former workers in the public sector, such as idly reading a small brochure which summarises the profiles of members of parliament. He repeatedly and overtly flattered me by saying that his final position was "not great at all, compared with being a first-class official at the NPA". He even said: "It is great, some first-class officials become general secretaries of the Ministries, they are the top, indeed, I heard that members of parliament are only dancing on the palms of first-class officials." Although I was relieved that he seemed to be willing to spend some time on the interview, I was also afraid that such flattering might indicate his intention to conduct the interview in a business-like manner, without showing private aspects of his life, especially controversial or shameful aspects which he would conceal in a business setting.

My fear as an interviewer was unnecessary. Sato talked about his life in detail, disclosing tough experiences. He repeatedly referred to himself as '*dame-ningen*' (a Japanese term that can be roughly translated as a loser, a waster, or a stupid person) and detailed why this was the case. He mentioned his recollection of his schooldays when he was too timid to ask: 'Sir, can I go to the washroom?', and wet his pants. His father, who was a university graduate, always scolded his mother, and the mother did not argue back because she believed she was at fault as she was stupider than the father. Despite his brilliant brother's financial support, Sato failed to gain admission to a university he wanted to attend. As explained above, he was abusive to his own wife and children just like his father was to him, ignoring their problems. He did not hesitate to share what he was like when he became addicted to *pachinko* (a type of slot machine common in Japan) and lost seven million yen (equivalent to £45,000) due to the stress at work. According to him, he stopped caring about his attire, wearing dress shoes with holes and keeping the same shirt for a few days.

After the first interview, I was generally happy that I had elicited a detailed account of the activist's life, including plentiful accounts of how he felt at each stage. At the same time, I had a strange feeling that 'I was used'. It was confusing because the interview went as I wanted and we seemed to have established a rapport, with Sato being friendly to me throughout the interview. (He even tweeted about the interview, saying it was a pleasant occasion.) First, I thought this might have been because Sato seemed to use the interview as a confession to a priest to work through his pains and his sense of guilt toward his family. However, I did not have the feeling that 'I was used' after interviews with other activists who told me about their problematic pasts.

The second interview took place after two weeks. Sato quickly switched back to the mode of reflecting on the past, filled with remorse toward his family. His flattering featured again, as he explained: "My speed of promotion was extremely slow compared with the first-class officials, but I was careful not to fall from the ladder." However, it was on this occasion that he mentioned his first-class boss. The second interview did not end on a friendly note like the first one, as I asked some follow-up questions such as: "Could you tell me when you have contacts with *zainichi* or foreigners?" "What did you mean by 'a quiet life' [the slogan on his webpage]?" Sato became gradually excited, if not angry, as he started to talk about his own political ideology. It felt as if the atmosphere of cooperation with each other, where Sato could engage with introspection, had faded.

Analysis

What was my feeling that 'I was used'? Why did the rapport with Sato change? And why did the second interview end like that?

Contradictions in the subject's narrative are the key to understanding their psyche (Gadd 2012). In Sato's case the contradiction was about the gap between his salaryman-like well-mannered attitude and his willingness to disclose his past, which he was deeply ashamed of. The key to explaining this contradiction was his desire, summarised in his words: "I could not say what I wanted to say ... When I saw the actions of Mr. Sakurai, who will never compromise, I just envied him." In order to understand his longing to share Sakurai's attitude, it is necessary to remember Sato's grudge against the norm of masculinity. While he complied with the norm and aspired to obtain a masculine self, he also hated those who symbolised it, whether it was his father or his bosses. His desire to be freed from it manifested itself in the way he quit the job, which bewildered his co-workers. Although he seemed to regard the interview as a meeting between two (former) salary-men, the way he contextualised his desire with reference to Sakurai clarified what it meant for him to talk about his shameful past. His desire to resist the salaryman norm and show his honest self might have been manifested in the way he became blunt about what his life was really like behind his successful salaryman façade.

What was my role for Sato? In retrospect, I noticed that although he was friendly to me, he always tried to position me as an 'elite' without exploring other possible topics, such as family, my life in Manchester, and so on. This was somewhat awkward considering that his adult life was a series of painful experiences resulting from the culture of salaryman masculinity which was produced and reproduced in the hierarchy with first-class officials at the top. The climax of this awkwardness was when he confessed (he added "to be honest" before he started the account) in the second interview that the immediate reason why he left the job was because of harassment by the first-class boss. It is noteworthy that just after this account he mentioned his tendency to oppress his family members and said: "I was unable to say anything during my work … looking back, such dissatisfaction surfaced [as his abusive attitude] toward family, maybe." It seemed as if he had wanted me, as someone representative of first-class officers, to acknowledge that the classification system they (and I) benefitted from had been responsible for undermining his life. If this interaction is understood from a psychoanalytic perspective, it could be said that his transference meant that he saw his former boss in me. Therefore, my feeling that 'I was used' was probably not merely my lack of appreciation of the interview. Rather it might have been the function of my 'receptive unconscious' (Bondi 2014) that reflected Sato's anger at being subordinated to the hierarchical system. This makes more sense of why the rapport deteriorated in the second interview, as I stopped being a listener and started to ask follow-up questions. In Sato's eyes, I might have looked more like an 'elite', like his father, who bullied him with his intellectual authority.

My own unconscious defensiveness might have been activated when I analysed the interview and wrote it up. The defensiveness stemmed from my experience of leaving the NPA. Sato might have appeared to me as similar to former colleagues who would confess to me how tired they were of their life at a police station, where they had to deal with moody bosses and rebellious subordinates, sacrifice their family lives to go for drinks with colleagues, and meet a strict quota every month. They often told me: "Change the force when you reach a high position." My acknowledgement of Sato's ambivalence toward salaryman masculinity was, in hindsight, a product of my own defensiveness towards the regret that I felt because now that I had quit the position, I could no longer seek to change the culture of the force.

Conclusion

The interaction between Sato and me illustrates the complex interplay between the unconscious of an interviewer and an interviewee. Although our shared experience at the public organisations provided us with some common ground, the different positions that he and I held in these organisations allowed his unconscious to imagine me to be like some characters from his previous life, namely his former bosses. And yet, that did not mean the interview did not go well. On the contrary, Sato (with his suppressed anger) might have given me the details of the difficulties he underwent precisely because he likened the interaction between us to that between him and his former bosses. He was trying to realise his desire to break the norm of the salaryman's manner, which could have dominated the interview. Further, it was possibly because I felt the interview was similar to meetings between myself and my former colleagues at a police station that I could be sensitive to Sato's suffering under the norm of salaryman masculinity.

The reflection on the interaction between Sato and myself warns against the simplification of far-right subjects, which might result in the dismissal of some essential parts of their subjectivities. Partly because of the huge differences in political values and norms, it is tempting to stress the commonality between the researchers and far-right activists outside the realm of politics. While this is a significant step away from their dehumanisation, it can also be harmful, making researchers capture only part of their lives. In fact, it would hinder our understanding of how their experiences play a significant role in their attraction to far-right movements, albeit appearing to be irrelevant to their political activities. The potential damage here is that researchers might lose sight of the problems with the social structure that have added to the activists' strains and caused the surge of offensive movements. In this regard, simplification comes close to dehumanisation.

My interaction with Sato illustrates that there can be differences and conflicts in the 'non-political' areas of our lives, as is the case with the daily interaction with others. The case study suggests that rather than adding to dehumanisation, acceptance of and reflection on such conflicts can provide us with some hints to grasp their meaning-making. The reflective process will even include recognition of researchers' negative feelings toward the research subject, which might provide a deep insight into the subject as well as the nature of the interaction. This recovery of the very 'human' – mixed with love and hate, friendliness and tension – nature of the interaction might help us provide a richer illustration of far-right subjects.

Note

1 The classification has changed since 2012.

References

Adorno, T. W., Frenkel-Brunswik, E., Levinson, D. J., and Sanford, R. N. 1969. *The Authoritarian Personality*. New York: The Norton Library (original work published 1950).

Akhtar, S. 2009. *Comprehensive Dictionary of Psychoanalysis*. London: Karnac.

Benjamin, J. 2017. *Beyond Doer and Done To: Recognition Theory, Intersubjectivity and the Third*. Abingdon: Routledge.

Bondi, L. 2014. 'Understanding Feelings: Engaging with Unconscious Communication and Embodied Knowledge', *Emotion, Space and Society*, 10(1), 44–54.

Busher, J. 2021. 'Negotiating Ethical Dilemmas during an Ethnographic Study of Anti-Minority Activism: A Personal Reflection on the Adoption of a "Non-Dehumanization" Principle'. In: Ashe, S. D., Busher, J., Macklin, G., and Winter, A. (eds). *Researching the Far Right: Theory, Method and Practice*. Abingdon: Routledge, 270–283.

Connell, R. 1995. *Masculinities*. Cambridge: Polity.

Dasgupta, R. 2013. *Re-Reading the Salaryman in Japan: Crafting Masculinity*. Abingdon: bookRoutledge.

Dobratz, B. A. and Waldner, L. A. 2021. 'Interviewing Members of the White Power Movement in the United States: Reflections on Research Strategies and Challenges of Right-Wing Extremists'. In: Ashe, S. D., Busher, J., Macklin, G., and Winter, A. (eds). *Researching the Far Right: Theory, Method and Practice*. Abingdon: Routledge, 212–224.

Freud, S. 1953. 'Fragment of an Analysis of a Case of Hysteria'. In: Strachey, J. (ed. and trans.). *The Standard Edition of the Complete Psychological Works of Sigmund Freud* (Vol. 7, 1–122). London: Hogarth Press (original work published 1905).

Fromm, E. 2001. *The Fear of Freedom*. London; New York: Routledge (original work published 1942).

Gadd, D. 2004. 'Making Sense of Interviewee-Interviewer Dynamics in Narratives about Violence in Intimate Relationships', *International Journal of Social Research Methodology: Theory and Practice*, 7(5), 383–401.

Gadd, D. 2012. 'In-Depth Interviewing and Psychosocial Case Study Analysis'. In: Gadd, D., Karstedt, S., and Massner, S. F. (eds) *The SAGE Handbook of Criminological Research Methods*. London: SAGE, 36–48.

Gadd, D. and Dixon, B. 2011. *Losing the Race: Thinking Psychosocially about Racially Motivated Crime*. London: Karnac Books.

Gammon, T. L. 2021. 'Making Sense of Discomfort: The Performance of Masculinity and (Counter-) Transference', *Journal of Psychosocial Studies*, 14(2), 89–103.

Hidaka, T. 2010. *Salaryman Masculinity: Continuity and Change in Hegemonic Masculinity in Japan*. Leiden: Extenza Turpin Distributer.

Hollway, W. and Jefferson, T. 2000. *Doing Qualitative Research Differently: A Psychosocial Approach*. London: SAGE.

Kawamura, S. and Iwabuchi, K. 2022. 'Making Neo-Nationalist Subject in Japan: The Intersection of Nationalism, Jingoism, and Populism in the Digital Age', *Communication and the Public*, 7(1), 15–26.

Leeb, C. 2018. *The Politics of Repressed Guilt: The Tragedy of Austrian Silence*. Edinburgh: Edinburgh University Press.

McAfee, N. 2019. *Fear of Breakdown: Politics and Psychoanalysis*. New York: Columbia University Press.

Pilkington, H. 2016. *Loud and Proud: Passion and Politics in the English Defence League*. Manchester: Manchester University Press.

Proudfoot, J. 2015. 'Anxiety and Phantasy in the Field: The Position of the Unconscious in Ethnographic Research', *Environment and Planning D: Society and Space*, 6, 1135–1152.

Ramalingam, V. 2021. 'Overcoming Racialisation in the Field: Practicing Ethnography on the Far Right as a Researcher of Colour'. In: Ashe, S. D., Busher, J., Macklin, G., and Winter, A. (eds). *Researching the Far Right: Theory, Method and Practice*. Abingdon: Routledge, 254–269.

Smyth, L. and Mitchell, C. 2008. 'Researching Conservative Groups: Rapport and Understanding across Moral and Political Boundaries', *International Journal of Social Research Methodology*, 11(5), 441–452.

Suzuki, A. 2019. 'Uncustomary Sisterhood: Feminist Research in Japanese Conservative Movements'. In: Toscano, E. (ed.). *Researching Far-Right Movements: Ethics, Methodologies, and Qualitative Inquiries*. Abingdon and New York: Routledge, 107–120.

Todd, J. D. 2021. 'Experiencing and Embodying Anxiety in Spaces of Academia and Social Research', *Gender, Place and Culture*, 28(4), 475–496.

Treadwell, J. and Garland, J. 2011. 'Masculinity, Marginalization and Violence: A Case Study of the English Defence League', *British Journal of Criminology*, 51(4), 621–634.

Yamaguchi, T. 2013. 'Xenophobia in Action: Ultranatinalism, Hate Speech, and the Internet in Japan', *Radical History Review*, 117, 98–118.

Yoshida, Y. 2020. 'Not Leather Boots But Dress Shoes: White-Collar Masculinity and the Far-Right Movement', *Journal of Contemporary Eastern Asia*, 19(2), 104–124.

25

Interviewing the 'unlovable': on the challenges of conducting feminist research on far-right women

Katherine Williams

In 2019, I undertook a period of overseas fieldwork to interview female members of the Alternative for Germany (AfD), the first far-right party to make significant electoral gains in the country since the Second World War. In taking a broadly feminist epistemological and methodological approach to my PhD research, I have encountered challenges which require extensive critical reflection. If, put simply, feminist research is attentive to power and its in/visibilities and the marginalisation of underrepresented groups, how can I reconcile its broadly emancipatory remit with potentially giving members of the far right a prominent platform? How can I challenge the dominant assumptions surrounding women's political engagement in this context without sounding as though I condone or support participants' anti-egalitarian views? In which ways can I report participants' responses without inadvertently normalising the hateful rhetoric of the far right? Here, I hope to offer insight into how I dealt with – and continue to deal with – these important questions in the critical interrogation of my research practices. I begin with a brief overview of my rationale for taking a feminist approach. I then touch upon some of the epistemological and methodological challenges I faced and how I attempted to negotiate them. These include participant selection, researcher privilege, and interacting with participants whose worldviews are antithetical to my own. I conclude by suggesting several practical strategies that may help researchers to better navigate this tricky epistemological terrain.

My approach, in a nutshell

Firstly, my approach centres women as research subjects in their own right in contrast to studies that have been dominated by the "salient" image of white working-class men (Bows 2018: 169). While there is a wealth of post-9/11 research which suggests that women's engagement with terrorism is more complex and certainly more politically or ideologically motivated than first imagined (see Alison 2009; Gowrinathan 2021; Hamilton 2007; Pearson et al. 2020), there is a relative paucity of qualitative empirical work relating to women's support of far-right, fascist, or extremist groups, parties, and movements.[1] Some studies suggest that women overwhelmingly *do not* support the far right electorally due to their alleged economic security (men being the so-called 'losers of modernisation') (Betz 1994); higher religiosity (Billiet 1995); acceptance of Western feminist norms and values (Inglehart and Norris 2003); and innate lack of interest in politics (Verba et al. 1997). Consequently, reappraising these assumptions regarding women's identification with the far right becomes a pressing task for researchers. Secondly, the concept of gender – "how women, men, and non-binary persons act according to feminine, masculine or fluid expectations of men and women" (Davey et al. 2019: 4) – is employed to unpack dominant discourses surrounding women's political agency and their often-contradictory engagement with far-right ideology, with gender understood here as a pervasive social construct that informs normative power relations (Butler 1999; Connell 1987; Harding 1991; Yuval-Davis 1997). On the ground, gender 'mattered' to participants to varying degrees; the women I interviewed in 2019 reported living their lives in markedly different ways from those that they advocate for other women – for example, encouraging others to have children while not wanting any themselves. Lastly, this approach consolidates the idea that women are important socio-political actors whose engagement with the social world has a "constitutive effect" (Locher and Prügl 2001: 116). Where do women position themselves in discourse? Which contextual factors underpin the development of women's political subjectivity?

While, as Tickner (2014) points out, there is no "unique" feminist method (94–95), feminist researchers often employ those most conducive to the documentation of participants' personal experiences. The majority of scholarly literature on electoral support for the far right, however, is quantitative. While this gives us a valuable insight into the macro-level issues that drive party engagement in this context (Damhuis and de Jonge 2022: 1), it does not give an insight into what Fielding (1981) terms the "perennial" issue of subject motivation (1). Resultantly, a renewed turn to the qualitative is necessary to glean a deeper view into the person behind the vote at the ballot box. Qualitative data – interviews, text, oral histories, field notes – thus comes to *constitute* knowledge, rather than just be a source of it (D'Costa 2006: 139). Using methods such as interviewing and documentary analysis, I feel better equipped to critically interrogate the relationship between discourse and what subjects think and feel, what they do, and the contextual factors that make this thinking and feeling possible. This provides a non-generalisable, but nonetheless valuable, insight into the development of women's political agency and their support for the AfD across time and space. However, it is not enough for feminist researchers like myself to simply 'accept' the agency of their participants; by unpacking the notion of choice, we can better recognise the complex interplay of politics and power through which the articulation of subjects' agency is made possible in the first place. How is knowledge produced? And by whom?

Challenging subjects

An important ethical question arises: does my research run the risk of privileging the 'voices' of the relatively powerful? As Ackerly (2009) points out, the identification and selection of participants is an act of "epistemological power" on the part of the researcher that can have a tangible impact on the wider project (34). In this regard, Blee (2018) suggests that researchers reflect on whether their research should even be conducted in the first place to avoid inflicting further harm (98). This involves examining what is "ethically permissible" and what is "ethically right"; this encourages researchers not just to act in accordance with what is expected of them by their institutions but to gain an insight into the possible impact of their research on participants, their personal and professional networks, and the groups targeted by the far right (Blee 2018). I attempted to mitigate this issue by focusing primarily on registered members of a legal political party, as, for the most part, they operate within the "confines" of the law (Klandersman and Mayer 2006: 52). In theory, this reduces the likelihood that participants will pose a 'risk' to others or disclose information relating to ongoing criminal investigations or terrorism. However, this is an uneasy compromise. As a result of its links to right-wing extremists, the AfD is now formally monitored by the Federal Office for the Protection of the Constitution (*Bundesamt für Verfassungsschutz,* BfV).[2] At the time of my fieldwork, however, the AfD was not subject to extended investigation by the BfV, although there were reports that the activities of its youth organisation were under close scrutiny. I tried to scope participants from reliable and credible sources, such as their official parliamentary profiles on the Bundestag (German federal parliament) and Landtag (German state parliament) webpages, and regional AfD branches. This left a paper trail and gave me some measure of accountability. Despite my best efforts, I had only managed to recruit one participant by the time I departed the UK; the rest responded to my interview call while I was in Germany.

While only contacting members of legal political parties strikes some balance between the responsible selection of participants and negotiating enduring issues surrounding risk and ethics, it is not a perfect solution. The relative successes of the far right at polling stations across Europe and the seemingly uncritical acceptance of their ideas in mainstream political discourse indicate that the far right is no longer relegated to the fringes of society; in my interactions with the AfD and its members, I might, however inadvertently, contribute to this mainstreaming of the far right. Furthermore, given the AfD's so-called "cumulative radicalisation" and their subsequent monitoring (Bochum 2020: 29), I have doubts as to whether a research project such as mine would be advisable today given what we now know about the AfD's links with right-wing extremists and what this 'cumulative radicalisation' means for the groups affected by far-right violence in Germany.

At this stage, I would be entirely remiss if I did not recognise my own privilege here as a white, cis-gendered person. This certainly helped me to recruit the participants I did manage to interview and facilitate rapport. If an interview did go well, I asked increasingly provocative or controversial questions without fear of repercussion; this included asking participants how they felt about being labelled *rechtspopulistisch* by political and media commentators. At no point during my overseas fieldwork did I feel unsafe or threatened; a researcher of colour or someone from a different background might have had a very different experience or been denied access altogether. Additionally, my reasonable command of German helped to reassure participants who did not feel confident speaking in English. Participants assumed that as a British person, I was unaware of contemporary German political debates and thus simplified their explanations, albeit with their own particular spin on a given issue. My presumed naïveté worked to my advantage; this made it possible for me to gain access to information that may otherwise have been unavailable, such as interviewees' own take on the contextual factors which led to their AfD engagement. However, such "pretence awareness" – what Glaser and Strauss (1967) describe as researchers conveying ignorance about what participants say while simultaneously promoting rapport – leads back to the question of how far participants can be said to give their informed consent (cited in Duncombe and Jessop 2014: 111). Given that all but one of my interviews was conducted in German, I felt some degree of logistical and epistemological flexibility was ultimately necessary to build rapport with participants and establish some measure of trust.

Writing about reflexivity and positionality is one thing, but in practice, this is often difficult, particularly when your participants express opinions that fundamentally challenge your own worldview. As Luff (1999) observes, "listening [and] nodding [...] to views that you strongly disagree with [...] may be true to a methodology that aims to listen seriously to the views and experiences of others, but can feel personally very difficult" (698). While I felt comfortable responding to participants' questions, like Tyagi (2017), I felt I needed to 'restrain' certain aspects of my own identity (330), namely, and somewhat paradoxically, my feminist outlook. Concordantly, one of the most challenging aspects of my exchanges with female AfD members was the lack of empathy some demonstrated towards other groups, namely, Syrian refugees and members of the LGBTQ+ community. I asked each participant if they believed that Germany had a humanitarian responsibility to help refugees; one participant simply replied "no". Additionally, it was difficult for me, the proud child of an LGBTQ+ parent, to listen to some participants outline their opposition to same-sex marriage; another participant casually described how the LGBTQ+ community is "tolerated" by the AfD but not necessarily "accepted". While some participants affirmed their support for the 'traditional' family by outlining their opposition to same-sex marriage, others did not toe the party line in this regard and expressed that they supported the right of LGBTQ+ people to get married. This is one of the most striking, and often confusing, aspects of participants' accounts: why do participants support the AfD when, in some cases, they appear to fundamentally disagree with cornerstone party issues? Consequently, it was hard to keep my silence in the face of this obvious contradiction that touched upon aspects of my own identity.

Navigating tricky terrain

My first suggestion is a relatively simple one: we, as researchers, have a responsibility to accurately report what our participants tell us. Throughout the course of my own PhD research, however, I have grappled with the tension that exists between the accurate reporting of participants' accounts and fact-checking their misrepresentation of government statistics and data to 'back up' their various claims. With regard to accurate reporting, for example, there is no reasonable way for researchers to find out whether a participant's retelling of a pivotal childhood experience is indeed 'true'. Some of my participants, for example, described how growing up in the former German Democratic Republic (GDR) left an indelible mark on their lives and has broadly influenced their political activism today. To this end, a feminist approach recognises that there is no singular 'truth' and that knowledge is historically contingent, with participants' accounts representing "active processes of reflection and construction" (Scott 1998: par. 7.1). However, the falsehoods "consciously deployed" by far-right political actors in an era of so-called post-truth politics exposes a "significant shift in a shared reality that we take for granted when engaging with politics" (Zerilli 2020: 7–8). In 'problematising' the issue of truth, researchers can make a critical distinction between fact-checking (i.e., investigating, for example, the empirical provenance of participants' statistical claims) and *who* is able to tell the 'truth'. Who gets to tell the 'truth'? To what end? Researchers should be prepared to let participants tell their own stories but these accounts are not immune from critical engagement or challenge. A pertinent example from my own research is the claims of some participants that they are good allies to LGBTQ+ people. Unpacking these claims, it soon became clear that while participants make token statements about LGBTQ+ people, they simultaneously attempt to deflect attention away from their own complicity in the AfD's maintenance and reproduction of an anti-LGBTQ+ discourse and do not challenge the blatant homophobia of their party peers, instead laughing off controversies as inconsequential faux pas. This dual positioning has enabled some of the women I interviewed to establish successful careers within the AfD at both federal and state levels. In my research, I unpack this discursive strategy and critically engage with the idea that subjects ultimately benefit from their strategic operationalisation of the AfD's heteronormative discourses as white, cis-gender women and their desire to further accumulate socio-political capital.

Secondly, I suggest that it is very important to reach out to others working on similar topics for support and advice. While in Germany, I touched base with PhD researchers as well as those working for prominent anti-racist organisations. It is important to note that some organisations working with vulnerable groups, for example, those attempting to leave extremist groups, do not work with researchers on an ad hoc basis. Some political foundations such as the Friedrich Ebert Stiftung and Amadeu Antonio Stiftung also make their research publications freely available online in both English and German. Additionally, if, as Mayer (2015) suggests, there is a degree of "moral reprobation" attached to support of the far right more generally (394–395), I posit here that the same can apply to scholarly research on the topic. It can be very difficult for researchers to 'manage' their positive identities due to the stigma attached to interacting with those who hold far-right or extremist views (Sanders McDonagh 2014: 242). This stigma relates both to the 'unlovability' of research subjects as well as whether researchers of the far right are themselves trustworthy. With regard to the latter, I vividly remember a fellow PhD candidate hesitating to sit next to me at a postgraduate training event after asking me about my research topic. The idea that peers and colleagues might think I support the far right because of my research topic is something that I have grappled with emotionally throughout my academic career to date. However, this assumption is not necessarily surprising or unreasonable given what we know about the far right and the real-world impact of their role in perpetuating political polarisation and attempts to undermine our democratic institutions. Being part of a broader research community helps to mitigate some of the impact our challenging research has on ourselves and others, particularly people of marginalised identities. I have also attempted to mitigate this assumption vis-à-vis my project through my critical engagement with the topic at hand and the materials which form the empirical evidence base of my project, as I have reflected on throughout this chapter. With all this in mind, I think that honesty is the best policy when it comes to addressing peoples' hesitancy or nervousness about researchers working on the far right. After chatting with this person for a while and explaining the remit of my project and my own motivations – a broad academic interest in the role of women in terrorism, political violence, and far-right parties and groups – their concerns appeared to be assuaged. Moving forward, I strive to openly engage with critical questions about my research and have made new friends and colleagues in the process.

Bearing in mind the emotional and physical rigours of overseas fieldwork and interacting with research participants with wildly different viewpoints than your own, my third suggestion is simply this: do not overwork and underplay. I, of course, did not take my own advice during my time in the field. I felt guilty when I was not working – so as to justify the expense and challenges of working away from my home and partner – and I frequently felt very anxious about my relative inexperience as an interviewer as well as securing the next interview. I am not suggesting that watching back-to-back episodes of *Criminal Minds* or atmospheric French crime dramas necessarily alleviates what Lee and Renzetti (1993) refer to as the "psychic costs" of interviewing "challenging" individuals and groups (4–5), but any port in a storm. On a more serious note, however, recognising the role of our own emotions throughout the research process is very important; as Tyagi (2017) points out, "feminist research has made a strong case for emotionality as a legitimate part of not only the research process but also, as a valid addition to the data gathered" (323). To this end, I kept a fieldwork diary to reflect on not only research matters but my own thoughts and state of mind at various stages of my trip. While my fieldwork was generally a success, my journal tells me that I often felt overwhelmed, lonely, and anxious despite having visited Germany many times, being able to speak German, and staying with a good friend for the duration of my trip. Consequently, it becomes incumbent on researchers to recognise and confront their emotions while in the field to gain further critical insight into their research settings as well as the people within them. Researchers bear unequal burdens (some of them face more danger due to their identities, for example) and more social support and collective processing of emotions for researchers may also be necessary.

Concluding thoughts

As Bows (2018) notes, it can be difficult for feminist researchers to reconcile feminism's core tenets of equality and diversity with women's engagement with the far right (181). However, it remains important to (re)examine how the far right attracts women and maintains their interest. This may involve actively engaging with women themselves, depending on the context of the research and the feasibility of the study itself. Feminist research confronts issues relating to power as well as the sometimes-contradictory intersections of gender, race, and class, and encourages researchers to engage in extensive critical reflection. To this end, qualitative research methods such as interviewing allow us to better scratch beneath the surface of dominant assumptions surrounding women's support for the far right and how they reconcile their own place in the world. Human behaviour and our understanding of it are constantly in flux; our research practices should ultimately reflect this.

Notes

1 There are, however, some notable exceptions. See, for example, Bacchetta and Power (2002), Blee (2001), Deckman (2016), and Gottlieb (2000).
2 In Germany, far-right parties or groups determined to be *verfassungsfeindlich* (hostile to the constitution) are closely observed by the German security domestic services and face being banned altogether.

References

Ackerly, B. 2009. 'Feminist Methodological Reflection'. In: Klotz, A. and Prakash, D. (eds). *Qualitative Methods in International Relations: A Pluralist Guide*. Basingstoke and New York: Palgrave Macmillan, 28–42.

Alison, M. 2009. *Women and Political Violence: Female Combatants in Ethno-National Conflict*. London and New York: Routledge.

Bacchetta, P. and Power, M. (eds). 2002. *Right-Wing Women: From Conservatives to Extremists around the World*. New York and London: Routledge, 1–19.

Betz, H. G. 1994. *Radical Right-Wing Populism in Western Europe*. New York: St. Martin's Press.

Billiet, J. 1995. 'Church Involvement, Ethnocentrism, and Voting for a Radical Right-Wing Party: Diverging Behavioural Outcomes of Equal Attitudinal Dispositions', *Sociology of Religion*, 56(3), 303–326.

Blee, K. 2001. *Inside Organised Racism: Women in the Hate Movement*. Berkeley and Los Angeles, CA: University of California Press.

Blee, K. M. 2018. *Understanding Racist Activism: Theory, Methods, and Research*. London and New York: Routledge.

Bochum, P. 2020. *We Are the People: The Rise of the AfD in Germany*. London: Haus Publishing.

Bows, H. 2018. 'Closing the Gender Gap: Women and the Far Right in Contemporary Britain'. In: Copsey, N. and Worley, M. (eds). *'Tomorrow Belongs to Us': The British Far Right since 1967*. Abingdon and New York: Routledge, 169–185.

Butler, J. 1999. *Gender Trouble: Feminism and the Subversion of Identity*. New York: Routledge.

Connell, R.W. 1987. *Gender and Power*. Cambridge: Polity.

D'Costa, B. 2006. 'Marginalised Identity: New Frontiers of Research for IR?' In: Ackerly, B. A., Stern, M., and True, J. (eds). *Feminist Methodologies for International Relations*. Cambridge: Cambridge University Press, 129–153.

Damhuis, K. and de Jonge, L. 2022. 'Going Nativist: How to Interview the Radical Right?', *International Journal of Qualitative Methods*, 21, 1–11.

Davey, J., Ebner, J., Kelmendi, V., Mahmood, S., and Margolin, D. 2019. *Perspectives on the Future of Women, Gender, and Violent Extremism*. https://www.google.com/url?sa=t&rct=j&q=&esrc=s&source=web&cd=16&ved=2ahUKEwivpI-MkqziAhUyThUIHYPiDqUQFjAPegQIBhAC&url=https%3A%2F%2Fextremism.gwu.edu%2Fsites%2Fg%2Ffiles%2Fzaxdzs2191%2Ff%2FPerspectives%2520on%2520the%2520Future%2520of%2520Women%252C%2520Gender%2520and%2520Violent%2520Extremism.pdf&usg=AOvVaw2kdpoUbf_dvyAOs5tG34ic (accessed 12 April 2022).

Deckman, M. 2016. *Tea Party Women: Mama Grizzlies, Grassroots Leaders, and the Changing Face of the American Right*. New York: New York University Press.

Duncombe, J. and Jessop, J. 2014. '"Doing Rapport" and the Ethics of "Faking Friendship"'. In: Miller, T., Birch, M., Mauthner, M., and Jessop, J. (eds). *Ethics in Qualitative Research*. London: SAGE Publications Ltd., 108–121.

Fielding, N. 1981. *The National Front*. London: Routledge and Kegan Paul.

Glaser, B. G., and Strauss, A. 1967. *The Discovery of Grounded Theory*. Chicago, IL: Aldine.

Gottlieb, J. 2000. *Feminine Fascism: Women in Britain's Fascist Movement, 1923–1945*. London: IB Tauris.

Gowrinathan, N. 2021. *Radicalizing Her: Why Women Choose Violence*. Boston, MA: Beacon Press.

Hamilton, C. 2007. *Women and ETA: The Gender Politics of Radical Basque Nationalism*. Manchester and New York: Manchester University Press.

Harding, S. 1991. *Whose Science? Whose Knowledge? Thinking from Women's Lives*. Milton Keynes: Open University Press.

Inglehart, R. and Norris, P. 2003. *Rising Tide: Gender Equality and Cultural Change Around the World*. New York: Cambridge University Press.

Klandersman, B. and Mayer, N. (eds). 2006. *Extreme Right Activists in Europe: Through the Magnifying Glass*. Abingdon: Routledge.

Locher, B. and Prügl, E. 2001. 'Feminism and Constructivism: Worlds Apart or Sharing the Middle Ground?', *International Studies Quarterly*, 45(1), 111–129.

Luff, D. 1999. 'Dialogue across the Divides: "Moments of Rapport" and Power in Feminist Research with Anti-Feminist Women', *Sociology*, 33(4), 687–703.

Mayer, N. 2015. 'The Closing of the Radical Right Gender Gap in France?', *French Politics*, 13(4), 391–414.

McDonagh, E. S. 2014. 'Conducting "Dirty Research" with Extreme Groups: Understanding Academia as a Dirty Work Site', *Qualitative Research in Organisations and Management: An International Journal*, 9(3), 241–253.

Pearson, E., Winterbotham, E., and Brown, K.E. 2020. *Countering Violent Extremism: Making Gender Matter*. Cham: Palgrave Macmillan.

Renzetti, C. M. and Lee, R. M. (eds). 1993. *Researching Sensitive Topics*. Newbury Park, London and New Delhi: SAGE Publications.

Scott, S. 1998. 'Here Be Dragons: Researching the Unbelievable, Hearing the Unthinkable. A Feminist Sociologist in Uncharted Territory', *Sociological Research Online*, 3(3), 98–109.

Tickner, J. 2014. *A Feminist Voyage through International Relations*. Oxford and New York: Oxford University Press.

Tyagi, A. 2017. 'Field, Ethics and Self: Negotiating Methodology in a Hindu Right-Wing Camp', *Contemporary Social Science*, 13(3–4), 323–336.

Verba, S., Burns, N., and Lehman Schlozman. 1997. 'Knowing and Caring about Politics: Gender and Political Engagement', *The Journal of Politics*, 59(4), 1051–1072.

Yuval-Davis, N. 1997. *Gender and Nation*. London, Thousand Oaks, CA, and New Delhi: SAGE Publications.

Zerilli, L. M. 2020. 'Fact-Checking and Truth-Telling in an Age of Alternative Facts', *Le foucauldien*, 6(1), 1–22.

26

Examining far-right empowerment experiences using YouTube and Parler data: managing researcher safety and ethical and methodological requirements

Carina Hoerst and John Drury

Early career researchers (ECRs) like myself[1] are establishing new ways of understanding the ethics of researching the far right. In this chapter, I will discuss how I – a UK-based PhD student in social psychology – consulted UK and European ethical and legal guidelines concerning best practices for investigating two major far-right rallies in the United States. The aim, thereby, was to investigate the occurrence of *collective psychological empowerment* as a key psychological underpinning of far-right mobilisation in the context of ingroup-relevant victories. By doing so, I will outline the difficulties of researching empowerment experiences among rally attendees whose identity is incompatible with that of the researcher and further discuss the challenges that ECRs can face when they study hateful content and pursue an academic career in this domain. Subsequently, I will discuss one way to establish credibility by reconciling methodological and ethical requirements.

Collective psychological empowerment as a (complementary) explanation for increased far-right mobilisation

With the onset of Donald Trump's campaign for the 2016 US presidential election, organised far-right street mobilisation found renewed traction (e.g., Beirich and Buchanan 2018). Scholars commonly explain collective action in terms of protestors' perceived ability to change their disadvantaged situation and their anger about this disadvantage (e.g., van Zomeren et al. 2008, 2012), and far-right mobilisation as based on – among others – grievances over a threatened status quo (e.g., Castelli Gattinara, Froio, and Pirrò 2021; see also Jetten 2019). However, since Trump's victory marked a success and reason for celebration among the far right, it may be difficult to explain increased mobilisation using these explanations alone. The social identity model of collective psychological empowerment (e.g., Drury and Reicher 2005, 2009) may account for this (victorious) context. It describes the subjective and positive experience of power transformation resulting from successful collective action over a previously dominant outgroup (commonly, police forces during ongoing crowd conflicts) which can motivate further action. Since the basis of empowerment is the perception of support for ingroup-normative action, I sought to examine whether empowerment can also derive from electoral events and thereby aid in explaining the notion that the far right was "emboldened" by Donald Trump's 2016 electoral campaign and victory (e.g., Potok 2017).

One rally infamously stood out in this context due to the unprecedented unification among hate groups it involved: the 2017 Charlottesville (VA) 'Unite the Right' rally. Given the rally context of affirmation of white nationalism and denigration of other identities, it provided promising ground to examine the occurrence of empowerment. However, it appeared useful to compare participants' experiences at a rally taking place in a context of success with one in the shadow of defeat (Hoerst and Drury 2023). For the latter, I chose the 2021 Washington, DC, Capitol insurrection. Overall, I found that in Charlottesville, attendees arrived already feeling empowered, and (initially) interpreted the rally as a success. By contrast, at the Capitol insurrection, empowerment may have rather been associated with attendees' perception of high numbers of fellow attendees joining the cause. In both cases, the fact that attendees could mobilise freely and (at least temporarily) occupy public spaces of relevance seemed to send an encouraging message to attendees and the wider social movement. This should put further emphasis on de-platforming and public disavowal of far-right agendas.

Researcher safety and research feasibility

Before conducting the above study, I faced several ethical and methodological challenges. Collective psychological empowerment has been studied predominantly through direct interaction with research subjects, i.e., ethnography at protests and conducting interviews (Drury and Reicher 1999, 2005; Drury et al. 2005). This was, among other reasons, possible because of the alignment between researchers' and protesters' identities and values, for example, regarding environmental and societal issues (Drury and Stott 2001). However, research on far-right movements, while trying to understand the underlying dynamics (and perhaps even its members), should also try to dismantle them. In my case, understanding what empowers far-right movements ought to help to *dis*empower them. Thus, far from siding with the movement, my position to counteract far-right movements, challenged me, as well as other researchers studying the far right, to gain access and accurate data (cf. Vestergren and Drury 2020). This is aggravated by the fact that we, as researchers, are not exempt from being targets of hate, while some are more vulnerable than others.

I do not intend to downplay the detrimental impact active interaction may have on male and/or established researchers based on being viewed as the outgroup, ranging from – at best – research subjects' refusal to cooperate with the "parasite" researcher (cf. Drury and Stott 2001: 62) to – at worst – physical harm or distress. Yet, with far-right scenes being dominated by white men, and far-right ideology being strongly intertwined with misogyny, they pose a particular risk to anyone and any researcher that is viewed as an outgroup based on presumed personal characteristics such as gender, religion, or ethnicity (Social Research Association 2001; Franzke et al. 2019). These researchers are, therefore, particularly vulnerable to suffering from abuse when aiming to engage with the far right directly. The vulnerability is exacerbated when the researchers are ECRs who are commonly disproportionately affected by precarity (cf. Conway 2021) and still need to establish themselves. If applying the best-suited methodology is not possible (as in my case), this may be disadvantageous for the researchers' credibility, but also for the research since it may be deprived of sufficient informative value. However, more than one method is commonly acceptable, and researchers may decide to make some compromises and use online surveys or online ethnography instead. In terms of safety though, this does not prevent them from facing hatred. The reasons for the latter are twofold: first, researchers' 'business cards' are their publications, which are often accompanied by an active off- and online promotion. However, public presence may attract attention from unwanted sources; research subjects may start threatening the researcher online, ranging from online harassment to doxing (Marwick, Blackwell, and Lo 2016; Conway 2021). Second, in the case of qualitative research, online material may worsen the impact on researchers' mental health due to exposure to sometimes uncontrollable content (Dickson-Swift et al. 2008).

Thus, the question is how ECRs can navigate these challenges while achieving credibility. As a (white) woman, the fact that I could be attacked based on my gender discouraged me from researching collective psychological empowerment among far-right movements in the way previous researchers have done with other movements. Instead, I decided to make the compromise and shifted online. And social media appeared to be a fruitful alternative for me.

The Capitol insurrection has been strongly associated with a right-wing 'Twitteresque' platform, called Parler (e.g., Munn 2021). Due to its lack of censoring, Parler was popular among several far-right groups (Aliapoulios et al. 2021; Munn 2021). The number of members grew strongly between October 2018 and December 2020, with a spike in activity beginning at the Capitol insurrection and hashtags like '#trump2020', '#stopthesteal', or '#electionfraud' were among the highest-rated twenty on Parler.

As Parler's provider Amazon Web Services (AWS) judged the degree to which users celebrated violence in the aftermath of the insurrection as incompatible with their Terms and Conditions (e.g., BBC News 2021), they decided to take the entire platform down. Because of Parler's alleged role in the event, though, it offered a unique source of data on how participants had organised it. As such, de-platforming risked losing this information. Before Parler was taken down, more than 56.7 terabytes of material from the platform were acquired which made up 99 per cent of the entire platform, including videos.[2] The data was subsequently made available for prosecution and research purposes (Nally 2021) and still serves US authorities in prosecuting attendees of the insurrection and many researchers in examining the event.

While researchers previously investigating empowerment in collective action engaged directly with their research subjects, I was inspired by the availability of video material on sites like ProPublica (an independent journalism platform which featured a video-based chronology based on the Parler data; Groeger et al. 2021), as well as on YouTube. I decided to undertake a qualitative examination of secondary data in the form of video material[3] featuring coverages that were 'interview-like'. For the Charlottesville rally case, I mostly used YouTube videos, and for the Capitol insurrection case, I used ProPublica's chronology alongside YouTube videos.

Gaining some access to data from the subject of investigation, I now found myself confronted with methodological requirements of qualitative research on the one hand and ethical ones on the other, whose clash posed some challenges to the scientific rigour of my study.

(Reconciling) methodological requirements and ethics principles for internet-mediated research

Qualitative researchers are required to equip their result sections with so-called data extracts – short unedited snippets of participants' statements – supposed to assess the accuracy of the data, support the findings, and provide transparency (Eldh, Årestedt, and Berterö 2020). The British Psychological Society (BPS 2021) states that respect for the autonomy, privacy, and dignity of individuals and communities are key considerations in psychological research. Although the publication of data extracts needs to be assessed in this light, commonly this requirement can be easily met by providing participants with all necessary information regarding the study and gaining their informed consent before they take part. Remote acquisition of research data (what the BPS coins 'internet-mediated research') is no exception. However, the BPS rightfully points out that sometimes participants may not be aware of being research subjects, such as (in my case) working with YouTube and Parler video material. This raised the question of how I could meet the ethical requirements of gaining informed consent from research subjects in a design that deliberately sought to avoid direct interaction with participants. Since the ethical concern here was with the protection of personal data – i.e., anything that could personally identify a participant, specifically, so-called 'special category personal data' which contains sensitive information such as identity or attitudes – this concerned the 'public vs. private' debate which mandates different treatment of data depending on whether it is classified as public or private (cf. Sugiura, Wiles, and Pope 2017). The BPS (2021) states that researchers may continue their observations without informed consent in spaces where the research subjects are likely to expect to be observed by strangers, which was certainly true for the two rallies since both took place in public. However, the fact that I had to rely on secondary data put me in an ethical grey area.

In the next subsections, I, therefore, discuss contemporary guidance on this matter, why it was insufficient in my case of studying empowerment among far-right rally attendees, and how I reconciled ethical and methodological issues to the best of my capabilities. I divide this discussion into 'how to collect data' and 'how to present data'.

How to collect data

Even though 99 per cent of the data from Parler is now available to the public, ethically speaking not everything that is in (or has made it into) the public domain can automatically be used for research without obtaining informed consent from the research subjects in the UK (Information Commissioner's Office (ICO) 2021; The University of Sheffield n.d.). Townsend and Wallace (2016) argue that the starting point for this debate thereby lies in users' engagement with and understanding of the Terms of Services/Terms of Conditions of the platforms they are using – or rather the lack thereof (Williams, Burnap, and Sloan 2017).

In my case, it was neither preferred to obtain informed consent from far-right rally attendees, since I would make myself visible to them (cf. Fuchs, 2018), nor was it feasible to reach out to a 'forum moderator'[4] as suggested by the BPS (2021) and the University of Sheffield (n.d.). And this became even more challenging in the case of YouTube data where recordings may appear online without the person featured in the video even owning an account.

The UK Concordat to Support Research Integrity (Universities UK 2019) provides national guidance on good research practices and how to control these. It advocates for the highest standards of rigour and integrity in all aspects of research at UK universities. Among others, this is sought to be achieved through promoting appropriate up-to-date ethical frameworks (commitment 2). I suggest that a recent call for ethics committees to provide the necessary expertise when dealing with ethical approval applications for research on terrorism (Morrison, Silke, and Bont 2021) could be seen as one measure to meet this commitment. Sufficient expertise among the ethics boards, Morrison et al. (2021) suggest, can thereby be achieved by collaborating with the researcher(s). In fact, in collaboration with my university's ethics committee and legal counsel, I justified the choice of my methods on the grounds of researcher safety, as well as the necessity of undertaking the study in the first place on it being 'in the public interest' (cf. ICO 2021; National Committee for Research Ethics in the Social Sciences and the Humanities (NESH) 2019). The latter was explained by the insights the study could provide (i.e., what empowered rally attendees), and hence, what could be done to counteract far-right extremism as a major threat to democracy. Gaining ethical approval was successful even over and above potential copyright concerns stemming from using individuals' statements (BPS 2021).

How to present data

Having established my study on utilitarian grounds as serving the public interest allowed me to collect data without gaining informed consent from research subjects. However, this did not free me from the responsibility to respect their privacy and confidentiality when presenting my findings. The EU law on data protection and privacy, the General Data Protection Regulation (GDPR), views all de-identified data as no longer personal (Data Protection Act 2018, Part 6, 171 (2) (a)). Deriving from this, where it is not possible to obtain informed consent, quotes should be omitted or paraphrased (BPS 2021). Noteworthy, Townsend and Wallace (2016) suggest paraphrasing as a means to protect the researcher. However, they also acknowledge that it is not always helpful when working qualitatively. In line with that, I feared that a study based only on paraphrased statements would neither provide information about who said what, nor allow the readers to fully grasp the empowerment experience[5] among rally attendees, and, therefore, the impact the US elections had on them.

A solution came from my approach to collecting interview-like data, hence, I gathered videos mainly showing attendees being interviewed by on-site journalists or activists, particularly in the case of the Charlottesville rally due to the dominance of YouTube videos (and for the Capitol insurrection where data was collected from YouTube). The NESH (2019: 11) states that "persons who are interviewed and/or referred to in ['edited media'], must take into account that the published information might be used for research purposes". This led me to use the answer to the question of whether attendees were aware of being recorded at the time of the interview and/or could foresee that the interview would be made public, as a decision criterion to include or exclude direct quotes of interviewees. I thereby used the undisguised presence of cameras and/or interviewers using their microphones to interview attendees and/or introducing themselves as journalists as indicators of such awareness.

However, I found it important to emphasise and mention it when a statement was from a person of influence in the scene (i.e., a hate group leader, main organiser etc.) who intends to reach a wider audience (cf. Townsend and Wallace 2016). Thus, whenever the criterion of awareness was met, and/or the research subject was a 'public figure' (cf. University of Sheffield, n.d.), I decided that the data was eligible to be quoted directly. Where this was not the case (i.e., to a large extent with Parler video data), I refrained from doing so and paraphrased the data instead.

Conclusion

In this chapter, I introduced my work on researching the experience of psychological collective empowerment among far-right rally attendees. I discussed the difficulty of researching this phenomenon and asked the question of how ECRs can achieve credibility when the methodology of choice seems unfeasible, and public visibility could risk researcher safety. I have outlined that working with secondary data bypassed some of these issues but also how this caused new issues regarding tensions between methodological and ethical requirements. I hope to have shown one way how this can be reconciled and how a researcher working with far-right material can establish credibility while protecting their mental and physical health as best as possible.

Notes

1 The chapter is written from the perspective of the first author, who was also the first author of the study this chapter is based on. Since she conducted this study under the supervision of the second author, and because this chapter is going to contribute to her doctoral thesis, the second author is acknowledged here too.

2 I adopt Clary's (2021) and Munn's (2021) argument that the data acquisition was not done by 'hacking' but by a legal web scrape and in the public interest.

3 In the case of the Capitol Insurrection, I initially considered working with text material (Booeshaghi 2021). However, I decided against it due to a preliminary inspection of 5 per cent of the data finding that the data dominantly featured narratives of mobilisation rather than empowerment (cf. 'preparatory media'; Munn 2021, para 3).

4 There is no content moderation on Parler (Masnick 2020), nor are YouTube content moderators comparable to forum moderators who may constitute a gateway to a specific community.

5 This is not to be confused with giving research subjects 'a voice' as remarked by Kaufmann (2019), who noted that paraphrasing (through potential distortion of first accounts) may disempower a group that feels already left behind.

References

Aliapoulios, M. et al. 2021. 'An Early Look at the Parler Online Social Network', [Preprint]. http://arxiv.org/abs/2101.03820 (accessed 17 December 2021).

BBC News. 2021. 'Parler: Amazon to Remove Site from Web Hosting Service', *BBC News*. https://www.bbc.com/news/technology-55608081 (accessed 31 March 2022).

Beirich, H. and Buchanan, S. 2018. '2017: The Year in Hate and Extremism, Southern Poverty Law Center', Southern Poverty Law Center (SPLC). https://www.splcenter.org/fighting-hate/intelligence-report/2018/2017-year-hate-and-extremism (accessed 25 September 2021).

Booeshaghi, S. 2021. 'Parlertrick', *GitHub*. https://github.com/sbooeshaghi/parlertrick (accessed 3 March 2021).

BPS (British Psychological Society). 2021. 'Ethics Guidelines for Internet-Mediated Research', British Psychological Society. https://www.bps.org.uk/news-and-policy/ethics-guidelines-internet-mediated-research (accessed 21 December 2020).

Castelli Gattinara, P. C., Froio, C., and Pirrò, A. L. P. 2021. 'Far-Right Protest Mobilisation in Europe: Grievances, Opportunities and Resources', *European Journal of Political Research*. https://doi.org/10.1111/1475-6765.12484 (accessed 29 May 2022).

Clary, G. 2021. 'Parler Wasn't Hacked, and Scraping Is Not a Crime', *Lawfare*. https://www.lawfareblog.com/parler-wasnt-hacked-and-scraping-not-crime (accessed 30 July 2022).

Conway, M. 2021. 'Online Extremism and Terrorism Research Ethics: Researcher Safety, Informed Consent, and the Need for Tailored Guidelines', *Terrorism and Political Violence*, 33(2), 367–380. https://doi.org/10.1080/09546553.2021.1880235 (accessed 23 December 2021).

Data Protection Act 2018 (n.d.). 'Data Protection Act 2018', *Statute Law Database*. https://www.legislation.gov.uk/ukpga/2018/12/part/6 (accessed 17 December 2020).

Dickson-Swift, V. et al. 2008. 'Risk to Researchers in Qualitative Research on Sensitive Topics: Issues and Strategies', *Qualitative Health Research*, 18(1), 133–144. https://doi.org/10.1177/1049732307309007 (accessed 8 January 2022).

Drury, J. et al. 2005. 'The Phenomenology of Empowerment in Collective Action', *British Journal of Social Psychology*, 44(3), 309–328. https://doi.org/10.1348/014466604X18523 (accessed 11 October 2019).

Drury, J. and Reicher, S. 1999. 'The Intergroup Dynamics of Collective Empowerment: Substantiating the Social Identity Model of Crowd Behavior', *Group Processes & Intergroup Relations*, 2(4), 381–402. https://doi.org/10.1177/1368430299024005 (accessed 25 February 2020).

Drury, J. and Reicher, S. 2005. 'Explaining Enduring Empowerment: A Comparative Study of Collective Action and Psychological Outcomes', *European Journal of Social Psychology*, 35(1), 35–58. https://doi.org/10.1002/ejsp.231 (accessed 11 October 2019).

Drury, J. and Reicher, S. 2009. 'Collective Psychological Empowerment as a Model of Social Change: Researching Crowds and Power', *Journal of Social Issues*, 65(4), 707–725. https://doi.org/10.1111/j.1540-4560.2009.01622.x (accessed 3 April 2020).

Drury, J. and Stott, C. 2001. 'Bias as a Research Strategy in Participant Observation: The Case of Intergroup Conflict', *Field Methods*, 13(1), 47–67. https://doi.org/10.1177/1525822X0101300103 (accessed 31 March 2022).

Eldh, A.C., Årestedt, L., and Berterö, C. 2020. 'Quotations in Qualitative Studies: Reflections on Constituents, Custom, and Purpose', *International Journal of Qualitative Methods*, 19. https://doi.org/10.1177/1609406920969268 (accessed 29 January 2022).

Franzke, A. S. et al. 2019. 'Internet Research: Ethical Guidelines 3.0.', Association of Internet Researchers (AoIR). https://aoir.org/reports/ethics3.pdf (accessed 7 January 2022).

Fuchs, C. 2018. '"Dear Mr. Neo-Nazi, Can You Please Give Me Your Informed Consent So That I Can Quote Your Fascist Tweet?": Questions of Social Media Research Ethics in Online Ideology Critique'. In: Meikle, G. (ed.). *The Routledge Companion to Media and Activism*. Abingdon: Routledge, 385–394.

Groeger, L. V. et al. 2021. 'What Parler Saw during the Attack on the Capitol', *ProPublica*. https://projects.propublica.org/parler-capitol-videos/ (accessed 20 January 2021).

Hoerst, C. and Drury, J. 2023. 'The Role of Subjective Power Dynamics in Far-Right Collective Action: The "Unite the Right" Rally and the Capitol Insurrection', *Journal of Social and Political Psychology*, 11(1), 330–347. https://doi.org/10.5964/jspp.9951

Information Commissioner's Office (ICO). 2021. 'What Common Issues Might Come up in Practice?', *ICO*. https://ico.org.uk/for-organisations/guide-to-data-protection/ guide-to-the-general-data-protection-regulation-gdpr/the-right-to-be-informed/what-common-issues-might-come-up-in-practice/ (accessed 10 December 2021).

Jetten, J. 2019. 'The Wealth Paradox: Prosperity and Opposition to Immigration', *European Journal of Social Psychology*, 1097–1113. https://doi.org/10.1002/ejsp.2552 (accessed 3 April 2020).

Kaufmann, K. 2019. 'Mobile Methods: Doing Migration Research with the Help of Smartphones'. In: Smets, K. et al. (ed.). *The SAGE Handbook of Media and Migration*. London: SAGE.

Marwick, A. E., Blackwell, L., and Lo, K. 2016. 'Best Practices for Conducting Risky Research and Protecting Yourself from Online Harassment', *Data & Society*. https://datasociety.net/library/best-practices-for-conducting-risky-research/ (accessed 8 January 2022).

Masnick, M. 2020. 'Parler Speedruns the Content Moderation Learning Curve; Goes from "We Allow Everything" to "We're the Good Censors" in Days', *Techdirt*. https://www.techdirt.com/2020/07/01/parler-speedruns-content-moderation -learning-curve-goes-we-allow-everything-to-were-good-censors-days/ (accessed 26 February 2021).

Morrison, J., Silke, A. and Bont, E. 2021. 'The Development of the Framework for Research Ethics in Terrorism Studies (FRETS)', *Terrorism and Political Violence*, 33(2), 271–289. https://doi.org/10.1080/09546553.2021.1880196 (accessed 29 January 2022).

Munn, L. 2021. 'More Than a Mob: Parler as Preparatory Media for the U.S. Capitol Storming', *First Monday*. https://doi.org/10.5210/fm.v26i3.11574 (accessed 28 February 2021).

Nally, L. 2021. 'The Hacker Who Archived Parler Explains How She Did It (and What Comes Next)', *Vice*. https://www.vice.com/en/article/n7vqew/the-hacker -who-archived-parler-explains-how-she-did-it-and-what-comes-next (accessed 26 February 2021).

The National Committee for Research Ethics in the Social Sciences and the Humanities. 2019. 'A Guide to Internet Research Ethics', *NESH* https://www .forskningsetikk.no/globalassets/dokumenter/4-publikasjoner-som-pdf/a-guide -to-internet-research-ethics.pdf (accessed 8 January 2022).

Potok, M. 2017. 'The Trump Effect', Southern Poverty Law Center. https://www .splcenter.org/fighting-hate/intelligence-report/2017/trump effect (accessed 23 February 2019).

Social Research Association. 2001. 'A Code of Practice for the Safety of Social Researchers', SRA. https://the-sra.org.uk/common/Uploaded%20files/SRA-safety-code-of-practice.pdf (accessed 8 January 2022).

Sugiura, L., Wiles, R., and Pope, C. 2017. 'Ethical Challenges in Online Research: Public/Private Perceptions', *Research Ethics*, 13(3–4), 184–199. https://doi.org/ 10.1177/1747016116650720 (accessed 26 July 2022).

Townsend, L. and Wallace, C. 2016. 'Social Media Research: A Guide to Ethics', University of Aberdeen, 1, 16. https://www.gla.ac.uk/media/Media_487729_ smxx.pdf (accessed 30 November 2020).

Universities UK. 2019. *The Concordat to Support Research Integrity*. https://www. universitiesuk.ac.uk/sites/default/files/field/downloads/2021–08/Updated% 20FINAL-the-concordat-to-support-research-integrity.pdf (accessed 15 January 2022).

The University of Sheffield. n.d. 'Research Involving Social Media Data', *Research Ethics Policy Note no. 14*. https://www.sheffield.ac.uk/polopoly_fs/1.670954!/file /Research-Ethics-Policy-Note-14.pdf (accessed 30 November 2020).

Vestergren, S. and Drury, J. 2020. 'Taking Sides with Swedish Protesters: Gaining and Maintaining Trust in the Field'. In: Gülsüm Acar, Y., Moss, S. M., and Ulug, O. M. (eds). *Researching Peace and Conflict: Field Experiences and Methodological Reflections*. Cham: Springer, 149–171.

van Zomeren, M., Postmes, T., and Spears, R. 2008. 'Toward an Integrative Social Identity Model of Collective Action: A Quantitative Research Synthesis of Three Socio-Psychological Perspectives', *Psychological Bulletin*, 134(4), 504–535. https://doi.org/10.1037/0033-2909.134.4.504 (accessed 21 October 2020).

van Zomeren, M., Leach, C. W., and Spears, R. 2012. 'Protesters as "Passionate Economists": A Dynamic Dual Pathway Model of Approach Coping with Collective Disadvantage', *Personality and Social Psychology Review*, 16(2), 180–199. https://doi.org/10.1177/1088868311430835 (accessed 11 August 2021).

Williams, M. L., Burnap, P., and Sloan, L. 2017. 'Towards an Ethical Framework for Publishing Twitter Data in Social Research: Taking into Account Users' Views, Online Context and Algorithmic Estimation', *Sociology*, 51(6), 1149–1168. https://doi.org/10.1177/0038038517708140 (accessed 21 October 2020).

Part VI

Activism and dissemination

27

Critically examining the role of the scholar in policymaking on the far right

Richard McNeil-Willson, Michael Vaughan, and Michael Zeller

Recent incidents of far-right violence and terrorism have perhaps awakened some governmental institutions to the threats and dangers posed by the far right. Despite the tardiness of this attention by policymakers, many researchers studying the far right – not to mention those directly affected by far-right activity – have tentatively welcomed the sprouting of some political will to address these issues. Moreover, the readiness and even occasional alacrity of some governmental and intergovernmental institutions to seek input from select researchers may also be viewed as encouraging. But this presents a question: how should researchers studying the far right relate with policy and policymakers, and what does an ethical approach to this relationship look like? In this chapter, we reflect on this topic and several of its components, viewed through the lens of researchers encountering policymaking arenas,[1] to help researchers cogitate about their participation in policy processes.

With greater focus in recent years on the development of policy at national and European levels to counter the far right, researchers who are approached to engage in such processes must reconnoitre terrain strewn with hazards. What duty do researchers have to engage with policymakers in its construction? Does engagement – particularly on policymaking designed to defang the far right – undermine our prospects, ethical responsibilities, and practical means for engaging in other research on the far right? What are the ethical questions to consider when political considerations of stakeholders come into tension with academic standards for rigorous research? And how should researchers engage with states or actors that have been accused of openly encouraging far-right movements, ideologies, or policies, and may distort research for malign purposes? Drawing on experience in several collaborative research projects supported by governmental institutions as well as participation in intergovernmental consultative bodies for policymaking to address far-right mobilisation, we consider these questions and offer guidance to other researchers pressed by similar considerations.

The chapter will first explore the context fuelling increased concern over the far right and relatedly increasing state policy discussions and responses, often within the counterterrorism paradigm. This is followed by a discussion of the sensitive nature of working with states: whether and how scholarly engagement with the state may risk lending legitimacy to existing racialised policy approaches bound up within the liberal state's long 'War on Terror', to hard-right elements within national governments, and even to far-right movements. Finally, the chapter sets out general principles and questions by which researchers can critically examine their work to determine the honesty, risk, costs, and incentives involved in scholarly engagement with policymaking. This is designed to support the researcher as they navigate situations and power structures during engagement in policy responses to the far right.

Counterterrorism, policymaking, and the far right

Issues of whether and how researchers studying the far right should involve themselves in policy work around extremism are becoming more critical, especially given long-standing criticisms of counterterror policy as stoking Islamophobia and racism, and spurring the securitisation of minorities, borders, and human rights. Concern arises from the development of counterterrorism and counter-extremism practices which have typically focused on Muslim communities or, when attempting to address far-right violence, have drawn upon implicitly racialised practices native to the War on Terror. Ultimately, this risks acting to enable the very same processes involved in far-right mobilisation.

Far-right threats have often been underemphasised in counterterror contexts that have treated Islamically framed terrorism with disproportionate concern. Counterterror and deradicalisation legislation introduced in Europe since the start of the War on Terror has overwhelmingly focused on Muslim communities (Kundnani 2012). This has reinforced the problematisation and securitisation of Muslims throughout Europe (Pantazis and Pemberton 2009; O'Toole et al. 2016; Abbas 2019). Whilst there have been recent attempts to address far-right threats – for instance, in the proscription of European far-right groups (Zeller and Vaughan 2021), the construction of an EU-wide definition of Violent Right-Wing Extremism, and work with major online platforms to challenge violent far-right content (McNeil-Willson 2022) – current European policy still contains a heavy Islamist bias (Weilnböck and Kossack 2019), alongside a systematic underestimation of neo-Nazism, white supremacism, and similar far-right movements.

When policy has addressed the far right, it often relies on existing structures imported from the War on Terror. Current Prevention or Countering Violent Extremism (P/CVE) approaches, for instance, emphasise the role of individual and localised factors in drawing those deemed as 'vulnerable' towards terrorism – and are criticised for pathologising radicalisation and disregarding the wider political context of violence (Coppock and McGovern 2014; Younis and Jadhav 2020; Aked, Younis, and Heath-Kelly 2021). This is particularly problematic in the context of far-right violence as it delineates and disassociates violent right-wing extremism from key contextual factors, such as interaction with and co-optation of extreme nationalistic anti-minority or anti-migrant language by mainstream politicians, governmental actors, and national media (Winter and Mondon 2020). The expansion of the securitised lens to include the countering of extremism as a means of combating the far right also risks researchers actively participating in policing the borders of legitimate political activity. The conception of a political mainstream as separated from radical and extreme currents constructs at least notionally discrete channels from a spectrum of political views and actions (Brown, Mondon, and Winter 2021). The distinction between radicals – at least tolerably committed to liberal democratic principles – and extremists – representing a rejection of and (in some degree) a threat to those principles – is partially rooted in terminology adopted and propagated by German security agencies (Butterwegge and Meier 2002). Such a framework has effectively trivialised state acts of racism and violence, whilst also allowing for the amalgamation of wildly incongruous phenomena – such as the alluring but misleading parallelism between 'right-wing extremism' and 'left-wing extremism', or comparisons with Islamically justified violence that obfuscate processes of government legitimisation towards the far right.

Researchers inevitably engage in policymaking processes dominated by such conceptual frameworks. Their input is often sought as advisory towards policy processes: presenting relevant research, suggesting approaches and options, and providing alternative perspectives. Often attributed status as an 'expert', researchers are nevertheless constrained by conditions of the policymaking arena. They enter into an environment which almost universally stresses a 'security-first' paradigm that aligns the approach to the far right with politicised governmental interests. For instance, the label of what is and is not far right largely depends on the government, media, and other relevant national or international actors present at that moment, and the type of solution that can be put forward is similarly bound to these actors. In sum, researchers face a phalanx of actors that encourage the advancement of specific state or governmental interests, whilst being discouraged and disincentivised from more critical work (Breen Smyth 2009: 209).

There are also questions as to what extent research and findings conducted within an academic study should be repurposed for policy design. Studies into politically sensitive areas of politics inevitably involve the navigation of knotty questions of academic research ethics, with projects required to undergo ethical reviews at an early stage to ensure they are based upon the Participant Protection Model (PPM) – in which the safety and security of the research subject is held as sacrosanct. Such safeguards are designed to ensure that the scholar does not act to harm the safety or reputation of a participant through their research, as well as allowing for further research in the field. Navigating this process is particularly difficult when the research subject holds views that are directly in conflict or even abhorrent to the researcher – such as in the case of the far right. While scholars are developing guidelines for researcher physical and mental wellbeing (e.g. Conway 2021), these in no way absolve researchers of responsibility towards their subject. Therefore, the scholar should examine their intentions, to consider whether the application of their research and research subject to advance policy and policy-based careers risks a disservice to academia and potentially hinders future research activity.

Researchers studying the far right, when asked to deploy their research within a policymaking setting, are thus faced with a problem. The requirement to engage with national policymakers and practitioners in the hope of tackling violent, virulent, or simply visible manifestations of the far right may potentially offer legitimacy to racialised governmental counterterror practices, lend credence to far-right actors purporting to moderation and tolerance, or may risk the safety of research subjects – a consideration no matter how unpleasant their views – and the degradation of academic ethics and research practice. Disengagement with policymakers, on the other hand, preserves academic purity but will likely limit the impact of academic research and leave policymakers reliant on less critical or scrupulous actors that operate in the field of security research. The decision to engage with policymakers is therefore a constant exercise in assessing to what extent engagement is possible, ethical, and impactful.

Working with sensitive states

To work with policymakers is to work with politicians and, inevitably, confront political considerations. This is the crux of the challenge confronting researchers involved in policymaking. Proffering recommendations or even submitting factual research may face resistance arising from actors' commitment to principles and programmes or to electorates. Without gainsaying political jockeying for electoral support – it is essentially democratic, even if we might wish politicians would be guided more by the better angels of their nature – it clearly deters actions that risk alienating constituents, whatever the merits of such actions. And a large and increasing number of policy arenas are occupied in part by far-right actors representing far-right constituents. The growth of political actors that claim to act as 'the voice of the people' against a constructed and contradictory imagining of 'the establishment' encompasses the adoption of aggressive political language as an election-winning strategy. As non-mainstream parties on the right have gained electoral success, and traditional parties have sought to outmanoeuvre this threat, parties in many countries have embraced key elements of far-right discourses, normalising and embedding them within government (Wodak 2019).

At both national and supranational levels, election to democratic office is cited as cause for withholding proscriptive and other punitive measures – and even stopping short of designating far-right actors as such. But this is disconsonant both with the lessons of historical experience and with the modern legal and juridical context of many states. Anti-system actors – that is, actors (of any ideological stripe) that wish to change fundamentally the political system in which they operate – widely enjoy a significant degree of popular support, which they have and continue to leverage into political representation. The fact that such actors gain representation through legitimate democratic means does not preclude the possibility that they are illegitimate actors insofar as they aim to subvert established liberal democratic systems of procedures and protections. Democratic legitimacy, merely winning electoral representation, should not be used as a fig leaf to conceal demonstrable facts about far-right actors nor prevent policy input from taking account of those facts.

Yet this is the situation researchers encounter in many policymaking contexts. There are policymaking institutions and processes partially compromised by the influence of far-right actors, but that does not mean there is no avenue therein for meaningful and beneficial research input. Evaluating the benefits of realistically possible policy outcomes against the risks of legitimising wilfully misleading policy processes and their outputs is a calculation that demands continuous attention from researchers. Though there is no definitive answer to this question – not least because of the varieties of policymaking contexts – we provide below guidance to thinking through it: when to engage, how to navigate and evaluate a policymaking context as a researcher of the far right, and when to leave. Through these considerations, though, we encourage researchers, empowered with the hard-won knowledge and critical insights of independent inquiry, to remain open to policymaking participation: not to sacrifice the good that may be won through policymaking on the altar of an ideal outcome.

Far-right political actors are empowered in many contexts, exercising influence on policy processes and in some cases dictating them. Across Europe and North America, radical right parties enjoy political representation, partially relying on extremist constituencies: from US Republicans to

Poland's Law and Justice party, Sweden Democrats, and Italy's Lega, Forza Italia, and Fratelli d'Italia. In a few cases, unabashedly extremist parties have won national political representation; this was the case with Golden Dawn in Greece until 2019 (and the subsequent court ruling that declared the party a 'criminal organisation'); it is the case with the Our Homeland party in Hungary and the People's Party Our Slovakia. The effects of such political realities confine the scope for research input to policymaking.

In national policymaking contexts where a far-right party has won representation, researchers broadly confront one of two situations. In one, a far-right party is in government. The opportunity for meaningful policymaking input is relatively closed. Even as progress may be possible in addressing violent right-wing extremism, work confronting less aggressive strains of the far right is probably limited by the commitments of governing far-right actors to constituents. Any policymaking engagement in such situations must seriously reckon with the risk of researcher participation conferring legitimacy on far-right actors. In the other, far-right parties are represented but not a part of the government. The opportunity for meaningful policymaking input is relatively open. Yet far-right actors may exercise influence or indeed vetoes in policy processes. Even without such encumbrances, the possible extent to address and mitigate the causes and consequences of the far right may stop at the point of legislatively represented actors. Nevertheless, when national governments are unoccupied by far-right actors, researchers may reasonably expect the greatest latitude for input to policymaking.

In supranational policymaking contexts, where consensual decision-making is more common (and the number of veto points much greater) researchers face a more complex quandary. Far-right influence from one national context may limit the form, extent, and full veridicality of research input relating to that national context. The variety of national approaches and conceptualisations of what is (and is not) 'far right' may hamper research input from different researchers or bodies and may require the adoption of differing standards to ensure transnational acceptance. In addition to attending to the quality of their input, researchers must continually assess the degree to which that input is subject to constraints imposed by far-right actors beyond their own context, to determine whether it will be acceptable.

Researchers engaged in policymaking processes confront at all times the choice identified by Albert Hirschman (1970): loyalty, voice, or exit. That is, researchers may find the process and its prospects satisfactory, may find it necessary to raise issues and problems in attempts to mitigate deficiencies and ameliorate conditions, or may withdraw from the process. Below we provide a guide to thinking through the considerations that underlie researchers' choices.

General principles and questions

How should researchers adjudicate the ethics of engaging with policymaking around the far right? Like other ethical questions, this is not a mechanical process and requires a high degree of contextual information and subjective judgement. With that caveat in mind, we offer four critical questions based on our experiences which can act to stimulate and structure the reflection of those working in the field.

Is my research honest?

A key concept in research ethics is *integrity* – meaning whether research is conducted honestly and according to recognised principles.[2] Scholars who are relatively comfortable applying these standards within a strictly academic context may nevertheless find unexpected challenges from working with policymakers. If researchers collaborate with government in producing some output, they may find that government actors have a role in research design, reviewing work in an ongoing way, or even approving final products. Does this influence significantly degrade the research input to the policy process?

As opposed to academic peer reviewers who should theoretically share the same priorities around research integrity, governmental actors operate according to a different logic. Some of the abiding tensions in far-right policymaking involve the definitions of extremism, the designation of particular actors as far right, or the efficacy of different policy solutions. In Denmark, for example – a country with a strong focus on the right of assembly – the bar for enacting proscription or similar legal sanctions against extremist groups is typically set high, limited to groups involved in demonstrably violent acts; those that only use hate speech and violent rhetoric, on the other hand, such as the *Stram Kurs* ('Hard Line') party or neo-Nazi organisations, generally do not face restrictions based on extremist views alone. Does the Danish government's stance significantly encumber useful policymaking? In policy aiming to track and counter far-right violence, perhaps not; in policy aiming to identify the causes of far-right violence, including macro-social factors like polarisation, probably yes (cf. McNeil-Willson et al. 2019). Researchers may find the possibilities for productive input more constrained in the latter case.

Government actors may also have a greater tendency towards lack of transparency, particularly concerning politically sensitive topics such as the far right, which conflicts with researchers' preferences for public accessibility and contribution to public knowledge. For example, the results of projects completed for the European Commission are typically owned by the EC itself. In projects that do not explicitly include a dissemination component, the EC may decide to withhold results from wider publication. Researchers do well to address this point early on: how will deliverables be handled and disseminated? Is it possible to publish, if not the direct outputs of a project, the data and to share other versions of analyses? Looking after the honesty and integrity of research input means exposing that research to review and criticism, so attending to dissemination among broader research communities and the general public is essential.

Who benefits and who bears risk?

A potentially more difficult test centres on *beneficence*, namely the risks and benefits associated with the research and how they are distributed among different groups. In contrast with questions about integrity which mostly involve factors endogenous to the research itself, assessing beneficence requires judgements about how research will interact with complex social and political systems.

At its most obvious, researchers can consider the intended goal of the policy under consideration, and its possible ramifications. For example, in 1972 the German government adopted the so-called *Radikalenerlass* ('radical decree'), which attempted to prevent people opposed to the liberal democratic system from civil service offices. Although the decree was directed against supporters of the far-right NPD (*Nationaldemokratischen Partei Deutschlands*) in civil service, in practice it almost exclusively affected supposedly radical leftists, working as teachers, judges, doctors and nurses, administrators, secretaries, engineers, and social workers. (Recently in Germany, some have suggested a new *Radikalenerlass* should be used to deal with far-right supporters in the army and other civil sectors.) Involvement in such processes may lead to the creation of policy that, though putatively aimed at countering far-right violence, may have wide-reaching impacts of securitisation on a variety of democratic actors. Using a more recent example of far-right violence, in some cases broadcast through social media, we can see greater pressure for more effective moderation of right-wing extremist content online. This is precisely the aim of the Christchurch Call to Eliminate Terrorist and Violent Extremist Content Online,[3] which has been taken up by bodies like the Global Internet Forum to Counter Terrorism (GIFCT) and the European Union Internet Forum (EUIF). This spurt of policymaking contains the potential to reduce the direct harms of hate speech and the indirect harms resulting from far-right mobilisation. But it also risks reinforcing a shift in the regulation of speech towards for-profit tech corporations or illiberal states with lesser transparency or accountability.

Both risks to the public (especially marginalised groups) and benefits for far-right actors constitute obvious grounds for revising or withdrawing from a project, especially where those consequences are direct, significant, or outweigh any prospective benefits. Yet in most cases, the calculus will likely be less clear-cut.

What are the costs of participation and non-participation?

Another consideration beyond the substantial issues of integrity and beneficence involves the cost of participating (or, indeed, not participating) in policymaking processes.

In terms of the cost of participation, we suggest that research activity inevitably involves an opportunity cost calculation. In other words, if you agree to participate in some policymaking process, what other research will be unexplored – either because of the reality of finite resources or because of the path dependency of your research agenda being steered in a particular direction catering to the demands of a policymaking audience? The answer to this question will vary from researcher to researcher; one may feel their agenda aligns completely with policymakers while another may perceive a risk of co-optation. Naturally, the cost of participation is also a question of scale: small, one-off projects will not reshape your research agenda to the same extent as a multi-year grant. Yet if, as a field, experts are consistently co-opted into government paradigms as discussed previously, it will likely reduce the capacity for scholars to act as critical agents.

Flipping the question, what are the costs of non-participation by researchers? If policymakers continued making decisions without the input of research experts, how would the policy system and its outcomes develop over time? Researchers are likely to have greater independence to challenge perceived assumptions than the policymakers themselves and, with many instances of policy engagement taking place outside of formal academic projects, are likely to be less constrained by hierarchical structures of those within governmental or intergovernmental bodies.

What incentives could be affecting my decision?

We also suggest it is worth reflecting on the professional incentives which could bias any ethical considerations.

Researchers are increasingly encouraged or incentivised to engage in 'transfer' activities which demonstrate their impact on broader society. Especially for researchers facing precarious working conditions, this may increase the appeal of engaging with policymakers. Yet measures of impact in academia can tend towards the quantitative – the more the better – and have lesser regard for the kind of nuances discussed above about who benefits and who bears the risk. Indeed, discerning different kinds of transfer is likely to only compound the problem: the highest impact is gained from working with the most powerful actors such as trans/national governments and major corporations; these are the groups most easily able to dictate the terms of any research collaboration (potentially encroaching on research integrity) and to occupy and therefore likely to be reproducing the patterns of domination which oppress currently marginalised groups (raising questions around beneficence of the research).

Finally, we want to draw attention to how timing affects ethical considerations, and in particular the trade-off between repercussions and information. For example, before a research project begins, the repercussions of non-participation are minimal, making such a choice on ethical grounds more straightforward. However, you will also be making that choice based on imperfect information: you may only be able to guess at the outcomes the policy system will produce, how your research will play a role, and what outcomes might result from your non-participation. As a research project progresses you may acquire clearer information about some of these dynamics, and yet the costs of withdrawal will also grow, whether sunk costs of time and resources or damaged relationships with policymakers.

Some evaluations, of course, are only possible in hindsight, when the cognitive cost of admitting mistakes is highest, such as: what were the final outcomes of the policy system you participated in? How did your research agenda and that of the field develop over time, and what avenues were left unexplored? For this reason, we suggest that the ethics of engaging with policymakers should be treated as an ongoing question rather than a preliminary screening test.

In conclusion, scholarly engagement with policymaking practices is a process that requires constant critical self-reflection, evaluation, and adjustment. The scholar is largely required to engage on terms determined by policymakers, within a counter-extremism paradigm consistently critiqued as stoking phenomena, such as Islamophobia, which feed the far right and may risk giving credence directly to far-right political actors and governments. We suggest that careful consideration of the honesty, risks, costs, and incentives for scholarly engagement with policymaking could help to mitigate some of these problems – although we recognise that many of the structural problems and inequalities between researcher and policymaker remain. Ultimately, the decision to engage or not is a personal one, and one that many scholars working to understand the far right have already had to grapple with during their work. It is a decision that, we believe, can be helped by more open and honest conversation amongst scholars on the perils, pitfalls, and indeed the potential of such engagement.

Notes

1 We focus on the relationship of researchers to state-based governing institutions and related policy processes. This relationship may be complicated by intersecting or parallel relationships with other researchers and research institutions, non-governmental organisations and civil society actors, and research participants and subjects. It is well, therefore, to read this chapter, especially our guidance to researchers in the penultimate section, as a framework to think through one set of issues in what may be more complex policymaking collaborations.
2 Australian National Statement on Ethical Conduct in Human Research, p. 10.
3 For more information, refer to the Call's webpage: https://www.christchurchcall.com/

References

Abbas, T. 2019. *Islamophobia and Radicalisation: A Vicious Cycle*. London: Hurst.

Aked, H., Younis, T. and Heath-Kelly, C. 2021. *Racism, Mental Health and Pre-Crime Policing – The Ethics of Vulnerability Support Hubs*. London: Medact.

Breen Smyth, M. 2009. 'Subjectivities, "Suspect Communities", Governments and the Ethics of Research on "Terrorism"'. In: Breen Smyth, M., Gunning, J., and Jackson, R. (eds). *Critical Terrorism Studies: A New Research Agenda*. London: Routledge.

Brown, K., Mondon, A., and Winter, A. 2021. 'The Far Right, the Mainstream and Mainstreaming: Towards a Heuristic Framework', *Journal of Political Ideologies*. https://doi.org/10.1080/13569317.2021.1949829

Butterwegge, C. and Meier, L. 2002. *Rechtsextremismus*. Freiburg: Herder.

Conway, M. 2021. 'Online Extremism and Terrorism Research Ethics: Researchers Safety, Informed Consent and the Need for Tailored Guidelines', *Terrorism and Political Violence*, 33(2), 367–380.

Coppock, V. and McGovern, M. 2014. '"Dangerous Minds"? Deconstructing Counter-Terrorism Discourse, Radicalisation and the "Psychological Vulnerability" of Muslim Children and Young People in Britain', *Children & Society*, 28(3), 242–256.

Hirschman, A. O. 1970. *Exit, Voice, and Loyalty: Responses to Decline in Firms, Organizations, and States* (Vol. 25). Cambridge, MA: Harvard University Press.

Kundnani, A. 2012. 'Blind Spot? Security Narratives and Far-Right Violence in Europe', International Centre for Counter-Terrorism (ICCT) – The Hague.

McNeil-Willson, R. 2022. '#plandemic: Online Resilience for Counter Far-Right COVID-19 Conspiracies', *First Monday*, 28.

McNeil-Willson, R., Gerrand, V., Scrinzi, F., and Triandafyllidou, A. 2019. *Polarisation, Violent Extremism and Resilience in Europe Today: An Analytical Framework for the BRaVE Project (Concept Paper)*. Global Governance, Robert Schuman Centre for Advanced Studies. Florence: European University Institute.

O'Toole, T., Meer, N., DeHanas, D. N., Jones, S. H., and Modood, T. 2016. 'Governing through Prevent? Regulation and Contested Practice in State–Muslim Engagement', *Sociology*, 50(1). 160–177.

Pantazis, C. and Pemberton, S. A. 2009. 'From the Old to the New Suspect Community: Examining the Impacts of Recent UK Counter-Terrorist Legislation', *British Journal of Criminology*, 79, 646–666.

Weilnböck, H. and Kossack, O. 2019. 'The EU's "Islamism" Bias and Its "Added Damage" in Central and Eastern Europe', *Open Democracy*, 26 November. https://www.opendemocracy.net/en/global-extremes/the-eus-islamism-bias-and -its-added-damage-in-central-and-eastern-europe/ (accessed 18 October 2023).

Winter, A. and Mondon, A. 2020. *Reactionary Democracy: How Racism and the Populist Far Right Became Mainstream*. London: Verso.

Wodak, R. 2019. 'Entering the "Post-Shame Era": The Rise of Illiberal Democracy, Populism and Neo-Authoritarianism in Europe', *Global Discourse* (Themed Issue: The Limits of EUrope: Identities, Spaces, Values), 9, 195–213.

Younis, T. and Jadhav, S. 2020. 'Islamophobia in the National Health Service: An Ethnography or Institutional Racism in PREVENT's Counter-Radicalisation Policy', *Sociology of Health and Illness*, 42, 610–26.

Zeller, M. and Vaughan, M. 2021. 'Proscribed Right-Wing Extremist Organisations', *Centre for Analysis of the Radical Right*. https://www.radicalrightanalysis.com/ resources/proscribed-right-wing-extremist-organisations/ (accessed 18 October 2023).

28

Critical reflexivity and research on state responses to the far right

Anna A. Meier

"If whiteness gains currency by being unnoticed, what does it mean to notice whiteness?" asks Sara Ahmed in the introduction to her essay, 'The phenomenology of whiteness' (Ahmed 2007: 149). In this short chapter, I attempt to 'notice' whiteness in research on white supremacist violence. Put differently, what does it mean to be a white researcher in white-dominated spaces researching topics deeply entangled with whiteness? How do we reckon, in Ahmed's words, with a "project of critique [that is] complicit with its object"?

Such questions are crucial not only due to heightened interest among research communities in recent years in studying white supremacist violence but also because white supremacist violence is often understood through the lens of counterterrorism, itself a white supremacist institution. Scholars of colour, and in particular racialised Muslim scholars, have long underscored that racism and Islamophobia in counterterrorism are intentional, not incidental, components of a national security apparatus that exists to preserve a status quo in white majority countries. This status quo uses violence against communities of colour to protect whites' sociopolitical status, even when particular national security actors do not intend to do this (e.g. Cainkar and Selod 2018; Kundnani 2014). I focus here on these actors: the bureaucrats, staffers, and other elites tasked with making and enforcing policy to *counter* violent white supremacy. Studying such actors, while important, raises questions of researcher access, positionality, and complicity at the heart of state institutions that may be more closely aligned with the ideologies of violent white supremacy than they would like to believe.

My argument in this short chapter is that research with policy elites is important for understanding not only what policy surrounding white supremacist violence looks like, but also why it continues to look that way. Nevertheless, the people best positioned to do this research – that is, white people – are also the most likely to reproduce white supremacy, even if inadvertently. On the one hand, white access to overwhelmingly white elites can reproduce dynamics likely to occur in policymaking spaces to which researchers do *not* have access, thereby providing opportunities to capture something closer to elites' true attitudes. Being racialised as white also affords safety when talking about sensitive issues such as racism. On the other, doing critical work on white supremacy in such a space requires constant reflexivity so as not to overlook how white supremacy itself constitutes those spaces. Succinctly, whiteness offers both unique access and unique limitations in the study of white supremacy.

To demonstrate this point, I use autoethnography to examine my own research with national security elites in Berlin, Germany, and Washington, DC. Autoethnography is a method that underscores the co-constitution of knowledge in research encounters by using the researcher's experience as a source of data (Brigg and Bleiker 2010; Lapadat 2017). I apply an autoethnographic sensibility to three encounters from 2019: one with a former bureaucrat in the German chancellor's office, one with a current staffer in the German Bundestag, and one with two former US Congressional staffers turned think-tank researchers. All occurred as part of a larger project on elite sense-making in designing and implementing counterterrorism policy. I use pseudonyms for all of my interlocutors.

In describing my own praxis, I follow Ahmed's call to leave open the door for critique, rather than prescribing solutions (Ahmed 2004: 165). Contrary to what conventional wisdom might suggest, the challenges of research with policy elites arose not from issues of access but rather from the need for constant, critical reflexivity. By 'critical reflexivity' I refer to a combination of structural intersectionality and practical reflexivity as laid out by Crenshaw (1991) and Berling and Bueger (2013). Critical reflexivity acknowledges the larger sociopolitical contexts in which researcher and researched are positioned, accompanied by a critical examination of how power operates in those contexts. More generally, reflexive analysis reminds us that research does not occur in a vacuum, and what we hear and how we interpret it will vary depending on our identities vis-à-vis those of our interlocutors and the settings in which we find ourselves (Townsend-Bell 2009).

In practice, I followed roughly the guidelines codified by Soedirgo and Glas (2020) for doing reflexive analysis, including frequent recording of assumptions, consideration of positionality pre-interview, and discussions of interview data (to the extent that it was ethical) with non-participant insiders and outsiders in order to address gaps in my own self-reflection. Such an approach does not guarantee anti-racist outcomes, but it does underscore that the power dynamics involved in researching white supremacy are never *not* present and can themselves be a source of insight into how white supremacy functions. Put simply, positionality structures possibility – both for policymakers and research on policy.

Encounter 1: racism in Berlin

"Oh, a specialist, I see."

No exchange with Otto in the hour we have spent together has gone well. First, I mistook what he thought was lunch for a meeting over coffee. Shortly after resolving the lunch mix-up, I messed up the simplest of German subject-verb agreements, triggering what would become a common interaction with my interlocutors. ("But your name; I thought you were German." "No; my great-great grandparents were immigrants." "Where from?" "Bavaria." "Oh, that is not Germany.") Now I have provoked something in the vicinity of sarcasm by being familiar with a book Otto likes. We are discussing counterterrorism in twenty-first-century Germany, already a sensitive topic, but that is not why our conversation has taken place on eggshells.

Otto is a former bureaucrat in the German chancellor's office. He worked on a national security portfolio during the 9/11 attacks and so has unique insight into how discourses of terrorism developed at the highest levels of the German government. I am in the early days of my research; nevertheless, getting access to Otto and people like him has been surprisingly straightforward. I get the sense that some view me as a curiosity, which makes me feel insecure. I am also conscious of being a young woman in the early days of my first scholarly fieldwork trip, interviewing mostly older men. Every interaction involves negotiating age, gender, and seniority – all heuristics for 'expertise'. I don't feel that I am passing Otto's test.

Eventually, however, Otto decides he is comfortable enough to speak relatively freely. He begins laying out reactions to the influx of asylum-seekers into Germany in the early days of the Syrian Civil War. "It was clear", he rationalises, "that some would be violent." Why? I wonder. Otto's assertion plays into nativist narratives from the German right about terrorist infiltrators, even though Otto is a lifelong member of a left-wing party. I am surprised to hear him accept this uncritically, but I don't say anything; I want him to keep talking. "This isn't a left or right issue", he continues. "The refugees are an issue, even though it isn't politically correct to say so."

Encapsulated in this anecdote is a key component of doing research on white supremacist violence with white elites as a white researcher. Whatever other identities I may hold, I am squarely in the insider camp on the dimension that matters: race. Otto is not the only elite I will encounter who will comfortably express racist views despite having just met me. These views are never intended to shock. I get the impression Otto, and others, either expect me to agree already or believe me capable of understanding and sympathising with their position. My interpretation is that, to them, such a position is completely normal in a conversation between two white 'specialists', who have independently assessed the national security landscape but come to similar conclusions coloured by race in unacknowledged ways, even as shared race makes the conversation possible in the first place.

Critical reflexivity requires noticing moments of surprise that are not intended to be surprising. Though my whiteness afforded me unique access to the racist views embedded in mainstream national security discourses, it also positioned me insofar as I did not expect to encounter those views with so little effort expended on my part. That I could still find a surprise in that space produces an opportunity for insight – to paraphrase feminist scholar Caron Gentry, discomfort *tells us something* (Gentry 2020). My discomfort instructed that if I had to work to 'see' a space dealing with white supremacy as structurally white supremacist, then my interlocutors might also not 'see' white supremacy as constitutive of their work, rather than simply a target of that work.

Taking a critically reflexive approach thus required changing the starting point of my inquiry. Rather than simply pay attention to how my interlocutors answered my questions, I also needed to understand something about the environments in which they worked and lived – in other words, how their social worlds shaped what was thinkable and normal to them. The importance of this came sharply into focus in an encounter with a very different sort of bureaucrat, which I describe below.

Encounter 2: the limits of the left

I meet Paul in his office at one of the many buildings housing operations for German MPs that ring Berlin's Pariser Platz, a tourist destination crowded with selfie sticks and street performers. Paul is a staff researcher for a leftist member of the Bundestag, and as a fellow young leftist, I find our conversation one of the most relaxed and natural I have had during my fieldwork.

Indeed, Paul's discussion of his own language surrounding white supremacist violence forces me to reflect on how I use 'white supremacist violence' to encompass a wide range of activities, sacrificing one kind of precision to focus on what, to me, is the key thread of structural oppression underlying the far right. He is conscious of his own political biases and how they shape his views of the world. I notice, for instance, that he uses the explicit language of 'terrorism' to describe white supremacist organisations – a rhetorical choice not common in Germany unless formal charges of terrorism have been filed. "I'm not perfect in my language", he says. "There is more than terrorism out there – neo-Nazi music, art, culture – and sometimes when I say 'terrorism' [*Terrorismus*], I'm referring to all of that." He continues: "I also say the 'extreme right' [*Rechtsextremismus*] sometimes. There's not a huge difference. … But I think these terms are only as useful as the policies that follow from them."

Yet Paul's reflections on policies countering white supremacist violence feel surprisingly non-radical. I ask all of my interlocutors, who universally agree that the German government has not taken white supremacist violence seriously, how they would know if the government *were* to take it seriously. "There would be more personnel working on the issue", Paul explains. He does not elaborate much. When pressed, he clarifies that he doesn't think intelligence and law enforcement officials know enough about the threat – though he is careful to note that what such officials know and don't know only becomes clear after attacks occur.

I find this response confusing for several reasons, which is a signal that I need to pay attention to it. A number of my interlocutors have explained, contrary to Paul's position, that hiring more personnel to work on issues of white supremacist violence is an insufficient move at best and a smokescreen at worst. That Paul offers this seemingly inadequate solution and suggests no others does not track with the expectations I have formed. I am surprised that Paul's otherwise careful attention to structural components of racism and white supremacy does not extend to the area of policy solutions. "Diversity is not part of the *Selbtsverstandnis* in Germany", he says in response to an earlier question, using a word that means an intuitive sense of what it means to be German. To make sense of what he views as a lack of government action, he points to the mainstreaming of far-right ideology and a refusal to reckon with racism. Yet his vision for an improved policy environment involves more of the same policy Band-Aids, rather than deeper anti-racist change.

It takes me several weeks to process my conversation with Paul, which was at once among the most enjoyable and most frustrating of my fieldwork. Eventually, I classify it as the most enlightening. What I have done with Paul, unintentionally, is replicate discussions in white leftist spaces that purport to be radical but that remain constrained by the bounded imagination of whiteness. I come to recognise the same dynamics repeating themselves in other activist spaces of which I am a part. I believe Paul, like so many of these activists, is genuinely interested in such solutions but finds it challenging to imagine what they might look like in practice – a challenge I find myself also confronting, even as I demand more of my interlocutors.

This difficulty in imagining solutions becomes legible when one considers the workings of structural white supremacy. After all, structural white supremacy persists by being unremarkable: those who do remark on it are characterised as misguided or, at worst, pathological (Davis and Ernst 2019). A critically reflexive approach to doing research on the far right, then, requires asking not *whether* white supremacy is present, but *how it manifests*. For some, like Otto, it may be in casual racism masquerading as objectivity. For others, like Paul, it may be in limitations on what Robin D. G. Kelley (2003) calls 'freedom dreaming' about the actions that will help us achieve anti-racist futures (see also Joseph-Salisbury and Connelly 2021). And for Black, Brown, and Indigenous individuals, it may be far more personal.

Encounter 3: ruptures in Washington

Far from temperate Berlin, I meet Claire and Jenna in a glass-walled office in Washington, DC at the crest of a heat wave. Both are former US Congressional staffers who now work at a think tank. Claire is a white woman; Jenna belongs to a historically excluded racial group.[1]

It is immediately clear that Claire and Jenna respect each other a great deal. This goes beyond professionalism in the presence of a stranger (me): they regularly reference each others' expertise as we talk and bounce examples back and forth to form the most comprehensive answers that they can. Nevertheless, Jenna's statements occasionally make Claire vocally uncomfortable. According to Jenna, the US counterterrorism apparatus post-9/11 views terrorism as an identity – 'terrorist' as something one is, rather than 'terrorism' as something one does. The endpoint of this logic, she explains, is eradication:

> Jenna: The response that we've had for terrorism as identity is, you hold that identity and you are irredeemable. ... If terrorism is identity, your [policy] answer is genocide.

Invoking the language of genocide to describe counterterrorism is contentious, and I had heard nothing similar even in leftist texts advocating for the abolition of counterterrorism institutions. It is clearly a carefully considered choice: Jenna slows the pace of her speech during this interlude and articulates every word. It is also clear that Claire is not quite sure what to do with this declaration from Jenna. She works through her thoughts verbally, breaking apart the category of 'terrorism' that Jenna has brought up:

> Claire: I'm not sure I totally agree, in the sense that I don't think the IRA and al-Qaeda are one in the same. ... In the case of al-Qaeda or ISIS, there is a political end ... but also they're willing to die for the cause and that is a goal in and of itself and you're fighting an entire ideology. ... They're very very very different groups.

In retrospect, this train of thought – responding as it does to Jenna's foundational assumption that terrorism is always equated with identity, rather than her assertion that this equation implies genocide – feels more like a non sequitur than it appeared in the moment. Yet by this point in my research, I am better equipped to analyse what may be happening here. By avoiding Jenna's invocation of the term 'genocide', Claire has moved our conversation in a more comfortable direction by trying to find examples where a more extreme policy response, even if not genocide, is appropriate because of something extreme about the actors themselves – in her view, actors such as al-Qaeda and ISIS. Jenna's analysis had unsettled Claire's understanding of counterterrorism as a space that frequently did harm but within which some actors were still fundamentally different and thus deserving of different treatment (while, conspicuously, avoiding the varying racialisation of the average IRA member vs. the average al-Qaeda member). Claire had therefore provided an explanation for that differentiation that was at odds with Jenna's *worldview* – one which replaced Jenna's frame of 'genocide', with all its important connotations, with one of different types of actors in order to make sense of counterterrorism's systematic violence against historically excluded communities.

This encounter further crystallised, for me, that worldviews are where we must begin when doing critical research on the far right. For white researchers and political elites alike, the default assumption is that racism *could* surface in policy spaces but will not *inevitably* do so – in other words, that white supremacy is not structural. Shifting to assume that white supremacy is constitutive of and perpetuated by national security institutions, which act as referenda on who is a threat and who is familiar, not only aligns research with empirical reality but also changes the questions we ask. 'Are institutions racist?' is a very different question from 'How does racism manifest in institutions?' Each starts us in a different place. Critical reflexivity demands that we at least entertain the second question; making space for inevitability, in turn, moves the challenge of not reproducing white supremacy front and centre.

Discussion: critical reflexivity and the white imagination

My encounters with Otto, Paul, Claire, and Jenna, alongside numerous others in the course of my research on elites working to counter white supremacist violence, carry significant implications for those doing work on national security policy. First and foremost is the need to do this research in the first place. Had I not physically walked into bureaucrats' offices and listened to them explain their work in their own words, I may have continued to believe narratives about resource constraints driving responses to white supremacist violence – or, conversely, the outright bad intentions of some policy elites. Both of these stories miss the complexity of making and enforcing policy against white supremacist violence while inhabiting structurally white supremacist institutions tasked with upholding imperial and racist systems.

Yet the risk of reproducing structural white supremacy remains, underscoring the need to actively work against it. Critical reflexivity, I argue, can render visible whiteness "for those who inhabit it" (Ahmed 2004). I caveat this statement forcefully, because the workings of whiteness-as-institution rely on those who benefit from the institution not noticing its tendrils, such that 'visibility' may never be complete. What to do, then, when those best positioned to *access* whiteness-as-institution are simultaneously the worst positioned to *understand* whiteness-as-institution?

Fundamentally, we must change our starting points. Ethical research requires not working, or writing, for an audience that discounts the reality of structural white supremacy shaping policymaking. Instead of leaving open the possibility for observing racism in my interviews, I learned to ask, instead: what would happen if I started from the position that racism *is* present, foundationally so, and what are the implications for how I as a racial insider can talk about policy in the first place? For me, this has meant adjusting the analytical frames that I turn to when interpreting my interview data. Insights from Black and queer political thought have proven indispensable at shedding light on national security dynamics I once found surprising (e.g. Shakur 1988; Puar 2007), and I hope their inclusion in literature on the far right becomes far more commonplace.

Following this is the need for attentiveness to the language we both hear and use ourselves. As a white insider, I can allow racist utterances in private conversations if they arise naturally without worrying about harm to myself, allowing me to capture something closer to my interlocutors' true attitudes absent any concern on their part about respectability or 'political correctness' that might arise were my racial identity different. That such exchanges likely occur in policy conversations to which researchers are not privy is important to acknowledge. Simultaneously, though, I must be cautious of the language I myself use to describe what I hear, an obligation made more complex when translating across languages. As Schaffer (2006) notes, uncritical reproduction of language assumes that everyone describes the world in the same way. Understanding how the people making policy surrounding white supremacist violence in turn describe 'white supremacist violence' shines light on how concepts are constructed in real time – and how linguistic choices may constrain what policy responses are viewed as possible or appropriate. To return to Gentry, hearing a policy described as 'genocidal' – and finding that description unexpected – *tells us something*, and it is the duty of the ethical researcher to take this utterance and its implications seriously.

I conclude with a note of caution via Sonia Ryang, who warns that centring oneself in one's analysis, as I have done here, risks reproducing Western notions of individualism and the positioning of the white individual as the default, rather than something that emerges from particular historical and socio-political contexts (Ryang 2000). Certainly, there is a risk of privileging one's own interpretations over those of one's interlocutors – and, moreover, of reading a research encounter as an opportunity for self-discovery rather than a chance to learn something valuable in the struggle against structural white supremacy. I suggest, however, that working as a white researcher on white supremacist violence is necessarily a process of unlearning particular ways of interpreting politics, which is assisted by a critically reflexive approach. Engaging ethically with that unlearning means noticing the moments of surprise from which insight springs, thereby allowing one's personal unlearning to guide, but not overshadow, one's eventual analysis.

Note

1 Thanks to Kelebogile Zvobgo for proposing the language of 'historically excluded' as an alternative to 'minority' or 'marginalised'.

References

Ahmed, S. 2004. 'Declarations of Whiteness: The Non-Performativity of Anti-Racism', *Borderlands*, 3(2).

Ahmed, S. 2007. 'A Phenomenology of Whiteness', *Feminist Theory*, 8(2), 149–168.

Berling, T. V. and Bueger, C. 2013. 'Practical Reflexivity and Political Science: Strategies for Relating Scholarship and Political Practice', *PS: Political Science and Politics*, 46(1), 115–119.

Brigg, M. and Bleiker, R. 2010. 'Autoethnographic International Relations: Exploring the Self as a Source of Knowledge', *Review of International Studies*, 36(3), 779–798.

Cainkar, L. and Selod, S. 2018. 'Review of Race Scholarship and the War on Terror', *Sociology of Race and Ethnicity*, 4(2), 165–177.

Crenshaw, K. 1991. 'Mapping the Margins: Intersectionality, Identity Politics, and Violence against Women of Color', *Stanford Law Review*, 43(6), 1241–1299.

Davis, A. M. and Ernst, R. 2019. 'Racial Gaslighting', *Politics, Groups, and Identities*, 7(4), 761–774.

Gentry, C. 2020. *Disordered Violence: How Gender, Race and Heteronormativity Structure Terrorism.* Edinburgh: Edinburgh University Press.

Joseph-Salisbury, R. and Connelly, L. 2021. *Anti-Racist Scholar-Activism.* Manchester: Manchester University Press.

Kelley, R.D.G. 2003. *Freedom Dreams: The Black Radical Imagination.* New York: Beacon.

Kundnani, A. 2014. *The Muslims Are Coming!* London: Verso.

Lapadat, J. C. 2017. 'Ethics in Autoethnography and Collaborative Autoethnography', *Qualitative Inquiry*, 23(8), 589–603.

Puar, J. 2007. *Terrorist Assemblages.* Durham, NC: Duke University Press.

Ryang, S. 2000. 'Ethnography or Self-Cultural Anthropology? Reflections on Writing about Ourselves', *Dialectical Anthropology*, 25(3/4), 297–320.

Schaffer, F. C. 2006. 'Ordinary Language Interviewing'. In Yanow, D. and Schwartz-Shea, P. (eds). *Interpretation and Method: Empirical Research Methods and the Interpretive Turn.* New York: Routledge, 150–160.

Shakur, A. 1988. *Assata: An Autobiography.* Chicago, IL: Lawrence Hill Books.

Soedirgo, J. and Glas, A. 2020. 'Toward Active Reflexivity: Positionality and Practice in the Production of Knowledge', *PS: Political Science and Politics*, 53(3), 527–531.

Townsend-Bell, E. 2009. 'Being True and Being You: Race, Gender, Class, and the Fieldwork Experience', *PS: Political Science and Politics*, 42(2), 311–314.

29

An anti-racist scholar-activist ethic: working in service to racial justice

Remi Joseph-Salisbury, Laura Connelly, and Aurelien Mondon

The practice of research raises a range of urgent ethical considerations, particularly when research focuses on social (in)justice. As argued elsewhere, including across other chapters in this collection, this point is particularly pertinent in relation to ethnicity and racism studies in general, and far right studies specifically. This is the case both for scholarship that (methodologically) engages directly with far-right political groups (Ashe 2020; Busher 2021) and scholarship that takes a more expansive approach, seeing the far right as a blurry-edged construct that is intimately connected to what is socially constructed as the mainstream (Brown et al. 2021; Mondon and Winter 2020). Whilst "there has been relatively little in the way of detailed discussion about the *practice* of researching the far right" (Ashe et al. 2020: 2), there is growing recognition that the complex ethical and political challenges researchers face are important subject matters.

Taking this as our entry point, this chapter emerges from dialogue between two authors who have researched and written about anti-racist scholar-activism (Joseph-Salisbury and Connelly 2021), and one who researches and writes about the far right and its mainstreaming (Mondon 2013; Mondon and Winter 2020). While all three write with social justice at the heart of their praxis, their approaches differ in a particularly interesting way: Remi and Laura focus on the perspective of resistance, while Aurelien's work centres on mapping the reactionary context. Emerging from that dialogue, this chapter offers a new lens – an anti-racist scholar-activist ethic – for navigating the ethical and political dilemmas of undertaking research on the far right. To do so, it centres the notion of working *in service to racial justice*, suggesting that it offers an anchoring, or orientation, that can guide anti-racist scholar-activist scholarship and praxis specifically, and more ethical (research) praxis generally. Elsewhere, Remi and Laura have developed the *in service to racial justice* orientation in relation to working with(in) racially minoritised communities and/or anti-racist movements (Joseph-Salisbury and Connelly 2021). Their collaboration with Aurelien here offers an opportunity to complicate these arguments by considering what working in service means when the focus is on politics which (and participants who) are diametrically opposed to racial justice.

With that in mind, after setting out the theoretical underpinnings of working in service to racial justice below, the chapter explores questions of *social usefulness* and *accountability* in its examination of the practice of an anti-racist scholar-activist ethic. While it is generally true across all disciplines, a key contention of this chapter is that it is crucial for those who research the far right to remain connected and committed to communities of resistance. There can be no neutral stance to this research. This conscious positioning ensures that we, as researchers, work in service to racial justice and remain accountable to those at the sharp end of racism.

Working in service to racial justice

The notion of working in service has featured, notably, in the work of Patricia Hill Collins (2012, 2013), Ambalavaner Sivanandan (2008b, 2019), and Walter Rodney (cited by Osuna 2017). In her conceptualisation of 'intellectual activism', Collins (2013: ix) refers to "the myriad ways in which people place the power of their ideas *in service* to social justice". She distinguishes working *in service to* social justice from working *in support of* social justice. The latter, she argues, "implies a lack of accountability", whilst the former invokes responsibilities associated with the notion of service itself. Specifically, working in service "may involve sacrifice" and "making choices that put one at odds with prevailing academic norms" (Collins 2013: 43). In this sense, Collins (2013: xii) casts the in-service orientation as counter-hegemonic: it rubs against the pressures omnipresent within Higher Education (HE) to "place our fancy degrees in service to conservative political agendas" and hegemonic power structures more broadly.

Turning to Sivanandan, under his forty-year directorship, the radical think tank the Institute of Race Relations (IRR) adopted more structurally focused understandings of race and racism that were contextualised by imperialism and colonialism (Fekete 2021; Sivanandan 2008a).[1] Reorienting the IRR to play an active role in servicing anti-racist struggle, Sivanandan retrospectively described his vision in the following way:

> there was a plethora of grassroots, community movements at the time (unlike now, alas) that we could serve. If we could not be at the barricades in the fight for racial justice, we could, at least, be servitors in that cause. We could do research that spoke to the issues and problems confronting Black communities. We could be a servicing station. We could put gas in the tanks of Black and Third World peoples on their way to liberation. That, in any case, was our pious hope. (Sivanandan 2008b: np)

What Sivanandan articulates here is a radical orientation, premised on the notion of working in service to communities of resistance,[2] rather than to the "interests of the ruling elite" that the IRR had previously served (Sivanandan 2008a: 22). Though Sivanandan refers specifically to his work at IRR, the fundamental ideas are resonant for scholar-activists working inside (and outside) the university (Joseph-Salisbury and Connelly 2021). He points to the importance of both an embeddedness within communities of resistance and of putting research to use for those communities and for wider struggles for liberation.

With parallels to Sivanandan and Collins, the anti-colonial activist and academic Walter Rodney contended that:

> If we [the petit-bourgeois intellectuals] have a role, it has to do with the shift of the initiative into the hands of workers and peasants and then for a change we begin to serve those classes. Because mostly we have been serving other classes anyhow. Mostly we have been serving the capitalist class. So for a change, we may begin to service the working people, service the working class. (Rodney cited by Osuna 2017: 37)

For Rodney, working in service to 'working people', or to communities of resistance in Sivanandan's (2019) terms, constitutes a break from the norm: such praxis is counter-hegemonic.

In the context of contemporary HE, this counter-hegemony takes on a particular character. It is antithetical to the dominant norms, values, and practices promulgated within what Remi and Laura have termed elsewhere the *neoliberal-imperial-institutionally-racist university* (see Joseph-Salisbury and Connelly 2021). The *neoliberal* university captures the chilling effects of market logic on higher education: the repositioning of the university as a commodity, education as a service for students to purchase, and universities and academics as service providers who must compete. The *imperial* university points to the way Western universities have been, and continue to be, located within a "network of state apparatuses of control, discipline, surveillance, carcerality, and violence" (Webb 2018: 96–97), and the *institutionally racist* university acknowledges how racisms underpin and are reproduced within universities. As the hyphenation denotes, these forces are deeply entangled. Acknowledging this context is important because it draws attention to the difficult institutional conditions within which university-based anti-racist scholar-activists operate. It centres the increasingly competitive working environments, governed by a high-stakes metric culture which means that time is increasingly squeezed and compromised. It also points to the presence of control, surveillance (Webb 2018), and the threat of racist and anti-anti-racist *backlash* (Joseph-Salisbury and Connelly

2021) that impact those who pursue racial justice, particularly minoritised academics. Most importantly, it highlights the oppositional relationship between the dominant logics of the university and the principles of anti-racist scholar-activism.

Before moving on, however, it is worth noting that – despite all of this – we should not mistake the university for a monolith. Rather, it is important to recognise that the university is an assemblage of competing and contradictory forces and visions (la paperson 2017). If this were not the case, we would surely have to concede that there is no value in anti-racist scholar-activists working in the university (which is not to say that we do not sometimes wonder about the extent of this value). With this in mind, as anti-racist scholar-activists we must identify, exploit, and grow the pockets of possibility the university presents in order to work in service to communities of resistance and racial justice more broadly.

The field of far right studies is an interesting case study through which to examine how research can serve different (hegemonic and counter-hegemonic) purposes. The field has always been a disproportionately popular one, particularly within political science. While many scholars generally have as a starting point a negative, even antagonistic, view of their topic of study, the scientification and datafication of the social sciences have promoted an increasingly detached approach and strengthened the grip of 'white logics' (see Zuberi and Bonilla-Silva 2008). Claims of objectivity and neutrality, core to positivist approaches, have at times served to replace the urgency of studying the far right to actively counter it, with simply studying the far right in an apparently apolitical manner. Worse still, at times, this has led to the legitimisation of the far right by using euphemistic descriptors to avoid terminologies considered 'too political' and 'loaded'.

As discussed in other chapters of this book, the politics of naming are key and yet often ignored. The increasing ubiquity of the term 'populism' in the field is a tribute to this. Although the concept itself is not new and has helped with understanding American and Russian movements in the late nineteenth century and left-wing movements in Latin America at the turn of the twenty-first century, it has increasingly been applied to the resurgent, reconstructed far-right movements in the 2000s. While the concept has shed light on some of the discursive strategies employed by far-right actors to claim an apparent democratic legitimacy, it has often become a substitute for other more stig-matising but also more appropriate and better-defined terms such as extreme right, racist, or even fascist right. Instead, in a strange effort to appease com-plaints emanating from the far right, many scholars have taken them at their word and adopted a descriptor far-right actors have themselves been push-ing for. The shift away from more stigmatising denominators has been facili-tated by the belief in a 'post-racial' society (Lentin 2016), which has created conditions whereby being accused of racism comes to be of greater concern than racism itself. In a 'post-racial' society, understandings of racism are also 'frozen' or limited to their most illiberal articulations, rather than being understood as an evolving ideology still core to far-right (and often mainstream) politics (see Lentin 2020; Mondon and Winter 2020). The avoidance of terms and topics considered overly political, such as racism, is directly linked to academics increasingly seeing themselves as detached actors rather than intimately and unavoidably embedded in the politics they research. In a racially unjust society, such pretensions can lead researchers to work in service to the status quo by not only accepting but strengthening hegemonic discourses which conceal or euphemise structures of oppression and even legitimise reaction.

What working in service means in practice

In practice, the notion of working in service to racial justice is particularly helpful in addressing some of the issues set out above. It can engender an anti-racist scholar-activist research ethic in several ways, for example, by raising questions about *social usefulness* and *accountability*. Here, each is explored in turn, thinking both about how they pertain to anti-racist scholarship generally and to far right research specifically.

Social usefulness

Considerations of usefulness – the extent to which our work is useful beyond academia – are far from novel. In the UK context, such considerations are even institutionalised through the Research Excellence Framework (REF) Impact agenda, albeit in a limiting and reductive form. The notion of working in service to racial justice, however, implores us to think about usefulness in a particular way. The key question becomes, to what or to whom is our work useful? Through this frame, our praxis can be considered useful not if it serves the interests of the status quo (and/or the far right), but if it empowers communities of resistance and bolsters anti-racism. There are echoes here of what Richard Johnson (1993: 19), writing on radical education, describes as *really useful knowledge*. As Johnson puts it, not usefulness as "a tool of social reproduction and a guardian of the status quo" but a usefulness that "demands changes by unveiling the causes of exploitation and tracing its origins within the ruling ideology".

In research with twenty-nine anti-racist scholar-activists, Remi and Laura found that a sense of urgency was often at the heart of considerations of social usefulness – that is to say, a sense of urgency regarding what is at stake in a given socio-political context necessitates socially useful work (Joseph-Salisbury and Connelly 2021). This has resonance for those researching the far right since, as Aurelien has noted elsewhere (Mondon and Winter 2020), there is an urgency to the threat posed not only by the growing influence of the far right themselves but also by the way in which they are increasingly being constructed as legitimate actors. This is aided in part – either consciously or unconsciously – by some research on the far right and through their media portrayal and platforming. For anti-racists, the threat posed by the far right presents an imperative to engage in work that helps us understand but also undermines or counters that threat, while ensuring that doing so does not amplify or legitimise such politics. For those for whom this means engaging directly with the far right, and particularly those who engage members of the far right as research participants, the pertinent question has to be: to what extent can an engagement with the far right serve, or be socially useful to, communities of resistance and racial justice? Whilst it might well be the case that serving racial justice can involve "dialogues with one's enemies as well as one's allies" (Back 2002: 23; Ashe 2020),[3] holding steadfast to that notion of (anti-racist) service – whilst remaining reflexive about the potential benefits and (unintended) harms of our work (Joseph-Salisbury 2018) – can help guide scholars through the ethical quagmire of research that engages the far right. As Ashe et al. (2020: 3) note, this question is not easily answered:

> Researchers of the far right [also] often find themselves grappling, struggling even, with questions about whether their own research practices might even be fuelling the very problems that they set out to understand and address.

It is therefore when a commitment to racial justice is not foregrounded or considered, or when the threat posed by far-right politics (particularly to those at the sharp end of such politics) is either euphemised or hyped to fit mainstream narratives, that research on the far right can perhaps become dangerous or harmful.

Thinking more generally about the relationship between research, researchers, and the far right, questions of usefulness should also lead us to give due consideration to how our work might be used, and by whom. Research on the far right that does not make clear that it stands against the far right risks euphemising the dangers such politics pose and/or serves to legitimise them, even if unwillingly. For example, research on the 'left behind' and 'white working class' has often served to legitimise the far right as if far-right actors speak on behalf of 'the people' (Begum et al. 2021; Bhambra 2017). At times, such research has been used by far-right parties and actors themselves in their own propaganda. This has often been based on a skewed, uncritical, or biased reading of data, with that data generally pointing to a much more nuanced picture as to where support comes from. For example, while Trumpism and Brexit were often touted as (white) working-class revolts, it has been empirically demonstrated that support for these politics predominantly came from wealthier sections of the population (Mondon and Winter 2018; Dorling 2016). This should not have surprised us as both these movements served the interests of the wealthy first and foremost. Linking such politics to the 'left behind' is not only simplistic (at best) or inaccurate empirically, but also lends a veneer of democratic legitimacy to politics which are innately elitist and sit squarely against working-class interests and solidarity by seeking to divide rather than unify. Ultimately, therefore, scholars need to ask themselves whose interests their work serves – the far right or anti-racist communities of resistance.

Accountability

In considering the usefulness of our work through the lens of working in service to racial justice, accountability becomes another important consideration. Accountability is a central principle in the research ethics processes of universities, with researchers encouraged to reflect on their obligations to research participants and other key stakeholders. Even neoliberal tools such as the REF Impact agenda and universities' promotion of 'knowledge exchange' and 'public engagement' can – at least at first glance – promote accountability to wider publics. Yet, in these institutionalised forms, accountability can be limited and superficial. Too often researchers' relationships with the communities that they research are short-term and extractive (Smith 2012), leading many from dispossessed and/or marginalised communities to be distrustful of researchers and universities more broadly. An *in service to racial justice* orientation, in stark contrast, encourages forms of accountability that are both inherently tied to a deep embeddedness in communities of resistance and are counter-hegemonic in nature. Whilst these forms may overlap for brief moments with those promoted by the Impact agenda, the nature and extent of accountability are incomparable.

Embeddedness in communities of resistance is a fundamental principle that guides the praxes of anti-racist scholar-activism. As Rodney (2019) urged, we should spend time outside of our university campuses doing work *with* and *within* – rather than *on* – those engaged in anti-racist resistance. We should sit down with, listen to, and learn from one another to co-produce theory and action that is useful to movements for racial justice. This embeddedness fosters opportunities for direct forms of accountability, including providing spaces in which non-academic activists can challenge scholar-activists when their work does not benefit their community or the wider anti-racist movement, a process which in turn encourages meaningful reflexivity. This can serve as an important corrective to ensure that our scholarship and praxes "stay connected to and informed by struggle" (Osuna 2017: 36). Whilst some (particularly racially minoritised) scholar-activists may be accountable to communities that they have grown up in, for others, embeddedness in communities of resistance is something that must be more deliberately cultivated, with sensitivity and patience. Building enduring and trusting relationships can require a significant time investment and thus bristles against pressures omnipresent within HE to be productive – that is, to use time 'wisely' within a metric culture that promotes 'ticking the boxes' and moving on. In this regard, forms of accountability deriving from embeddedness in communities of resistance are counter-hegemonic in nature.

Of course, how we understand embeddedness and its relationship with accountability will change in relation to different methodologies and research foci. Indeed, embeddedness as it is conceived here can help to ensure accountability to communities of resistance with whom we share values, but how can we ensure our work remains accountable to anti-racist movements when our research is with those who hold competing values to our own? How can research undertaken with members of the far right maintain a commitment to working in service to racial justice? We would suggest here that even (or perhaps especially) for those who research far-right groups, there is a need to remain connected to, and embedded in, communities of resistance. Such grounding enables us as researchers to constantly keep in mind what it means to work in service to racial justice and can ensure that we remain accountable to those at the sharp end of racism. This is a particularly pressing issue for those researching the far right, as research has too often failed to engage with those on the sharp end of such politics, focusing instead on the perpetrators, at times giving them undue space.

In this particular context, and not to diminish the importance of striving for direct accountability, it may also be generative to think about accountability to *imagined communities of resistance* (Joseph-Salisbury and Connelly 2021). The diversity of work within far right and anti-racist studies necessitates a broader conceptualisation of accountability that extends beyond those with whom we have direct contact. It is in this vein that Busher (2021: 280) talks of employing an 'acid test' that considers how they would feel if they were reading their work out "in a room in which a significant minority of the audience were… people who have experienced fear or anxiety as a result of the actions of EDL activists". This accountability to an imagined community is essential. Whilst it requires some careful balancing alongside a "scholarly ethics of fairness" (Blee 2007: 125) in representing far-right participants, ultimately, we must remember "whose side we are on" (Becker 1967: 23). This requires a move away from flawed notions of neutrality and objectivity in research which imply that a researcher must remain 'in the middle', as if this middle ground was not a political construction itself. An expanded notion of community in *imagined communities of resistance* also attends to a particular challenge for those engaged in far right studies whereby directly engaging affected communities in research about the far right (in order to be accountable) could risk their (re)traumatisation. Lastly, this idea can better enable us to adopt an internationalist accountability that ties liberation struggles in the UK to those around the world. In this sense, accountability should not only be tied to the communities of resistance in which we organise but to the wider project of racial justice.

Conclusion

This chapter demonstrates that the notion of *working in service to racial justice* provides an anchoring, or orientation, that can guide anti-racist scholar-activists through ethically difficult terrains. This orientation implores reflexive researchers to ask a range of questions about their praxes, including those centred in this chapter around social usefulness and accountability. In terms of social usefulness, we might ask ourselves to whom is our work useful and how, as well as how our work might be (mis)used. We might also think about who we are accountable to, in what ways, and how our accountability might extend beyond those with whom we have direct contact. Although the in service to racial justice principle should be generative for all anti-racist scholars and particularly scholar-activists, this chapter pays particular attention to the implications the orientation has for those who research the far right. Though typically under-considered, such research is fraught with ethical difficulties and tensions, and this chapter is intended to offer a new lens through which to approach these challenges. More so, it urges researchers to push back against approaches within far right studies that risk amplifying and legitimising the far right by placing ourselves firmly on the side of communities of resistance and racial justice more broadly.

Notes

1 These radical and structurally focused understandings of racism are central to the praxis of anti-racist scholar-activism and to the working in service orientation we advance in this chapter.

2 We take this term from Sivanandan to refer to the powerful anti-racist collectives and coalitions that were/are driven by the interests of racially minoritised communities, historically under the banner of political blackness (see Sivanandan 2019; Virdee 2014).

3 Important though this may be, there may be questions to be asked in the far right studies field, with regard to how much energy is spent talking to the far right in comparison to how much time is spent talking to those minoritised communities negatively affected by the far right.

References

Ashe, S. 2020. 'Whiteness, Class and the "Communicative Community"'. In: Ashe, S., Busher, J., Macklin, G., and Winter, A. (eds). *Researching the Far Right*. London: Routledge, 284–306.

Ashe, S., Busher, J., Macklin, G., and Winter, A. 2020. 'Introduction'. In: Ashe, S., Busher, J., Macklin, G., and Winter, A. (eds). *Researching the Far Right*. London: Routledge, 1–14.

Back, L. 2002. 'Guess Who's Coming to Dinner? The Political Morality of Investigating Whiteness in the Gray Zone'. In: Ware, V. and Back, L. (eds). *Out of Whiteness: Color, Politics and Culture*. Chicago, IL: University of Chicago Press.

Becker, H. S. 1967. 'Whose Side Are We On?', *Social Problems*, 14(3), 239–247.

Begum, N., Mondon, A. and Winter, A. 2021. 'Between the "Left Behind" and "the People": Racism, Populism and the Construction of the "White Working Class" in the Context of Brexit'. In: Hunter, S. and van der Westhuizen, C. (eds). *Routledge Handbook of Critical Whiteness Studies*. London: Routledge.

Bhambra, G. 2017. 'Brexit, Trump, and "Methodological Whiteness": On the Misrecognition of Race and Class', *British Journal of Sociology: Special Issue on the Trump/Brexit Moment: Causes and Consequences*, 68(S1), S214–S232.

Blee, K. 2007. 'Ethnographies of the Far Right', *Journal of Contemporary Ethnography*, 36(2), 119–128.

Brown, K., Mondon, A., and Winter, A. 2021. 'The Far Right, the Mainstream and Mainstreaming: Towards a Heuristic Framework', *Journal of Political Ideologies*, 1–18.

Busher, J. 2021. 'Negotiating Ethical Dilemmas during an Ethnographic Study of Anti-Minority Activism: A Personal Reflection on the Adoption of a "Non-Dehumanization" Principle'. In: Ashe, S., Busher, J., Macklin, G., and Winter, A. (eds). *Researching the Far Right: Theory, Method and Practice*. London: Routledge, 270–283.

Collins, P. H. 2012. 'Looking Back, Moving Ahead: Scholarship in Service to Social Justice', *Gender and Society*, 26(1), 14–22.

Collins, P. H. 2013. *On Intellectual Activism*. Philadelphia, PA: Temple University Press.

Dorling, D. 2016. 'Brexit: The Decision of a Divided Country', *BMJ*, 354. doi:10.1136/bmj.i3697

Fekete, L. 2021. 'S1/E1 Liz Fekete: A Brief History of the Institute of Race Relations'. In: Lewis, C. and Regis, T. *Surviving Society* Podcast, 8 March. https://soundcloud .com/user-622675754/s1e1-liz-fekete-a-brief-hsitory-of-the-institute-of-race -relations (accessed 12 October 2023).

Johnson, R. 1993. '"Really Useful Knowledge": 1790–1850'. In: Edwards, R., Hanson, A., and Thorpe, M. (eds). *Culture and Processes of Adult Learning*. London: Routledge, 17–29.

Joseph-Salisbury, R. 2018. 'Confronting My Duty as an Academic: We Should All Be Activists'. In: Johnson, A., Joseph-Salisbury, R., and Kamunge, B. (eds). *The Fire Now: Anti-Racist Scholarship in Times of Explicit Racial Violence*. London: Zed, 44–55.

Joseph-Salisbury, R. and Connelly, L. 2021. *Anti-Racist Scholar-Activism*. Manchester: Manchester University Press.

la paperson. 2017. *A Third University Is Possible*. Minneapolis, MN: University of Minnesota Press.

Lentin, A. 2016. 'Racism in Public or Public Racism: Doing Anti-Racism in "Post-Racial" Times', *Ethnic and Racial Studies*, 39(1), 33–48.

Lentin, A. 2020. *Why Race Still Matters*. Cambridge: Polity Press.

Mondon, A. 2013. *A Populist Hegemony? Mainstreaming the Extreme Right in France and Australia*. Farnham: Ashgate.

Mondon, A. and Winter, A. 2018. 'Whiteness, Populism and the Racialisation of the Working-Class in the United Kingdom and the United States'. *Identities: Global Studies in Culture and Power*, 26(5), 510–528.

Mondon, A. and Winter, A. 2020. *Reactionary Democracy: How Racism and the Populist Far Right Became Mainstream*. London: Verso.

Mondon, A. and Winter, A. 2021. 'From Demonization to Normalization: Reflecting on Far Right Research'. In: Ashe, S., Busher, J., Macklin, G., and Winter, A. (eds). *Researching the Far Right*. London: Routledge.

Osuna, S. 2017. 'Class Suicide: The Black Radical Tradition, Radical Scholarship, and the Neoliberal Turn'. In: Johnson, G. T. and Lubin, A. (eds). *Futures of Black Radicalism*. London: Verso. 10–21.

Rodney, W. 2019. *The Groundings with My Brothers*. London: Verso.

Sivanandan, A. 2008a. 'Race and Resistance: The IRR Story', *Race & Class*, 50(2), 1–30.

Sivanandan, A. 2008b. 'Catching History on the Wing', Institute of Race Relations, 50th Anniversary Conference.

Sivanandan, A. 2019. *Communities of Resistance: Writings of Black Struggles for Socialism*. London: Verso.

Smith, L. T. 2012. *Decolonizing Methodologies*, 2nd ed. London: Zed.

Virdee, S. 2014. *Race, Class and the Racialised Outsider*. Basingstoke: Palgrave.

Webb, D. 2018. 'Bolt-Holes and Breathing Spaces in the System: On Forms of Academic Resistance (or, Can the University Be a Site of Utopian Possibility?)', *The Review of Education, Pedagogy and Cultural Studies*, 40(2), 96–118.

Zuberi, T. and Bonilla-Silva, E. 2008. *White Logic, White Methods: Racism and Methodology*. Lanham, MD: Rowman & Littlefield.

30

The far right from the underside of history: decolonising far right studies

Isis Giraldo

In February 2000, 450 paramilitary troops from the powerful Autodefensas Unidas de Colombia (AUC) perpetrated a massacre that can be described as one of "the most horrifying in a country that has made of horror a historical fixture of hyperbolic excess" (Giraldo 2021).[1] While the murder spree had started on 16 February en route towards El Salado (a town whose inhabitants had been accused of siding with guerrillas), it was really on 18 February that the 'Feast of Blood' (Ruíz 2008) began. On that day, heavily armed troops entered the village from three different directions. Shouting and kicking doors down, they forced the inhabitants who had been unable to flee the previous day out of their homes. They gathered them in the town's main square, separated women, men, and children, and after having designated a team of women to cook for them during their occupation, dragged a young man towards the middle of the square. They covered his head with a plastic bag, cut one of his ears, and battered him as he screamed and pleaded with them to spare his life. While kicking him, they warned their forced audience to witness their eventual fate if they did not give them the information about the guerrillas they were looking for. This information the inhabitants did not have.

Once the killing was accomplished, the troops who had previously taken drums, accordions, and bagpipes from the Casa de la Cultura started to play them as if they were at a party. The surviving victims described how the paramilitaries kept torturing and killing men (twenty-three in total) and women (five in total) – many of whom were selected by drawing lots – and playing music. They also reported that it was unequivocal that the perpetrators, who competed among themselves to carry out the killings and sang songs after each one of them, took a lot of pleasure in their cruelty (CNMH 2009: 127). The outcome of the massacre was fifty-nine cruelly murdered people (aged seven to sixty-seven), around 4,000 forcibly displaced, and two women raped (CNMH 2009: 42).

By the time of the events in El Salado, paramilitary organisations had already been established in Colombia as key violent actors against certain sectors of civil society: black, indigenous, and mestizo rural communities and peasants; human rights defenders; trade unionists; and left-wing militants. They had already been identified as key producers of what Ulrich Oslender (2008) denotes as 'geographies of terror'. Indeed, during the peak period of their rising and expansion as the AUC (the 1990s), they were the main perpetrators of massacres, selective killings, and forced displacement and were associated in the Colombian imaginary with extremely cruel actions – throat-cutting, dismemberment, decapitation, evisceration, incineration, castration, burning with acids or blowtorches, rape – and weapons of torture, including chainsaws and machetes (CNMH 2013: 55).

Yet, merely ten days after El Salado, Carlos Castaño, AUC's top leader, was offered a one-hour-long interview on Caracol – one of the two national TV channels – by Darío Arizmendi, then one of the most powerful journalists in Colombia. The interview was a golden opportunity for Castaño to invite himself into every household with the aim, as Estrada Gallego (2001: 43) suggests, of seeking support for his actions and organisation. Dressed in a grey suit and having crafted his performance as a first-person account where he was the protagonist, Castaño appears as a very normal middle-class man who shares the wider values of urban Colombian society, embodies middle-class dominant masculinity (firm, polite, and paternalistic) and loves country and family.[2] Both the interview and the TV channel became the platform for Castaño to, first, reaffirm the lies upon which the paramilitaries – with the help of the regular Army – had justified their terror campaign in rural Colombia, namely that rural communities and peasants were "virtual guerrillas" and, second, make a case for presenting the AUC as the "armed wing of the middle classes" (Caracol Televisión 2000a; Caracol Televisión 2000b). According to the national newspaper *El Tiempo* (2000), which published an editorial commenting on the interview, this last point was indeed Castaño's "strongest feature" because it furnished those classes' support.

Castaño's appearance on national television furthered the mainstreaming of far-right ideology in Colombia, a process whose origin can be traced back to the establishment of the Republic in the early nineteenth century (see Giraldo n.d.). It opened the path for the election of Álvaro Uribe Vélez in 2002 and his re-election in 2006 with a programme focused on "a crackdown on guerrillas" (Rojas 2009) that facilitated, between 2002 and 2008, the murder by the regular Army of at least 6,402 particularly vulnerable civilians, the "disposable persons" (*los desechables*, the slang term in Colombia to refer to homeless people), in the name of the security of the "fine citizens" (*los ciudadanos de bien*, a very common term in the Colombian context that was heavily deployed by Uribe before, during, and after his two mandates) (Giraldo 2021: 67).[3] By 2010, when Uribe left the presidency with historically high approval ratings, the *Falsos Positivos*

– as these crimes are known in Colombia – were already, albeit not at their actual colossal scale, widely known.

By all standards – particularly under Uribe, who took the elitist defence of capital accumulation and inequality by violent means to new heights – Colombia has been an exemplary model for the implementation of 'far-right' policies within a (formally) stable liberal democratic framework.[4] Yet the very term 'far right' has been conspicuously absent in predominant discourse on Colombia both at home and abroad. This has brought dreadful consequences for large swathes of the Colombian population and for global environmental justice. Regarding the ethics of researching the far right, the paucity of works on the far rightness of successive Colombian governments, for decades on end, has arguably had calamitous effects.[5] In this piece, I aim to bridge this gap. Further, I aim to contribute to research on the far right by taking as a point of departure a case from the margins to outline a critique of the dominant framework. Put otherwise: the piece aims to approach the far right from the 'underside of history' and thus destabilise the usual logics of knowledge production.[6] This is important both for ethical reasons (particularly regarding rural Colombia) and for political ones (in Colombia and beyond). My argument is that the mainstream liberal framework to address the 'far right' has had two nefarious effects in ethico-political terms. First, it has helped euphemising and, therefore, downplaying and naturalising Colombia's far rightness. Second, it has buttressed some of the myths upon which contemporary far-right blocs in Europe and the US justify their existence, politics, and strategies.

There is no universally agreed-upon definition of the far right. Even worse, other expressions such as 'radical right' (Bell 2002), 'extreme right' (Hainsworth 2008), 'populist radical right' (Mudde 2017), 'religious right' (Cowan 2021), and 'alt-right' (Wendling 2018) are used somewhat interchangeably, although the latter is tied to the specific context of the contemporary US.[7] While there might be agreement over issues scholars often identify with far-right ideology, movements, and parties, there is no agreement regarding how to name such issues. Yet, and as I claim the Colombian case also exemplifies, attending to ethical considerations in the study of the far right requires stripping the mainstream scholarly terminology of pervading euphemisms. Deploying an intently *de*-euphemised glossary, I identify as some of the issues present in far-right ideologies the following: hostility to any form of democracy and a preference for totalitarianism and highly stratified societies along every social category; ethnonationalism; white supremacy; Judeophobia;[8] Islamophobia; authoritarianism; religious fundamentalism(s); denialism regarding the relationship between capitalism and environmental collapse; the deployment of 'the people' exclusively as a rhetorical device; and a fierce defence of colonialism and lost empires.

Although these depend on time and place, strong opposition to equality – even in its 1789 restricted understanding which excluded colonised and enslaved people – is the common thread. The year 1789 is in fact a key point of reference in dominant approaches to the far right because the very term 'right' refers to the spatial organisation of the 1789 French Constituent Assembly where those supporting the *ancien régime* and against the Revolution were located at the furthest end of the president's right (Camus and Lebourg 2015: 8). Hence, the study of the 'far right' (and the 'right' for that matter) remains anchored within a self-centred European history that takes the French Revolution and its resistance to it by the counter-revolutionary bloc as a foundational moment. Unsurprisingly, scholarly approaches to the far right are anchored within a liberal framework inspired by the Enlightenment whose drawbacks, apart from its being Western-centred, include that it is usually tepid in its critique of capitalism; is "obsessed with an ill-defined 'populism' – in turn perceived as the most immediate danger to democracy itself understood solely through a liberal lens" (Giraldo 2022b: 49); and uncritically deploys terms – e.g. 'nativism' instead of 'settler colonialism', 'populism'/'national populism' instead of 'ethnonationalism' or 'white supremacy' – that have been coined by far-right movements themselves in their struggle to control the narrative and which contribute to falsify history, on the one hand, and feed the myths upon which the far right builds its ideology, on the other.

The case of Colombia is complex because it has historically combined both integral Catholic[9] and secular anti-egalitarianism – which has produced a highly hierarchised society (see Giraldo 2022a); authoritarianism; myriad manifestations of political violence; aggressive capitalism; developmentalism and extractivism; and simultaneous colonialism (land-grabbing and forced displacement) and coloniality (Giraldo 2021; Giraldo n.d.).[10]

This has been enforced for such a long time and through so many means that for a large proportion of the urban social body, it constitutes *the natural* way of governing/being governed.[11] Because of its colonial history, Colombia has been profoundly marked by the French Revolution and the reaction to it given that a great many nineteenth-century high-profile intellectuals – including classical scholar Miguel Antonio Caro, a Catholic integralist whose role was paramount in the writing of the 1886 Constitution that remained in place until 1991 – belonged to the European counter-revolutionary politico-religious current of thought. Indeed, the establishment of the Colombian Republic in 1810 and upon Independence from the Spanish Crown entailed a constant intense power struggle between the counter-revolutionary and Catholic integralist conservative branch and the Enlightenment-inspired liberal one for the most part of the nineteenth century and half of the twentieth. This struggle emerged with particular violence: the Thousand Days

War (1899–1902) and the period of La Violencia (1946–1966) were both bloody conflicts around partisan loyalties and in which approaches to the state, itself a European construct, were also key.[12] Besides this historical inter-party political violence over the state (particularly its relationship with the Catholic religion and the question of liberal law), succeeding governments have also unleashed state and parastate violence against the dozens of indigenous, black, and *mestizo* peasant communities that live in and defend diverse modes of social organisation – many of which are non-liberal (yet not illiberal), non-modern (yet not premodern), and at odds with capitalism and developmentalism.

Recentring the Colombian case within dominant scholarship on the far right is important because it renders explicit what appears rather implicitly in far-right ideology in other contexts, particularly those with Catholic/ Christian traditions. First is elitism (not 'populism'), which emerges as the favouring of capital accumulation and exploitation (of resources, earth, and labour) on the one hand and of stark inequalities along every possible axis on the other. Second is an understanding of democracy solely in its 'liberal' declination, i.e. as being inexorably linked to capitalism (as a mode of production and social organisation) and neoliberalism (as a 'political rationality' (Brown 2006)). Such an understanding denies the very possibility of more communal-based and non-Western democratic practices (see Rivera Cusicanqui 1990). Third is contemporary colonialism via land grabbing and forced displacement for individual/corporative capital accumulation, which is enacted in the name of national economic growth and development. These three elements have operated in connection with and in complement to each other.

Elitism, not populism

Attaching the epithet 'populist' to 'right' or 'far-right' has been pivotal in helping dilute Colombian far-rightness, particularly under Uribe. As I show elsewhere (Giraldo 2021), the citizenry under his rule was organised according to an 'affective economy' (Ahmed 2004) in which the term *ciudadano de bien* (the 'fine citizen') was explicitly deployed to identify that portion of the social body that Uribe represented which in turn delimited those who were deserving of rights. The concept of the 'fine citizen' – projected in the national imaginary as encapsulating determination, success, innovation, and entrepreneurship (Giraldo n.d.) – stands in opposition to, first, the *populacho* ('the masses' or rather 'the rabble') and, second, the *terroristas*, i.e. those defending or claiming to defend the rights of the *populacho*. Human rights activists, social leaders, and left-wing politicians and intellectuals fall into the former category, guerrillas into the latter. Both were military targets. Instead of being populist and very much in full alignment with integral Catholicism (now also back in full force in Italy, while gathering strength in Spain and France), such a conception of the nation is overtly elitist.

Equating democracy with neoliberalism

It is elitism that has allowed for the aspiring and accomplished middle-class subjectivities to be delimited by a free-market and entrepreneurial logic and for the notions of productivity and profitability to be established as the key governance criteria. This, in turn, has impinged upon citizenship "by implicitly tying it to modernity-coloniality and its derivatives[,] capital, productivity, development" (Giraldo 2021: 74). Further, upon how democracy is understood, namely, on the basis of "an asymmetrical distribution of rights according to gendered[, racialised,] and classed notions of marketable entrepreneurship" (López-Pedreros 2019: 242). From this emerges a broad acceptance and justification of violence by the social body as an inevitable consequence of or as a means to an end: economic growth and capitalist expansion (Giraldo 2021). It is elitism in its articulation with neoliberalism that facilitated how a state crime as colossal and horrific as the *Falsos Positivos*, as I claim elsewhere (Giraldo 2021), was read by an enormous proportion of the Colombian urban social body as being insignificant: those who were murdered were not perceived by those inhabiting or wishing to inhabit the category of the *fine citizen* as having the right to claim rights, which is how Hannah Arendt defines citizenship (Arendt 1949: 296, cited in Rojas 2009: 229).

Contemporary (post-independence) colonialism

The third element – contemporary colonialism – has been in fact at the heart of the formation and expansion of Colombian paramilitary organisations which were originally created by rural elites to defend their privileges and became the main actors in "a large scale land grabbing process that merits the qualification of 'agrarian counter-reform'" (Grajales 2011: 771). For this process to work, paramilitary organisations have relied, firstly, on violence – to grab the land of peasants – and, secondly, a large social network composed of elected officials and public servants – to convert the land grabbed into legitimate property (Grajales 2011: 772). This means that the violent role of paramilitary organisations in Colombia needs to be understood not as is usually the case in dominant approaches to the question, i.e. as organisations that proliferate thanks to the weakness of the state, but, as Jacobo Grajales has proposed, as a key component of a capitalist state formation that follows the "logics of competition, accumulation and economic development" (Grajales 2011: 774). Although on the surface the Colombian case might appear as a particular one not permitting generalisation, a closer look sheds light on larger drawbacks of the mainstream terminology and scholarly approach to the far right, even in the context of the global North. A major one is 'populism'. It is true that recent far-right political projects, parties, and leaders in Europe and the US have not been as overtly elitist as Colombia's Uribe. Further, they have explicitly mobilised the trope of 'the people' which stands in opposition to 'the elite' and which is supposed to refer to those large majorities that have been – so the narrative goes – *left behind* by the promises of neoliberal globalisation. However, the trope of the people as it is deployed by such political actors is implicitly (yet patently) grounded on a conception of the 'nation' that is white and excludes the non-white citizens belonging to such societies (racially diverse partly because of their respective colonial histories). Yet the actual evidence tells a different story: the success of far-right projects (e.g. Brexit in the UK) or politicians (e.g. Donald Trump in the US) was not due to the massive mobilisation of 'the people' – in the sense of working-class masses – but of white middle-class blocs (Bhambra 2017: 216–217). Sidestepping these crucial details translates into aligning the analytical framework to address the far right with the political vision and mission of its object of study. When it comes to naming, conceptualising, and analysing what is at stake with regard to the far right in certain contexts, the term 'ethnonationalism' – which in Europe and the US actually emerges as 'white supremacy' – is more technically precise (let alone evidence-based) than the widely disseminated 'populism' or 'national populism', both of which actually work as euphemisms that favour the far right.

The same goes for the deployment of 'nativism' whose problem is that it panders to the myths upon which far-right blocs justify their political engagements. This is extremely problematic because the wider success of these blocs is contingent upon revised history. Although not explicitly employed in the specific case of Colombia, the term 'nativism' still outlines two important elements in Colombia and beyond: colonialism (key for capital accumulation and developmentalism) and historical revisionism (key for the control of the narrative and the legitimation of violence against certain groups). In the specific case of settler colonial contexts, the 'nativist' claim to the land erases the incontestable historical fact that the *actual natives* are non-white and those carrying out the displacement are the white settlers. Making 'nativism' a key concept of the analytical framework of the far right occludes this. Moreover, it reinforces the blatant lie upon which false theories, such as 'The Great Replacement', are based. The scholarly deployment of 'nativism' – particularly in the context of settler colonial states – can be read as an instance of what Gurminder K. Bhambra has termed "methodological whiteness": where "data and arguments are [...] distorted to support a particular narrative of the exceptional distress of [the white population] that is not borne out by the evidence" (2017: 226). This takes the argument back to the drawbacks of the liberal framework inherent to the mainstream scholarly approach to the far right I have been addressing. This framework is, firstly, Eurocentric, so it takes whiteness (and Christianity) as its baseline. Secondly, it is the offspring of the Enlightenment. Accordingly, it assumes a disembodied subject of knowledge that locates itself at the 'point zero' (Castro-Gómez 2010) of knowledge production and misguidedly presumes itself as *objective* and *race blind*. This is key because occluding how the relations of domination on the basis of race that were established in the past – via colonial enterprises – have been fundamental in configuring the world as we know it today both perpetuates "the coloniality of power" (Quijano 2000) and produces analytically flawed, empirically unsustainable, and politically questionable scholarly work.

Notes

1 The late-twentieth-century Colombian paramilitary organisations are armed groups that were "created and funded by wealthy sectors of society" with the aim of eliminating and neutralising anyone threatening or hindering the "interests of those with economic and political power" (Hristov 2014). They have been militarily and logistically supported by the state (see Avilés 2006) and are part and parcel of the Colombian political struggle rather than extraneous to it (Grajales 2011: 773). Furthermore, they "are the complex result of the confluence of a great variety of actors, such as landholders, drug smugglers, and army officers" (Grajales 2011: 773). The AUC were created in 1997, under the leadership of Carlos Castaño, as an overarching organisation unifying a number of already existing paramilitary organisations.

2 It is worth noting that an equivalent of Castaño's interview would have been unimaginable with a leader of any guerrilla organisation, whose cruel actions, as evidence has unmistakably shown, paled in contrast with those of paramilitaries.

3 As Governor of Antioquia County in the 1990s, Uribe had arguably institutionalised paramilitarism via the legal implementation of groups of armed civilians created with a "defensive function" aimed at "supporting the armed forces with intelligence about local communities" (Avilés 2006: 398). For updates on

the most recent balance of total number of victims in this specific case, see JEP (2021).

4 Colombia's is in fact the longest democracy in Latin America.

5 Uribe's gathered and maintained support in Colombia and abroad by means of continuous and intense marketing campaigns (in which euphemisms played a primary role) during and in the aftermath of his presidency. In 2011, for instance, he was invited to the London School of Economics to give a talk titled 'The three pillars of Colombia's recent progress' (Uribe Vélez 2011). These 'pillars', presented in the language of liberal democracy, are the elements I identify here as being key to far-right ideology.

6 The expression 'the underside of history' belongs with the language developed by the thoroughly anti-capitalist and anti-imperialist Theology of Liberation that emerged in the 1970s in Latin America (see Mendieta 2020).

7 'Radical right' is also more common in the US context, however, "within Europe, distinctions have been made between the extreme and radical rights" (Hainsworth 2008: 8). See Paul Hainsworth (2008) for a definitional groundwork on the terms 'extreme right' and 'extreme rightism'.

8 Following Shlomo Sand, I prefer 'Judeophobia' over 'antisemitism' (see Sand 2018: 35).

9 Integral Catholicism is an all-comprising politico-theological doctrine that rests on the notion of natural order that in turn determines social order: social functions and stations are divinely predetermined and immutable (see Camus and Lebourg 2015: 10).

10 'Coloniality' refers to "the invisible threads of power that emerge in colonial situations but extend well beyond a strictly colonial setting and period" (Giraldo 2016). In other words, coloniality is the logic while colonialism the enactment (Mignolo 2011: 22).

11 It is important to make the distinction between the hegemonic Colombian nation-state, on the one hand, and the heterogeneous peoples that inhabit the vast territory and hold Colombian citizenship yet do not recognise themselves as part of the hegemonic idea of the Colombian nation. Rural populations have been and continue to be extraordinarily large. After the Second World War, for instance, about "three fourths of the population was composed of peasants" (Sánchez 1992), which is why the issue of the agrarian reform was pivotal in the conflict.

12 Independence from Spain gave birth to the Republic of New Granada which included present-day Venezuela, Ecuador, and Panama. The two former became independent states in 1830, while Panama did so in 1903. There is considerable debate on the dating of the period known as La Violencia from which the late FARC emerged in 1964.

References

Ahmed, S. 2004. 'Affective Economies', *Social Text*, 22.2(79), 117–139.

Arendt, H. 1949. *The Origins of Totalitarianism*. London: Penguin.

Avilés, W. 2006. 'Paramilitarism and Colombia's Low-Intensity Democracy', *Journal of Latin American Studies*, 38(2), 379–408.

Bell, D. (ed.). 2002. *The Radical Right*. New York and London: Routledge.

Bhambra, G. K. 2017. 'Brexit, Trump, and "Methodological Whiteness": On the Misrecognition of Race and Class', *The British Journal of Sociology*, 68 Supplement 1, S214–S232.

Brown, W. 2006. 'American Nightmare: Neoliberalism, Neoconservatism, and De-Democratization', *Political Theory*, 34(6), 690–714.

Camus, J. Y. and Lebourg, N. 2015. *Les droites extrêmes en Europe*. Paris: Seuil.

Caracol Televisión. 2000a. *Cara a Cara con Carlos Castaño (Parte I)*. 1 March. https://www.youtube.com/watch?v=FtISPNDRVYI (accessed 30 October 2023).

Caracol Televisión. 2000b. *Cara a Cara con Carlos Castaño (Parte II)*. 1 March. https://www.youtube.com/watch?v=Cc7wrFDiHh0 (accessed 30 October 2023).

Castro-Gómez, S. 2010. *La Hybris del Punto Cero. Ciencia, raza e ilustración en la Nueva Granada (1750–1816)*. Bogotá: Editorial Pontificia Universidad Javeriana.

CNMH. 2009. *La masacre de El Salado: Esa guerra no era nuestra*. Bogotá: Centro Nacional de Memoria Histórica.

CNMH. 2013. *¡Basta Ya! Colombia memorias de guerra y dignidad*. Bogotá: Centro Nacional de Memoria Histórica.

Cowan, Benjamin A. 2021. *Moral Majorities across the Americas: Brazil, the United States, and the Creation of the Religious Right*. Chapel Hill, NC: The University of North Carolina Press.

El Tiempo. 2000. 'El rostro de Carlos Castaño'. 5 March. https:/www.eltiempo.com /archivo/documento/MAM-1304335 (accessed 27 March 2023).

Estrada Gallego, F. 2001. 'La retórica del paramilitarismo. Análisis del discurso en el conflicto armado', *Análisis Político*, 44, 39–57.

Giraldo, I. 2016. 'Coloniality at Work: Decolonial Critique and the Postfeminist Regime', *Feminist Theory*, 17(2), 157–173.

Giraldo, I. 2021. '"Pedagogies of Cruelty", Masculinity, and the Patriarchal Order of the Colombian Nation-State: The Falsos Positivos as a Paradigmatic Example', *Postcolonial Studies*, 24(1), 63–81.

Giraldo, I. 2022a. 'SoHo as "Virtual Theatre": Performing Gender, Class, and Race in 21st-Century Urban Colombia', *Cultural Studies*, 36(1), 41–73.

Giraldo, I. 2022b. 'The Weaponization of "Gender" beyond Gender: The Entrenchment of "Coloniality of Power" and "Pedagogies of Cruelty"'. In: Burke, P. J. et al. (eds) *Gender in an Era of Post-Truth Populism: Pedagogies, Challenges and Strategies*. London: Bloomsbury, 43–63.

Giraldo, I. n.d. *Regimes of Colombianidad: Beauty, Citizenship, and Sex*. Work in progress.

Grajales, J. 2011. *The Journal of Peasant Studies*, 38(4), 771–792.

Hainsworth, P. 2008. *The Extreme Right in Western Europe*. Abingdon: Routledge.

Hristov, J. 2014. *Paramilitarism and Neoliberalism: Violent Systems of Capital Accumulation in Colombia and Beyond*. London: Pluto Press.

JEP. 2021. *La JEP hace pública la estrategia de priorización dentro del Caso 03, conocido como el de falsos positivos*. Bogotá: Jurisdicción Especial para la Paz.

López-Pedreros, A. R. 2019. *Makers of Democracy: A Transnational History of the Middle Classes in Colombia*. Durham, NC and London: Duke University Press.

Mendieta, E. 2020. 'Philosophy of Liberation'. In: Zalta, E. N. (ed.). *The Stanford Encyclopedia of Philosophy*. Winter 2020. Metaphysics Research Lab, Stanford University. https://plato.stanford.edu/entries/liberation/ (accessed 30 October 2023).

Mignolo, W. 2011. *The Darker Side of Western Modernity: Global Futures, Decolonial Options*. Durham, NC and London: Duke University Press.

Mudde, C. (ed.). 2017. *The Populist Radical Right*. London and New York: Routledge.

Oslender, U. 2008. 'Another History of Violence: The Production of "Geographies of Terror" in Colombia's Pacific Coast Region', *Latin American Perspectives*, 35(5), 77–102.

Quijano, A. 2000. 'Colonialidad del poder, eurocentrismo y América Latina'. In: Lander, E. (ed.). *La colonialidad del saber: Eurocentrismo y ciencias sociales. Perspectivas Latinoamericanas*. Buenos Aires: CLACSO, 201–246.

Rivera Cusicanqui, S. 1990. 'Liberal Democracy and *Ayllu* Democracy in Bolivia: The Case of Northern Potosí', *The Journal of Development Studies*, 26(4), 97–121.

Rojas, C. 2009. 'Securing the State and Developing Social Insecurities: The Securitisation of Citizenship in Contemporary Colombia', *Third World Quarterly*, 30(1), 227–245.

Ruíz, M. 2008. *Fiesta de sangre: Así fue la masacre de El Salado*. La Semana. 30 August. https://www.semana.com/nacion/articulo/masacre-de-el-salado-como-la-planearon-y-ejecutaron-los-paramilitares/557580 (accessed 30 October 2023).

Sánchez, G. 1992. 'The Violence: An Interpretative Synthesis'. In: Bergquist, C., Peñaranda, R., and Sánchez, G. *Violence in Colombia: The Contemporary Crisis in Historical Perspective*. Wilmington, DE: SR Books.

Sand, S. 2018. *The End of the French Intellectual: From Zola to Houellebecq*. Trans. by David Fernbach. London and New York: Verso.

Uribe Vélez, Á. 2011. *The Three Pillars of Colombia's Recent Progress*. LSE Podcasts. https://soundcloud.com/lsepodcasts/the-three-pillars-of-colombias (accessed 30 October 2023).

Wendling, M. 2018. *Alt-Right: From 4chan to the White House*. London: Pluto Press.

31

How should journalists engage
with the far right?

Gary Younge

My first 'job' in journalism was as an intern on an international magazine programme, broadcast on Channel Four, where I was hired because I spoke several foreign languages. In that capacity I was asked, by the director, to call the far-right Front National (FN) in France and invite then-leader Jean-Marie Le Pen on the show. I refused.

I had two main reasons. The first was journalistic. At the time, the FN had about 12 per cent of the vote and no seats in the legislature. We had the whole world to choose from. Why bother with them?

The second was moral. The media, I felt, should not smooth the path of the far right to respectability by giving them a platform and treating them like everyone else. The prospect of creating a spectacle, which in turn attracts viewers and clicks, should not override an ethical responsibility to avoid spreading hate speech and offensive propaganda. I did not make the call – it was too early in my career (literally the last day of my probationary period) and too lowly a job to sacrifice a principle I held dear – and Le Pen did not come on the programme, though I doubt that was because of my refusal since I was too lowly an employee to stop anything from happening.

Twenty-four years later, as a much more experienced journalist, I interviewed the white supremacist and self-appointed American leader of the alt-right, Richard Spencer, for the same channel for a documentary called *Angry, White and American* on the roots of white anxiety in the US (Channel 4 2017a). The interview, which took place in a car park outside a white supremacist conference in Tennessee, started with me asking him why he'd want to live in a white ethno-state and ended with me walking away, after telling him: "I was looking for someone who could give me some intellectual ballast about what is going on in this country in terms of race and in terms of white people but I found the wrong guy, because you don't know what you're talking about." A clip of the interview in which he insists: "You will never be an Englishman" and I reply: "You don't get to tell me who I am" went viral on social media. At the time of writing, one version of it had been retweeted 21,200 times on Twitter and viewed 823,016 times on YouTube.

The aim here is not to justify either of those decisions but to examine the ethical risks inherent in both engaging and refusing to engage with the far right and weigh the political risks and journalistic challenges involved. Such an examination demands an assessment of the relative strength of the far-right forces being covered, the relative seniority of the subjects in question, the purpose of the coverage, and a relational appreciation of what constitutes the far right in any given moment. (The political spectrum is not static. Ronald Reagan was considered by many to be far right, but many of his policies – including amnesty for undocumented migrants and a top marginal tax bracket of 50 per cent – would now be read as liberal, particularly compared to Donald Trump.) While this assessment is essentially political, the methods employed should, at all times, adhere to the standard principles of responsible journalism – fairness, independence, a commitment to accuracy, and accountability.

The first thing to acknowledge is that the far right pose an ethical risk in journalism, even if journalists do not engage them. The function of journalism is to describe, explain, and reflect the world we live in and the far right have long been part of that world. Journalists could choose to ignore the far right completely – but to do so arguably involves even greater risk than engaging them in some way.

It is important to assert, at the outset, that with the possible exception of public sector broadcasters who are bound by certain rules around electoral representation, the media is not obliged to cover the far right. Since you can't cover everything, journalism involves choices. It is not a matter of censorship or 'cancel culture' if they refuse to cover them, any more than it would be if they failed to cover Trotskyists. There are any number of reasons at any given time why the media might decide not to cover the far right and, while those decisions should be subject to critique, they are not in themselves problematic. The far right is not entitled to the airwaves or the pages of newspapers.

That said, the decisions cannot simply be arbitrary. Just because you have the power to make a decision does not mean that others lack the agency to question it. Decisions to exclude or marginalise the far right that appear cavalier, precocious, or simply vindictive have the potential to backfire, providing more sympathy for the very people one might be seeking to alienate on the grounds that journalists are being unfair.

To ignore the far right, one would have to find some other explanation for organised racist violence, as well as other political violence against left opponents and minorities; for the myths, conspiracy theories, and prejudices that emerge from that part of the political spectrum; for the fear among minorities and progressives engendered by the presence of the far right; for the impact of the far right on the electoral programmes and rhetoric of the rest of the political culture. In short, one would have to imagine a world where the far right did not exist and then describe that world to readers and viewers. And since that world does not exist, one would have strayed, consciously and determinedly, into the world of fiction.

This is a particularly ineffective, and arguably counter-productive, approach at a time when, thanks to social media, organisations of the far right can create their own media ecosystems, offering their agenda unfiltered, without any context or correction. To simply ignore them would effectively allow their falsehoods and hate speech to go unchallenged in any meaningful way – because how can you effectively challenge a message when you have refused to acknowledge the messenger?

Another option would be not to ignore the far right but simply refuse to engage them directly in any way, relying instead on second-hand material from other sources. Journalists rely on secondary sources all the time, but generally not as a matter of principle but pragmatism concerning access, time, and space. To adopt this as a principle simply relies on someone else engaging with the far right, shifting the responsibility and risk to other entities. It also leaves the journalist at the mercy of someone else's lens. It basically commits the journalist or enterprise to coverage of the far right by hearsay.

The risk in either refusing to cover the far right at all, or covering it through an intermediary, is that the critical function of journalism is deliberately forgone, or undermined, in a critical field at a critical moment. For it is only through understanding the appeal of the far right that a society will be able to provide a politically effective counter to it. If one refuses to talk to anybody, how can we know what motivates their base, what strategies they employ, or what their trajectory might be? Understanding the Tea Party in the United States was crucial to understanding how and why Donald Trump could become president; understanding the surge of the British National Party during the noughties is essential to understanding how and why Britain voted to leave the European Union. Just because you pretend a storm isn't coming doesn't prevent the thunder and lightning; it just means you are not prepared when it arrives.

But engagement carries its own challenges. All journalistic encounters in some way involve a transactional bet. The journalist wants to talk to someone in the hope that they will tell them something; the interviewee wants to talk to the journalist in the hope that they will be able to amplify a point of view. There is no guarantee that either will get what they want. This transactional element is particularly explicit in politics, where the interviewee often has talking points and a media strategy.

So it should be clearly understood and conceded that when the media talk to the far right, even when they are arguing with them, it gives the far right the opportunity to put their case. My interview with Spencer, for example, gave him a platform to tell an international audience (the documentary was subsequently screened in Denmark and New Zealand and was made available on Amazon Prime) that Black people could not be British and that Africans, including enslaved people, benefitted from white supremacy. A great deal of political effort has gone into countering views like this over the years; one must question the sagacity of giving them space to a global audience even if they were instantly and vigorously contested.

Moreover, the more mainstream the outlet engaging the far right, the greater the opportunity the far right has to appear mainstream and respectable as opposed to extremist and anti-democratic. The desire to shed the image of street violence and bigotry and appear as just a more forthright and outspoken element of the establishment is a familiar electoral trajectory among the far right. Along with occasionally changing the name of the party, a process of prettification has eased the path for the far right to enter government in Italy, Austria, and Switzerland, become the main presidential contender in France, and ensure a significant and enduring presence in Belgium, Denmark, Germany, Norway, the Netherlands, and Sweden, among others. Over the last two decades, fascism has effectively returned as a mainstream ideology in Europe. With it has come an escalation in the physical attacks against minorities. Between 2000 and 2005 officially reported racist violence rose 71 per cent in Denmark, 34 per cent in France, and 21 per cent in Ireland. The media should question its role in that trend and ask itself if it wants to make it easier and faster than it has already been.

This was effectively the question asked by British anti-racists when the BBC decided to invite Nick Griffin, the leader of the British National Party, onto its flagship political debate panel show, *Question Time*. To convey such political real estate on Griffin, an open and unapologetic bigot, it was argued, endowed him with conventional respectability and gave his racist views an audience they would never have had otherwise while placing him on a par with other mainstream politicians. (I will return to this argument later.)

So if both engagement and non-engagement carry risk, the issue becomes how we weigh those risks. There is no definitive answer to that question since the risks are contingent on the balance of forces at any given moment as well as the medium and the precise nature of the journalism involved.

But some parameters can be drawn. A vital distinction should be made between followers of the far right and leaders of the far right. Those who are tempted by its message, who have been to rallies, who may even be card-carrying members but who hold no official positions and have no power or authority within the organisation should be held to a different ethical journalistic standard than those who are office bearers and party or movement leaders. The former offer insight into where and how the message of the far right lands, what they are looking for in it, and how it relates to their lives. They are political participants, but they are not politicians. They may spout talking points, but they do not write them. It is possible to listen to such people without indulging them and to question them without interrogating them; in fact, it is important to do so. This is all the more important because journalists are increasingly more likely to come from an elite background divorced from the worlds they are covering.

In the US, the median personal income is $41,353; 33 per cent of those over twenty-five have a bachelor's degree or higher (US Bureau of Labor Statistics 2022); racial minorities comprise 42 per cent of the population (US Census Bureau 2021) and 42 per cent of those who live in poverty. American journalists earn an average salary of $48,370 (US Bureau of Labor Statistics 2021); 17 per cent of newsroom staff are from minorities (Arana 2018); and 79 per cent have degrees (Pew Research Center 2018). So newsrooms are whiter, wealthier, and better educated than the population.

In Britain, a third of columnists went to private school and then either Oxford or Cambridge (compared to less than 1 per cent of the nation as a whole), which makes them more elite than the House of Lords. The news media in general is not much more representative, with 43 per cent going to private school and 36 per cent attending Oxford or Cambridge (The Sutton Trust 2019).

So the growing inequalities, pervasive in the West, are often amplified within the media which has left them ill-equipped to engage with both left and right populism over the last decade and more comfortable dismissing and deriding their subjects rather than attempting to understand them. This was as true in their coverage of UK Labour leader Jeremy Corbyn and US Democratic contender Bernie Sanders as it was of the Brexit campaign and Donald Trump supporters. It should come as little surprise that in many of these cases, their inability or unwillingness to show any curiosity about what these movements and moments represented trapped them in a fetid ecosystem which led to woeful misjudgements about the political dynamics at play.

For example, when reporting on the US election in 2016, I interviewed a range of Republicans in the small Indiana town of Muncie. During those interviews, it became very clear that they were well aware of his faults and actually agreed with many of the criticisms of him. They just loathed Hillary Clinton more. Each had their reasons. I questioned them and asked how they felt about the various things he'd said. But my job was not to argue with them but to try and fathom what motivated their support. At the time I wrote:

> More than 50 million people are likely to vote for Trump, even if he goes down in flames. It would be unhelpful to generalise about all of them, reducing them to caricature only to dismiss them. Something is happening here and it behoves people to try to understand it, whether or not they like it. From interviews with a range of Trump voters in Muncie, it's clear most are not blind to his flaws, even if they wouldn't necessarily describe them in the manner of his detractors. (Younge 2016)

This dislocation between journalists and the public was made painfully clear on the night before the 2017 general election in Britain when at 9.53 pm Twitter revealed that Piers Morgan's prediction was "Conservatives to win by 90–100 seat majority", while the *Sun*'s Steve Hawkes tweeted four minutes later "Rumour Tories could be looking at 400 seats" – only to learn from an exit poll a few minutes later that the country was on course for a hung Parliament. They just hadn't done the reporting to justify these predictions, instead working on the 'received wisdom' they had received from each other.

In this regard, it is important that the general principles of journalism are applied when talking to the far right. Interviewees should be treated with respect; they should not be wilfully misinterpreted, misled, ridiculed, lampooned, caricatured, or otherwise misrepresented. The journalist should avoid cliché and stereotype both in their choice of subject, location, and line of questioning. This too is an ethical matter. Journalistic work that disparages and misrepresents its subjects not only devalues their humanity but devalues the journalism itself.

The point here is not to give anyone a free ride. Quite the opposite. In fact, it is only by taking the followers of the far right seriously that it is possible to embark on some kind of understanding of where they are coming from and where they want to go. In this process the journalist may take the interviewee to task – but they may just let them speak (Younge and Topham 2020a). The object is to find out what they think, not win an argument.

In this context, there is nothing inherently unethical about not challenging a lie. An interview is not a debate. The question of why people think Barack Obama was not born in America, refugees and asylum seekers are receiving preferential treatment in housing and benefits, or halal food is now compulsory in school dinners is more revealing than arguing with them about whether those facts are true. When I have heard followers of the far right saying things that are untrue I have been more likely to ask "Where did you get that fact from?" "Why do you think that?" or "How do you know that's true?" than to assert "That's a lie" (Younge and Topham 2020b). The latter shuts down the conversation, whereas the questions get to the heart of their information sources, belief systems, and rumour mills.

Americans believe there are fifteen times as many Muslims in the US as there are; Poles believe there are thirty times more immigrants in Poland than there are; Italians believe there are more than thirty times as many teenage pregnancies as there are (Nardelli and Arnett 2014). These misconceptions come from somewhere. It is not just useful and interesting but important to know where and why people believe things that are untrue. In my experience, you don't get there by telling them they are wrong.

There's also nothing unethical about not challenging open bigotry in an interview setting. When interviewing far-right devotees and other problematic characters, I constantly remind myself that they are not my friends. This is not a conversation, it's an interview. While it is difficult to hear personally, the interview is not being conducted in a personal capacity. While investigating the roots of Obamaphobia in late 2009 for the BBC World Service, one McCain voter told me: "I've voted for the American. At least he's a white guy" (Younge 2011). Up until that point there had only been people saying racism was a factor in Obama's unpopularity. It was useful to have someone say it. I felt it didn't need challenging. It spoke for itself.

Television has to play by different rules. Whereas in print, you can insert the correct figure (perhaps with a link for sourcing), falsehoods on television, whenever possible, should be corrected in real time. But even then it is possible to challenge with a less combative: "The number I have heard is closer to x, where did you get your number from" rather than "that's a lie". During *Angry, White, and American*, one interviewee claimed that the Ku Klux Klan were liberal Democrats and that Robert E. Lee did not own slaves. I contested the Ku Klux Klan claim with a joke ("Well they hung black people from trees so they couldn't be that liberal") while my verbal questioning about Robert E. Lee was edited out leaving just a quizzical expression. I dealt with both statements in the voiceover. "I liked Jean. The trouble is what she said simply wasn't true. Lee did own slaves; the Klan weren't liberal. Facts matter." This then provoked a spirited back and forth with the lawyer who questioned whether the interviewee had the right to reply. I argued that she did in real time and if we didn't include the voiceover we couldn't include the statements since they were untrue. Ultimately, on this point, I prevailed. But these are some of the challenges with television you don't have with print.

So there is significant room for manoeuvre with the followers of the far right. For the leaders, however, there must be different standards. As the architects of movements that peddle falsehoods, promote violence, and violate democratic norms, the issue of whether, how, and why to interview them becomes particularly acute.

They are not regular politicians. Violence is central to their method; exclusion is central to their meaning. How we engage them – and why – is an issue of political morality. This is an imperative that sits uneasily with flaccid notions of journalistic objectivity, in which those views that make it through the filter are considered equal, regardless of their factual or moral integrity. "On the one hand, on the other hand" doesn't work here: you can't weigh genocide against relatively stable democracy as though any reasonable person might disagree on the outcome.

In these moments – and with the rise of the far right across the Western world, there are many of them – the claim that journalists sit above society, as though in a hermetically sealed chamber, responsible only to their editors and 'the story', becomes increasingly thin. We have responsibilities, both professional and human, to resist the allure of spectacle. There is too much at stake.

The question of whether to interview them at all is, I believe, entirely dependent on their political strength. Five years before I refused to call the Front National, Jean-Marie Le Pen got only 14.39 per cent of the vote and came fourth in the first round of the presidential election. Two years after my refusal, he got 15 per cent and was still fourth. There was no good journalistic case for interviewing him. To give him a platform on an international news magazine programme would, I believed, elevate him beyond his actual news value, contribute to his normalisation, and effectively promote him unnecessarily.

Spencer, I believed, was different because he was embedded in the political world that was sustaining Trump. He coined the term 'alt right' – a synonym for the extreme right. Steve Bannon, Trump's chief strategist at the time of the interview, used to run *Breitbart News*, which he had boasted was a platform for the alt right. It felt as though these far-right ideas had travelled quite rapidly from the margins to the mainstream, and were infecting the US body politic at the highest level. If these people were, as they claimed, providing the intellectual underpinning for the Trump administration, then it seemed to me it is more dangerous to ignore them than engage and hopefully expose them – particularly in a documentary about the roots of white anxiety. Three weeks after the interview, neo-Nazis and their fellow travellers, including Spencer, descended on Charlottesville, Virginia, leaving one dead and several injured as many chanted antisemitic and racist slogans. Donald Trump effectively defended them, drawing an equivalence between fascists and those fighting fascism and saying there were some 'very fine people' among the extreme right who marched that day.

Presented with the same choices in the current context, I think I would do the opposite. There would be a strong case for interviewing the leader of the Front National (now the Rassemblement National), Marine Le Pen (Jean-Marie's daughter), who has now twice got through to the presidential run-off and in 2022 gained 41.5 per cent of the vote and emerged as the third largest party in Parliament. They are no longer marginal, they have already been normalised by the electorate. They have influence and power, controlling around ten municipalities including the 120,000-strong population of Perpignan. As such it would be important to hold her and her party to account.

Herein lay the challenge with Griffin on *Question Time*. One might argue that the root of the problem was not that the BBC had put him on the programme but that voters had put him in a situation where it became difficult to keep him off it.

Spencer, on the other hand, has seen his organisation dissolved and has been crippled financially by legal rulings relating to the role he played in Charlottesville. Meanwhile, Trump is out of office and Bannon has been banished. The far right are still a significant presence in the US, but Spencer is no longer a meaningful participant in it (Williamson 2021). If I were doing the same documentary again, I would have to find someone else.

In short, I think the ethical justification of whether to engage far-right leadership should be judged by the proximity to power. The closer they are to power, the greater the case for engagement because it is important that they are held to account, challenged, and confronted publicly. The further they are from power, the weaker the case in terms of public interest and the greater the likelihood that engaging them will in fact offer them a means of amplification and respectability they did not have before.

The question of how to interview far-right leaders should start with the same premise as interviewing the followers. The basic principles of journalism still apply – interviewees should be asked relevant questions, given the chance to respond, and not be misrepresented. But none of that negates the necessity to confront, challenge, and, where possible, expose far-right leaders: in the absence of that there is really no justification for engaging them in the first place.

One good example of how not to do it (Younge 2017a) appeared in the *New York Times* a few weeks after my interview with Spencer, where reporter Richard Fausset (2017) profiled Tony Hovater, one of the founders of the white supremacist Traditionalist Worker Party, who was characterised as a "polite and low-key" "Nazi sympathiser next door". Fausset told us how Tony and his wife, Maria, registered for their wedding at Target. We learned that Tony likes *Seinfeld* and *King of the Hill*, that he described his time playing with a metal band over a turkey sandwich at Panera Bread, and that Maria wore a sleeveless jean jacket and ordered the boneless wings during an interview at Applebee's.

Given the tiny size of the TWP and the fact that it disbanded just a few months after the interview, there was a very weak case for doing the article anyway. But there was no excuse for doing it this badly. Its effect was not to expose the obscenity of their views (he thinks Hitler was "chill" about Slavs and gays, and considers the claim that six million Jews were slaughtered during World War II "overblown"; she's "pretty lined up" politically with him), but rather to underscore the normality of their existence. It offered this as a revelation, as though Hannah Arendt's coverage of Adolf Eichmann's trial never happened.

The idea that Nazis go shopping, watch television, and eat at chain restaurants shouldn't surprise us: they generally live 'next door' to someone. Fascism, as the British poet Michael Rosen pointed out, doesn't arrive in fancy dress. Fascists do not need horns and a trident, any more than the proud advocates of segregation sixty years ago were anything other than ordinary white Americans who felt their privilege being threatened.

Television once again presents different challenges. The choreography is important. I would not sit down with Spencer or shake his hand and would not engage in the kind of warm-up chit-chat I would normally do with an interviewee. (I have seen Louis Theroux be more cordial with white nationalists and still go on to do a good job.) Confrontations have to be immediate; abusive language and behaviour have to be called out immediately. The potential for escalation is considerable. They generally produce more heat than light, people talking over each other and shouting, as was the case with me and Spencer. The problematic gendering of these moments cannot be overlooked – the exchange between Spencer and me could effectively be reduced to two men shouting at each other in a car park.

The one approach that rarely, if ever, works on television is to aim to outsmart a far-right leader. That's not because they are necessarily smart, though some are, but because their intelligence is not the issue. Such an approach generally backfires because either the interviewee gets the better of the presenter – they are far more used to talking to mainstream journalists than mainstream journalists are at talking to them – or because the presenter comes across as a bullying clever dick abusing their position. Once again, interviews are not debates.

In any case, and this some journalists find difficult to accept, it's ultimately not about them. In the final analysis, the risk resides in whether, on balance, people who see or read the interview are more or less likely to identify with the views and personality of the far right.

There can, of course, be no definitive answer to that. With Spencer I thought it was telling that he did not circulate the video clip of the encounter himself, suggesting he was not happy with how it went. He also later claimed that he had somehow been tricked into doing the video, which is untrue – he just expected a white reporter.

But we don't know how and where these things land, how they might be used, by whom, and to what end. Nor does that assessment answer whether it was a risk worth taking.

The risk that by reporting the far right a journalist might give them the oxygen of publicity must be weighed against the risk that ignoring them will hamper our capacity to fathom their appeal. We need to understand where they're coming from, what motivates them, and what their strategies are. Ignoring organised bigotry doesn't make it go away. But the media should not smooth their path to respectability by giving them a platform they would otherwise not have and treating them like other politicians. Their politics of discrimination and scapegoating, often connected to violence, are antithetical to democratic norms and they should therefore not be normalised.

In weighing those risks (Younge 2017b) one must further assess the extent to which any coverage serves to publicise their agenda as opposed to exposing it and who gains and loses as a result of that coverage. It is occasionally only possible to assess the relative benefits and downsides of these competing risks by actually doing it. But it is important to understand the risks you are taking before you take them.

References

Arana, G. 2018. 'Decades of Failure', *Columbia Journalism Review*, Fall 2018. https://www.cjr.org/special_report/race-ethnicity-newsrooms-data.php (accessed 4 July 2022).

Channel 4. 2017a. *Angry, White and American*, 9 November. https://www.channel4 .com/programmes/angry-white-and-american (accessed 4 July 2022).

Channel 4. 2017b. 'On a Personal Journey across White America …', Twitter, 7 November. https://twitter.com/channel4news/status/927843442457276417?lang =en (accessed 4 July 2022).

Fausset, R. 2017. 'A Voice of Hate from America's Heartland', *New York Times*, 25 November. https://www.nytimes.com/2017/11/25/us/ohio-hovater-white -nationalist.html (accessed 4 July 2022).

'Gary Younge Interviews Richard Spencer: "Africans Have Benefitted from White Supremacy"'. 2017. *The Guardian*, 7 November. https://www.youtube.com/ watch?v=puJ-arJgkZU (accessed 4 July 2022).

Nardelli, A. and Arnett, G. 2014. 'Today's Key Fact', *The Guardian*, 29 October. https://www.theguardian.com/news/datablog/2014/oct/29/todays-key-fact-you -are-probably-wrong-about-almost-everything (accessed 4 July 2022).

Pew Research Center. 2018. 'Newsroom Employees Earn Less Than Other College-Educated Workers', 4 October. https://www.pewresearch.org/fact-tank/2018/10 /04/newsroom-employees-earn-less-than-other-college-educated-workers-in-u-s/ (accessed 4 July 2022).

The Sutton Trust. 2019. *Elitist Britain*, 24 June. https://www.suttontrust.com/our -research/elitist-britain-2019/ (accessed 4 July 2022).

US Bureau of Labor Statistics. 2021. 'Occupation, Employment and Wages'. https:// www.bls.gov/oes/current/oes273023.htm (accessed 29 November 2022).

US Bureau of Labor Statistics. 2022. 'Usual Weekly Earnings of Wage and Salary Workers First Quarter 2022'. https://www.bls.gov/news.release/pdf/wkyeng.pdf (accessed 15 April 2022).

US Census Bureau. 2021. 'Quick Facts'. https://www.census.gov/quickfacts/US (accessed 29 November 2022), accessed 4 July 2022.

Williamson, E. 2021. 'How a Small Town Silenced a Neo-Nazi Hate Campaign', *New York Times*, 5 September. https://www.nytimes.com/2021/09/05/us/politics /nazi-whitefish-charlottesville.html?referringSource=articleShare, accessed 4 July 2022

Younge, G. 2011. 'Opposing Obama', BBC World Service, 21 January. https://www .bbc.co.uk/worldservice/documentaries/2010/01/100128_opposing_obama_part _1.shtml (accessed 4 July 2022).

Younge, G. 2016. 'The View from Middletown: Trump Speaks to Us in a Way Other People Don't', *The Guardian*, 27 October. https://www.theguardian.com /membership/2016/oct/27/middletown-trump-muncie-clinton (accessed 4 July 2022).

Younge, G. 2017a. 'How to Interview a Nazi', *The Nation*, 29 November. https:// www.thenation.com/article/archive/how-to-interview-a-nazi/ (accessed 4 July 2022).

Younge, G. 2017b. 'Why Interviewing Richard Spencer Was a Risk Worth Taking', *The Guardian*, 8 November. https://www.theguardian.com/commentisfree/2017 /nov/08/interviewing-richard-spencer-white-supremacist (accessed 4 July 2022).

Younge, G. and Topham, L. 2020a. 'Younge America: The Old Farts Club', *The Guardian*, 1 November. https://www.theguardian.com/world/video/2010/nov/01 /younge-america-old-farts-club-video (accessed 4 July 2022).

Younge, G. and Topham, L. 2020b. 'Younge America: The Great Divide', *The Guardian*, 29 October. https://www.theguardian.com/world/video/2010/oct/29/ younge-america-great-divide (accessed 4 July 2022).

32

Researching the far right: towards an ethics of talking 'about'

Katy Brown

The far right, under its many names and guises, has become a hugely popular area of research within political science and other disciplines (Gattinara 2020; Carter 2018). Despite such sustained interest, and scant evidence to suggest that it is waning, this attention has certainly not been matched by levels of engagement with the specific ethical implications of researching the far right. With the way that academia can contribute to the political dynamics for which it offers interpretations, there is an urgent need to deal with these questions and reflect on our practices at every stage of the research process.

Such considerations take on particular significance in the context of the far right today. Over recent years, we have seen its growing mainstreaming (Brown, Mondon, and Winter 2023; Wodak 2020), where not only have some far-right parties enjoyed greater electoral success (Akkerman, de Lange, and Rooduijn 2016) but where more pervasively, far-right discourse has become normalised in mainstream circles (Krzyżanowski 2020). It is not simply far-right groups that are responsible for such shifts but those at the heart of what is considered 'mainstream', whether that be prominent politicians vying for the most exclusionary immigration policy, media outlets platforming far-right actors, or other popular figures such as authors, sportspeople, and celebrities defending exclusionary positions. Academia, too, is implicated in these processes, with different levels of consciousness and reflection in this regard. Here, the focus is not on those who have actively stoked far-right ideas, but rather the everyday ways that academia may be involved in mainstreaming.

To do so, this piece focuses on developing an ethics of talking 'about' the far right, whereby the way that we discuss and disseminate our findings forms a key area of reflection in the field. First, the chapter outlines the importance of taking a principled and explicitly political approach as a baseline for building this ethical position. Next, it provides an overview of the ethical questions we may ask ourselves when studying the far right, taking into consideration the before, during, and after components of reflexivity. With particular attention to this final element, the lens of mainstreaming offers a way for us to visualise the role that academia may play when talking 'about' the far right, using the case of the populist hype to evidence some of the dangers that come from limited reflection on this topic. By engaging with these questions, it is hoped that we can start to build towards a more comprehensive ethics of talking 'about' the far right within academia. Throughout this chapter, I make use of the pronoun 'we' in order to convey that this is a joint endeavour in which we all must be invested, so it is an invitation to take these principles forward together.

Political commitment as a necessity

Fundamental to this call is an understanding of our own role as academics within the research process. It is clear within the field of political science that the legacies of positivism and the pursuit of 'objective' and 'neutral' enquiry are still often held as the benchmarks for 'rigorous' and 'reliable' research. These questions have taken on recent significance within far right studies, when the Centre for the Analysis of the Radical Right (CARR) announced its commitment to neutrality after an article published on its site attracted condemnation for claiming that anti-fascists had "become what they oppose". While the director doubled down, some CARR fellows denounced the position and resigned from the organisation, reinforcing their own commitment to opposing the far right. This principled stand from many early career researchers illustrates the kind of conscious engagement with these questions that is much needed in this area.

If we are to reflect seriously on the responsibility that we have as researchers, we must reject not only the plausibility of neutrality but its desirability too. Taking inspiration from more radical traditions, such as critical, anti-racist, feminist, and decolonial scholarship, we can challenge the premise and value of these supposed standards of 'rigour'. Many scholars have offered fervent critiques of the claim to objectivity and neutrality, for instance in upholding white supremacy, privileging Western thought, and placing white men's experiences as universal (e.g., Meer 2019: 501–502; Zuberi and Bonilla-Silva 2008; Smith 1999: 56; Mills 1999: 17–18; Harding 1988: 7), yet these harmful benchmarks of validity still prevail in many circles. Here, instead of trying to appease such unattainable, and indeed undesirable, requirements for 'scientific' research, we must stand firm and unashamed in our political stance. In the face of injustice, political commitment is a necessity, whereby research should strive to help combat sites of exclusion and inequality (Wodak and Meyer 2009; van Dijk 2009: 63). Indeed, the only ethical position to take in such work is one of sustained opposition, because if research does not seek to challenge these sources of oppression, then what purpose does it serve?

When it comes to the far right and its mainstreaming, detachment should not be regarded as a sign of virtue. As Remi Joseph-Salisbury and Laura Connelly (2021: 12) underline in relation to racism, "there is simply too much at stake to engage in pretensions of neutrality". When faced with issues of exclusion and injustice, a dispassionate and 'value-free' approach is an indicator not of work marked by integrity and credibility but of complicity with systems of oppression. It is not just a moral issue within research either, as there is marked analytical value in being political; if we are to approach the complexities of such systems effectively, we must absolutely start from an understanding of the inequalities that are embedded within them. Only then can we begin to unpick and understand the dynamics that are at play. As such, supposed objectivity and neutrality equate in practice to no such thing, nor do they offer adept frameworks for interpreting the world in which we live. Counter to hegemonic claims, therefore, critical scholarship is not singularly marred by biases or analytical failings from which alternatives are free but instead offers a more transparent, sophisticated, and ethical approach to research:

> Rather than undermining academic rigour, the explicitly political and partisan nature of anti-racist scholar-activism offers a higher level of integrity and honesty than scholarship that purports to be objective. It makes clear – rather than hides – the assumptions and positions that underpin scholarship. (Joseph-Salisbury and Connelly 2021: 13)

Guided by these principles, our approach to studying the far right must be fundamentally shaped by opposition to the harmful effects of mainstreaming, using this commitment to fundamentally drive our research at every stage. Of course, these are complex and multifarious issues with no simple solutions, but the desire to challenge them is what must remain at the heart of what propels such research forward.

Reflexivity at every stage

If we accept, therefore, that we are not and should not be neutral observers in the field of far right studies, or indeed other areas, we must necessarily engage with our positionality as researchers. Reflexivity refers to the "active acknowledgement by the researcher that her/his own actions and decisions will inevitably impact upon the meaning and context of the experience under investigation" (Horsburgh 2003: 308). To work reflexively, the analyst must engage in a process of "continual internal dialogue and self-evaluation of [their] positionality" (Berger 2015: 220). This entails asking and answering the following questions candidly when approaching a research project:

1) *What am I coming to the research with?*

    This question addresses the *before* phase of a project, taking into account prior influences, characteristics, and motivations which may influence the approach that is taken from the outset.

2) *How does this affect the way in which I conduct my research?*

    This consideration centres on the *during* phase of a project, reflecting on how the answer to the first question may continuously impact the way that research is carried out, how it proceeds, and how analysis is interpreted.

3) *What am I leaving the field with?*

    This final question deals with the *after* phase of research, evaluating the potential impact a project may have, how it might be received, and what it could be used for. It encourages consideration of the lasting effects of our work beyond the simple publication of findings.

All three questions are of course intimately linked, each relying on the previous to inform the approach to the next. They are all integral to critically engaged research and so form the foundation from which an ethical approach can be built. This chapter is particularly concerned with the third question, not because it takes precedence over the others but because it has received so little attention and we actually have significant power over how we choose to approach such issues. If we look at this through the lens of mainstreaming in particular, we can attempt to actively embed our responsibility to counter the far right in how we go about communicating our research and shaping the legacy of our findings.

Talking 'with' and 'about' the far right

As indicated, the lens of mainstreaming proves useful in understanding the impact of the decisions we make when communicating research, particularly pointing to the discursive implications of our choices. Building on our prior definition (Brown, Mondon, and Winter 2023: 170), mainstreaming can be understood in the following way:

> The process by which parties/actors, discourses and/or attitudes move from a position of unacceptability (outside the norm) to one of legitimacy (within the norm). These norms themselves are not fixed and are subject to discursive construction and reconstruction.

It is thereby a dynamic and complex process, with many contributing factors and intersecting components. Research on mainstreaming to date has largely centred around the actions of the far right itself in carving out its own electoral success (Akkerman, de Lange, and Rooduijn 2016); a number of fascinating studies point to the way that far-right parties (for instance, the Front/Rassemblement National under Marine Le Pen) have sought to modify and soften their positions to appear more 'mainstream' (Paxton and Peace 2021; Peker 2021; Hutchins and Halikiopoulou 2020; Almeida 2017; Dézé 2015; Shields 2014; Mişcoiu 2012). While certainly an important facet, comparatively less attention has been paid to the mainstream and its role in normalising far-right discourse. Some work has explored mainstream party strategies in response to the supposed threat of 'niche' parties (Abou-Chadi 2016; Meguid 2005), yet still, the far right is often placed in the driving seat, almost painted as forcing the mainstream into positions that would otherwise be unnatural to it. One of the prominent forms of imagery within political science research that has been used to symbolise the relationship between the far right and mainstream is the notion of 'contagion' (e.g., Meijers 2017; Rooduijn, de Lange, and van der Brug 2014; van Spanje 2010). With the power of metaphors to frame political issues (Boeynaems et al. 2017; Bougher 2012; Mio 1997), the implication of 'contagion' is that mainstream parties or actors are almost infected by the far right, placing the latter in a position of power while the former may be considered innocent victims of a societal force over which they have no control. By overemphasising the far right's influence, therefore, the mainstream's powerful role is sometimes minimised and obscured.

In order to redress that imbalance, a holistic approach to mainstreaming must necessarily account for and centralise the role of the mainstream itself, i.e., putting the mainstream in mainstreaming (Brown 2022). Of course, this is complicated by the fact that the mainstream is notoriously hard to define, but I propose the following as a way to conceptualise it:

> a contingent identity that is hegemonically positioned, both through internal and external construction, as representative of the norm or centre however defined in a particular context.

Crucially, this accounts for the way that what or who is considered mainstream may change over time, place, and context. What is key in terms of mainstream actors is that they benefit from reputational and material advantage, with perceptions of respectability lending greater credence to their claims, and heightened access to discursive platforms and resources accelerating their capacity to set the agenda. Jana Goyvaerts' (2021) work on the intersections between different sectors (politics, media, and academia) underscores how the mainstream too may be composed of various groups which overlap in different ways. Notably, with academia's role in knowledge production (Andersen 2003: 3), our work on the far right does not sit outside of mainstreaming processes so we must pay attention to what we are contributing to this discussion.

To characterise the way that mainstream discourse may function in this process, including academic work, I identify two interrelated components: talking 'with' and 'about' the far right. Talking 'with' refers to shared discourses between the mainstream and far right, encompassing any similarities between them, both in terms of content and style. This encourages us to avoid exceptionalising the far right and its discourses, instead identifying how exclusionary positions can also be found at the heart of the mainstream. Of course, this does not mean downplaying the deeply harmful politics of far-right groups in any way but rather emphasising that the mainstream too is responsible for furthering inequality and has great power to do so. It should be noted at this stage that there is no expectation that these ideas necessarily originate within the far right or are forced upon the mainstream as a response to the far right; indeed, the mainstream possesses significant agency to act of its own volition. The second component, talking 'about', denotes the way in which mainstream actors discursively construct the far right, either explicitly through direct references or implicitly through more subtle allusions. It thereby seeks to understand how the subject position of the far right is constructed by various actors, with its implications not only for the far right itself but the image of the mainstream too. For instance, mainstream politicians may attempt to draw closer or distance themselves from the far right in certain instances by talking 'about' in different ways. In so doing, they may shift the perceived relative positioning between the two. Crucially for this piece and in other contexts, talking 'with' and 'about' are interdependent and symbiotic. The way that we talk 'about' the far right can actually talk 'with' it in some ways, by legitimising its position and core discourses. These issues are pertinent in academia as it is clear that our research constitutes a form of talking 'about' and is therefore subject to the same potential implications.

Academia, talking 'about', and populist hype

Clearly, academia's role in conveying and mediating people's understanding of political events means that we have a responsibility to talk 'about' in a way that does not talk 'with'. Some within the profession have actively and quite explicitly chosen to talk 'with', but more pervasively, there are less obvious ways that our decisions can feed into particular narratives and contribute towards greater mainstreaming. As previously discussed, the idea of contagion and the way that mainstream parties are commonly portrayed as responding to the far right rather than acting of their own accord already have harmful implications for how we understand the power dynamics in these situations. The field of far right studies therefore has a need to engage with these questions and the process of mainstreaming within our reflexive practices.

To examine and illustrate some of the issues associated with talking 'about', this section explores the role of the 'populist hype' (Glynos and Mondon 2019) in talking 'with' the far right to some extent. Studies underscore how populism has come to be associated significantly with far-right politics and how its application as a concept and signifier has created some problematic associations (Galanopoulos and Venizelos 2022; Hunger and Paxton 2022; Mondon 2022a; Thornborrow, Ekstrom, and Patrona 2021). Of course, there are ways to engage with it carefully in the field, drawing on precise definitions (Katsambekis 2022), but a broader lack of reflection can serve to reinforce certain perceptions of the far right. In particular, this section highlights how it can legitimise the idea that the far right is guided by public opinion, euphemise racist politics, and reinforce the mainstream as the solution. By addressing the specific problems that the populist hype poses, we can understand the broader importance of developing and implementing an ethics of talking 'about' in our work.

First, by choosing to label far-right politics as 'populist' above other descriptors, credence is given to the idea that the far right is a people-led or people-inspired phenomenon in pursuit of a genuinely anti-elitist agenda. While, of course, far-right politics can attract a broad base of support (Halikiopoulou and Vlandas 2020), the populist signifier facilitates its framing as a movement rising from the bottom-up, particularly (white) working-class communities, and thereby deflects attention from the elitist politicians that often lead such parties (Mondon 2022b). Despite the evidenced limitations of characterising far-right voters as predominantly from white working-class communities (Mondon and Winter 2019; Bhambra 2017), the way in which 'populism' has been picked up in the media, too, for example, has led to an uncritical acceptance of this as a confirmed association (Brown and Mondon 2021: 284). This way of talking 'about' far-right support has therefore further entrenched some of its claims in terms of representation, by legitimising its position as something arising from the concerns of 'the people'. Our use of 'populist' to describe the far right must therefore be carefully qualified and contextualised to avoid simplistic associations.

Linked to this, populism can act as a euphemisation for the far right if not applied with caution, as while it is generally portrayed negatively (Goyvaerts 2021; Goyvaerts and De Cleen 2020), it acts as a less stigmatising qualifier than 'racist' or 'far right', for instance. This has seen far-right politicians such as Marine Le Pen, Matteo Salvini, and Steve Bannon openly embrace the term (Brown and Mondon 2021: 287) by emphasising how it links them to 'the people'. In his last speech to the European Parliament, Nigel Farage (BBC 2020) claimed a historic battle was afoot between globalism and populism, stating: "You may loathe populism, but I tell you a funny thing, it's becoming very popular. And it has great benefits." Thus, the signifier's phonetic resonance with 'popular' and its ideological association with the people-vs-elite antagonism allow far-right actors to lay claim to it and add their own inflection onto what it means. It is hard to imagine a scenario where an actor would talk about the 'great benefits' of racism (at least explicitly); even the extreme right Britain First (BF) had a webpage dedicated to the claim that they were 'not racist' (Lentin 2020: 55). Thus, even if 'populist' is generally employed in a pejorative manner, its more positive inflection leaves it open to reinterpretation and manipulation. With the links between politics, media, and academia (Goyvaerts 2021), it is important for us to reflect on whether 'populist' is the most accurate term to use in the case we are describing. Using it ourselves without clear contextualisation and a careful delineation of its meaning can lend further to this reframing and the far right's desired image.

The final point that arises from the populist signifier is its reinforcement of the 'mainstream'. With the effects described in the two previous paragraphs, it may seem somewhat counterintuitive to suggest that the use of 'populism' also serves to reinforce the status quo, but the two phenomena are linked. As populism in its reified form is often associated with a bottom-up revolt, it is commonly portrayed as dangerous, illiberal, and irrational, in contrast to the 'moderate and sensible' mainstream. Both Bice Maiguashca (2019) and Emmy Eklundh (2020) put forward fascinating arguments about how understandings of populism shape the perceived solutions to it. Maiguashca (2019: 783) argues that its blanket use to describe radical politics has had detrimental effects on progressive causes by framing the solution as "re-energising and relegitimising [...] the 'centre ground' of politics". Eklundh (2020: 119) underscores how populism's framing as low and unrefined is marked by a commitment to rationality "which has in the past produced a highly unequal and often violent reality for excluded groups, such as women, non-Europeans, or young people". What both accounts emphasise is that populism has been portrayed as the source of danger, but that this has drawn attention away and detracted from the exclusionary politics characterising far-right groups. In creating a frontier between anti-populist and populist, between good and bad, between rational and irrational politics, any progressive alternatives which do not rely on 'the centre' are similarly cast aside. With the central claim here in relation to mainstreaming, that the mainstream has been influential in normalising far-right politics and that there has been little scrutiny of this phenomenon, such perceptions clearly reinforce rather than challenge dominant narratives. Thus, the effects identified here in relation to the populist hype indicate that our decisions when talking 'about' are certainly not free from consequence and can feed into the dynamics that we are studying.

An ethics of talking 'about'

This discussion speaks more broadly to the responsibility we have in consciously reflecting on these issues. Our modes of talking 'about' must not serve to legitimise the far right, further facilitate its mainstreaming, or talk 'with' it in any way. It is not simply about which words we do or do not use, but how we conceptualise them, how we question common-sense categories, how we communicate our reflexive and methodological processes, how we choose to present our data, and whether we directly quote far-right actors or not. The decisions that we make when talking 'about' are numerous and complex, with no easy answers, but we must work together to build better practices going forward. As a starting point, I propose that when we start to answer the third question in our reflexive process, we engage with the concept of mainstreaming; we think about the power dynamics and interactions involved in the normalisation of far-right politics and consider the messages that we are adding to those debates. We can ask ourselves:

1. Is this the most appropriate way to conceptualise this form of politics?
2. Where am I suggesting that power lies?
3. Which other groups are involved and who/what am I framing as the solution?
4. Am I accounting for key factors which speak to its wider relevance and implications?
5. Who is affected by this politics and am I taking into account the impact?
6. How does my framing relate to the desired image of the far right and/or mainstream in this scenario?

These questions are by no means exhaustive, of course, but by discussing these issues, we can start to reflect more carefully on our position. A key point is to welcome critique on these issues and accept where improvements can be made. Certainly, this is not a purely individual issue, as the demands of the neoliberal university do not encourage such careful reflection. The pressure to publish, generate impact, and build a public profile often runs counter to this aim, particularly when job prospects in this increasingly casualised sector are tied so closely to these measures (Goyvaerts et al. 2024).

However, by working collectively towards an ethics of talking 'about', with an active and sustained rejection of talking 'with', we can hope to build effective strategies moving forward.

References

Abou-Chadi, T. 2016. 'Niche Party Success and Mainstream Party Policy Shifts – How Green and radical right parties differ in their impact', *British Journal of Political Science*, 46(2), 417–436.

Akkerman, T., de Lange, S. L., and Rooduijn, M. (eds). 2016. *Radical Right-Wing Populist Parties in Western Europe: Into the Mainstream?* Abingdon: Routledge.

Almeida, D. 2017. 'Exclusionary Secularism: The Front National and the Reinvention of Laïcité', *Modern & Contemporary France*, 25(3), 249–263.

Andersen, N. Å. 2003. *Discursive Analytical Strategies: Understanding Foucault, Koselleck, Laclau, Luhmann*. Bristol: Policy.

BBC News. 2020. 'Nigel Farage's Last Words to the European Parliament', *BBC News* [Online], 29 January. https://www.bbc.co.uk/news/av/uk-51294356 (accessed 13 March 2022).

Berger, P. 2015. 'Now I See It, Now I Don't: Researcher's Position and Reflexivity in Qualitative Research', *Qualitative Research*, 15(2), 219–234.

Bhambra, G. K. 2017. 'Brexit, Trump, and "Methodological Whiteness": On the Misrecognition of Race and Class', *The British Journal of Sociology*, 68(1), Supplement 1: 214–232.

Boeynaems, A., Burgers, C., Konijn, E. A., and Steen, G. J. 2017. 'The Effects of Metaphorical Framing on Political Persuasion: A Systematic Literature Review', *Metaphor and Symbol*, 32(2), 118–134.

Bougher, L. D. 2012. 'The Case for Metaphor in Political Reasoning and Cognition', *Political Psychology*, 33(1), 145–163.

Brown, K. 2022. *Talking 'with' and 'about' the Far Right: Putting the Mainstream in Mainstreaming*. Bath: University of Bath.

Brown, K. and Mondon, A. 2021. 'Populism, the Media, and the Mainstreaming of the Far Right: The Guardian's Coverage of Populism as a Case Study', *Politics*, 41(3), 279–295.

Brown, K., Mondon, A., and Winter, A. 2023. 'The Far Right, the Mainstream and Mainstreaming: Towards a Heuristic Framework', *Journal of Political Ideologies*, 28(2), 162–179. https://doi.org/10.1080/13569317.2021.1949829

Carter, E. 2018. 'Right-Wing Extremism/Radicalism: Reconstructing the Concept', *Journal of Political Ideologies*, 23(2), 157–182.

Dézé, A. 2015. 'La "Dédiabolisation" une Nouvelle Stratégie?' In: Crépon, S., Dézé, A., and Mayer, N. (eds). *Les faux-semblants du Front national*. Paris: Presses de Sciences Po, 27–50.

van Dijk, T. A. 2009. 'Critical Discourse Studies: A Sociocognitive Approach'. In: Wodak, R. and Meyer, M. (eds). *Methods of Critical Discourse Analysis*. 2nd ed. London: SAGE, 62–85.

Eklundh, E. 2020. 'Excluding Emotions: The Performative Function of Populism', *Partecipazione e Conflitto*, 13(1), 107–131.

Galanopoulos, A. and Venizelos, G. 2022. 'Anti-Populism and Populist Hype during the COVID-19 Pandemic', *Representation*, 58(2), 251–268.

Gattinara, P. C. 2020. 'The Study of the Far Right and Its Three E's: Why Scholarship Must Go beyond Eurocentrism, Electoralism and Externalism', *French Politics*, 18(3), 314–333.

Glynos, J. and Mondon, A. 2019. 'The Political Logic of Populist Hype: The Case of Right-Wing Populism's "Meteoric Rise" and Its Relation to the Status Quo'. In: Cossarini, P. and Vallespín, F. (eds). *Populism and Passions*. Abingdon: Routledge, 82–101.

Goyvaerts, J. 2021. *The Academic Voice in Media Debates on Populism (POPULISMUS Working Paper No. 12)*.

Goyvaerts, J., Brown, K., Mondon, A., Glynos, J., and De Cleen, B. 2024. 'On the Politics of "Populism" – The Case of Populist Hype'. In: Katsambekis, G. and Stavrakakis, Y. (eds). *Elgar Handbook of Populism*. London: Edward Elgar.

Goyvaerts, J. and De Cleen, B. 2020. 'Media, Anti-Populist Discourse and the Dynamics of the Populism Debate'. In: Krämer, B. and Holtz-Bacha, C. (eds). *Perspectives on Populism and the Media: Avenues for Research*. Baden-Baden: Nomos Verlag, 83–108.

Halikiopoulou, D. and Vlandas, T. 2020. 'When Economic and Cultural Interests Align: The Anti-Immigration Voter Coalitions Driving Far Right Party Success in Europe', *European Political Science Review*, 12(4), 427–448.

Harding, S. 1988. *Feminism and Methodology*. Bloomington, IN: Indiana University Press.

Horsburgh, D. 2003. 'Evaluation of Qualitative Research', *Journal of Clinical Nursing*, 12(2), 307–312.

Hunger, S. and Paxton, F. 2022. 'What's in a Buzzword? A Systematic Review of the State of Populism Research in Political Science', *Political Science Research and Methods*, 10(3), 617–633.

Hutchins, R. D. and Halikiopoulou, D. 2020. 'Enemies of Liberty? Nationalism, Immigration, and the Framing of Terrorism in the Agenda of the Front National', *Nations and Nationalism*, 26(1), 67–84.

Joseph-Salisbury, R. and Connelly, L. 2021. *Anti-Racist Scholar-Activism*. Manchester: Manchester University Press.

Katsambekis, G. 2022. 'Constructing "the People" of Populism: A Critique of the Ideational Approach from a Discursive Perspective', *Journal of Political Ideologies*, 27(1), 53–74.

Krzyżanowski, M. 2020. 'Discursive Shifts and the Normalisation of Racism: Imaginaries of Immigration, Moral Panics and the Discourse of Contemporary Right-Wing Populism', *Social Semiotics*, 30(4), 503–527.

Lentin, A. 2020. *Why Race Still Matters*. Cambridge: Polity.

Maiguashca, B. 2019. 'Resisting the "Populist Hype": A Feminist Critique of a Globalising Concept', *Review of International Studies*, 45(5), 768–785.

Meer, N. 2019. 'The Wreckage of White Supremacy', *Identities*, 26(5), 501–509.

Meguid, B. M. 2005. 'Competition between Unequals: The Role of Mainstream Party Strategy in Niche Party Success', *American Political Science Review*, 99(3), 347–359.

Meijers, M. J. 2017. 'Contagious Euroscepticism: The Impact of Eurosceptic Support on Mainstream Party Positions on European Integration', *Party Politics*, 23(4), 413–423.

Mills, C. W. 1999. *The Racial Contract*. Ithaca, NY: Cornell University Press.

Mio, J. S. 1997. 'Metaphor and Politics', *Metaphor and Symbol*, 12(2), 113–133.

Mișcoiu, S. 2012. 'De l'antisémitisme foncier à la normalisation stratégique. Le Front National à l'époque de Marine Le Pen', *Holocaust. Studii și cercetări*, IV(05), 190–200.

Mondon, A. 2022a. 'Populist Hype'. In: *The Populism Interviews*. Abingdon: Routledge.

Mondon, A. 2022b. 'Populism, Public Opinion, and the Mainstreaming of the Far Right: The "Immigration Issue" and the Construction of a Reactionary "People"', *Politics*, 1–18. https://doi.org/10.1177/02633957221104726

Mondon, A. and Winter, A. 2019. 'Whiteness, Populism and the Racialisation of the Working Class in the United Kingdom and the United States', *Identities*, 26(5), 510–528.

Paxton, F. and Peace, T. 2021. 'Window Dressing? The Mainstreaming Strategy of the Rassemblement National in Power in French Local Government', *Government and Opposition*, 56(3), 545–562.

Peker, E. 2021. 'Right-Wing Populism and the Securitisation of Laïcité Narratives in French Education Policy', *Social Policy and Society*, 20(2), 326–339.

Rooduijn, M., de Lange, S. L., and van der Brug, W. 2014. 'A Populist Zeitgeist? Programmatic Contagion by Populist Parties in Western Europe', *Party Politics*, 20(4), 563–575.

Shields, J. 2014. 'The Front National: From Systematic Opposition to Systemic Integration?', *Modern & Contemporary France*, 22(4), 491–511.

Smith, L. T. 1999. *Decolonizing Methodologies: Research and Indigenous Peoples*. London, New York, and Dunedin: Zed Books.

Thornborrow, J., Ekstrom, M., and Patrona, M. 2021. 'Discursive Constructions of Populism in Opinion-Based Journalism: A Comparative European Study', *Discourse, Context & Media*, 44(1), 1–9.

van Spanje, J. 2010. 'Contagious Parties: Anti-Immigration Parties and Their Impact on Other Parties' Immigration Stances in Contemporary Western Europe', *Party Politics*, 16(5), 563–586.

Wodak, R. 2020. *The Politics of Fear: The Shameless Normalization of Far-Right Discourse*. 2nd ed. Los Angeles, CA: SAGE Publications.

Wodak, R. and Meyer, M. (eds). 2009. 'Introducing Qualitative Methods'. In: *Methods of Critical Discourse Analysis*. 2nd ed. London: SAGE.

Zuberi, T. and Bonilla-Silva, E. (eds). 2008. *White Logic, White Methods: Racism and Methodology*. Lanham, MD: Rowman & Littlefield.

Index

Note: 'n' after a page number indicates a note on that page.

Milton Keynes UK
Ingram Content Group UK Ltd.
UKHW021417280524
443389UK00008B/188